THE CHRISTIAN YEAR

SERMONS OF THE FATHERS

vol. 1

from Advent to Pentecost

THE CHRISTIAN YEAR

SERMONS OF THE FATHERS

vol. 1

from Advent to Pentecost

compiled and edited by
George W. Forell

*To Pat with love
on the occasion of
her ordination
May 6, 1973
Geo. W. Forell*

THOMAS NELSON & SONS

London   NEW YORK   Toronto

Library of Congress Catalog Card Number: 64–25283

Printed in the United States of America

FOREWORD

Every year all over Christendom countless books of sermons are published and sold. While some of the sermons they contain are literary masterpieces, others are desperately dull and unimaginative. They range in theological perception from the profound yet simple works of our great contemporary theologians to the ever popular variations on themes from *Poor Richard's Almanack*. The variety is impressive not only as far as content is concerned but also in the different ways in which these books are offered to the prospective buyer. Some sermon books are advertised as containing "great" sermons; others are said to be merely "edifying" or theologically "orthodox." Yet, strangely enough, almost all of these books do find some use for the working parish-minister who has to prepare from fifty to one hundred different sermons a year, is hungry for ideas and always hopes against hope that the new sermon book will contain at least one or two useful suggestions that will help him in his task.

The pressure on the minister who is conscientious in his sermon preparation is very great. Today he no longer competes for attention only with the other clergymen in his community but in the age of mass communications he feels the competition of the high-priced communications specialists on radio and television. It is against these experts that his rhetorical skill is measured. Meanwhile other duties continue to encroach on the time he has set apart for sermon preparation and so it is not surprising that he will turn for help to any likely book that promises to make his difficult task easier. The sermons offered here are different. They are selected to bring a new perspective to the task of the preacher by illumining each text in the light of the history of its exposition. This does not mean that these sermons are necessarily all "great" or "interesting" or even "orthodox."

Since the authors range from Pope Leo the Great to Jonathan Edwards, and from Bernard of Clairvaux to Friedrich Schleiermacher, they are obviously not "orthodox" according to any ecclesiastically recognized canon of orthodoxy. Nevertheless, the sermons here submitted have one thing in common: they are the work of preachers, and the men who preached them, each in his own way, were very serious about the task of preaching. They considered it a calling from God, a responsibility they could not shirk. They were all professional preachers. This is as true of John Chrysostom as of John Donne, of Martin Luther as of Phillips Brooks. Thus this collection of sermons represents a gallery in which 1,500 years of sermons are hung for our inspection. After examining this gallery of sermons the reader will probably conclude that he likes some and does not like others. Some of these sermons he may find moving, others irritating, and some just boring. This is as it should be.

But if the reader is himself accustomed to listening to sermons or delivering them—and it is this reader for whom this collection has been especially prepared—these sermons should help him to obtain some perspective on Christian preaching in general.

Preaching depends for its ultimate effectiveness upon the work of the Holy Spirit. It is the common experience of the Christian Church that technically incompetent preaching has been used by God to reach man with the Gospel, and rhetorically impressive efforts have failed.

But preaching is also an art and one of the humanities. And while it is true that God can and does use incompetent preachers (as He can use immoral ones) for this purpose, the preacher has a responsibility for technical competence as well as moral uprightness. To pride oneself on making the Holy Spirit work harder because of one's laziness of intellect and imagination is scarcely more praiseworthy than the antinomian attitude of sinning so that grace may abound.

If, then, the task of preaching is a most serious responsibility, this book is designed to offer a special kind of assistance.

In all of the humanities the creative person does not develop without a great deal of hard work. Much of this work in literature, in music, in painting, consists in becoming familiar with the past. A writer has to read a great deal. A composer must listen to the music of other composers as far back as he can discover it. A painter must study as many paintings as he possibly can, from those found in the caves of our prehistoric ancestors to those of the twentieth century.

This involvement in the past is a condition of the creative process in all of the humanities. It is not an effort to imitate the past but to understand it and learn from it in preparation for the expression of one's own artistic vision in one's own personal idiom. This is particularly true of those artists who seem most original and even idiosyncratic to us. A closer study of their work will often reveal their profound and dialectic involvement with the past. Indeed, one could say that the difference between a great modern artist and a contemporary primitive is that the great artist has comprehended the past and it is reflected creatively in his own work, in his own style. The difference, for example, between a Pablo Picasso and a Grandma Moses is in their relationship to the past. In the work of Picasso the entire history of the human race is artistically remembered and expressed. Grandma Moses remembered her own childhood only. The very personal and unique style of a Picasso is, therefore, because of its sophisticated relationship to the past, vastly more universal. The same could be said for a James Joyce or a Hindemith.

This does not mean that the remembrance of the past implies imitation. It does imply awareness and reflection. The problem revealed in much modern preaching appears to be that it lacks awareness of the Christian past. It is very largely of the Grandma Moses variety, rehearsing the personal remembrances and experiences of the individual preacher.

Strangely enough, this is equally true of both the extremes of the theological spectrum. So-called "evangelicals" tend to preach their own conversion experience. Every sermon is a variation on a theme of their own past. This can be done very impressively and movingly, but it is utterly subjective. Similarly, the so-called "liberals" tend to repeat constantly and publicly their own struggle for emancipation from some orthodoxy, to the needless annoyance of those who do not share their views, and the embarrassment of those among their hearers who are more secure in their own "emancipation" and would like to go on from there.

Both types of preachers share a basically unhistorical and subjective view of the task of preaching in spite of the seeming dissimilarities of the content of their sermons. If such a preacher or listener reads and uses the sermon books that are so abundantly available they will tend to increase his awareness on the level on which he exists already. They will seldom relate him to Christian preaching as the speech of the Church concerning God's deed in Jesus Christ through the centuries. Thus the help he receives tends to obscure the historical dimension of preaching, the long line of men called by God to speak His word since Pentecost.

Reading the sermons of an Augustine or a Schleiermacher is an inspiration because they faced their task in their age with courage and imagination; it is a comfort because their preaching consists of very human words, as human as any spoken by a contemporary preacher. Nevertheless, the Holy Spirit used these words to call men to repentance and faith. Thus even the relatively boring or theologically awkward sermon may give modern man perspective and courage in the face of his own lack of brilliance or theological acumen.

Of course, there will be those who will consider any reading of sermons illegitimate and suggest that a thorough exegesis of the Bible, preferably the reconstruction of the *ipsissima verba* of Jesus, is all that is actually needed. They consider the 2,000 years of Christian history irrelevant to the present task of the preacher.

Yet it is hard to see that the God who speaks decisively and authoritatively to man in the history of the Jewish people and of the Apostolic Church would suddenly lose interest in His people and their history at the somewhat elusive moment when the Biblical canon was closed.

The preachers whose sermons are here presented placed themselves under the authority of the canonical scriptures of the Old and New Testaments. Under this authority and not independent of it, they addressed the men and women of their time. While we cannot merely imitate their faith or repeat their message, knowing this message might enable modern men to understand and address their age with greater depth and a wider perspective.

The basic plan of this volume is very simple. It follows the assigned Sunday gospel lessons of the Western Church (based on the so-called "Roman lessons" which were established by Charlemagne) for the first part of the liturgical year from Advent to Pentecost. Preference has been given to expository sermons dealing with these texts, although topical sermons have been used at times.

While trying to respect the thrust of the message, almost all sermons have been abbreviated. Brief biographies of the preachers whose sermons have been selected will be found in the appendix, with a short list of the sources of the sermons used. In a few cases the translation of sermons are the editor's. Care has been taken to be uniform in style and in most cases this has been possible.

In the preparation of this volume many people have been of assistance. Miss Sharon Bauer, Miss Meredith Medler, and Pastor James R. Anderson deserve special mention.

GEORGE W. FORELL

EPIPHANY 1964

CONTENTS

THE FIRST SUNDAY IN ADVENT

Text: Luke 3:1-6

1. John Chrysostom

John cometh, doing nothing else but bringing his people to a sense of their own sins. This, among other things, his very garb declared, being that of repentance and confession. This was indicated also by what he preached, for nothing else did he say, but "bring forth fruits meet for repentance." Forasmuch then as their not condemning their own sins, as Paul also hath explained, made them start off from Christ, while their coming to a sense thereof would set them upon longing to seek after their Redeemer, and to desire remission; this John came to bring about, and to persuade them to repent, not in order that they might be punished, but that having become by repentance more humble, and condemning themselves, they might hasten to receive remission.

But let us see how exactly he hath expressed it; how, having said that he "came preaching the baptism of repentance in the wilderness of Judaea," he adds, "for remission," as though he said, "For this end he exhorted them to confess and repent of their sins; not that they should be punished, but that they might more easily receive the subsequent remission." For had they not condemned themselves, they could not have sought after His grace: and not seeking, they could not have obtained remission.

Thus that baptism led the way for this; wherefore also he said, that "they should believe on Him which should come after him"; together with that which hath been mentioned setting forth this other cause of His baptism. For neither would it have been as much for him to have gone about to their houses, and to have led Christ around, taking Him by the hand, and to have said, "Believe in This Man"; as for that blessed voice to be uttered, and all those other things performed in the presence and sight of all.

On account of this He cometh to the baptism. Since in fact both the credit of him that was baptizing, and the purport of the thing itself, was attracting the whole city, and calling it unto Jordan; and it became a great spectacle.

Therefore he humbles them also when they are come, and persuades them to have no high fancies about themselves; showing them liable to the utmost evils, unless they would repent, and leaving their forefathers, and all vaunting in them, would receive Him that was coming.

Because in fact the things concerning Christ had been up to that time veiled, and many thought He was dead, owing to the massacre which took

11

place at Bethlehem. For though at twelve years old He discovered Himself, yet did He also quickly veil Himself again. And for this cause there was need of that splendid exordium and of a loftier beginning. Wherefore also then for the first time He with clear voice proclaims things which the Jews had never heard, neither from prophets, nor from any besides; making mention of Heaven, and of the kingdom there, and no longer saying anything touching the earth.

. . . . .

See, at least, how both the prophet and the Baptist go upon the same ideas, although not upon the same words.

Thus the prophet saith that he shall come saying, "Prepare ye the way of the Lord, make his paths straight." And he himself when he was come said, "Bring forth fruits meet for repentance," which corresponds with, "Prepare ye the way of the Lord." Seest thou that both by the words of the prophet, and by his own preaching, this one thing is manifested alone; that he was come, making a way and preparing beforehand, not bestowing the gift, which was the remission, but ordering in good time the souls of such as should receive the God of all?

But Luke expresses somewhat further: not repeating the exordium, and so passing on, but setting down likewise all the prophecy. "For every valley," saith he, "shall be filled; and every mountain and hill shall be brought low; and the crooked shall be made straight, and the rough ways smooth; and all flesh shall be the salvation of God." Dost thou perceive how the prophet hath anticipated all by his words; the concourse of the people, the change of things for the better, the easiness of that which was preached, the first cause of all that was occurring, even if he hath expressed it rather as in figure, it being in truth a prophecy which he was uttering? Thus, when he saith, "Every valley shall be filled, and every mountain and hill shall be brought low, and the rough ways shall be made smooth," he is signifying the exaltation of the lowly, the humiliation of the self-willed, the hardness of the law changed into easiness of faith. For it is no longer toils and labors, saith he, but grace, and forgiveness of sins, affording great facility of salvation.

. . . . .

But if John, who was so pure, and more glorious than the heaven, and above all prophets, than whom none greater was born, and who had such great boldness of speech, thus exercised himself in austerity, scorning so exceedingly all dissolute delicacy, and training himself to this hard life; what excuse shall we have, who after so great a benefit, and the unnumbered burdens of our sins, do not show forth so much as the least part of his penance, but are drinking and surfeiting, and smelling of perfumes, and in no better trim than the harlot women on the stage, and are by all means softening ourselves, and making ourselves an easy prey to the devil?

. . . . .

Seest thou how great power was in the coming of the prophet? How he stirred up all the people? How he led them to a consideration of their own sins? For it was indeed worthy of wonder to behold him in human form showing forth such things and using so great freedom of speech, and rising up in condemnation of all as children, and having his great grace beaming out from his countenance. And, moreover, the appearance of a prophet after the great interval of time contributed to their amazement, because the gift had failed them, and returned to them after a long time. And the nature of his preaching too was strange and unusual. For they heard of none of those things to which they were accustomed; such as wars and battles and victories below, and famine and pestilence, and Babylonians and Persians, and the taking of the city, and the other things with which they were familiar, but of Heaven and of the kingdom there, and of the punishment in hell. And it was for this cause, let me add, that although they that committed revolt in the wilderness, those in the company of Judas, and of Theudas, had been all of them slain no great while before, yet they were not the more backward to go out thither. For neither was it for the same objects that he summoned them, as for dominion, or revolt, or revolution; but in order to lead them by the hand to the kingdom on high. Wherefore neither did he keep them in the wilderness to take them about with him, but baptizing them, and teaching them the rules concerning self-denial, he dismissed them; by all means instructing them to scorn whatever things are on earth, and to raise themselves up to the things to come, and press on every day.

This man then let us also emulate, and forsaking luxury and drunkenness let us go over unto the life of restraint. For this surely is the time of confession both for the uninitiated and for the baptized; for the one, that upon their repentance they may partake of the sacred mysteries; for the others, that having washed away their stain after baptism, they may approach the table with a clean conscience. Let us them forsake this soft and effeminate way of living.

2. Bernard of Clairvaux

The Coming of Christ in the Incarnation

People living in the world, my brethren, know the name of Advent well enough, just as they know the names of other solemnities, but with the reason for the name it may be otherwise. And sometimes even those who would assist these hapless sons of Adam so share their ignorance that they are powerless to help either themselves or them. It behooves you, therefore, to whom, as to little children, God reveals things that are hidden from the wise and prudent, to consider diligently why we keep this Advent, and specially to ponder *Who* it is Who comes, *whence* He comes, and *whither*, *why* He comes and *when*, and *by what way*.

Gabriel bears witness that *He Who comes* is the Son of the Highest; He is moreover the Co-Highest, equal to the Father in exaltation and in dignity. But why is it the Son Who comes, and not the Father or the Holy

Spirit? This surely did not happen without reason, nor did the advent of the Son take place apart from the deep purpose of the Trinity. And, if we consider how our exile came about, we may be able to understand a little how fitting it was for the Son to be the One to set us free. Lucifer was hurled by God from heaven, because he tried to make himself God's equal, the which equality is proper only to the Son; the Father, therefore, jealous on the Son's behalf, seems by that act to say, "Vengeance is Mine, I will repay." (And observe here that Lucifer did nothing, he performed no act, his pride was in his thought alone; yet in a moment, in the bat of an eyelid, he was cast down beyond recall, because "he stood not in the truth." So you, my brethren, must flee pride for all that you are worth; for it was pride that plunged him who shone more brightly than all the stars of heaven so swiftly into everlasting darkness, and turned the first of angels into a devil; and pride is the beginning of all sin.) But to resume: Satan, because he hated man, forthwith brought forth in him the evil that he had conceived within himself, persuading him that he would be like God, if only he would eat of the forbidden tree; although it is the Son of the Most High alone Who is the Key of David that shuts and no man opens, and in Whom are hidden all the treasures of wisdom and of knowledge. You see, therefore, the truth of the Lord's saying that the devil is a liar and the father of lies; he was a liar when he said, "I will be like to the Most High," he was the father of lies when he injected into man the poisoned sperm of his own falsity.

That was how our first parents came to disobey and to be thieves, trying at the serpent's (that is, the devil's) instigation to filch to themselves that which is proper to the Son of God. And the Father did not overlook the wrong that was done to Him, but took revenge on man continually— that is to say, on us, for we all sinned in Adam and received his sentence of damnation. What does the Son do, seeing the Father thus jealous for His sake, and sparing never a creature? "See now," He says, "because of Me the Father is losing the creatures He has made. The foremost angel aspired to My loftiness, and has gained possession of the race of people that believed in him. Angels and men are the only two rational species, capable of blessedness, that the Father has created, and now on My account He has lost many angels and the whole race of men. Therefore, that they may know that I too love the Father, let Him receive through Me those whom He seemingly has lost because of Me. They all envy Me. Behold, I come and show Myself to them in such a way that anyone who is disposed to envy Me or longs to copy Me shall have his emulation turned to good. I know that the renegade angels, whose sin did not proceed from ignorance or weakness, must perish because their pride forbids the remedy of penitence. But the Father Himself created men from the beginning in order to supply the fallen angels' places, and so to build again the ruins of Jerusalem."

You have heard Who the Comer is; now you must consider *whence* He comes and *whither*. He comes from the heart of God the Father into the Virgin's womb; He comes from the height of heaven to the lowest parts of earth. On earth we also have to pass our lives, but that is all right if He stays there too. For where will it be well with us without Him, or ill with us, so long as He is there? But He came down not only to the earth, but also down to very hell, not as a captive bound, but as One free among the dead, as Light that shines in darkness and the darkness overwhelmed it not. Wherefore His soul is not allowed to stay in hell, nor does His holy body see corruption on the earth; for Christ Who descended is the Same as He Who ascended, that He might fill all things.

When you consider Who He is Who comes, you get a revelation of unspeakable majesty and might. When you consider whence He comes, a road of great length opens to your eyes, even as says the prophet, "Behold, the Name of the Lord cometh from afar." And when you look to see whither He comes, you are faced with a condescension beyond all thought or measure, in that such Highness deigned to come down into the horrors of this prison-house.

Now as to *why* He came. We may be sure that some great matter was at stake to make such Majesty deign thus to come from so far off to such a worthless place—a great cause, certainly, because mercy is great, because pity is much and love is overflowing. But we shall not need to cudgel our brains to find out what it was, for His own words and works proclaim it openly. *He hastened from the mountains to seek the hundredth sheep, that was astray.* O wondrous condescension on the part of God the Seeker! O mighty dignity of Man the sought! If anyone would make his boast of that, he will not be a fool; because that dignity is grounded on nothing of man's own, but only on the fact that God accounted him so dear. All the riches and glory of the world put together are less than this glory, nor is there anything to be compared with it.

I want to know, however, why He was pleased to come to us, rather than that we should go to Him. Ours was the need, and it is not the custom for the rich to go to the poor. It would have been more suitable for us to go to Him, but a twofold obstacle made this impossible. Our eyes were darkened; and He dwells in light to which no human being may approach. We, lying paralyzed upon our bed, had not the power to reach the heights of God. So the most kind Saviour and Physician of souls came down from His lofty place, and tempered His brightness to the weakness of our eyes. In that most pure and glorious body that He took He covered His own light as in a lamp.

We must now consider when the Saviour came. He came, as you well know, not at time's beginning, nor in the midst of it, but at its end. Wisely did Wisdom ordain that, when the need was greatest, He should first bring help, forgetting not the thankless sons of Adam. Evening had come, the day was declining, the light of the knowledge of God was dim and charity was waxing cold before the prevalence of wickedness; no angels were appearing nor prophets uttering, for the hardness of men's hearts had been too much for them. "Then said I," says the Son, "behold, I come!" Thus, "while all things were in silence and night in the midst of her course," came Thine Almighty Word, Oh Lord, out of the royal throne. "When the fullness of the time was come, God sent His Son."

You know Who comes, the places whence and whither He proceeds, the reason of His coming and the time. One only thing remains to think about, *the way by which He comes.* Just as, in order to effect salvation in the midst of earth, He came once visibly in flesh, so also He comes daily, unseen and in the spirit, to save the souls of individuals. Although the sick man cannot travel far to meet the great Physician, let him at least try to raise his head when he draws near! You have no need, Oh man, to cross the sea or pierce the clouds or go across the Alps. You are not asked to take a lengthy road; go only to yourself, and you will find your God. "The Word is near thee, in thy mouth and in thy heart." Let then the heart's contrition and the mouth's confession release you from the dunghill of your wretched conscience, that is not worthy to receive the Fount of purity.

3. Martin Luther

"We want to begin now to preach about Holy Baptism. For it is proper for us who want to be Christians to know and understand what this means. Then we can speak and confess even before the devil and do not run to the sacrament like a sow to the trough. We will be able to deal with it with awe and honor.

I AM THE VOICE OF ONE CRYING IN THE WILDERNESS. . . . We are told that when John was about 28 or 29 years old he preached in the desert: "The kingdom of God is at hand." The two things that John preached, all prophets proclaimed. All the fathers entered heaven through the forgiveness of sins for Christ's sake, e.g. our ancestors Adam and Eve. But while all preached the same message the difference is that all these prophets spoke of the Christ who was to come. The fathers saw him from afar off. They died and are blessed in the hope of the coming Christ and they shall be raised with us on the last day. (The question whether they have been raised already cannot be dealt with now.)

John is the first one who uses the words that he has come to preach repentance which should serve to bring us into the kingdom of heaven. He is the first one to use this phrase. By preaching of the kingdom of heaven he makes a clear distinction between the earthly and the heavenly kingdom. Even this earthly kingdom was ruled by God. Here, too, He gave His people law and order, but in addition He committed it to reason as we read in Genesis 1:28, "and subdue it"—be it gold or silver. This then is the concern of the worldly realm. The gospel of the preaching of John has nothing to do with that. He does not teach the publicans how to do their business. This a publican knows by himself. He does tell them to be faithful in their office (*Amt*). They should act as the emperor has ordered it.

It is the same with the soldiers (Luke 3:14), as if to say: "You are soldiers to protect and keep the peace, to defend the poor widows and to punish the evil. Your office teaches you that." He does not take over the worldly regiment in order to rule it.

The books of the jurists are made by reason, in fact they are the product of the very best reason; yet they are often more like pigs. Reason can say, "Do not do injustice, obey your parents, do not steal." This reason has from the very best of its resources and it is sufficient for the worldly realm. John doesn't get involved here—yet he confirms this realm.

But he preaches something else. When the earthly kingdom ends we must have another. Indeed, we have it even now, for we are always in death—not only in his teeth but in his very belly. John preaches the kingdom to those who are in the jaws of death. If all the kings and emperors with all their supporters and their power would join together they could not help here for a moment. Another kingdom is needed that is more powerful than death though he can do hundred thousands of things against life. The heathen became tired counting the many kinds of sickness at death's disposal. Yet they could not count them all. Thus death is the mightiest lord, he takes the child in the womb of the mother, he torments the living all during their life, and we assist him all the time.

Thus the worldly regiment is so miserable because it is subjected to death, sickness, swords, guns, and fire. Yet our Lord God has given so much in this poor life that everything in this world belongs to it and we can eat and drink to excess. And this makes us so proud that we imagine that we will live forever—and yet life is dying. . . . And even though God has decorated this life with gold and silver and all His creatures, it is nevertheless pitiful and serves the devil. This kingdom we leave to man's council, the jurists, and the parents.

God lets death exercise His power and rule in this life in order that we might not live as miserly paunches and usurers but rather observing the miserable shooting and dying which begins in the womb and lasts to end of life and remember that our life has no permanency. Thus our text says that John preached that they should all look toward another life. The heathen did not know this. We have the grace and mercy, knowledge and wisdom that we know of an eternal life. Death will cease and another life will come. The heathen Cicero and Plato had a scent of it. But they had no assurance. But we can say, after this life, rather, in the midst of this life, there is another life, the kingdom of heaven, which is eternal.

And John also preaches the road and the street that leads in this direction. And he gives the light that illumines the way. He teaches the defense against the devil who tries in every way to obstruct the road. The worldly kingdom teaches nothing about all this. Here Satan does not fight us with physical death but he interferes with us spiritually and obstructs the road to the heavenly kingdom with much false pride and false belief. These arrows and weapons are more effective for the devil than his physical weapons. He rains down his arrows. Think of all the idolatries in one heart! But the Christian knows how one can break through all these arrows and weapons, cannons and guns—as Paul says (Ephesians 6:10ff), "Put on the armor of God," put on your boots and you can step into the mud. Put on your helmet, and so on.

But these are other weapons than those of human gladiators. Those are mere toys in comparison. It is with these spiritual weapons that the Christian breaks through and the devil cannot hinder him. The Christian must know and confess and help that we reach eternal life in order that we might not only be citizens in this life, where we live with our body and possessions, but even now also citizens in heaven. This one must know.

4. John Calvin

THE WORD OF THE LORD CAME UPON JOHN. Before relating, as the other Evangelists do, that John began to exercise his office of teaching, Luke asserts that he was divinely called to that office. He does so, in order to assure us, that the ministry of John carried undoubted authority. Why the interpreters have chosen to translate the word, ἐπὶ Ἰωάννην, "UPON John," instead of "TO John," I do not see: but because there is no ambiguity as to the meaning, that this commission was entrusted to him, and that he received a command to preach, I have followed the received version. Hence infer, that there are no regular teachers, but those on whom God has conferred the office; and that it is not enough to have the Word of God, if there be not likewise a special calling.

Matthew and Mark do not speak of the preaching of John as extending beyond *the wilderness,* while Luke says, that he *came into all the country around Jordan.* These statements may be reconciled by observing that John discharged the office of teaching among the neighbours with whom he dwelt, but that his Gospel spread more widely and became known in many places, so that the report of it, in a short time, reached Jerusalem. Indeed, the whole of that tract of the Jordan might be called a *wilderness*: for the word does not mean "a solitude," but "a rough and mountainous, and thinly inhabited, district."

PREACHING THE BAPTISM OF REPENTANCE. This form of expression shows first, generally, what is the right use of the Sacraments; and next, why *baptism* was instituted, and in what it consists. A sacrament, then, is not a dumb ceremony, exhibiting some unmeaning pomp without doctrine; but the Word of God is joined to it, and gives life to the outward ceremony. By *the Word* I mean, not mutterings of a magical character, made by some exorcist between his teeth, but what is pronounced with a clear and distinct voice and leads to the edification of faith. For we are not simply told that John *baptized unto repentance,* as if the grace of God were contained in a visible sign, but that he explained, in his preaching, the advantage of baptism, that the sign, through the word preached, might produce its effect. This is the peculiarity of baptism, that it is said to be an outward representation of *repentance for the forgiveness of sins.* Now, as the meaning, power, and nature of that baptism are the same as ours, if we judge of the figure from its true import, it is incorrect to say that the baptism of John is different from the baptism of Christ.

AND ALL FLESH SHALL SEE THE SALVATION OF GOD. That salvation will not be at all obscure, or experienced by a small number of persons, but will strike every eye and will be common to all. Hence it follows that this prediction was far from being accomplished when the people returned from Babylon; for though the Lord gave, at that time, a memorable display of His grace, yet He did not reveal His *salvation* to the whole world. On the contrary, the prophet's design which was to be manifested, in contrast with God's former benefits, and thus to inform believers, that the dispensations of God toward His Church had never been so remarkable nor His power so illustriously displayed in their deliverance. *Flesh* is here put for *men*, without being intended to denote their depravity.

5. Friedrich Schleiermacher

John, the precursor of our Lord, recalling the words of the prophet, proclaimed to his people, "prepare the way of the Lord." In order that He might come to you everything that is high and raises itself up must be brought low. First of all, he had in mind the glorying before God which was the custom of the more particular and conscientious of the children of Israel because of their faithful observance of the law and because of the privileges of their descent from the oldest of God's chosen. They felt that all this made them superior to other people and guaranteed them the grace of God. For this reason John proclaimed to them: "Whoever proudly raises his head, whatever the reason, shall be humbled and every imaginary peak shall be brought low so that the spiritual king of the true Zion might enter. . . . You pride yourselves to be Abraham's children. God is able from these stones to raise up children for Abraham. You pride yourselves that God's revelation dwells among you. Even now the ax is laid to the root of the tree. It will be cut down if it does not bring fruit. You pride yourselves that you do faithfully and conscientiously do all that the law of God demands of you. Remember the words, 'This people draw near with their mouths and honor me with their lips while their hearts are far from me, I shall cast them out.'" This was John's preaching of repentance. If we now ask whether we are still in need of such preaching, what is the answer? We are even more members of a particularly blessed part of our generation than these Jewish people were. Among us the saving Gospel of Jesus, the world's Saviour, has long been proclaimed. Are there among all those who carry His name none who seek their salvation elsewhere than in living communion with Him? Are there none who live out of some other trust than the trust in what they are in Him and may become ever more through Him?

Do we not claim a self-made righteousness based upon the ever ambiguous proofs of our own works? Is there no false confidence in the pure letter of doctrine? Is the correct understanding and enthusiastic defense of such doctrine more than at most an uncertain sign that the saving truth has deeply entered our heart?

If we ask these questions we will have to confess that there is many a hill that must be brought low in order that the King may enter. . . .

Thus this proclamation, "Every mountain and hill shall be brought low," is for us also a preaching of repentance. For if the Christian rests in his self-satisfied contentment because of the measure of godliness and perfection which he has received, the reason can only be that he simply overlooks the sinfulness of his own heart. . . . The Lord demands the entire soul in order to re-create and enlighten it through His Spirit. He who has known the Saviour can desire nothing less than to present his whole being to Him, so that He may conform it to His image. He who is satisfied with some minor improvement has not understood himself nor the Saviour.

Secondly, the prophet says, and John with him, "Every valley shall be filled." In the mountainous regions of this earth one finds narrow and deep valleys, so unfortunately located that the sun reaches them only rarely and for a few hours each year. Those who live there have a feeble notion of the splendor of the sky, of the richness of light, and of the joy and pleasure with which others bathe in the rays of the sun.

When sometimes the sun reaches these valleys it creates a deep desire in the heart of the inhabitants to have a richer experience of the glory they see only fleetingly. But the narrow concerns of their life in the remote valley soon capture them again, their fleeting wish is extinguished and they adjust to their old darkness and limitation. . . . These valleys shall be filled and all those who still live in the shadow of death shall be drawn out of the darkness of a meager earthly existence into the bright light of a new spiritual life. And when all shall rejoice in this light and behold the Lord as He blesses all with His grace—that is His most glorious Advent.

But there are still others who do not live in such deep valleys and yet in places where the land must be evened out. The majority of the people who have been reached by the Gospel enjoy a great many precious gifts. Even though not all of them recognize it, these gifts have their origin in this one heavenly source. Many things that darken and destroy the life of man have been removed. Destructive passions and desires have been modified through law and order. Many people have acquired a sense of shame about taking unfair advantage of others. They consider it an honor to belong to an order where law and decency dwells. They are willing to work and live for this order and even to die for it. . . . But among the multitude which enjoy these gifts there are only a few who find even the greatest accomplishments of human power too little. They desire more than a good conscience based on peace with the order of society. These are the people for whom the fellowship with Christ is the highest good. They rejoice that He has come to dwell in their hearts and that according to His word the Father came with Him. They can exclaim, "Lord, if I have only Thee, what do I ask for in heaven and on earth."

And the great multitude of the other cultured and moral people knows and feels that such godliness implies a blessing all its own. They know they do not have it, but deceive themselves with the comforting notion that such godliness is only for those who have a certain gift—which is not given to everyone. They are satisfied with faithful and eager service in their calling. . . . But we who consider the blessings of godliness to be above everything else cannot be content with such explanations. We must proclaim even to these brethren that the valleys must be filled where you dwell. The deceptions which imprison you must cease. Godliness is not the property of a special group. Rise to the courageous faith that you also are called into the blessed life of godliness. Learn that all your accomplishments, spiritual and glorious as they may be, cannot satisfy the human heart whose highest calling is to behold God.

They may consider this an inappropriate call to repentance but we want to proclaim to them that God has not been without witness. The outward and the inner world lead to Him the more deeply they are understood. . . . He alone must be your love, your peace; He alone deserves praise and glory. And if you are unable to hold on to Him and even to rejoice in Him, why do you not raise your hands and pray: "Descend to us, tear apart the heavens and dwell among us!" If you do this, the valley has been filled and the King of Glory may come in. . . .

But, indeed, this too is a preaching of repentance. For the congenital awareness of human nature of a highest being is never truly understood. The soul is still godless and idolatrous when it does not see that this feeling should rule our entire life and that it should appropriate and incorporate everything else within us. And it is equally certain that the call to true godliness cannot be heard without a devastating feeling of our own impotence and a deep desire for the Word which became flesh to dwell among us. For the truth that the consciousness of God should possess and govern man completely; this truth is only in the only-begotten Son of God. To recognize the one and to seek the other is one and the same thing—but, thanks be to God, to seek Him and to find Him are also one and the same.

And finally the prophet proclaims, "the crooked shall be made straight." If we consider how human beings guide each other from the lower to the higher, from the worse to the better, we cannot deny that the common path is crooked. To influence a man to listen to justice, order, and law, we explain to him that this is in his own interest. To influence him to put his trust in God, we explain to him that many occasions will arise where he will find no other comfort but this trust. When we meet people to whom the Gospel is an offense or foolishness we often try to excuse that which we in the very depths of our heart praise and acknowledge. We say that what they consider offensive is not so important; it isn't the main thing—and we offer some little thing that we hope they will accept and appropriate more easily.

If we think that this is to prepare the way of the Lord we err indeed. These are the crooked ways which the King of Glory cannot honestly choose. The principle that a detour, if only better paved, easier, and smoother, is to be preferred to the straight way is what the King disdains. . . . He wants to enter the human heart on the straight road of truth. Only if people are led on this way do they come into the possession of the heavenly gifts He is willing to offer and are they able to receive Him.

This was the way of the first messengers. They did not hesitate because to some of their hearers the message of the Cross was an offense and to others foolishness. They insisted that they did not want to know anything but Christ and Him crucified. They did not try to hide this message with something for some reason more pleasing to their audience. No, this Jesus whom you delivered up, God has raised from the dead and made Him Lord and Christ. It was on this straight road that they brought men to say, "Brethren, what shall we do to be saved?" Even today and forever there is no other way to introduce the Lord into human hearts than this short and straight way of open truth. If we want to advance His entry we must make straight all that is crooked. He who would like to smuggle the Christian faith under some pretense into the soul of man, he who recommends this faith as a means to some other end, he who thinks that this faith can be cut and adjusted to measure—he does not prepare the way of the Lord but belongs to those of whom it is said "Many will come and say 'Lo, here is the Christ,' or 'There he is.'" Do not believe them.

We must walk straight as the first disciples, then only do we prepare the way. Do you feel that you are called to a blessedness which you do not have now? Do you know that there is an eternal life for man which is not yet yours? Can you reach this by yourself? Can you light the light to illuminate your way? Do you know how to escape the mud and mire? Say "yes" or "no"! The simple truth is thus held before the souls of men. Whatever the answer may be, the crooked has been made straight. When the right time comes the resistance will be broken and quietly or loudly, eagerly or reluctantly, the inner voice will make the humble confession for which the Lord is waiting in order to draw the soul to Himself. Nothing should then prevent the acceptance of the invitation: "Come to me, all who labor and are heavy laden, and I will give you rest. Take my yoke upon you, and learn from me; for I am gentle and lowly in heart, and you will find rest for your souls. For my yoke is easy, and my burden is light."

THE SECOND SUNDAY IN ADVENT

Text: Luke 21:25-33

1. John Chrysostom

Forasmuch as He had said, "Immediately after the tribulation of those days"; but they sought of this, after how long a time it should be, and desired to know in particular the very day. Therefore He puts also the similitude of the fig tree, indicating that the interval was not great, but that in quick succession would occur His advent also. And this He declared not by the parable alone, but by the words that follow, saying, "know that it is near, even at the doors."

Whereby He foretells another thing also, a spiritual summer, and a calm that should be on that day (after the present tempest) for the righteous; but to the sinners the contrary, winter after summer, which He declares in what follows, saying, "the day shall come upon them, when they are living in luxury."

But not for this intent only did He put forward this about the fig tree, in order to declare the interval; for it was possible to have set this before them in other ways as well; but that he might hereby also confirm His saying, as assuredly thus to come to pass. For as this *of the fig tree* is of necessity, so that too. For thus, wherever He is minded to speak of that which will assuredly come to pass, He brings forward the necessary courses of nature, both Himself, and the blessed Paul imitating Him. Therefore also when speaking of His resurrection, He saith, "When the corn of wheat hath fallen into the earth, except it die, it abideth alone; but if it die, it bringeth forth much fruit." Whereby also the blessed Paul being instructed uses the same similitude: "Thou fool," he saith, "that which thou sowest is not quickened, except it die."

After this, that they might not straightway return to it again, and say, "When?" he brings to their remembrance the things that had been said, saying, "Verily I say unto you, This generation shall not pass, till all these things be fulfilled!" All these things. What things? I pray thee. Those about Jerusalem, those about the wars, about the famines, about the pestilences, about the earthquakes, about the false Christs, about the false prophets, about the sowing of the Gospel everywhere, the seditions, the tumults, all the other things, which He said were to occur until His coming. How then, one may ask, did He say, "This generation?" Speaking not of the generation then living, but of that of the believers. For He is wont to distinguish a generation not by times only, but also by the mode of religious service, and practice; as when He saith, "This is the generation of them that seek the Lord."

23

For what He said above, "All these must come to pass," and again, "The Gospel shall be preached," He declares here also, saying, "All these things shall surely come to pass, and the generation of the faithful shall remain, cut off by none of the things that have been mentioned. For both Jerusalem shall perish, and the more part of the Jews shall be destroyed, but over this generation shall nothing prevail, not famine, not pestilence, not earthquake, nor the tumults of wars, not false Christs, not false prophets, not deceivers, not traitors, not those that cause to offend, not the false brethren, nor any other such like temptation whatever."

Then to lead them on more in faith, He saith, "Heaven and earth shall pass away, but my words shall not pass away"; that is, it were more easy for these firm, fixed, and immovable bodies to be blotted out, than for aught of My words to fall to the ground. And he who gainsays these things, let him test His sayings, and when he hath found them true (for so he surely will find them) from what is past, let him believe also the things to come, and let him search out all things with diligence, and he will see the actual events bearing witness to the truth of the prophecy. And the elements He hath brought forward, at once to declare, that the Church is of more honor than Heaven and earth, and at the same time to indicate Himself by this also to be Maker of all. For since He was speaking of the end, a thing disbelieved by many, He brought forward Heaven and earth, indicating His unspeakable power, and showing with great authority, that He is Lord of all, and by these things rendering His sayings deserving of credit, even with those who are much given to doubt.

"But of that day and hour knoweth no man, no, not the angels of Heaven, neither the Son, but the Father." By saying, "not the angels," He stopped their mouths, that they should not seek to learn what these angels know not; and by saying, "neither the Son," forbids them not only to learn, but even to inquire. For in proof that therefore He said this, see after His resurrection, when He saw they were become over curious, how He stopped their mouths more decidedly. For now indeed He hath mentioned infallible signs, many and endless; but then He saith merely, "It is not for you to know times or seasons." And then that they might not say, "we are driven to perplexity, we are utterly scorned, we are not held worthy so much as of this," He says, "which the Father hath put in His own power." And this, because He was exceedingly careful to honor them, and to conceal nothing from them. Therefore He refers it to His Father, both to make the thing awful, and to exclude that of which He had spoken from their inquiry. Since if it be not this, but He is ignorant of it, when will He know it? Will it be together with us? But who would say this? And the Father He knoweth clearly, even as clearly as He knoweth the Son; and of the day is He ignorant? Moreover, "the Spirit indeed searcheth even the deep things of God," and doth not He know so much as the time of the judgment? But how He ought to judge He knoweth, and of the secrets of each He hath a full perception; and what is far more common than that, of this could He be ignorant? And how, if "all things were made by Him, and without Him was not even one thing made," was He ignorant of the day? For He who made the worlds, it is quite plain that He made the times also; and if the times, even that day. How then is He ignorant of that which He made?

And ye indeed say that ye know even His substance, "but that the Son not even the day," the Son, who is always in the bosom of the Father; and yet His substance is much greater than the days, even infinitely greater. How then, while assigning to yourselves the greater things, do you not allow even the less to the Son, "in whom are hid all the treasures of wisdom and knowledge." But neither do you know what God is in His substance, though ten thousand times ye talk thus madly, neither is the Son ignorant of the day, but is even in full certainty thereof.

For this cause, I say, when He had told all things, both the times and the seasons, and had brought it to the very doors ("for it is near," He saith, "even at the doors"), He was silent as to the day. "For if thou seek after the day and hour, thou shalt not hear them of me," saith He; "but if of times and preludes, without hiding anything, I will tell thee all exactly. . . . For that indeed I am not ignorant of it, I have shown by many things; having mentioned intervals, and all the things that are to occur, and how short from this present time until the day itself (for this did the parable of the fig tree indicate), and I lead thee to the very vestibule; and if I do not open unto thee the doors this also I do for your good."

And that thou mayest learn by another thing also, that the silence is not a mark of what we have mentioned, how He sets forth another sign also. "But as in the days of Noah they were eating and drinking, marrying and giving in marriage, until the day that the flood came, and took all away; so shall also the coming of the Son of Man be." And these things He spake, showing that He should come on a sudden, and unexpectedly, and when the more part were living luxuriously. For Paul too saith this, writing on this wise, "When they shall speak of peace and safety, then sudden destruction cometh upon them"; and to show how unexpected, He said, "as travail upon a woman with child." How then doth He say, "after the tribulation of those days"? For if there be luxury then, and peace, and safety, as Paul saith, how doth He say, "after the tribulation of those days"? If there be luxury, how is there tribulation? Luxury for them that are in a state of insensibility and peace. Therefore He said not, "when there is peace," but "when they speak of peace and safety," indicating their insensibility to be such as of those in Noah's time, for that amid such evils they lived in luxury.

But not so the righteous, but they were passing their time in tribulation and dejection. Whereby He shows, that when Antichrist is come, the pursuit of unlawful pleasures shall be more eager among the transgressors, and those that have learned to despair of their own salvation. Then shall be gluttony, then revelings, and drunkenness. Wherefore also most of all He puts forth an example corresponding to the thing. For like as when the ark was making, they believed not, saith He; but while it was set in the midst of them, proclaiming beforehand the evils that are to come, they, when they saw it, lived in pleasure, just as though nothing dreadful were about to take place; so also now, Antichrist indeed shall appear, after whom is the end, and the punishments at the end, and vengeance intolerable; but they that are held by the intoxication of wickedness shall not so much as perceive the dreadful nature of the things that are on the point of being done. Wherefore also Paul saith, "as travail upon a woman with child," even so shall those fearful and incurable evils come upon them.

And wherefore did He not speak of the ills in Sodom? It was His will to introduce an example embracing all men, and disbelieved after it was foretold. So therefore, as by the more part the things to come are disbelieved, He confirms those things by the past, terrifying their minds. And together with the points I have mentioned, He shows this also, that of the former things also He was the doer. Then again He sets another sign, by all which things He makes it evident, that He is not ignorant of the day. And what is the sign? "Then shall two be in the field; one shall be taken, and one left. Two women shall be grinding at the mill, one shall be taken, and one left. Watch therefore, for ye know not what hour your Lord doth come." And all these things are both proofs that He knew, and calculated to turn them from their inquiry. So for this cause He spake also of the days of Noah, for this cause He said, too, "Two shall be on the bed," signifying this, that He should come upon them thus unexpectedly, when they were thus without thought, and "two women grinding at the mill," which also of itself is not the employment of them that are taking thought.

And, together with this, He declares that servants as well as masters should be both taken and left, both those who are at ease, and those in toil, as well from the one rank as from the other; even as in the Old Testament He saith, "From him that sitteth upon the throne to the captive woman that is at the mill." For since He had said, that hardly are the rich saved, He shows that not even these are altogether lost, neither are the poor saved all of them, but both out of these and out of those are men saved, and lost.

And to me He seems to declare that at night will be the Advent. For this Luke too saith, "Seest thou how accurately He knows all things"?

After this again, that they may not ask about it, He added, "Watch therefore, for ye know not what hour your Lord doth come." He said not, "I know not," but, "ye know not." For when He had brought them well nigh to the very hour, and had placed them there, again He deters them from the inquiry, from a desire that they should be striving always. Therefore He saith, "Watch," showing that for the sake of this, He did not tell it.

"But know this, that if the good man of the house had known in what watch the thief would come, he would have watched, and would not have suffered his house to be broken up. Therefore be ye also ready, for in such an hour as ye think not the Son of Man cometh."

For this intent He tells them not, in order that they may watch, that they may be always ready; therefore He saith, "When ye look not for it, then He will come," desiring that they should be anxiously waiting, and continually in virtuous action.

But His meaning is like this: If the common sort of men knew when they were to die, they would surely strive earnestly at that hour.

In order therefore that they may strive, not at that hour only, therefore He tells them not either the common hour, or the hour of each, desiring them to be ever looking for this, that they may be always striving. Wherefore He made the end of each man's life also uncertain.

2. Martin Luther

AND WHEN THESE THINGS BEGIN TO COME TO PASS, LOOK UP, AND LIFT UP YOUR HEADS; BECAUSE YOUR REDEMPTION DRAWETH NIGH. Here you may ask, Who can lift up his head in the face of such terrible wrath and judgment? If the whole world is filled with fear at that day, and lets fall its head and countenance out of terror and anxiety, how shall we look up and lift up our heads, which evidently means, how shall we manifest any joy in and longing for these signs? In answer I would say that all this is spoken only to those who are really Christians and not to heathen and Jews. True Christians are so afflicted with all manner of temptations and persecutions that in this life they are miserable. Therefore they wait and long and pray for redemption from sin and all evil; as we also pray in the Lord's Prayer, "Thy kingdom come," and "Deliver us from evil." If we are true Christians we will earnestly and heartily join in this prayer. If we do not so pray, we are not yet true Christians.

If we pray aright, our condition must truly be such that, however terrible these signs may be, we will look up to them with joy and earnest desire, as Christ admonishes: "When these things begin to come to pass, look up." He does not say, "Be filled with fear or drop your heads; for there is coming that for which we have been so earnestly praying." If we really wish to be freed from sin and death and hell, we must look forward to this coming of the Lord with joy and pleasure.

Saint Paul also says, in 2 Timothy 4:8, "Henceforth there is laid up for me the crown of righteousness, which the Lord, the righteous judge, shall give to me at that day: and not only to me, but also to all them that have loved his appearing." If He gives the crown to those who love His appearing, what will He give to those who hate and dread it? Without doubt, to enemies, eternal condemnation. Titus 2:13 says, "Looking for the blessed hope and appearing of the glory of the Great God and our Saviour Jesus Christ." And Luke 12:36, "And be ye yourselves like unto men looking for their lord, when he shall return from the marriage feast."

But what do those do who are filled with fear and do not desire to have Him come, when they pray, "Thy kingdom come, thy will be done," "deliver us from the evil one"? Do they not stand in the presence of God and lie to their own hurt? Do they not strive against the will of God who will have this day for the redemption of the saints? It is necessary, therefore, that we exercise great care lest we be found to hate and to dread that day. Such dread is a bad omen and belongs to the damned, whose cold minds and hard hearts must be terrified and broken, if perchance they might reform.

But to believers that day will be comforting and sweet. That day will be the highest joy and safety to the believer, and the deepest terror and anguish to the unbeliever; just as also in this life the truths of the Gospel are exceedingly sweet to the godly and exceedingly hateful to the wicked. Why should the believer fear and not rather exceedingly rejoice, since he trusts in Christ Who comes as Judge to redeem him and to be his everlasting portion?

But you say I would indeed await His coming with joy, if I were holy and without sin. I should answer, what relief do you find in fear and flight? It would not redeem you from sin if you were to be filled with terror for a thousand years. The damned are eternally filled with fear of that day, but this does not take away their sin; yea, this fear rather increases sin and renders man unfit to appear without sin on that day when it comes. Fear must pass out of the soul and there must enter in a desire for righteousness and for that day. But if you really desire to be free from sin and to be holy, then give thanks to God and continue to desire to be more free from sin. Would to God that such desire were so sincere and powerful in you as to bring you to your death.

There is no one so well prepared for the judgment day as he who longs to be without sin. If you have such desire, what do you fear? You are then in perfect accord with the purpose of that day. It comes to set free from sin all who desire it, and you belong to that number. Return thanks to God and abide in that desire. Christ says His coming is for our redemption. But do not deceive yourself and be satisfied, perhaps, with the simple desire to be free from sin and to await the coming of that day without fear. Perhaps your heart is false and you are filled with fear, not because you would be free from sin, but because in the face of that day you cannot sin free and untrammeled. See to it that the light within you be not darkness. For a heart that would be truly free from sin will certainly rejoice in the day that fulfills its desire. If the heart does not so rejoice there is no true desire to be loosed from its sin.

Therefore we must above all things lay aside all hatred and abhorrence of this day, and exercise diligence that we may really desire to have our sins taken away. When this is done, we may not only calmly await the day, but with heartfelt desire and joy pray for it and say, "Thy kingdom come, thy will be done." In this you must cast aside all feelings and conceit, hold fast to the comforting words of Christ, and rest in them alone.

Could He admonish, comfort, and strengthen you in a more delicate and loving manner? In the first place He says, "You will hear of wars, but you should have no fears." And when He tells you to have no fears, what else does He mean than that He commands you to be of good cheer and to discern the signs with joy? Secondly, He tells you to look up; thirdly, to lift up your heads; and fourthly, He speaks of your redemption. What can comfort and strengthen you if such a word does not? Do you think He would deceive you and try to lead you into a false confidence? My dear hearer, let such a word not have been said in vain: thank God and trust in it—there is no other comfort or advice if you cast this to the winds. It is not your condemnation but your redemption of which Christ speaks. Will you turn His words around and say, "It is not your redemption but your condemnation"? Will you flee from your own salvation? Will you not greet and thank your God Who comes out to meet and to greet you?

He has no doubt also spoken this word for the faint-hearted who, although they are devout and prepared for the last day, are yet filled with great anxiety and are hindered in taking part in His coming with that desire which should be found at the end of the world; therefore He calls attention to their redemption. For when at the end of the world sin will hold such sway—and by the side of sin the punishment for sin with pestilence, war, and famine—it will be necessary to give to believers strength and comfort against both evils, sin and its punishment. Therefore He uses the sweet and comforting word "redemption" which is so dear to the heart of man. What is redemption? Who would not be redeemed? Who would have a desire to abide in the desert of sin and punishment? Who would not wish an end to such misery and woe, such perils for souls, such ruin for man? Especially should this be the case when the Saviour allures, invites, and comforts us in such an endearing way.

The godless fanatical preachers are to be censured, those who in their sermons deprive people of these words of Christ and faith in them, who desire to make people devout by terrifying them, and who teach them to prepare for the last day by relying upon their good works as satisfaction for their sins. Here despair, fear, and terror must remain and grow and with it hatred, aversion, and abhorrence for the coming of the Lord, and enmity against God be established in the heart; for they picture Christ as but a stern judge whose wrath must be appeased by works, and they never present Him as the Redeemer, as He calls and offers Himself, of Whom we are to expect that out of pure grace He will redeem us from sin and evil.

Such is always the result where the Gospel is not rightly proclaimed. When hearts are driven only by commands and threats, they will only be estranged from God and be led to abhor Him. We ought to terrify, but only the obstinate and hardened; and when these have become terrified and dejected also, we ought to strengthen and comfort.

From all this we learn how few there are who pray the Lord's Prayer acceptably even though it is prayed unceasingly in all the world. There are few who would not rather that the day would never come. This is nothing else than to desire that the kingdom of God may not come. Therefore the heart prays contrary to the lips, and while God judges according to the heart, they judge according to the lips. For this reason they institute so many prayers, fill all the churches with their bawling, and think they pray aright when in reality their prayer is: "May the kingdom not come, or not just yet." Tell me, is not such a prayer blasphemy? Is it not of such a prayer that the Psalmist speaks in Psalms 109:7, "Let his prayer be turned into sin." How men are applying all the wealth of the world to fill every nook and corner of it with such blasphemy, and then are calling it a divine service!

Yet he who feels such fear must not despair, but rather use it wisely. He uses it wisely who permits such fear to urge and admonish him to pray for grace that this fear might be taken away and he be given joy and delight in that day. Christ has promised (Matthew 7:8), "Everyone that asketh receiveth." Therefore those who are fearful are nearer their salvation than the hard-hearted and reprobate, who neither fear nor find comfort in that day. For though they do not have a desire for it, they have a something within which admonishes them to pray for such a desire.

On the other hand, he uses fear unwisely who allows it to increase and abides in the same, as though he could thereby be cleansed from sin. This leads to nothing good. Not fear which, as John says (1 John 4:18), must be cast out, will remain in that day, but love which St. Paul says (1 Corinthians 13:8) must abide. Fear is to be a power to drive us to seek such love and pray for it. Where fear is not cast out it opposes the will of God and antagonizes your own salvation; it thus becomes a sin against the Holy Spirit. It is, however, not necessary to say that the individual must be altogether without fear, for we still have human nature abiding in us. This is weak and cannot exist altogether without the fear of death and the judgment; but the spirit must be uppermost in the mind, as Christ says (Matthew 26:41), "The spirit indeed is willing, but the flesh is weak."

AND HE SPAKE TO THEM A PARABLE: BEHOLD THE FIG TREE, AND ALL THE TREES: WHEN THEY NOW SHOOT FORTH, YE SEE IT AND KNOW OF YOUR OWN SELVES THAT THE SUMMER IS NOW NIGH. EVEN SO YE ALSO, WHEN YE SEE THESE THINGS COMING TO PASS, KNOW YE THAT THE KINGDOM OF GOD IS NIGH. Pure words of comfort are these. He does not put forth a parable from the fall or winter season when all the trees are bare and the dreary days begin, but a parable from the spring and summer season, when everything is joyous, when all creation buds forth and rejoices. By this He clearly teaches that we are to look forward to the last day with as much joy and delight as all creation shows in spring and summer. What is the meaning of this parable if in it He does not teach us this? He could have found others that were not so joyous.

In applying it, He does not say your hell or condemnation is at hand, but the kingdom of God. What else does it signify that the kingdom of God is at hand than that our redemption is near? The kingdom of God is but ourselves, as Christ says (Luke 17:21), "For lo, the kingdom of God is within you"; therefore, it draweth nigh when we are nearing our redemption from sin and evil. In this life it begins in the spirit; but since we must still battle with sin and suffer much evil, and since death is still before us, the kingdom of God is not yet perfect in us. But when once sin and death and all evil are taken away, then will it be perfect. This the last day will bring and not this life.

Therefore, my dear hearer, examine your life, probe your heart to ascertain how it is disposed toward this day. Do not put your trust in your own good life, for that would soon be put to shame; but think of and strengthen your faith in order that the day may not be a terror to you as to the damned, but be your joy as the day of your salvation and of the kingdom of God in you. Then when you think or hear of the same, your heart will leap for joy and earnestly long for its coming. If you do not wish to pronounce judgment upon yourself, then do not think that you would be able to stand in that day even with the meritorious deeds of all the saints.

3. John Calvin

THEN SHALL APPEAR THE SIGN OF THE SON OF MAN. By this term Christ points out more clearly the difference between the present condition of His kingdom and its future glory; for it is a sort of admission that, amidst the "darkness" of "tribulations," the majesty of Christ will not fully appear, and men will not perceive the redemption which He has brought. The confused mixture of things which we now perceive does certainly, on the one hand, "darken" our minds and, on the other hand, bury the grace of Christ, and make it almost vanish from our sight, so that the salvation obtained by Him, so far as relates to the perception of the flesh, is not comprehended. And therefore He declares that He will appear openly at His last coming and, surrounded by the heavenly power, which will be a "sign" erected on an elevated spot, He will turn the eyes of the whole world upon Himself.

Perceiving that the greater part of men would despise His doctrine and oppose His reign, He threatens also against all nations "mourning" and "lamentation"; because it is proper, that by His presence He should crush and destroy the rebels who, while He was absent, despised His authority. He says this partly to bring the haughty and refractory to repentance by striking them with terror, and partly to confirm the minds of His followers amidst so great obstinacy existing in the world. For it is no slight ground of offense to see the ungodly living without concern because they think that their mockery of God will remain unpunished; and again, there is nothing to which we are more prone than to be captivated by the allurements of the prosperity which they enjoy, so as to lose the fear of God. That the joy by which they are intoxicated may not excite the envy of believers, Christ declares that it will at length be turned into "mourning" and "gnashing of teeth."

He alludes, I think, to Zechariah 12:11-14 where God, informing them that a striking display of His judgment will soon be made, declares that there will be "lamentation in every family," such as is not usually seen at the funeral of a first-born son. There is no reason, therefore, why any person should expect the conversion of the world, for at length—when it will be too late and will yield them no advantage—"they shall look on him whom they pierced" (Zechariah 12:10). Next follows the explanation of that sign, that "they shall see the Son of man coming in the clouds," Who at that time was living on earth in the garb of a despised servant, and thus might lead them further on in the path of hope and patience. According to this argument, Christ keeps the minds of believers in a state of suspense till the last day, that they may not imagine those declarations, which the prophets made about the future restoration, to have failed of their accomplishment, because they lie buried for a long period under the thick darkness of tribulations.

THE TRIBULATION OF THOSE DAYS. This is improperly interpreted by some commentators to mean the destruction of Jerusalem; for, on the contrary, it is a general recapitulation of all the evils of which Christ had previously spoken. To encourage His followers to patience, He employs this argument, that the tribulations will at length have a happy and joyful result. As if he had said, "So long as the Church shall continue its pilgrimage in the world, there will be dark and cloudy weather; but as soon as an end shall have been put to those distresses, a day will arrive when the majesty of the Church shall be illustriously displayed." In what manner "the sun will be darkened" we cannot now conjecture, but the event will show. Indeed, He does not mean that "the stars" will actually fall, but according to the apprehension of men; and accordingly Luke predicts only that "there will be signs in the sun, and in the moon, and in the stars." The meaning, therefore, is that there will be such a violent commotion of the firmament of heaven, that the stars themselves will be supposed to fall. Luke also adds that there will be a dreadful commotion of the sea, "the sea and the waves roaring, so that men will faint through fear" and alarm. In a word, all the creatures above and below will be, as it were, heralds to summon men to that tribunal, which they will continue to treat with ungodly and wanton contempt till the last day.

.   .   .   .   .

AND WHEN THESE THINGS BEGIN TO TAKE PLACE. Luke expresses more clearly the consolation by which Christ animates the minds of His followers; for, though this sentence contains nothing different from the words of Matthew, which we have just now explained, yet it shows better for what purpose "the angels will come," as we are told, "to gather the elect." For it was necessary to contrast the joy of the godly with the general sorrow and distress of the world, and to point out the difference between them and the reprobate, that they might not view with horror the coming of Christ. We know that Scripture, when it speaks not only of the last judgment, but of all the judgments which God executes every day, describes them in a variety of ways, according as the discourse is addressed to believers or to unbelievers. "To what purpose is the day of the Lord to you?" asks the prophet Amos (5:18). "It is a day of darkness and gloominess, not of light"; of sorrow, not of joy; of destruction, not of salvation. On the other hand, Zechariah (9:9) bids the "daughter of Zion rejoice" on account of the "coming" of her "King"; and justly, for—as Isaiah 35.4 tells us—the same day that brings wrath and vengeance to the reprobate brings good-will and redemption to believers.

Christ therefore shows that, at His coming, the light of joy will arise on His disciples, that they may rejoice in the approaching salvation, while the wicked are overwhelmed with terror. Accordingly, Paul distinguishes them by this mark, that they "wait for the day or coming of the Lord" (1 Corinthians 1:7) for that which is their crown, and perfect happiness and solace, is delayed till "that day" (2 Timothy 4:8). It is therefore called here (as in Romans 8:23) "redemption"; because we shall then obtain truly and perfectly the consequences of the deliverance obtained through Christ. Let our ears therefore be awake to the sound of the angel's trumpet which will then sound, not only to strike the reprobate with the dread of death, but to arouse the elect to a second life; that is, to call by the voice of His Gospel; for it is a sign of infidelity to be afraid when the Son of God comes in person for our salvation.

.   .   .   .   .

I do not suppose the meaning of this to be merely that, during the state of confusion which has been mentioned, there will be as evident a sign that the coming of Christ is nigh, as that by which we know with certainty that the summer is at hand, when the trees begin to grow green; but, in my opinion, Christ expresses something else. For as in winter the trees, contracted by the severity of the cold, show greater vigor, but in spring lose their toughness and appear more feeble, and are even cleft asunder to open up a passage for fresh twigs, so the afflictions by which, according to the perception of the flesh, the Church is softened, do not in any way impair its vigor. As the inward sap diffused through the whole tree, after having produced this softness, collects strength to throw itself out for renovating what was dead, so the Lord draws from the corruption of the outward man the perfect restoration of His people. The general instruction conveyed is that the weak and frail condition of the Church ought not to lead us to conclude that it is dying, but rather to expect the immortal glory for which the Lord prepares His people by the Cross and by afflictions; for what Paul maintains in reference to each of the members must be fulfilled in the whole body, that "if the outward man is decayed, the inward man is renewed day by day" (2 Corinthians 4:16).

What Matthew and Mark had stated more obscurely, "know you that it is nigh at the door," is more fully explained by Luke, "know you that THE KINGDOM OF GOD is at hand"; and in this passage "the kingdom of God is not represented—as in many other passages—at its commencement, but at its perfection, and that according to the views of those whom Christ was teaching. For they did not view "the kingdom of God" in the Gospel as consisting in the "peace and joy" of faith, and in spiritual "righteousness" (Romans 14:17) but sought that blessed rest and glory which is concealed under hope till the last day.

THIS GENERATION SHALL NOT PASS AWAY. Though Christ employs a general expression, He does not extend the discourses to all the miseries that would befall the Church, but merely informs them, that before a single generation shall have been completed, they will learn by experience the truth of what He has said. For within fifty years the city was destroyed and the Temple was razed, the whole country was reduced to a hideous desert, and the obstinacy of the world rose up against God. Nay more, their rage was inflamed to exterminate the doctrine of salvation, false teachers arose to corrupt the pure gospel by their impostures, religion sustained amazing shocks, and the whole company of the godly was miserably distressed. Now though the same evils were perpetrated in uninterrupted succession for many ages afterward, yet what Christ said was true—that, before the close of a single generation, believers would feel in reality, and by undoubted experience, the truth of His prediction; for the apostles endured the same things that we see in the present day. And yet it was not the design of Christ to promise to His followers that their calamities would be terminated within a short time (for then he would have contradicted himself, having previously warned them that "the end was not yet"); but, in order to encourage them to perseverance, He expressly foretold that those things related to their own age. The meaning therefore is: "This prophecy does not relate to evils that are distant, which posterity will see after the lapse of many centuries, but those that are now hanging over you, and ready to fall in one mass; so that there is no part of it which the present generation will not experience." So then, while our Lord heaps upon a single generation every kind of calamities, He does not by any means exempt future ages from the same kind of sufferings, but only enjoins the disciples to be prepared for enduring them all with firmness.

HEAVEN AND EARTH SHALL PASS AWAY. In order to secure greater confidence in His statements, He illustrates their certainty by this comparison—that it is more firm and stable than the entire structure of the world. But this form of expression is explained by commentators in a variety of ways. Some refer it to the passing away of heaven and earth at the last day, by which their frail constitution will be brought to an end; others explain it to mean that the entire structure of the world sooner shall perish, than the prophecy which we have just heard shall fail to be accomplished. But as there can be no doubt that Christ expressly intended to raise the minds of His followers above the contemplation of the world, I think that He refers to the continual changes we see in the world, and affirms that we ought not to judge of His sayings by the changeful character of the world, which resembles the billows of the sea; for we know how easily our minds are carried away by the affairs of the world when it is undergoing incessant change. For this reason, Christ enjoins His disciples not to allow their attention to be occupied by the world, but to look down, from what may be called the lofty watch-tower of divine Providence, on all that He foretold would happen. Yet from this passage we draw a useful doctrine, that our salvation, because it is founded on the promises of Christ, does not fluctuate according to the various agitations of the world, but remains unshaken provided only that our faith rises above heaven and earth and ascends to Christ Himself.

4. John Keble

Would it be a joy or a grief to me, were the Advent now to happen? Now when I say that the answer to such a question as this may be a rule and measure for a man, how he is himself prepared for death and judgment, I perceive that I am saying a thing which may cause pain and sadness to some whom God would not have saddened. Therefore I beseech you earnestly to attend to the differences I am going to point out. The question is not whether one should be alarmed or not at the sudden coming of our Lord. It may be that the holiest and best, who then shall be alive, will be most deeply moved with the remembrance of their own sins and infirmities. But the question is: were that Day now at hand, should we sorrow as men without hope at the final departure of the good things of this world? Well may we tremble to appear before our Judge! But if we be at all such as He would have us, our trembling and amazement will be tempered with a comfortable sense of His fatherly care over us, and a hope that He will be merciful to us, and that we have not quite forfeited our interest in Him. On the other hand, if we have permitted our hearts and members to go astray from Him, and have not returned by due and timely repentance, our fear in that day will be not like the fear of sons. It will be a desperate horror, as of persons made aware that their last stake has failed them, and they have no chance of happiness or relief forever. This then is the question I could wish to ask of my own conscience, and of all your consciences, my brethren. If the cry were now made, "the Bridegroom cometh," no doubt we feel that we should go forth to meet Him in fear. But in what sort of fear? The fear which a penitent child might have of an offended father, or the mere selfish fear of punishment, such as the worst of men may feel when he is found out, and the sentence of the law is taking hold of him? Is it a miserable, slavish fear, or a contrite fear, a fear mingled with love? You will say, "How am I to know?" I will try and tell you some signs of the right sort of fear of the last day. It is such a fear as causes a person not to turn away his mind altogether from the thought of that day, but rather to prepare himself for it without loss of time. Suppose servants, in their master's absence, carrying on badly; of course they would be filled with fear when anything happened to make them feel that he might look in upon them at any moment. It would be a good and useful fear if it caused them to turn their minds in earnest toward amending their ways, if it stirred up the indolent to set about his work, if it quieted the noisy and unruly, if it restrained the dissolute and daring from improper liberties. But if the same servants, when the fear came across them, should presently try to drive it away by plunging deeper in excess of riot, or if those who could not quite rid themselves of it should yet care so much for the ridicule of the rest, or be so enslaved by their own old bad habits, as still to go on in the courses they knew would most grieve and provoke their master, then every one would say, their fear was not worth much, it was altogether of the wrong sort, and would not save them from a heavy reckoning at last. For what sort of an excuse would that be, when the master of the house came home, for the servant to go and say to him, "It is true, I neglected your work; I disobeyed your commands; I kept bad company; I wasted your goods; I did such and such wrong things; but I feared all the time you would be angry when you came to know it"? Would not the master say at once to him, "Out of thine own mouth will I judge thee; thou fearedst mine anger: why then didst thou go on offending me"? And who would say that such a servant was dealt with hardly if he were driven from his master's house for good and all?

By this then we may judge ourselves, my brethren, concerning our own fear of the coming of Christ, or of our own latter end. If it cause us to break off our iniquities, to do right things, and leave wrong things undone, it is a wholesome and godly fear, and the longer, and more diligently we obey its motions, the more may we thank God and take courage. A man, we will suppose, is in grievous sin before God: he is a thief, and has put his hand to his neighbor's goods; or he is unclean, having given himself up to the indulgence of some unlawful lust; or he is slothful and irreligious, neglecting his prayers, not coming to God's solemn worship. He comes to worship, and hears something in a lesson, or in a sermon, about the hour of death or the day of judgment which strikes him, makes him uneasy, will not let him rest. Or he takes up a book, and lights upon words which Providence seems to have thrown on purpose in his way, words that seem to him to speak of, and to mean, his very self and no other person. Or some fearful change perchance happens in his own home, or closely within his knowledge, that is to him as the finger of God: he cannot doubt the purpose and meaning of it. He is frightened for the time; he mourns to think of the Son of Man coming, and finding him as he is. Is it a good and wholesome fear or not? Wait a little and we shall see; I cannot tell you just yet. But I will tell you by and by, when I know for certain whether or not he is leaving off his sin. I am sure that only in such measure as he really leaves it off and desires the blessing of God on his endeavors, in such measure his fear of the last day will cease to be a slavish fear and will be mingled more and more with a dutiful love of God, as being still his Father, though wronged and displeased; and as still holding out the sweet hope of pardon and acceptance, through His Son Jesus Christ.

But alas! It is too plain that the generality of people calling themselves Christians do indeed fear death and judgment, when those awful realities are brought before their minds, but with no good and holy fear, else there would be better and more abundant fruits of penitence. Men do not so much fear God, they do not so much shrink from the thought of what their sins may bring them to hereafter, but they are uneasy at recollecting that, whether they will or not, they must part with this present world. Their way of going on shows too clearly, what is that causes them so to hate the remembrance of the end. There then will be no more of the pursuits and pleasures on which they have set their hearts. No more feastings then; no more sports and games; no more dress and show; no more managing and money-getting; no more marrying and giving in marriage; no more buying, selling, trading, planting and building. No more living upon vain shows and false pretenses; no plausible, comfortable ways of hiding our faults from ourselves and from one another, and so flattering ourselves that God will overlook them too. But all that is unreal will vanish away; all that is untrue will be exposed and brought to light. No wonder that we shrink from this, we who have contented ourselves with shadows and delight to have it so. No wonder that the unfaithful servant hides his eyes from his master's coming; no wonder if the negligent scholar had rather not see the face of his teacher. "Men love darkness rather than light, because their deeds are evil. For he that doeth evil hateth the light, neither cometh to the light, lest his deeds should be reproved." Therefore solemn thoughts are a trouble to us; therefore we draw back from holy things; therefore we are glad of any excitement of business or diversion that may fill our minds for the time and drive the true and eternal things out of them. "And what will ye do in the end thereof?" Which way will ye look in that day, when all around will be the earth, which you have idolized, burning; underneath the bottomless pit, for which you will have prepared yourselves, opening; above, the sign of the Son of Man, the Cross, which you have slighted, appearing in Heaven?

THE THIRD SUNDAY IN ADVENT

Text: Matthew 11:2-11

1. St. Augustine

The lesson of the holy Gospel has set before us a question touching John the Baptist. May the Lord assist me to resolve it to you, as He hath resolved it to us. John was commended, as ye have heard, by the testimony of Christ, and in such terms commended as that there had not risen a greater among those who were born of women. But a greater than he had been born of a Virgin. How much greater? Let the herald himself declare how great the difference is between himself and his Judge, whose herald he is. For John went before Christ both in his birth and preaching; but it was in obedience that he went before Him, not in preferring himself before Him. For so the whole train of attendants walks before the judge; yet they who walk before are really after him. How signal a testimony then did John give to Christ? Even to saying that he "was not worthy to loose the latchet of his shoes." And what more? "Of his fullness," saith he, "have all we received." He confessed that he was but a lamp lighted at His light, and so he took refuge at His feet lest, venturing on high, he should be extinguished by the wind of pride. So great indeed was he, that he was taken for Christ; and if he had not himself testified that he was not He, the mistake would have continued and he would have been reputed to be the Christ. What striking humility! Honor was proffered him by the people, and he himself refused it. Men were at fault in his greatness, and he humbled himself. He had no wish to increase by the words of men, seeing he had comprehended the Word of God.

This then did John say concerning Christ. And what said Christ of John? We have just now heard. "He began to say to the multitude concerning John, What went ye out into the wilderness to see? A reed shaken with the wind?" Surely not; for John was not "blown about by every wind of doctrine." "But what went ye out for to see? A man clothed in soft raiment?" No, for John was clothed in rough apparel; he had his raiment of camel's hair, not of down. "But what went ye out for to see? A prophet? Yea, and more than a prophet." Why "more than a prophet"? The Prophets foretold that the Lord would come, whom they desired to see and saw not; but to him was vouchsafed what they sought. John saw the Lord; he saw Him, pointed his finger toward Him, and said, "Behold the Lamb of God, who taketh away the sins of the world"; behold, here He is. Now had He come and was not acknowledged; and so a mistake was made also as to John himself. Behold then here is He whom the Patriarchs desired to see, whom the Prophets foretold, whom the Law prefigured. "Behold the Lamb

37

of God, who taketh away the sins of the world." And he gave a goodly testimony to the Lord, and the Lord to him. "Among them that are born of women," saith the Lord, "there hath not risen a greater than John the Baptist: notwithstanding, he that is less in the kingdom of heaven is greater than he"; less in time, but greater in majesty. This He said, meaning Himself to be understood. Now exceedingly great among men is John the Baptist, than whom among men Christ alone is greater. It may also be thus stated and explained, "Among them that are born of women there hath not risen a greater than John the Baptist: notwithstanding, he that is the least in the kingdom of heaven is greater than he." Not in the sense that I have before explained it. "Notwithstanding, he that is the least in the kingdom of heaven is greater than he"; the kingdom of heaven he meant is where the Angels are; he then that is the least among the Angels, is greater than John. Thus He set forth to us the excellence "of that kingdom which we should long for"; set before us a city of which we should desire to be citizens. What sort of citizens are there? How great are they? Whoso is the least there, is greater than John. Than what John? "Than whom there hath not risen a greater among them that are born of women."

Thus have we heard the true and good record both of John concerning Christ, and of Christ concerning John. What then is the meaning of this; that John sent his disciples to Him when He was shut up in prison, on the eve of being put to death, and said to them, "Go, say to him, Art thou he that should come, or do we look for another?" Is this then all that praise? That praise is it turned to doubting? What sayest thou, John? To Whom art thou speaking? What sayest thou? Thou speakest to thy Judge, thyself the herald. Thou stretchedst out the finger, and pointedst Him out; thou saidst, "Behold the Lamb of God, behold him who taketh away the sins of the world." Thou saidst, "Of his fullness have we all received." Thou saidst, "I am not worthy to unloose the latchet of his shoes." And dost thou now say, "Art thou he that should come, or do we look for another?" Is not this the same Christ? And who art thou? Art thou not His forerunner? Art thou not he of whom it was foretold, "Behold, I send my messenger before thy face, who shall prepare thy way before thee"? How dost thou prepare the way, and thou art thyself straying from the way? So then the disciples of John came; and the Lord said to them, "Go, tell John, the blind see, the deaf hear, the lame walk, the lepers are cleansed, the poor have the gospel preached to them"; and "blessed is he whosoever shall not be offended in me." Do not suspect that John was offended in Christ. And yet his words do sound so; "Art thou he that should come?" Ask my works: "The blind see, the deaf hear, the lame walk, the lepers are cleansed, the dead are raised, the poor have the gospel preached to them"; and dost thou ask whether I am He? My works, saith He, are My words. "Go, show him again. And as they departed." Lest haply any one should say that John was good at first, and the Spirit of God forsook him, therefore after their departure, he spake these words; after their departure whom John had sent, Christ commended John.

What is the meaning then of this obscure question? May that Sun shine upon us, from which that lamp derived its flame. And so the resolution of it is altogether plain. John had separate disciples of his own; not as in separation from Christ, but prepared as a witness to him. For meet it was that such a one should give his testimony to Christ, one who was also gathering disciples and who might have been envious of Him, for that he could not see Him. Therefore because John's disciples highly esteemed their master, they heard from John his record concerning Christ, and marveled; and as he was about to die, it was his wish that they should be confirmed by Him. No doubt they were saying among themselves, Such great things doth he say of Him, but none of himself. "Go, then, ask him"; not because I doubt, but that ye may be instructed. "Go, ask him," hear from Him what I am in the habit of telling you; ye have heard the herald, be confirmed by the Judge. "Go, ask him, Art thou he that should come, or do we look for another?" They went accordingly and asked; not for John's sake, but for their own. And for their sakes did Christ say, "The blind see, the lame walk, the deaf hear, the lepers are cleansed, the dead are raised, the poor have the gospel preached to them." Ye see Me, acknowledge Me then; ye see the works, acknowledge the Doer. "And blessed is he whosoever shall not be offended in me." But it is of you I speak, not of John. For that we might know that He spake not this of John, as they departed, "He began to speak to the multitudes concerning John"; the True, the Truth Himself, proclaimed his true praises.

I think this question has been sufficiently explained. Now keep the poor in mind. Give, ye who have not given hitherto; believe me, ye will not lose it. Yes, truly, that only it seems ye lose, which ye do not carry to the circus. Now must we render unto the poor the offerings of such of you as have offered anything, and the amount which we have is much less than your usual offerings. Shake off this sloth. I am become a beggar for beggars; what is that to me? I would be a beggar for beggars, that ye may be reckoned among the number of children.

2. Martin Luther

Now when John heard in the prison the works of the Christ, he sent by his disciples and said unto him, Art thou he that cometh, or look we for another? As though John would say to his disciples: "There, you hear of His works, such as I never accomplished, nor anyone else before Him. Now go to Him and ask him whether or not He is the One that cometh. Put away the gross worldly deception that He would ride on steeds in armor. He is increasing, but I must now decrease; my work must cease, but His must continue; you must leave me and cling to Him."

How necessary it was for John to point his disciples away from himself to Christ is very clear. For what benefit would it have been to them if they had depended a thousand times on John's piety and had not embraced Christ? Without Christ there is no help or remedy, no matter how pious men may be. So at the present day what benefit is it to the monks and nuns to observe the rules of St. Benedict, St. Bernard, St. Francis, St. Dominic, and St. Augustine if they do not embrace Christ, and Him only, and depart also from their John? All Benedictines, Carthusians, Barefoot-Friars, Ecclesiasts, Augustinians, Carmelites, all monks and nuns are surely lost, as only Christians are saved. Whoever is not a Christian cannot be helped even by John the Baptist who, indeed, according to Christ, was the greatest of all saints.

However, John deals kindly with his disciples, has patience with their weak faith till they shall have grown strong. He does not condemn them because they do not firmly believe him. Thus we should deal with the consciences of men ensnared by the examples and regulations of pious men, until they are freed from them.

. . . . .

But what does it mean when Christ says: "The poor have good tidings preached to them?" Is it not preached also to the rich and to the whole world? Again, why is the Gospel so great a thing, so great a blessing as Christ teaches, seeing that so many people despise and oppose it? Here we must know what Gospel really is, otherwise we cannot understand this passage. We must, therefore, diligently observe that from the beginning God has sent into the world a twofold word or message, *the Law* and *the Gospel*. These two messages must be rightly distinguished one from the other and properly understood, for other than the Scriptures there never has been a book written to this day, not even by a saint, in which these two messages, the Law and the Gospel, have been properly explained and distinguished, and yet so very much depends on such an explanation.

The Law is that word by which God teaches what we shall do, as, for instance, the Ten Commandments. Now, if human nature is not aided by God's grace, it is impossible to keep the Law, for the reason that man since the fall of Adam in Paradise is depraved and full of sinful desires, so that he cannot from his heart's desire find pleasure in the Law, which fact we all experience in ourselves. For no one lives who does not prefer that there were no Law, and everyone feels and knows in himself that it is difficult to lead a pious life and do good and, on the other hand, that it is easy to lead a wicked life and to do evil. But this difficulty or unwillingness to do the good is the reason we do not keep the Law of God. For whatever is done with aversion and unwillingness is considered by God as not done at all. Thus the Law of God convicts us, even by our own experience, that by nature we are evil, disobedient, lovers of sin, and hostile to God's laws.

From all this either self-confidence or despair must follow. Self-confidence follows when a man strives to fulfill the law by his own good works, by trying hard to do as the words of the Law command. He serves God, he swears not, he honors father and mother, he kills not, he does not commit adultery, and so on. But meanwhile he does not look into his heart, does not realize with what motives he leads a good life, and conceals the old Adam in his heart. For if he would truly examine his heart, he would realize that he is doing all unwillingly and with compulsion, that he fears hell or seeks heaven, if he be not prompted by things of less importance, as honor, goods, health, and fear of being humiliated, of being punished or of being visited by a plague. In short, he would have to confess that he would rather lead a wicked life if it were not that he fears the consequences, for the Law only restrains him. But because he does not realize his bad motives he lives securely, looks only at his outward works and not into his heart, prides himself on keeping the Law of God perfectly, and thus the countenance of Moses remains covered to him; that is, he does not understand the meaning of the Law, namely, that it must be kept with a happy, free, and willing mind.

Just as an immoral person, if you should ask him why he commits adultery, can answer only that he is doing it for the sake of the carnal pleasure he finds in it. For he does not do it for reward or punishment, he expects no gain from it, nor does he hope to escape from the evil of it. Such willingness the Law requires in us, so that if you should ask a virtuous man why he leads a chaste life, he would answer: "Not for the sake of heaven or hell, honor or disgrace, but for the sole reason that he considers it honorable, and that it pleases him exceedingly, even if it were not commanded." Behold, such a heart delights in God's Law and keeps it with pleasure. Such people love God and righteousness, they hate and fear naught but unrighteousness. However, no one is thus by nature. The unrighteous love reward and profit, fear and hate punishment and pain, therefore they also hate God and righteousness, love themselves and unrighteousness. They are hypocrites, disguisers, deceivers, liars, and self-conceited. So are all men without grace, but above all, the saints who rely on their good works. For the reason the Scriptures conclude, "All men are liars" (Psalm 116:11); "Every man at his best estate is altogether vanity" (Psalm 39:5); "There is none that doeth good, no, not one" (Psalm 14:3).

Despair follows when man becomes conscious of his evil motives and realizes that it is impossible for him to love the Law of God, finding nothing good in himself, but only hatred of the good and delight in doing evil. Now he realizes that the Law cannot be kept only by works hence he despairs of his works and does not rely upon them. He should have love; but he finds none, nor can have any through his own efforts or out of his own heart. How he must be a poor, miserable, and humiliated spirit whose conscience is burdened and in anguish because of the Law, commanding and demanding payment in full when he does not possess even a farthing with which to pay. Only to such persons is the Law beneficial, because it has been given for the purpose of working such knowledge and humiliation; that is its real mission. These persons well know how to judge the works of hypocrites and fraudulent saints, namely, as nothing but lies and deception. David referred to this when he said, "I said in my haste, all men are liars" (Psalm 116:11).

For this reason Paul calls the Law a law unto death, saying, "And the commandment, which was unto life, this I found to be unto death" (Romans 7:10); and a power of sin, "And the power of sin is the law" (1 Corinthians 15:56), and in 2 Corinthians 3:6, he says, "For the letter killeth, but the spirit giveth life." All this means that if the Law and human nature be brought into a right relationship, the one to the other, then will sin and a troubled conscience first become manifest. Man, then, sees how desperately wicked his heart is, how great his sins are, even as to things he formerly considered good works and no sin. He now is compelled to confess that by and of himself he is a child of perdition, a child of God's wrath and of hell. Then there is only fear and trembling, all self-conceit vanishes, while fear and despair fill his heart. Thus man is crushed and put to naught, and truly humbled.

Inasmuch as all this is caused only by the Law, St. Paul truly says that it is a law unto death and a letter that killeth, and that through the commandment sin becomes exceedingly sinful (Romans 7:13), provoking God's wrath. For the Law gives and helps us in no way whatever; it only demands and drives and shows us our misery and depravity.

The other word of God is neither Law nor commandments, and demands nothing of us. But when that has been done by the first word, namely, the Law, and has worked deep despair and wretchedness in our hearts, then God comes and offers us His blessed and life-giving word and promises; He pledges and obligates Himself to grant grace and help in order to deliver us from misery, not only to pardon all our sins, but even to blot them out, and in addition to this to create in us love and delight in keeping His Law.

Behold, this divine promise of grace and forgiveness of sin is rightly called the Gospel. And I say here, again, that by the Gospel you must by no means understand anything else than the divine promise of God's grace and His forgiveness of sin. For thus it was that Paul's epistles were never understood, nor can they be understood by the Papists, because they do not know what the Law and the Gospel really mean. They hold Christ to be a law-maker, and the Gospel a mere doctrine of a new law. That is nothing else than locking up the Gospel and entirely concealing it.

3. John Calvin

Now WHEN JOHN HAD HEARD. The Evangelists do not mean that John was excited by the miracles to acknowledge Christ at that time as Mediator; but, perceiving that Christ had acquired great reputation, and concluding that this was a fit and seasonable time for putting to the test his own declaration concerning Him, he sent to Him his disciples. The opinion entertained by some, that he sent them partly on his own account, is exceedingly foolish; as if he had not been fully convinced, or had not obtained distinct information, that Jesus is the Christ. Equally absurd is the speculation of those who imagine that the Baptist was near death, and therefore inquired what message he should carry, from Christ's mouth as it were, to the deceased fathers. It is very evident that the holy herald of Christ, perceiving that he was not far from the end of his journey, and that his disciples, though he had bestowed great pains in instructing them, still remained in a state of hesitation, resorted to this last expedient for curing their weakness. He had faithfully labored, as I have said, that his disciples should embrace Christ without delay. His continued entreaties had produced so little effect that he had good reason for dreading that, after his death, they would entirely fall away; and therefore he earnestly attempted to arouse them from their sloth by sending them to Christ. Besides, the pastors of the Church are here reminded of their duty. They ought not to endeavor to bind and attach disciples to themselves, but to direct them to Christ, Who is the only Teacher. From the beginning, John had openly avowed that he was not "the bridegroom" (John 3:39). As the faithful "friend of the bridegroom," he presents the bride chaste and uncontaminated to Christ, who alone is the bridegroom of the Church. Paul tells us that he kept the same object in view (2 Corinthians 11:2), and the example of both is held out for imitation to all the ministers of the Gospel.

ART THOU HE WHO WAS TO COME? John takes for granted what the disciples had known from their childhood; for it was the first lesson of religion, and common among all the Jews, that Christ *was to come*, bringing salvation and perfect happiness. On this point, accordingly, he does not raise a doubt, but only inquires if Jesus be that promised Redeemer; for, having been persuaded of the redemption promised in the Law and the Prophets, they were bound to receive it when exhibited in the person of Christ. He adds, "Do we look for another?" By this expression, he indirectly glances at their sloth which allowed them, after having been distinctly informed, to remain so long in doubt and hesitation. At the same time, he shows what is the nature and power of faith. Resting on the truth of God, it does not gaze on all sides, does not vary, but is satisfied with Christ alone and will not be turned to another.

GO AND RELATE TO JOHN. As John had assumed for the time a new character, so Christ enjoins them to carry to him that message which more properly ought to have been addressed to his disciples. He gives an indirect reply, and for two reasons: first, because it was better that the thing should speak for itself; and, secondly, because He thus afforded to His herald a larger subject of instruction. Nor does He merely supply him with bare and rough materials in the miracles, but adapts the miracles to His purpose by quotations from the Prophets. He notices more particularly one passage from the thirty-fifth chapter and another from the sixty-first chapter of Isaiah for the purpose of informing John's disciples that what the Prophets declared respecting the reign of Christ was accomplished and fulfilled. The former passage contains a description of Christ's reign, under which God promises that He will be so kind and gracious as to grant relief and assistance for every kind of disease. He speaks, no doubt, of spiritual deliverance from all diseases and remedies; but under outward symbols, as has been already mentioned, Christ shows that He came as a spiritual physician to cure souls. The disciples would consequently go away without any hesitation, having obtained a reply that was clear and free from all ambiguity.

The latter passage resembles the former in this respect. It shows that the treasures of the grace of God would be exhibited to the world in Christ, and declares that Christ is expressly set apart for the poor and afflicted. This passage is purposely quoted by Christ, partly to teach all His followers the first lesson of humility, and partly to remove the offense that the flesh and sense might be apt to raise against His despicable flock. We are by nature proud, and scarcely anything is much valued by us if it is not attended by a great degree of outward show. But the Church of Christ is composed of poor men, and nothing could be farther removed from dazzling or imposing ornament. Hence many are led to despise the Gospel, because it is not embraced by many persons of eminent station and exalted rank. How perverse and unjust that opinion is, Christ shows from the very nature of the Gospel, since it was designed only for the poor and despised. Hence it follows that it is no new occurrence, nor one that ought to disturb our minds, if the Gospel is despised by all the great, who, puffed up with their wealth, have no room to spare for the grace of God. Nay, if it is rejected by the greater part of men, there is no reason to wonder; for there is scarcely one person in a hundred who does not swell with wicked confidence. As Christ here guards His Gospel against contempt, He likewise reminds us who they are that are qualified to appreciate the grace of salvation which it offers to them; and in this manner, kindly inviting wretched sinners to the hope of salvation, raises them to full confidence.

THE POOR RECEIVE THE MESSAGE OF THE GOSPEL. By "the poor" are undoubtedly meant those whose condition is wretched and despicable, and who are held in no estimation. However mean any person may be, his poverty is so far from being a ground of despair that it ought rather to animate him with courage to seek Christ. But let us remember that none are accounted *poor* but those who are really such, or, in other words, who lie low and are overwhelmed by a conviction of their poverty.

AND BLESSED IS HE WHO SHALL NOT BE OFFENDED IN ME. By this concluding statement Christ intended to remind them that he who would adhere firmly and steadfastly to the faith of the Gospel must encounter *offenses*, which will tend to interrupt the progress of faith. This is said by way of anticipation, to fortify us against offenses; for we shall never want reasons for rejecting it, until our minds are raised above every offense. The first lesson, therefore, to be learned is that we must contend with offenses, if we would continue in the faith of Christ; for Christ Himself is justly denominated "a rock of offense and stone of stumbling, by which many fall" (1 Peter 2:8). This happens, no doubt, through our own fault; but that very fault is remedied when He pronounces those to be "blessed who shall not be offended in him"; from which, too, we infer that unbelievers have no excuse, though they plead the existence of innumerable offenses. For what hinders them from coming to Christ? Or what drives them to revolt from Christ? It is because He appears with His cross, disfigured and despised, and exposed to the reproaches of the world; because He calls us to share in His afflictions; because His glory and majesty, being spiritual, are despised by the world; and, in a word, because His doctrine is totally at variance with our senses. Again, it is because, through the stratagems of Satan, many disturbances arise, with the view of slandering and rendering hateful the name of Christ and the Gospel; and because everyone, as if on purpose, rears up a mass of offenses, being instigated by not less malignity than zeal to withdraw from Christ.

AND WHILE THEY WERE DEPARTING. Christ praises John before the people, in order that they may state from recollection what they have heard from him, and may give credit to his testimony. For John's name was widely celebrated, and men spoke of him in lofty terms: but his doctrine was held in less estimation, and there even were few that waited on his ministrations. Christ reminds them that those who "went out to see him in the wilderness" lost their pains, if they did not devoutly apply their minds and faculties to his doctrine. The meaning of the words, "you went out into the wilderness," is this: "Your journey would have been an act of foolish and ridiculous levity, if you had not a fixed object in view. But it was neither worldly splendor nor any sort of amusement that you were in quest of: your design was to hear the voice of God from the mouth of the Prophet. If therefore you would reap advantage from your undertaking, it is necessary that what he spoke should remain fixed in your memory."

CLOTHED WITH SOFT GARMENTS. Those who think that Christ here condemns the extravagance of a court are mistaken. There are many other passages in which luxury of dress and excessive attention to outward appearance are censured. But this passage simply means that there was nothing in the wilderness to attract the people from every quarter; that everything there was rude and unpolished, and fitted only to inspire disgust; and that such elegance of dress as delights the eyes is rather to be looked for in the courts of kings.

VERILY I SAY TO YOU. These words not only maintain the authority of John, but elevate his doctrine above the ancient Prophets, that the people may keep in view the right end of his ministry; for they mistook the design of his mission and, in consequence of this, derived almost no advantage from his discourses. Accordingly, Christ extols and places him above the rank of the Prophets, and gives the people to understand that he had received a special and more excellent commission. When he elsewhere says respecting himself that he was "not a prophet" (John 1:21) it is not inconsistent with the designation here bestowed upon him by Christ. He was, no doubt, a Prophet, like others whom God had appointed in His Church to be expounders of the Law, and messengers of His will. But he was *more excellent* than the Prophets in this respect: he did not, like them, make known redemption at a distance and obscurely under shadows, but proclaimed that the time of redemption was now manifest and at hand. Such too is the import of Malachi's prediction (3:1) that is immediately added, that the pre-eminence of John consisted in his being the herald and forerunner of Christ; for although the ancient Prophets spoke of His kingdom, they were not, like John, placed "before his face," to point Him out as present. As to the other parts of the passage, the reader may consult what has been said on the first chapter of Luke's Gospel.

THERE HATH NOT ARISEN. Our Lord proceeds further, and declares that the ministers of the Gospel will be as far superior to John as John was superior to the Prophets. Those who think that Christ draws a comparison between Himself and John have fallen into a strange blunder; for nothing is said here about personal rank, but commendation is bestowed on the pre-eminence of office. This appears more clearly from the words employed by Luke "there is not a greater prophet"; for they expressly restrict his eminence to the office of teaching. In a word, this magnificent eulogium is bestowed on John that the Jews may observe more attentively the commission which he bore. Again, the teachers who were afterward to follow are placed above him, to show the surpassing majesty of the Gospel above the Law, and above that preaching which came between them. Now, as Christ intended to prepare the Jews for receiving the Gospel, we ought also, in the present day, to be aroused to listen with reverence to Christ speaking to us from the lofty throne of His heavenly glory; lest He take revenge for our contempt of Him by that fearful curse which He pronounces on unbelievers by Malachi in the same passage.

"The kingdom of heaven" and "the kingdom of God" denote the new condition of the Church, as in other passages that have already occurred; for it was promised that at the coming of Christ all things would be restored.

HE THAT IS LEAST IN THE KINGDOM. The Greek word I have rendered "least," is in the comparative degree, and signifies "less"; but the meaning is more clearly brought out that all the ministers of the Gospel are included. Many of them undoubtedly have received a small portion of faith, and are therefore greatly inferior to John; but this does not prevent their preaching from being superior to his, because it holds out Christ as having rendered complete and eternal satisfaction by His one sacrifice, as the Conqueror of death and the Lord of life, and because it withdraws the veil and elevates believers to the heavenly sanctuary.

4. Phillips Brooks

Nature and Circumstances

VERILY I SAY UNTO YOU, AMONG THEM THAT ARE BORN OF WOMEN THERE HATH NOT RISEN A GREATER THAN JOHN THE BAPTIST; NOTWITH-STANDING HE THAT IS LEAST IN THE KINGDOM OF HEAVEN IS GREATER THAN HE. It is Jesus Who is talking about John the Baptist; and the question of which He is speaking is one that must have almost neces-sarily arisen with regard to two such teachers. Jesus had come to estab-lish on the earth a higher life for man. He had been telling men that they must enter into the new spiritual culture which, while it was the sequel and fulfillment of the education of the world that had gone before, was yet indeed new in Him, was the creation of His personal nature and His revelation of God. He was engaged in setting up the kingdom of God, into which all the servants of God were to be gathered and where their lives were to be trained. And in the midst of this great work it could not be but that men would look around and would look back. Jesus was telling them that the true greatness of human life must come by following Him. It was inevitable, then, that men should ask, "How is it about those great men who are not His followers; those great men who have gone before Him; those great men who are wholly outside of His influence—are they not truly great? And if they are, what has become of His saying that true greatness lies only in Him, and in the kingdom of God to which He is so earnestly summoning us?" This was the question that must have come into many minds as Jesus spoke. To this question Jesus gave His answer: "Among them that are born of women there hath not risen a greater than John the

Baptist: notwithstanding he that is least in the kingdom of heaven is greater than he." Because the question that brought forth this answer is not obsolete, but is on men's minds in many shapes today, I propose to you that we should study Christ's answer.

We see two elements: There is the greatness of nature, and there is the greatness of circumstances. They are distinct from one another; they do not make each other. A man may be great in nature and yet live among the meagerest surroundings. A man may live in the most sumptuous profusion of privileges, and yet be a very little man. They are distinct. One does not make the other; and yet the two have close relationships; each has a tendency toward the production of the other. The higher plane of living is always trying to make the man greater so that he may be worthy of it; on the other hand, the more the man grows great, the more he struggles to discover and attain some higher plane of life. In every fullest picture of human life the two combine; the great man in the fullest atmosphere alone entirely satisfies our imagination. But if they must be separated, as to some degree they always must, nothing can destroy the honor that belongs to personal character struggling under the most adverse circumstances to assert its greatness and to do its work.

But now, if these definitions have made the conditions of the problem plain, we are ready to go on to the truth that is included in what Christ says about John the Baptist. Christ recognizes the two elements of personal greatness and of lofty condition, and He seems almost to suggest another truth—one at any rate familiar to our experience of life—which is, that personal power which has been manifest in some lower region of life seems sometimes to be temporarily lost and dimmed with the advance of the person who possesses it into a higher condition. What really is a progress seems, for a time at least, to involve a loss. Think how this appears in our observation of the world. The college student graduates next week, and from the calm seclusion of scholastic life he goes out into the wrestling with business forces or the eager rivalry of his profession. He has really passed up into a higher life; but sometimes he looks back and sighs for the peace and dignity the old life enjoyed. The thinker, anywhere, tries to apply his thought, and though the contact with men, into which that effort brings him, disturbs his equanimity and throws him into perplexities which he knew nothing of before, he too has really mounted to a higher life. The esthetic student tries to be useful; and it is only through painful shocks to his sensibilities, and a disturbance of the symmetry of life in which his soul delights, that he passes into the loftier condition where he can help his fellow men. Everywhere that which seems to have perfected itself in the lower sphere displays its imperfection when it passes up to higher tasks. Thought, which has grown clear and self-complacent in the study of the physical world, bewilders itself and is baffled when it attempts to study God. Government, which seems to have mastered the problems of despotism, loses its equilibrium and is feeble once more when it attempts the higher tasks of freedom.

It is a strange perplexing fact of life—this fact that as a being or a work, which has seemed perfect in some lower region, goes up to some

higher region, it seems to grow imperfect; at least it manifests its imperfection. We can see at once what a temptation it must offer to the human
powers to linger in some lower sphere, in which they seem to be equal to
their work, instead of going freely up into a loftier world where they shall
learn their limitations and their feebleness. There is reason enough to fear
that man's power of thought, revelling today in the clearness with which
it seems to see the lower world of physical existence, will refuse some of
the higher duties that belong to it, the duties which most tax its capacity
and show its feebleness, the duties of understanding the soul of man and
reaching after the comprehension of God. Sad will it be if it is so, if studious
humanity, delighted with its achievements in the mere region of physical
research, shall turn its back on the lofty tasks in which man's intellect finds
its greatest glory as well as its most complete humility—the struggle to
know God.

In ordinary life the power of this temptation, the temptation to be
satisfied with greatness in some lower sphere and not to aspire to the highest
sort of existence, is constantly appearing. What multitudes of men there
are all through society who seem to have limited and shut in their lives to
some little range of occupations which they can fulfill with reasonable
credit to themselves, and who never seem to think that there is any call
for them to do more than to complete themselves in that poor little scheme
of life, never seem to dream that they ought to go up to a distinctly other
life with higher tasks and more difficult exactions. An idle, good-natured
creature, who has accepted his place and fills it, who amuses and is amused,
who keeps the world about him in good humor, and who is great in the
adornment of his own person and the management of petty etiquette—one
of the coolest things on earth, I think, is the quiet effrontery with which
such a man rests absolutely satisfied with his insect greatness, and criticizes
the blunders and feebleness which men of course develop who are setting
themselves to do some really useful work in the world. He treats them and
talks of them as if they belonged to a different world than his, and there
could be no possible call for him to undertake the same effort with all its risks
and exposures. One of the most wonderful things in the world is this power
of men to draw themselves a line beyond which they never dream of counting themselves responsible, across which they look and judge with cruelest
criticisms the men who are really fighting the world's sins and troubles on
the other side, as if of them there were no more to be asked than just that
they should be perfect in their own self-limited world of elegant useless-
ness. Never a brave reformer tries to break down a popular sin or to build
up some new and needed progress, taking on himself the responsibility
that a true man ought to take, but these self-satisfied critics gather around
him to criticize his methods and to ridicule his blunders, but never to lift
a hand to show how they also would blunder if they let themselves step
outside their safe and limited and petty life.

This, I think, is the way in which most men of the world look at
Christianity and at the efforts of their brother men to live a Christian life.
"I am no Christian," says the practical man, "I do not pretend to be pious
or religious." And then he looks up in your face as if he had settled the

whole question, as if his entire business thenceforth were just to stand by and see what sort of a Christian you were and how your piety came on. "I do my duty as a plain unreligious man," he says, "I make no professions." There is a tone of scornful pity as he speaks. He realizes—but not more keenly than the poor Christian himself realizes—how the believer in Christ, the man who is trying to honor and obey a Divine Master, stumbles and blunders in his attempt to keep company with the Infinite. For himself he has abandoned any such attempt, and seems by some strange self-delusion to have brought himself to feel that his abandonment of the attempt has released him from any responsibility about it. You see how foolish and how base such a position is. It is the soldier who has shirked the battle criticizing the torn uniform and broken armor and bleeding limbs of his comrade who comes staggering out of the fight. It is the ship that has lain snugly and use-lessly beside the wharf jeering at the broken bulwarks and torn sails with which its sister ship comes reeling in from her long voyage. He who lingers in some lower life, because there he is able to keep his complacency and not to fall so far short of his manifest duty as to cover himself with shame, has no right to compare himself with the feeblest and most unsuccessful of the children of God who, unable to be satisfied as long as there is a spiritual life that he is not living, has set boldly forth and entered at least into the outskirts of the kingdom of heaven, into the determination and struggle to live a religious life.

The progress from one kind of life into a higher kind, from one realm into a yet deeper and more central region of God's kingdom, is always press-ing; it can never be outgrown. Not merely when a man becomes a Christian, but always afterward, when some deeper and holier and maturer region of Christian life opens before him, the summons comes to move on, to advance into that higher realm. When the religion which has been living on mere authority is called upon to become a religion of clear personal conviction, when to the religion of sentiment is offered the test and privilege of active duty, when the religion of the single experience is bidden to graduate into a wide human sympathy—in all these cases, the same sort of thing occurs that occurs when the man of the world is first summoned to enter into the kingdom of heaven, to become a Christian. The door of a new room of life is thrown open, and the soul that has lived faithfully in the first room is bidden not to rest satisfied with that faithfulness, but to pass on into the second. May God give us grace and faith and courage and ambition always to be ready for that call, and to pass on and up to higher kinds of life, to new kingdoms of heaven as He shall open them to us forever.

THE FOURTH SUNDAY IN ADVENT

Text: John 1:19-28

1. St. Augustine

You have very often heard, holy brethren, and you know well, that John the Baptist, in proportion as he was greater than those born of women, and was more humble in his acknowledgment of the Lord, obtained the grace of being the friend of the Bridegroom; zealous for the Bridegroom, not for himself; not seeking his own honor, but that of his Judge, whom as a herald he preceded. Therefore, to the prophets who went before, it was granted to predict concerning Christ, but to this man, to point Him out with the finger. For as Christ was unknown by those who did not believe the prophets before He came, He remained unknown to them even when present. For He had come humbly and concealed from the first; the more concealed in proportion as He was more humble: but the people, despising in their pride the humility of God, crucified their Saviour, and made Him their condemner.

But will not He who at first came concealed, because humble, come again manifested, because exalted? You have just listened to the Psalm: "God shall come manifestly, and our God shall not keep silence." He was silent that He might be judged. He will not be silent when He begins to judge. It would not have been said, "He will come manifestly," unless at first He had come concealed; nor would it have been said, "He shall not keep silence," unless He had first kept silence. How was He silent? Interrogate Isaiah: "He was brought as a sheep to the slaughter, and as a lamb before his shearer was dumb, so He opened not His mouth." "But He shall come manifestly, and shall not keep silence." In what manner "manifestly"? "A fire shall go before Him, and round about Him a strong tempest." That tempest has to carry away all the chaff from the floor, which is now being threshed; and the fire has to burn what the tempest carries away. But now He is silent; silent in judgment, but not silent in precept. For if Christ is silent, what is the purpose of the apostles, what of the canticles of the Psalms, what of the declarations of the prophets? In all these Christ is not silent. But now He is silent in not taking vengeance: He is not silent in not giving warning. But He will come in glory to take vengeance, and will manifest Himself even to all who do not believe on Him. But now, because when present He was concealed, it behooved that He should be despised. For unless He had been despised, He would not have been crucified; if He had not been crucified, He would not have shed His blood—the price by which He redeemed us. But that He might give a price for us, He was

51

crucified; that He might be crucified, He was despised; that He might be despised, He appeared in humility.

Yet because He appeared as it were in the night, in a mortal body, He lighted for Himself a lamp by which He might be seen. That lamp was John, concerning whom you lately heard many things: and the present passage of the evangelist contains the words of John; in the first place, and it is the chief point, his confession that he was not the Christ. But so great was the excellence of John, that men might have believed him to be the Christ: and in this he gave a proof of his humility, that he said he was not when he might have been believed to have been the Christ; therefore, "This is the testimony of John, when the Jews sent priests and Levites to him from Jerusalem to ask him, Who art thou?" But they would not have sent unless they had been moved by the excellence of his authority who ventured to baptize. "And he confessed, and denied not." What did he confess? "And he confessed, I am not the Christ."

"And they asked him, What then? Art thou Elias?" For they knew that Elias was to precede Christ. For to no Jew was the name of Christ unknown. They did not think that he was the Christ; but they did not think that Christ would not come at all. When they were hoping that He would come, they were offended at Him when He was present, and stumbled at Him as on a low stone. For He was as yet a small stone, already indeed cut out of the mountain without hands; as saith Daniel the prophet, that he saw a stone cut out of the mountain without hands. But what follows? "And that stone," said he, "grew, and became a great mountain, and filled the whole face of the earth." Mark then, my beloved brethren, what I say: Christ, before the Jews, was already cut out from the mountain. The prophet wishes that by the mountain should be understood the Jewish kingdom. But the kingdom of the Jews had not filled the whole face of the earth. The stone was cut out from thence, because from thence was the Lord born on His advent among men. And wherefore without hands? Because without the co-operation of man did the Virgin bear Christ. Now then was that stone cut out without hands before the eyes of the Jews; but it was humble. Not without reason; because not yet had that stone increased and filled the whole earth: that He showed in His kingdom, which is the Church, with which He has filled the whole face of the earth. Because then it had not yet increased, they stumbled at Him as at a stone: and that happened in them which is written, "Whosoever shall fall upon that stone shall be broken; but on whomsoever that stone shall fall, it will grind them to powder." At first they fell upon Him lowly: as the lofty One He shall come upon them; but that He may grind them to powder when He comes in His exaltation, He first broke them in His lowliness. They stumbled at Him, and were broken; they were not ground, but broken: He will come exalted and will grind them. But the Jews were to be pardoned because they stumbled at a stone that had not yet increased. What sort of persons are those who stumble at the mountain itself? Already you know who they are of whom I speak. Those who deny the Church, diffused through the whole world, do not stumble at the lowly stone, but at the mountain itself:

because this the stone became as it grew. The blind Jews did not see the lowly stone: but how great blindness not to see the mountain!

They saw Him then lowly, and did not know Him. He was pointed out to them by a lamp. For in the first place he, than whom no greater had arisen of those born of women, said, "I am not the Christ." It was asked of him, "Art thou Elias?" He answered, "I am not." For Christ sends Elias before Him: and he said, "I am not," and occasioned a question for us. For it is to be feared lest men, insufficiently understanding, think that John contradicted what Christ said. For in a certain place, when the Lord Jesus Christ said certain things in the Gospel regarding Himself, His disciples answered Him: "How then say the scribes," that is, those skilled in the Law, "that Elias must first come?" And the Lord said, "Elias is already come, and they have done unto him what they listed"; and, if you wish to know, John the Baptist is he. The Lord Jesus Christ said, "Elias is already come, and John the Baptist" is he; but John, being interrogated, confessed that he was not Elias. In the same manner that he confessed that he was not Christ was true, so was his confession that he was not Elias. How then shall we compare the words of the herald with the words of the Judge? Away with the thought that the herald speaks falsehood; for that which he speaks he hears from the Judge. Wherefore then did he say, "I am not Elias"; and the Lord, "He is Elias"? Because the Lord Jesus Christ wished in him to prefigure His own advent, and to say that John was in the spirit of Elias. And what John was to the first Advent, that will Elias be to the second Advent. As there are two advents of the Judge, so are there two heralds. The Judge indeed was the same, but the heralds two, but not two judges. It was needful that in the first instance the Judge should come to be judged. He sent before Him His first herald; He called him Elias, because Elias will be in the second Advent what John was in the first.

For mark, beloved brethren, how true it is what I say. When John was conceived, or rather when he was born, the Holy Spirit prophesied that this would be fulfilled in him: "And he shall be," he said, "the forerunner of the Highest, in the spirit and power of Elias." What signifieth "in the spirit and power of Elias"? In the same Holy Spirit in the room of Elias. Wherefore in the room of Elias? Because what Elias will be to the second, that John was to the first Advent. Rightly therefore, speaking literally, did John reply. For the Lord spoke figuratively, "Elias, the same is John." But he, as I have said, spoke literally when he said, "I am not Elias." Neither did John speak falsely, nor did the Lord speak falsely; neither was the word of the herald nor of the Judge false, if only thou understand. But who shall understand? He who shall have imitated the lowliness of the herald, and shall have acknowledged the loftiness of the Judge. For nothing was more lowly than the herald. My brethren, in nothing had John greater merit than in this humility, inasmuch as when he was able to deceive men, and to be thought Christ, and to have been received in the place of Christ (for so great were his grace and his excellency), nevertheless he openly confessed and said, "I am not the Christ." "Art thou Elias?" If he had said I am Elias, it would have been as if Christ were already coming in His second Advent to judge, not in His first to be judged. As if saying, Elias is yet to come, "I am not," said he, "Elias." But give heed to the lowly One before whom John came, that you may not feel the lofty One before whom Elias came. For thus also did the Lord complete the saying: "John the Baptist is he which is to come." He came as a figure of that in which Elias is to come in his own person. Then Elias will in his own proper person be Elias, now in similitude he was John. Now John in his own proper person is John, in similitude Elias. The two heralds gave to each other their similitudes, and kept their own proper persons; but the Judge is one Lord, whether preceded by this herald or by that.

"And they asked him, What then? Art thou Elias? And he said, No. And they said unto him, Art thou a prophet? and he answered, No! They said therefore unto him, Who art thou? that we may give an answer to them that sent us. What sayest thou of thyself? He saith, I am the voice of one crying in the wilderness." That said Isaiah. This prophecy was fulfilled in John, "I am the voice of one crying in the wilderness." Crying what? "Prepare ye the way of the Lord, make straight the paths of our God." Would it not have seemed to you that a herald would have cried, "Go away, make room"? Instead of the herald's cry, "Go away," John says, "Come." The herald makes men stand back from the Judge; to the Judge John calls. Yes, indeed, John calls men to the lowly One, that they may not experience what He will be as the exalted Judge. "I am the voice of one crying in the wilderness, Prepare ye the way of the Lord, as said the prophet Isaiah." He did not say, "I am John, I am Elias, I am a prophet." But what did he say? "This I am called, 'The voice of one crying in the wilderness, Prepare the way for the Lord: I am the prophecy itself.' "

"And they which were sent were of the Pharisees," that is, of the chief men among the Jews; "and they asked him and said unto him, Why baptizest thou then, if thou be not the Christ, nor Elias, nor a prophet?" As if it seemed to them audacity to baptize; as if they meant to inquire, in what character baptizest thou? We ask whether thou art the Christ; thou sayest that thou art not. We ask whether thou perchance art His precursor, for we know that before the advent of Christ, Elias will come; thou answerest that thou art not. We ask, if perchance thou art some herald come long before, that is, a prophet, and hast received that power, and thou sayest that thou art not a prophet. And John was not a prophet; he was greater than a prophet. The Lord gave such testimony concerning him: "What went ye out into the wilderness to see? A reed shaken with the wind?" Of course implying that he was not shaken by the wind; because John was not such an one as is moved by the wind; for he who is moved by the wind is blown upon by every seductive blast. "But what went ye out for to see? A man clothed in soft raiment?" For John was clothed in rough garments; that is, his tunic was of camel's hair. "Behold, they who are clothed in soft raiment are in kings' houses." You did not then go out to see a man clothed in soft raiment. "But what went ye out for to see? A prophet? Yea, I say unto you, one greater than a prophet is here;" for the prophets prophesied of Christ a long time before, John pointed Him out as present.

"Why baptizest thou then, if thou be not the Christ, nor Elias, nor a prophet? John answered them, saying, I baptize with water; but there standeth One among you whom ye know not." For, very truly, He was not seen, being humble, and therefore was the lamp lighted. Observe how John gives place, who might have been accounted other than he was. "He it is who cometh after me, who is made before me" (that is, as we have already said, is "preferred before me"), whose shoe's latchet I am not worthy to unloose." How greatly did he humble himself! And therefore he was greatly lifted up; for he that humbleth himself shall be exalted. Hence, holy brethren, you ought to note that if John so humbled himself as to say, "I am not worthy to unloose His shoe's latchet," what need they have to be humbled who say, "We baptize; what we give is ours, and what is ours is holy." He said, "Not I, but He"; they say, "We." John is not worthy to unloose His shoe's latchet; and if he had said he was worthy, how humble would he still have been! And if he had said he was worthy, and had spoken thus, "He came after me who is made before me, the latchet of whose shoe I am only worthy to unloose," he would have greatly humbled himself. But when he says that he is not worthy even to do this, truly was he full of the Holy Spirit, who is such fashion as a servant acknowledged his Lord, and merited to be made a friend instead of a servant.

2. Martin Luther

Now here are found two kinds of people: some believe the crying of John and confess it to be what he says. These are the people to whom the Lord comes, in them His way is prepared and made even, as St. Peter says in 1 Peter 5:5: "God giveth grace to the humble"; and the Lord himself says in Luke 18:14: "He that humbleth himself shall be exalted." You must here diligently learn and understand spiritually what the way of the Lord is, how it is prepared, and what prevents him from finding room in us. The way of the Lord, as you have heard, is that He does all things within you, so that all our works are not ours but His, which comes by faith.

This, however, is not possible if you desire worthily to prepare yourself by praying, fasting, self-mortification, and your own works, as is now generally and foolishly taught during the time of Advent. A spiritual preparation is meant, consisting in a thoroughgoing knowledge and confession of your being unfit, a sinner, poor, damned, and miserable, with all the works you may perform. The more a heart is thus minded, the better it prepares the way of the Lord, although meanwhile possibly drinking fine wines, walking on roses, and not praying a word.

The hindrance, however, that obstructs the Lord's way is formed not only in the coarse and palpable sin of adultery, wrath, haughtiness, avarice, and so on, but rather in spiritual conceit and pharisaical pride, which thinks highly of its own life and good works, feels secure, does not condemn itself, and would remain uncondemned by another.

Such, then, is the other class of men, namely, those that do not believe the crying of John, but call it the devil's, since it forbids good works and condemns the service of God, as they say. These are the people to whom most of all and most urgently it is said, "Prepare the way of the Lord," and who least of all accept it.

Therefore John speaks to them with cutting words in Luke 3:7-8: "Ye offspring of vipers, who warned you to flee from the wrath to come? Bring forth therefore fruits worthy of repentance." But, as said above, the more just people are urged to prepare the Lord's way, the more they obstruct it and the more unreasonable they become. They will not be told that their doings are not the Lord's, and finally, to the glory and honor of God, they annihilate the truth and the word of John himself and his Master also.

Judge, then, whether it was not a mighty confession on the part of John, when he dared to open his mouth and proclaim that he was not Christ, but a voice to which they did not like to listen, chiding the great teachers and leaders of the people for not doing that which was right and the Lord's pleasure. And as it went with John, so it still goes, from the beginning of the world unto the end. For such conceited piety will not be told that it must first and foremost prepare the way of the Lord, imagining itself to sit in God's lap and desiring to be petted and flattered by having long ago finished the way, before God even thought of finding a way for them—those precious saints! The pope and his followers likewise have condemned the crying of John to prepare the Lord's way. Aye, it is an intolerable crying—except to poor, penitent sinners with aggrieved consciences, for whom it is the best of cordials.

. . . . .

It seems as though the Evangelist had omitted something in these words, and as if John's complete answer ought to be: "I baptize with water; but he has come among you who baptizes with fire." Thus Luke (3:16) says: "I baptize you with water: but he shall baptize you with fire." And in Acts 1:5 we read, "John baptized with water, but ye shall be baptized with the Holy Ghost." But, although he here says nothing of this other baptism, he sufficiently indicates that there is to be another baptism, since he speaks of Another Who is coming after him and who, undoubtedly, will not baptize with water.

Now begins the second onset, whereby John was tried on the other side. For not being able to move him by allurements they attack him with threats. And here is uncovered their false humility, manifesting itself as pride and haughtiness. The same they would have done had John followed them, after they had had enough of him. Learn therefore here to be on your guard against men, particularly when they feign to be gentle and kind; as Christ says (Matthew 10:16-47): "Beware of men, be wise as serpents, and harmless as doves." That is to say, "Do not trust those that are smooth, and do no evil to your enemies."

Behold, these Pharisees, who professed their willingness to accept John as the Christ, veer around when things turn out as they desired and censure John's baptism. They say, as it were, "Since you are not Christ, nor Elijah, nor a prophet, you are to know that we are your superiors according to the law of Moses and you are therefore to conduct yourself as our subordinate. You are not to act independently, without our command, our knowledge, and our permission. Who has given you power to introduce something new among our people with your baptizing? You are bringing yourself into trouble with your criminal disobedience."

John, however, as he had despised their hypocrisy, likewise scorns their threats, remains firm, and confesses Christ as before. Moreover he boldly attacks them and charges them with ignorance, saying, as it were: "I have no authority from you to baptize with water. But what of that? There is Another from Whom I have power; Him you do not know, but He is amply sufficient for me. If you knew Him, or wished to know Him, you would not ask whence I have the power to baptize, but you would come to be baptized yourselves. For He is so much greater than I, that I am not worthy to unloose His shoe's latchet."

John's words, "He it is who, coming after me, is preferred before me," three times quoted by the Evangelist in this chapter, have been misinterpreted and obscured by some who referred them to Christ's divine and eternal birth, as though John meant to say that Christ had been born before him in eternity. But what is remarkable in the fact that He was born before John in eternity, seeing that He was born before the world and all other things? Thus He was also to come not only after him, but after all things, since He is the first and the last (Revelation 1:11). Therefore, His past and His future agree. John's words are clear and simple, referring to Christ when He already was a man. The words "He will come after me" cannot be taken to mean that He would be born after him; John, like Christ, was at that time about thirty years old.

These words then evidently apply to His preaching. He means to say: "I have come—that is, I have begun to preach but I shall soon stop, and Another will come and preach after me." Thus St. Luke says (Acts 1:22) that Christ began from the baptism of John; and (Luke 3:23) that Jesus was thirty years old when He began. "Art thou he that should come" (Matthew 11:3), that is, He Who should begin to preach; for Christ's office does not begin till after His baptism, at which His Father had acknowledged and glorified Him. Then also began the New Testament and the time of grace, not at the birth of Christ, as He Himself says (Mark 1:15): "The time is fulfilled, and the kingdom of God is at hand." Had He not begun to preach, His birth would have been of no use; but when He did begin to act and to teach, then were fulfilled all prophecies, all Scriptures, then came a new light, and a new world.

So we see what John means by saying, "He will come after me." But the meaning of the words, "He is preferred before me; he was before me," is not yet clear, some referring them to Christ's eternal birth. We maintain in all simplicity that those words also were spoken concerning their preaching. Thus the meaning is: "Although He is not yet preaching, but is coming after me, and I am preaching before Him: nevertheless He is already at hand, and so close by that, before I began to preach, He has already been there and has been appointed to preach." The words "before me" therefore point to John's office and not to his person. Thus, "He has been before my preaching and baptism for about thirty years; but He has not yet come, and has not yet begun." John thereby indicates his office, namely, that he is not a prophet foretelling the coming of Christ, but one who precedes Him who is already present, Who is so near that He has already been in existence so many years before His beginning and coming.

Therefore he also says: "In the midst of you standeth one whom ye know not." He means to say: "Do not permit your eyes to wander off into future ages. He of whom the prophets speak has been among you in the Jewish nation for well nigh thirty years. Take care and do not miss Him. You do not know Him, therefore I have come to point Him out to you." The words, "In the midst of you standeth one," are spoken after the manner of the Scriptures, which say, "A prophet will arise or stand up." Thus, in Matthew 24:24, "There shall arise false prophets" and in Deuteronomy 18:15, God says, "The Lord thy God will raise up unto thee a prophet." John now wishes to show that this "raising up," "arising," and "standing," was fulfilled in Christ, Who was already standing among them, as God had prophesied. The people however knew Him not.

This then is the other office of John and of every preacher of the Gospel, not alone to make all the world sinners, as we have heard (John 1:24ff), but also to give comfort and to show how we may get rid of our sins; this he does in pointing to Him Who is to come. Hereby he directs us to Christ, Who is to redeem us from our sins, if we accept Him in true faith. The first office says: "You are all sinners, and are wanting in the way of the Lord." When we believe this, the other office follows and says: "Listen, and accept Christ, believe in Him, He will free you of your sins." If we believe this, we have it. Of this we shall say more anon.

3. John Calvin

And this is the testimony. Hitherto the Evangelist has related the preaching of John about Christ; he now comes down to a more illustrious testimony, which was delivered to the ambassadors of the Priests that they might convey it to Jerusalem. He says, therefore, that John openly confessed for what purpose he was sent by God. The first inquiry here is, For what purpose did the Priests put questions to him? It is generally believed that, out of hatred to Christ, they gave to John an honor which did not belong to him; but this could not be the reason, for Christ was not yet known to them. Others say that they were better pleased with John, because he was of the lineage and order of the priesthood; but neither do I think that this is probable; for since they expected from Christ all prosperity, why did they voluntarily contrive a false Christ? I think, therefore, that there was another reason that induced them. It was now a long time since they had the prophets; John came suddenly and contrary to expectation; and the minds of all were aroused to expect the Messiah. Besides, all entertained the belief that the coming of the Messiah was at hand.

That they may not appear to be careless about their duty, if they neglect or disguise a matter of so great importance, they ask John, "Who art thou?" At first, therefore, they did not act from malice but, on the contrary, were actuated by the desire of redemption; they wish to know if John be the Christ, because he begins to change the order that had been customary in the Church. And yet I do not deny that ambition, and a wish to retain their authority, had some influence over them; but nothing certainly was further from their intention than to transfer the honor of Christ to another. Nor is their conduct in this matter inconsistent with the office they sustain; for since they held the government of the Church of God, it was their duty to take care that no one rashly obtruded himself, that no founder of a new sect should arise, that the unity of faith should not be broken in the Church, and that none should introduce new and foreign ceremonies. It is evident, therefore, that a report about John was widely spread and had aroused the minds of all. All this was arranged by the wonderful Providence of God, that this testimony might be more strikingly complete.

AND HE CONFESSED, AND DENIED NOT. That is, he confessed openly, and without any ambiguity or hypocrisy. The word confess, in the first instance, means, generally, that he stated the fact as it really was. In the second instance, it is repeated in order to express the form of the confession. He replied expressly, that he was not the Christ.

ART THOU ELIJAH? Why do they name Elijah rather than Moses? It was because they learned from the prediction of Malachi (4:2,5) that, when the Messiah, "the sun of righteousness," should arise, Elijah would be the morning star to announce His approach. But the question is founded on a false opinion they had long held; for, holding the opinion that the soul of a man departs out of one body into another, when the prophet Malachi announced that Elijah would be sent, they imagined that the same Elijah, who lived in the reign of king Ahab (1 Kings 17:1), was to come. It is therefore a just and true reply that John makes, he is not Elijah; for he speaks according to the opinion they attached to the words; but Christ, giving the true interpretation of the prophet, affirms that John is Elijah (Matthew 11:14; Mark 9:13).

ART THOU A PROPHET? Erasmus gives an inaccurate explanation of these words by limiting them to Christ; for the addition of the article carries no emphasis in this passage. The messengers afterward declare plainly enough that they meant a different prophet than Christ, for they sum up the whole by saying (vs. 25), "if thou art neither the Christ, nor Elijah, nor a prophet." Thus we see that they intended to point out different persons. Others think that they inquired if he was one of the ancient prophets; but neither do I approve of that exposition. Rather do they by this term point out the office of John, and ask if God had appointed him to be a prophet. When he replies, "*I am not,*" he does not for the sake of modesty tell a lie, but honestly and sincerely detaches himself from the company of the prophets. And yet this reply is not inconsistent with the honorable attestation that Christ gives him. Christ bestows on John the designation of prophet, and even adds that he is "more than a prophet" (Matthew 9:9); but by these words He does nothing more than demand credit and authority for John's doctrine, and at the same time describes, in lofty terms, the excellence of the office which had been conferred on him. But in this passage John has a different object in view, which is, to show that he has no special message, as was usually the case with the prophets, but that he was merely appointed to be the herald of Christ.

This will be made still more clear by a comparison. All ambassadors—even those who are not sent on matters of great importance—obtain the name and authority of ambassadors because they hold special commissions. Such were all the prophets who, having been enjoined to deliver certain predictions, discharged the prophetic office. But if some weighty matter comes to be transacted, and if two ambassadors are sent, one of whom announces the speedy arrival of another who possesses full power to transact the whole matter, and if this latter has received injunctions to bring it to a conclusion, will not the former embassy be reckoned a part and appendage of the latter, which is the principal? Such was the case with John the Baptist, to whom God had given no other injunction than to prepare the Jews for listening to Christ, and becoming His disciples. That this is the meaning will still more fully appear from the context; for we must investigate the opposite clause, which immediately follows. "I am not a prophet," says he, "but a voice crying in the wilderness." The distinction lies in this, that "the voice crying, that a way may be prepared for the Lord," is not a prophet, but merely a subordinate minister, so to speak; and his doctrine is only a sort of preparation for listening to another Teacher. In this way John, though he is more excellent than all the prophets, still is not a prophet.

THE VOICE OF HIM WHO CRIETH. As he would have been chargeable with rashness in undertaking the office of teaching if he had not received a commission, he shows what the duty was that he had to perform, and proves it by a quotation from the prophet Isaiah (11:3). Hence it follows that he does nothing but what God commanded him to do. *Isaiah* does not, indeed, speak there of John alone but, promising the restoration of the Church, he predicts that there will yet be heard joyful voices, commanding to "prepare the way for the Lord." Though he points out the coming of God, when he brought back the people from their captivity in Babylon, yet the true accomplishment was the manifestation of Christ in flesh. Among the heralds who announced that the Lord was at hand, John held the chief place.

To enter into ingenious inquiries, as some have done, into the meaning of the word "voice" would be frivolous. John is called "a voice," because he was enjoined to cry. It is in a figurative sense, undoubtedly, that Isaiah gives the name "wilderness" to the miserable desolation of the Church, which seemed to preclude the return of the people; as if he had said that a passage would indeed be opened up for the captive people, but that the Lord would find a road through regions in which there was no road. But that visible wilderness, in which John preached, was a figure or image of the awful desolation that took away all hope of deliverance. If this comparison be considered, it will easily be seen that no torture has been given to the words of the prophet in this application of them; for God arranged everything in such a manner as to place before the eyes of His people, who were overwhelmed with their calamities, a mirror of this prediction.

WERE OF THE PHARISEES. He says that they were Pharisees, who at that time held the highest rank in the Church; and he says so in order to inform us that they were not some contemptible persons of the order of the Levites, but men clothed with authority. This is the reason why they raise a question about his "baptism." Ordinary ministers would have been satisfied with any kind of answer; but those men, because they cannot draw from John what they desired, accuse him of rashness for venturing to introduce a new religious observance.

WHY THEN DOST THOU BAPTIZE? By laying down those three degrees, they appear to form a very conclusive argument: "if thou art not the Christ, nor Elijah, nor a prophet"; for it does not belong to every man to institute the practice of baptism. The *Messiah* was to be one who possessed all authority. Of *Elijah*, who was to come, they had formed this opinion, that he would commence the restoration both of the royal authority and of the Church. The *prophets* of God, they readily grant, have a right to discharge the office committed to them. They conclude, therefore, that for John to baptize is an unlawful novelty, since he has received from God no public station. But they are wrong in not acknowledging him to be that Elijah who is mentioned by Malachi (4:5); though he denies that he is that Elijah of whom they foolishly dreamed.

I BAPTIZE WITH WATER. This ought to have been abundantly sufficient for the correction of their mistake, but a reproof otherwise clear is of no advantage to the deaf; for, when he sends them to Christ, and declares that Christ is present, this is a clear proof not only that he was divinely appointed to be a minister of Christ, but that he is the true Elijah, who is sent to testify that the time is come for the renovation of the Church. There is a contrast here that is not fully stated; for the spiritual baptism of Christ is not expressly contrasted with the external baptism of John, but that latter clause about the baptism of the Spirit might easily be supplied, and shortly afterward both are set down by the Evangelist.

This answer may be reduced to two heads: First, that John claims nothing for himself but what he has a right to claim because he has Christ for the Author of his baptism, in which consists the truth of the sign; and, secondly, that he has nothing but the administration of the outward sign, while the whole power and efficacy is in the hands of Christ alone. Thus he defends his baptism, so far as its truth depends on anything else; but, at the same time, by declaring that he has not the power of the Spirit, he exalts the dignity of Christ, that the eyes of men may be fixed on Him alone. This is the highest and best regulated moderation, when a minister borrows from Christ whatever authority he claims for himself, in such a manner as to trace it to Him, ascribing to Him alone all that he possesses.

It is a foolish mistake, however, into which some people have been led, of supposing that John's baptism was different from ours; for John does not argue here about the advantage and usefulness of his baptism, but merely compares his own person with the person of Christ. In like manner, if we were inquiring, at the present day, what part belongs to us and what belongs to Christ, in baptism, we must acknowledge that Christ alone performs what baptism figuratively represents, and that we have nothing beyond the bare administration of the sign. There is a twofold way of speaking in Scripture about the sacraments. Sometimes it tells us that they are "the laver of regeneration" (Titus 3:5); that by them "our sins are washed away" (1 Peter 3:21); "that we are ingrafted into the body of Christ," that "our old man is crucified," and that "we rise again to newness of life" (Romans 6:4,5,6); and, in those cases, Scripture joins the power of Christ with the ministry of man; as, indeed, man is nothing else than the hand of Christ. Such modes of expression show, not what man can of himself accomplish, but what Christ performs by man, and by the sign, as His instruments. But as there is a strong tendency to fall into superstition and as men, through the pride that is natural to them, take from God the honor due to Him and basely appropriate it to themselves, so Scripture, in order to restrain this blasphemous arrogance, sometimes distinguishes ministers from Christ, as in this passage, that we may learn that ministers are nothing and can do nothing.

ONE STANDETH IN THE MIDST OF YOU. He indirectly charges them with stupidity in not knowing Christ, to whom their minds ought to have been earnestly directed; and he always insists earnestly on this point, that nothing can be known about his ministry until men have come to him who is the Author of it. When he says that Christ standeth in the midst of them, it is that he may excite their desire and their exertion to know Him. The amount of what he says is that he wishes to place himself as low as possible, lest any degree of honor improperly bestowed on him might obscure the excellence of Christ. It is probable that he had these sentences frequently in his mouth, when he saw himself immoderately extolled by the perverse opinions of men.

WHO COMING AFTER ME. Here he says two things: first, that Christ was behind him in the order of time; but, secondly, that He was far before him in rank and dignity, because the Father preferred Him to all. Soon after he will add a third statement, that Christ was preferred to all others, because He is in reality more exalted than all others.

THESE THINGS WERE DONE IN BETHABARA. The place is mentioned, not only to authenticate the narrative, but also to inform us that this answer was given amidst a numerous assembly of people. There were many who flocked to John's baptism, and this was his ordinary place for baptizing. It is likewise supposed by some to be a passage across Jordan and, from this circumstance, they derive the name, for they interpret it "the house of passage." Some may prefer the opinion of those who refer to the memorable passage of the people (Joshua 3:13), when God opened up a way for them in the midst of the waters, under the direction of Joshua. Others say that it ought rather to be read "Betharaba." Instead of "Bethabara," some have inserted here the name "Bethany," but this is a mistake; for we shall afterward see how near Bethany was to Jerusalem. The situation of Bethabara, as laid down by those who have described the country, agrees best with the words of the Evangelist; though I have no wish to dispute about the pronunciation of the word.

4. John Keble

It must have sounded very strange to them, when John said, "He standeth already among you: ye know Him not, but I know Him: He is come from heaven, He is here on earth, He is in this country, nay more, He is even now in this company. There He is, standing bodily among you, little thought or dreamed of by you." No doubt, when they heard this, many thoughts arose in their hearts; but few if any, came at all near the truth. Few, if any, could discern which of that crowd was God Almighty present on earth. Some might look among the chief priests, the scribes and Pharisees, those who seemed to be most learned, most depended on for their knowledge of holy Scripture. Others might look among the rich and great ones, Herod's nobles, if there were any there, or the chief of the soldiers who listened to St. John. But all the while there was in the multitude a poor, humble, quiet young Man, supposed to be a carpenter's son; of Nazareth, a place of no great credit; Who had lived now thirty years, working at the carpenter's trade, going about the village like any other poor but respectable artisan. When people met Him, they saw nothing particular in Him—no form nor comeliness, no beauty nor glory, that they should desire Him. He was very likely one of the last persons in the crowd around St. John, toward whom the generality would have turned their eyes, thinking, What if this should be He? What if this Jesus of Nazareth should prove to be the very Christ? And yet He was so, and no other. The poor young carpenter, so mean in outward appearance, was the Christ; the very Christ, the Son of God, begotten from everlasting of the Father; the only Sacrifice for the sins of the world, the King and God of the whole creation, the Judge, both of quick and dead. He, of Whom all this is true, was in that company, but they knew Him not. He was in the crowd; He was close to some of them; very likely they thronged and pressed Him, but they knew Him not. Some of them might know something about Him: for example, if there were any there from Nazareth, they would know Him to be the person whom they called the "carpenter's son." Some few of them might have the same kind of knowledge of Him as St. John seems to have had before he baptized Him. The Baptist must have known our Lord from the beginning as a very very holy Person. He must have heard what the shepherds had said of Him; yet he says, "I knew him not: but when I saw the Spirit descending and remaining on him, I saw, and bare record, that this is the Son of God." He knew not Christ's full glory until the Holy Ghost had descended upon Him. Those among the crowd who knew most of Jesus could not well know more than St. John knew, before he baptized Him: and St. John himself says: At that time "I knew him not." Well, therefore, might he say to the multitudes, "There standeth One among you, Whom ye know not." Those among you, who know most of Him, account Him only a very holy Man, raised up for some very great and gracious purpose: but in truth, He is the Most High God, God Incarnate, God the Son come down from heaven and made Man, to die for us. There He stands in the midst of you, but ye know Him not.

Thus it was when the Baptist spake; and it was the same all along, in all the stages of our Saviour's life on earth. Whether He was among friends or enemies, or indifferent persons, He was not fully known: and when He had died and risen again, and His Holy Spirit had made Him known, as the true God, to all believers, He could no longer be seen. He was gone away into heaven. Always, and in every case, He was "a God, who hideth himself."

If it were so then, my brethren, be sure it is so now. It is still exactly and literally true, in respect of every assembly of Christian people, few or many, whether they be come together for good or for evil, for business or diversion; "There standeth One among you, Whom ye know not." Jesus Christ is always among us, to watch both over good and over evil, both over business and over diversion. We do not see Him, we only see one another, but He is not the less certainly among us. If we disobey Him, we disobey Him to His Face; if we affront Him, we affront Him to His Face; if we forget Him, yet He is close at hand, listening to every word we say, and noting all down in His awful Book. Let us turn this over in our minds; let us go on thinking of it, until we have got it well fixed in our hearts: so that, whatever company we go into, we may always remember that Christ is one of that company.

For example, here we are now, in Church; and we see a certain number of our friends and neighbors around us. We see them, but we do not see Christ, yet we know that Christ is here; for it is His own promise, and we have been told of it over and over: "Where two or three are gathered together in my name, there am I in the midst of them." Christ is here in the midst of us, but we know Him not; not even those among us who most earnestly desire and labor to behave well, not even the most devout of His worshipers can thoroughly know Him, He is so unspeakably high, holy, and pure. How much less can the ordinary sort, those who in general are but outwardly well-behaved. How can they be said to know Him? And least of all is He known to the profane and willfully inattentive. Yet is He among us all.

. . . . .

Above all things, when the memorial Sacrifice of Christ, when His Sacrament of Holy Communion comes on; when you leave your place and come into the chancel, to kneel down, and to partake of that saving Body and Blood, let all endeavor to feel in their very hearts that *here*, above all other places on earth, our Lord Jesus, God and Man, is present in a peculiar manner. As to those who come worthily He is present with such grace as is promised to nothing else that is done here below: For they do verily and indeed eat His Flesh and drink His Blood; they dwell in Him, and He in them; they are one with Him, and He with them. So the Holy Scripture teaches, that they who come unworthily find Him also present in such sense as that they are guilty of His Body and Blood. Their sin is the same, as if they had gone by whilst Joseph was laying Him in the grave, and had insulted His blessed Body. Therefore to all careless communicants the Church seems to cry aloud: "There standeth one among you, whom ye know not"; take care how you deal with Him. For He comes, longing to dwell in your hearts, He cannot bear to be neglected; much less to be affronted and reproachfully used. And to all penitent but sad and dejected communicants, she still utters the same words: "There standeth one among you," yea, there abideth in the midst of you, even in the very deep of your heart there abideth, One "whom ye know not." The God of all comfort is there, though as yet you taste not His comfort: but wait on Him in loving obedience, and all will be right.

Now we will suppose that the Holy Sacrament is over, and the Christian people are gone home to their houses; you are gathered together —families, fellow servants, friends, or neighbors—for innocent and loving conversation and refreshment. It is well. This also is God's blessing; but take good heed, I beseech you, that in these your home gatherings, as well as in your solemn assemblies, there is always present One more than your eyes can see; Christ is there, though you see Him not. He expects you to turn toward Him, and give Him thanks, at the beginning of the meals which He allows you. He expects you, during the meal, to recollect that He is there. And as you would not act rudely and unmannerly if you were at a great man's table, at a feast, where a king was present, so Christ expects of you to be sober and temperate out of true reverence to Him, and to guard your tongue from scandal and backbiting especially, because He is there, setting down every word. Keep these rules, my brethren: Behave at your common meals and meetings for diversion as persons who do not forget that they carry Christ about with them, having received Him in His Holy Sacrament, and a great blessing will attend you, even on those ordinary occasions. You will not be the less cheerful, but your cheerfulness will be far more innocent and happy.

Next imagine the Sunday over, the time of rest and refreshment at an end, and that you are gathered together for some purpose of worldly business; at market, for instance, or in a shop, or working together in any manner. Here again the saying will be true, "There standeth one among you, whom ye know not." He Who once spake from Heaven in thunder, "Thou shalt not steal"; He Who cannot bear any manner of cheating, fraud, injustice, or wrong; He is with the tradesman behind the counter, with the dealer in the fair or market, with the thresher in the barn, with the servant in the storehouse or garden. He knows all the liberties we ever take, either in helping ourselves secretly or in bargaining unfairly to our own advantage. He knows all the falsehoods men tell in such matters, all the grudging and envious thoughts, the bitter and angry words, to which they are tempted. He knows when the hired laborer neglects his due portion of work, as well as He knows when the employer underpays him, or grudges him his just wages in proper time. In all such temptations (and most of us at times are exposed to one or another of them), the great safeguard is to be aware of His eye fixed upon us. If we knew that some Saint, some very holy person was watching us, should we not think a good deal of it? Would it not make a great difference in our conduct? How much more, when He standeth among us invisibly, Who is the Lord of all Saints! How pure should we strive to be, in sight of the God of purity.

Indeed, my brethren, the thought of His so standing among us would be too awful if really considered; it would be too much for us, it could not be borne; were it not that He has graciously told us how good and forgiving He is also. We should surely die, upon thus seeing God, were it not that it is the same God Who made Himself Man for our sake, the same Christ Who died for us. But then we must be making much both of His birth and of His death, not neglecting them, or making them void. Christmas, like other holy seasons, is given us for our trial in this respect. May we so keep it, this time at least, that it may not tell to our condemnation.

CHRISTMAS DAY—THE NATIVITY OF OUR LORD

Text: Luke 2:1-14

1. Leo the Great

THE INCARNATION FULFILLS ALL ITS TYPES AND PROMISES. The Divine goodness, dearly beloved, has indeed always taken thought for mankind in divers manners, and in many portions, and of His mercy has imparted many gifts of His providence to the ages of old; but in these last times has exceeded all the abundance of His usual kindness, when in Christ the very Mercy has descended to sinners, the very Truth to those that are astray, the very Life to those that are dead: so that the Word, which is co-eternal and co-equal with the Father, might take our humble nature into union with His Godhead, and being born God of God, might also be born Man of man. This was indeed promised from the foundation of the world, and had always been prophesied by many intimations of facts and words: But how small a portion of mankind would these types and foreshadowed mysteries have saved, had not the coming of Christ fulfilled those long and secret promises, and had not that which then benefited but a few believers in the prospect, now benefited myriads of the faithful in its accomplishment? Now no longer then are we led to believe by signs and types, but being confirmed by the gospel story we worship that which we believe to have been done; the prophetic lore assisting our knowledge, so that we have no manner of doubt about that which we know to have been predicted by such sure oracles. For hence it is that the Lord says to Abraham, "In thy seed shall all nations be blessed"; hence David, in the spirit of prophecy, sings, saying: "The Lord swore truth to David, and he shall not frustrate it: of the fruit of thy loins will I set upon thy seat"; hence the Lord again says through Isaiah: "behold, a virgin shall conceive in her womb, and shall bear a Son, and his name shall be called Emmanuel, which is interpreted, God with us," and again, "a rod shall come forth from the root of Jesse, and a flower shall arise from his root." In which rod, no doubt the blessed Virgin Mary is predicted, who sprung from the stock of Jesse and David and fecundated by the Holy Ghost, brought forth a new flower of human flesh, becoming a virgin-mother.

THE INCARNATION WAS THE ONLY EFFECTIVE REMEDY TO THE FALL. Let the righteous then rejoice in the Lord, and let the hearts of believers turn to God's praise, and the sons of men confess His wondrous acts; since in this work of God especially our humble estate realizes how highly its Maker values it: in that, after His great gift to mankind in making us after His image, He contributed far more largely to our restoration when

the Lord Himself took on Him "the form of a slave." For though all that
the Creator expends upon His creature is part of one and the same Fatherly
love, yet it is less wonderful that man should advance to divine things than
that God should descend to humanity. But unless the Almighty God did
deign to do this, no kind of righteousness, no form of wisdom, could rescue
anyone from the devil's bondage and from the depths of eternal death.
For the condemnation that passes with sin from one upon all would remain, and our nature, corroded by its deadly wound, would discover no
remedy, because it could not alter its state in its own strength. For the first
man received the substance of flesh from the earth, and was quickened
with a rational spirit by the inbreathing of his Creator, so that living after
the image and likeness of his Maker, he might preserve the form of God's
goodness and righteousness as in a bright mirror. And, if he had per-
severingly maintained this high dignity of his nature by observing the
Law that was given him, his uncorrupt mind would have raised the character even of his earthly body to heavenly glory. But because in unhappy
rashness he trusted the envious deceiver, and agreeing to his presumptuous
counsels, preferred to forestall rather than to win the increase of honor
that was in store for him, not only did that one man, but in him all that
came after him also hear the verdict: "Earth thou art, and unto earth shalt
thou go"; "as in the earthy," therefore, "such are they also that are earthy";
and no one is immortal, because no one is heavenly.

WE ALL BECOME PARTAKERS IN THE BIRTH OF CHRIST BY THE REBIRTH
OF BAPTISM. And so to undo this chain of sin and death, the Almighty
Son of God, that fills all things and contains all things, altogether equal
to the Father and co-eternal in one essence from Him and with Him, took
on Him man's nature, and the Creator and Lord of all things deigned to
be a mortal; choosing for His mother one whom He had made, one who,
without loss of her maiden honor, supplied so much of bodily substance
that without the pollution of human seed the New Man might be possessed of purity and truth. In Christ, therefore, born of the Virgin's womb,
the nature does not differ from ours, because His nativity is wonderful.
For He Who is true God is also true man: and there is no lie in either
nature. "The Word became flesh" by exaltation of the flesh, not by failure
of the Godhead, which so tempered its power and goodness as to exalt our
nature by taking it, and not to lose His own by imparting it. In this nativity
of Christ, according to the prophecy of David, "truth sprang out of the
earth, and righteousness looked down from heaven." In this nativity also,
Isaiah's saying is fulfilled, "Let the earth produce and bring forth salvation, and let righteousness spring up together." For the earth of human
flesh, which in the first transgressor was cursed, in this Offspring of the
Blessed Virgin only produced a seed that was blessed and free from the
fault of its stock. And each one is a partaker of this spiritual origin in regeneration; and to everyone when he is reborn, the water of baptism is like
the Virgin's womb; for the same Holy Spirit fills the font, Who filled the
Virgin, that the sin, which that sacred conception overthrew, may be taken
away by this mystical washing.

2. Bernard of Clairvaux

Great indeed, beloved, is the Feast of the Lord's birth that we observe today; but a short day requires us to shorten our discourse. And it is no wonder that our word is brief, when even God the Father shortened His! Would you know how long, how short He made His Word? "I fill heaven and earth," this Word says of Himself; and now He is made flesh, they put Him in a narrow manger! "Thou art God from everlasting," says the prophet; and lo, He has become an infant of a day! Why did He do this, brethren? What was it that compelled the Lord of majesty to empty and to humble and to shorten Himself thus, if not that you might do the same? He cries by His example now what later He will preach by word of mouth, "Learn of Me, for I am meek and lowly of heart." I beg and beseech you, therefore, brethren, that you suffer not so precious a pattern to be shown to you in vain, but rather conform yourselves thereto, and be renewed in the spirit of your mind. Cherish humility, which is the groundwork and guardian of the virtues; follow after that, which alone can save your souls.

That, then, is the reason why He Who, being in the form of God, was equal to the Father, emptied Himself and took a servant's form; but He emptied Himself only of majesty and power, not of goodness and mercy. For what says the apostle? "The kindness and humanity of God our Saviour hath appeared." His power had appeared already in creation, His wisdom in the ordering of things created; but the kindness of mercy has appeared now in His humanity. The Jews received the revelation of His power through signs and wonders, and the philosophers perceived His majesty; but the power only awed the one, and the glory of the majesty only oppressed the other. Power demands subjection and majesty wonder; but neither calls for imitation. Let then Thy goodness, Lord, appear, that to it Man, made in Thine image, may conform himself. For we cannot imitate Thy majesty, power, and wisdom, nor is it meet for us to try; but "Thy mercy, O Lord, reacheth unto the heavens and thy truth unto the clouds." Let Thy mercy, then, extend its borders, enlarge its tents and open wide its arms, that it may reach from one end to the other, and sweetly order all things. Thy judgment, Lord, restricts Thy love's embrace; take off Thy girdle then, and come, with mercies like a flowing stream and charity a flood.

What do you fear, O Man? Why do you tremble before the Face of the Lord when He comes? He comes not to judge the world, but to save it. Flee not, nor fear. He comes unarmed; He wants to save you, not to punish you. And lest you should say now, "I heard thy voice and hid myself," behold He is an Infant, with no voice; for the cry of a baby is something to pity, not to be frightened of. He is made a little Child, the Virgin Mother wraps His tender limbs in swaddling bands; do you still quake with fear? This tells you He has come to save you, not to lose you; to rescue you and not to fetter you. Already He is fighting your two enemies, sin and death—death of both body and soul. He has come to vanquish both of them and, never you fear, He will save you from them both. He has already conquered sin in His own Person, in that He took our nature without spot of sin. Thenceforward He follows on your enemies and overtakes them, and He does not turn again until they are consumed. He fights sin by His life, He attacks it likewise by His word and His example; but in His Passion He binds it, yes, binds the strong man and despoils his goods. In the same way it is in Himself that He first conquers death, when He arises as the First-fruits of them that sleep and the First-born from the dead; thereafter He will vanquish it in all of us when He raises our mortal bodies and death, the last enemy, is then destroyed. In His rising, therefore, He is clothed with honor, not wrapped in swaddling bands as at His birth. And as His all-embracing mercy then judged nobody, now in His resurrection He girds Himself in, as it were, and seems with the girdle of righteousness in some sense to restrict His mercy's embrace; for from henceforth we must get ready for the Judgment, which will take place when we ourselves are raised. He came as a little Child before, that He might offer mercy in advance; and now He anticipates the final Judgment yet to be, that He may temper that with mercy too.

3. Martin Luther

Faith is first, and it is right that we recognize it as the most important in every word of God. It is of no value only to believe that this history is true as it is written; for all sinners, even those condemned, believe that. The Scripture, God's Word, does not teach concerning faith, that it is a natural work, without grace. The right and gracious faith which God demands is, that you firmly believe that Christ is born for you, and that this birth took place for your welfare. The Gospel teaches that Christ was born, and that He did and suffered everything in our behalf, as is here declared by the angel: "Behold, I bring you good tidings of great joy which shall be to all the people; for there is born to you this day a Saviour, who is Christ the Lord." In these words you clearly see that He is born for us.

He does not simply say, Christ is born, but to *you* he is born; neither does he say, I bring glad tidings, but to *you* I bring glad tidings of great joy. Furthermore, this joy was not to remain in Christ but it shall be to all the people. This faith no condemned or wicked man has, nor can he have it; for the right ground of salvation which unites Christ and the believing heart is that they have all things in common. But what have they?

Christ has a pure, innocent, and holy birth. Man has an unclean, sinful, condemned birth, as David says (Psalm 51:5), "Behold I was brought forth in iniquity; and in sin did my mother conceive me." Nothing can help this unholy birth except the pure birth of Christ. But Christ's birth cannot be distributed in a material sense, neither would that avail anything; it is therefore imparted spiritually, through the Word, as the angel says, given to all who firmly believe so that no harm will come to them because of their impure birth. This is the way and manner in which we are to be cleansed from the miserable birth we have from Adam. For this purpose Christ willed to be born, that through Him we might be born again, as He says in John 3:3, that it takes place through faith; as also St. James says in 1:18: "Of his own will he brought us forth by the word of truth, that we should be a kind of first fruits of his creatures."

We see here how Christ, as it were, takes our birth from us and absorbs it in His birth, and grants us His, that in it we might become pure and holy, as if it were our own, so that every Christian may rejoice and glory in Christ's birth as much as if he had himself been born of Mary as was Christ. Whoever does not believe this, or doubts, is no Christian.

Oh, this is the great joy of which the angel speaks. This is the comfort and exceeding goodness of God that, if a man believes this, he can boast of the treasure that Mary is his rightful mother, Christ his brother, and God his father. For these things actually occurred and are true; but we must believe. This is the principal thing and the principal treasure in every Gospel, before any doctrine of good works can be taken out of it. Christ must above all things become our own and we become His, before we can do good works.

But this cannot occur except through the faith that teaches us rightly to understand the Gospel and properly to lay hold of it. This is the only way in which Christ can be rightly known so that the conscience is satisfied and made to rejoice. Out of this grow love and praise to God who in Christ has bestowed upon us such unspeakable gifts. This gives courage to do or leave undone, and living or dying, to suffer everything that is well pleasing to God. This is what is meant by Isaiah 9:6, "Unto us a child is born, unto us a son is given," to us, to us, to us is born, and to us is given this Child.

Therefore see to it that you do not find pleasure in the Gospel only as a history, for that is only transient; neither regard it only as an example, for it is of no value without faith; but see to it that you make this birth your own and that Christ be born in you. This will be the case if you believe, then you will repose in the lap of the Virgin Mary and be her dear Child. But you must exercise this faith and pray while you live, you cannot establish it too firmly. This is our foundation and inheritance, upon which good works must be built.

If Christ has now thus become your own, and you have by such faith been cleansed through Him and have received your inheritance without any personal merit, but alone through the love of God who gives to you as your own the treasure and work of His Son, it follows that you will do good works by doing to your neighbor as Christ has done to you. Here good works are their own teacher. What are the good works of Christ? Is it not true that they are good because they have been done for your benefit, for God's sake, who commanded Him to do the works in your behalf? In this then Christ was obedient to the Father, in that He loved and served us.

Therefore since you have received enough and become rich, you have no other commandment to serve Christ and render obedience to Him, than so to direct your works that they may be of benefit to your neighbor, just as the works of Christ are of benefit and use to you. For the reason Jesus said at the Last Supper: "This is my commandment that ye love one another, even as I have loved you" (John 13:34). Here it is seen that He loved us and did everything for our benefit, in order that we may do the same, not to Him, for he needs it not, but to our neighbor; this is His commandment, and this is our obedience. Therefore it is through faith that Christ becomes our own, and His love is the cause that we are His. He loves, we believe; thus both are united into one. Again, our neighbor believes and expects our love, we are therefore to love him also in return and not let him long for it in vain. One is the same as the other; as Christ helps us so we in return help our neighbor, and all have enough.

Observe now from this how far those have gone out of the way who have united good works with stone, wood, clothing, eating, and drinking. Of what benefit is it to your neighbor if you build a church entirely out of gold? Of what benefit to him is the frequent ringing of great church bells? Of what benefit to him is the glitter and the ceremonies in the churches, the priests' gowns, the sanctuary, the silver pictures and vessels? Of what benefit to him are the many candles and much incense? Of what benefit to him is the much chanting and mumbling, the singing of vigils and masses? Do you think that God will permit Himself to be paid with the sound of bells, the smoke of candles, the glitter of gold, and such fancies? He has commanded none of these; but if you see your neighbor going astray, sinning, or suffering in body or soul, you are to leave everything else and at once help him in every way in your power and if you can do no more, help him with words of comfort and prayer. Thus has Christ done to you and given you an example to follow.

These are the two things in which a Christian is to exercise himself, the one that he draws Christ into himself, and that by faith he makes Him his own, appropriates to himself the treasures of Christ and confidently builds upon them; the other that he condescends to his neighbor and lets him share in that which he has received, even as he shares in the treasures of Christ. He who does not exercise himself in these two things will receive no benefit even if he should fast unto death, suffer torture or even give his body to be burned, and were able to do all miracles, as St. Paul teaches (1 Corinthians 13ff).

4. Friedrich Schleiermacher

In accordance with this text let us look at the first appearance of the Saviour as the proclamation of a joy which awaits mankind. Two things we want to take to heart: First, the joy in the appearing of the Saviour is the true pattern for all joy concerning the future; and second, faith which grasps this future joy is the only security concerning all our cares for the future.

First of all, the joy in the future that was to begin with the appearance of the Saviour but which was not visible at His birth is the pattern of all joy in regard to the future. While we are all accustomed to look from the present into the future, the more experience we gather, the more certain we become that such joy is very uncertain. This was the case with the joy occasioned by the address of the angel in those who heard his words. He spoke of a joy that will come to all people. Their ideas, however, concerning the results of the birth of this Child were limited to their own nation. They thought back into the past and remembered the splendid figure of David. They were led to assume a similarity between that ancient king of their people and the One who was now born to be their future Lord. The more literally they were to take these words, the more easily they would err. The pictures they formed in their minds on the basis of those words were quite different from what was actually going to happen. Joy that will come to all people was proclaimed to them. To this day it has not come to all the people of which the angel spoke at that time. . . . Yet many other nations have acknowledged this light, have been warmed by it, and have been raised to a higher way of life. Those who first heard these words could not possibly even suspect this development. Even if, as Scripture assures us, a time shall come when all Israel will be saved—and there is no other salvation than that which is offered in the One Name—this is still something in the future.

Thus the shepherds, trusting in the words of the proclamation, were nevertheless unable to get a firm view of the exact time of these events in God's counsel. This seems to be the character of all prophecy which fills the books of the Old Covenant. And it is equally true of the few prophecies we find in the books of the New Covenant. The ingenuity which attempted to interpret these passages has vainly tried to gain a definite picture of what is meant by them. The same is true for us. When we think of the joy which the appearance of the Saviour still implies for us we must resign ourselves that our picture of the future consists of uncertain imaginations. . . . Does that mean that such joy loses all value? Something, indeed, is necessary that it may have value for us and we must not hide the fact. Everything we are able to see in the future, everything that has been communicated and proclaimed to us about it, is only true for us, is only our possession if it coincides with our innermost desire, if it satisfies the direction of our own soul and thus gives us rest.

As for the shepherds who heard the message of the angel—we do not know whether they belonged to those who were waiting for the salvation promised in the prophecies of the Old Covenant . . . our narrative does not tell us. While they did not refuse the message and said, "Let us go over to Bethlehem and see this thing that has happened, which the Lord has made known to us," we do not know whether this message remained a truth for them which guided their lives. Did they consider following this humble Child? Did they ever belong among His disciples? It is quite possible that this proclamation came to them without reference to their own personal condition just to make them bearers of a tale that could never be forgotten again.

There is another narrative from the infancy of our Saviour which makes a more beautiful and certain impression. The old man who saw the Saviour when His mother and Joseph brought Him to the Temple to bring the prescribed sacrifice was certainly one of those who waited for the salvation of Israel. He had received the word that he would not see death before he had seen the Saviour of the world. His soul was so filled by this encounter that it satisfied him for the remainder of his life even though he had seen Jesus only in His infancy and without a sign of His divine dignity. But for Simeon this word became the basis for peace because it conformed to the innermost desire of his heart. And the same is true of that prophetess who happened to be present and who, in accordance with her hopes and out of the fullness of her needs and her faith, became quite a different kind of bearer of this proclamation than probably did those shepherds.

The same is true about us. We must confess that the present, in comparison with the future, is as incomplete as the human appearance of the Saviour at that time when His eyes first opened to the earthly light. We are all forced in a thousand different ways to look into the future. But the real joy in the future as shaped from this salvation in Christ is reserved for those who have a deep desire for a peace they cannot attain by their own power, for a spiritual wholeness and fullness which may be the goal of their striving but which they know to be outside their reach.

Thus the Saviour always says that He came as the Physician for the sick. Every word of comfort, every invitation was always—if it grasped someone and became true in a human soul—an intimation of a further development reserved for the future. It could only become living truth in receptive, and that means needy, souls. . . .

If our soul follows another direction than the divine Wisdom, if we desire something other than what God has decreed in His eternal counsel, we will be unable to see the traces of the future in the present. We will be deceived by the impulse of our own heart. Only those can experience true and healing joy in the future who desire nothing else than the simple salvation that Christ has brought to all men, who strive for nothing else than the peace of man with God secured in the completion of His divine work.

Secondly, let us see how the joy of our festival is turned toward the future because it rests on that which has already happened and thus affords security and confidence in regard to all cares which we may have about this future.

Here we must remember that this whole relationship is a matter of faith. What has happened then can only be grasped in faith and thus the comfort we have for the future rests on faith. Look at the words of the angel to the shepherds: "This will be a sign for you: you will find a babe wrapped in swaddling clothes and lying in a manger." Some sign! How could this possibly give them even a hint of the "joy which will come to all the people"? What kind of sign is this that "today is born a Saviour, who is Christ, the Lord"?

If the marvellous appearance had not opened the minds of the shepherds to a believing confidence, the sign would have tended to discount the proclamations. And this is the way it has always been. Only faith could see in the figure of the Saviour the joy which has come to all men. After He had begun His ministry, unbelief said, "Does any one of the chiefs of the people believe in him?" "What good can come from Nazareth?" "Has ever a prophet come from Galilee?" And their hearts were deceived, the signs of the Most High were misunderstood and unbelief on the basis of what it saw could not get a hold on the future. . . .

But if the shepherds held on to the faith awakened in them they will have said about those things that happened later in Bethlehem—the little boy will have escaped the murderous attempts of Herod. And in every need of the time they will have thought, we know that He who will be our royal Lord was born in the city of David and He will protect us. . . . Once we have become secure in the true Christmas joy, that our Saviour is born and that we do not have to wait for another, nothing that happens can make us doubt the future He has proclaimed. . . .

THE FIRST SUNDAY AFTER CHRISTMAS DAY

Text: Luke 2:33-40

1. St. Augustine

That day is called the birthday of the Lord on which the Wisdom of God manifested Himself as a speechless Child and the Word of God wordlessly uttered the sound of a human voice. His divinity, although hidden, was revealed by heavenly witness to the Magi and was announced to the shepherds by angelic voices. With yearly ceremony, therefore, we celebrate this day which saw the fulfillment of the prophecy: "Truth is sprung out of the earth: and justice hath looked down from heaven." Truth, eternally existing in the bosom of the Father, has sprung from the earth so that He might be placed in a manger. For whose benefit did such unparalleled greatness come in such lowliness? Certainly for no personal advantage, but definitely for our great good, if only we believe. Arouse yourself, Oh man; for you God has become man. "Awake, sleeper, and arise from among the dead, and Christ will enlighten thee." For you, I repeat, God has become man. If He had not thus been born in time, you would have been dead for all eternity. Never would you have been freed from sinful flesh if He had not taken upon Himself the likeness of sinful flesh. Everlasting misery would have engulfed you if He had not taken this merciful form. You would not have been restored to life had He not submitted to your death; you would have fallen had He not succored you; you would have perished had He not come.

Let us joyfully celebrate the coming of our salvation and redemption. Let us celebrate the festal day on which the great and timeless One came from the great and timeless day to this brief span of our day. He "has become for us . . . justice, and sanctification, and redemption; so that, just as it is written, 'Let him who takes pride, take pride in the Lord.' " For, so that we might not resemble the proud Jews who, "ignorant of the justice of God and seeking to establish their own, have not submitted to the justice of God," when the Psalmist had said: "Truth is sprung out of the earth," he quickly added: "and justice hath looked down from heaven." He did this lest mortal frailty, arrogating this justice to itself, should call these blessings its own, and lest man should reject the justice of God in his belief that he is justified, that is, made just through his own efforts. "Truth is sprung out of the earth" because Christ, who said: "I am the truth," was born of a virgin; and "justice hath looked down from heaven" because, by believing in Him who was so born, man has been justified not by his own efforts but by God. "Truth is sprung out of the earth" because "the Word was made flesh," and "justice hath looked down from heaven" because "every good and perfect gift is from above." "Truth is sprung out of the earth," that is, His flesh was taken from Mary; and "justice hath looked down from heaven" because "no one can receive anything unless it is given to him from heaven."

"Having been justified therefore by faith, let us have peace with God through our Lord Jesus Christ, through whom we also have access by faith unto that grace in which we stand and exult in the hope of the glory . . . of God." With these few words, which you recognize as those of the Apostle, it gives me pleasure, my brethren, to mingle a few passages of the psalm (which we are considering) and to find that they agree in sentiment. "Having been justified by faith, let us have peace with God" because "justice and peace have kissed"; "through our Lord Jesus Christ" because "truth is sprung out of the earth"; "through whom we also have access by faith unto that grace in which we stand, and exult in the hope of the glory of God"—he does not say "of our glory," but "of the glory of God" because justice has not proceeded from us but "hath looked down from heaven." Therefore, "let him who takes pride, take pride in the Lord" not in himself. Hence, when the Lord whose birthday we are celebrating today was born of the Virgin, the announcement of the angelic choir was made in the words: "Glory to God in the highest, and on earth peace among men of good will." How can peace exist on earth unless it be because "truth is sprung out of the earth," that is, because Christ has been born in the flesh? Moreover, "He Himself is our peace, He it is who has made both one" so that we might become men of good will, bound together by the pleasing fetters of unity. Let us rejoice, then, in this grace so that our glory may be the testimony of our conscience wherein we glory not in ourselves but in the Lord. Hence the Psalmist (in speaking of the Lord) has said: "My glory and the lifter up of my head." For what greater grace of God could have shone upon us than that, having an only begotten Son, God should make Him the Son of Man, and thus, in turn, make the son of man the Son of God? Examine it as a benefit, as an inducement, as a token of justice, and see whether you find anything but a gratuitous gift of God.

2. Martin Luther

AND THE CHILD GREW, AND WAXED STRONG, FILLED WITH WISDOM: AND THE GRACE OF GOD WAS UPON HIM. Some inquisitive people who were not satisfied with the information given in the Scriptures have desired to know what Christ did in His childhood, and have received their reward for their curiosity. Some fool or knave has fabricated a legendary book on the childhood of Christ, and has not been afraid nor slow to write down his lies and frauds, relating how Christ went to school and a great deal more of absurd and blasphemous tomfoolery. Thus he jests with his lies at the expense of the Lord, whom all the angels adore and fear, and before whom all creatures tremble, so that this rascal would have deserved that a great millstone had been hanged about his neck and he had been sunk in the depth of the sea, because he did not esteem the Lord of all more than to make him an object of his absurd buffoonery. Yet people may still be found who print this book, read and believe it, which, in fact, was the object of this miscreant. Therefore I say that such books ought to be burned by the pope, the bishops, and the universities, if they would follow Christ. But they produce books that are a great deal worse, are blind leaders and remain such.

Christ never went to school, for no schools like ours existed at that time. He did not even have an elementary education; as we read in the Gospel of St. John 7:15, the Jews were marveling, saying: "How knoweth this man letters, having never learned?" We also read in Mark 6:2-3 that they were astonished at His wisdom and said: "What is the wisdom that is given unto this man, and what mean such mighty works wrought by his hands? Is not this the carpenter, the son of Mary?" They thought it strange that a layman and the son of a carpenter should have such great knowledge, having never studied. Therefore they were offended in Him, as the Evangelist relates, and thought that He must be possessed of an evil spirit.

Let us therefore be satisfied with the narrative of the Gospel, which tells us enough of his childhood. Luke writes that "the child grew, and waxed strong, filled with wisdom." Later on he writes that He was subject to His parents. What else should he have related? The time was not yet come when He performed miracles. He was brought up like other children, with the exception, that as some children excel others in ability, Christ also was an extraordinarily clever child. Thus no more could be written concerning Him than is recorded by Luke. If he had related how He ate, drank, and what He did every day, how He walked, stood, slept, and watched, what kind of a narrative would it have been?

It is not necessary to believe, neither do I think it is true, that His coat which was woven from the top throughout, grew with Him in size from His youth. Probably His mother made it, and in that country it was the common garment of the poor. We should have a pure faith that accepts nothing that is not found in the Scriptures. Enough is contained in the Scriptures that we may believe, especially since Christ did not begin to perform His miracles and mighty deeds until after His baptism, as it is written in John 2:11 and Acts 10:37.

Some hairsplitters are perplexed by the words of Luke according to which Christ, although He was God, waxed strong, filled with wisdom. That He grew, they admit, which is indeed surprising, as they are very swift in inventing miracles where there are none and despise those in which they should believe. The reason for their perplexity and their anxious questions is this, that they have invented an article of faith according to which Christ from the first moment of conception was filled with wisdom and the spirit to the highest possible degree, just as if the soul were a wineskin which may be completely filled. They themselves do not understand what they say, nor whereof they confidently affirm, as St. Paul writes in 1 Timothy 1:7.

Even if I could not understand what Luke means when he says that Christ waxed strong, filled with wisdom, I should yet believe his word because it is the Word of God, and should honor it as the truth, although I might never find out how it could be true; and I should abandon my imaginary article of faith as human foolishness, which is far too worthless to be a standard of divine truth. We all must acknowledge that Christ was not always cheerful, notwithstanding the fact that he who is filled with the Spirit is also full of joy, since joy is the fruit of the Spirit, according to Galatians 5:22. Neither was Christ always gentle and calm, but sometimes He was indignant and vexed, as for instance when He cast the Jews out of the Temple (John 2:15-17), and when He was angry and grieved at the hardening of their hearts (Mark 3:5).

Therefore we must understand the words of Luke simply as applying to the human nature of Christ, which was an instrument and temple of the Godhead. And although He was always filled with the Spirit and with grace, yet the Spirit did not always move Him, but prompted Him now to do this, now something else, just as necessity required. Although the Spirit was in Him from the first moment of the conception, yet as His body grew and His reason naturally developed as in other men, so also was He filled and moved by the Spirit more and more. It is no delusion when Luke says that He waxed strong and advanced in wisdom, but the words tell us plainly in age and in stature, and as He grew in stature His reason developed, and with the development of His reason He became stronger in the Spirit and filled with wisdom before God, in Himself and before men, which needs no further explanation. This is a Christian explanation which can be accepted without any danger, and it does not matter whether it overthrows any other imaginary articles of faith.

Saint Paul agrees with this when he says (Philippians 2:7) that Christ, who existed in the form of God, emptied Himself, taking the form of a servant, being made in the likeness of men, and being found in fashion as a man. Saint Paul does not speak here of the likeness of Christ's human nature to our own, but he says: "Christ, the man, after He had taken upon Himself human nature, was made in the likeness of men, and found in fashion as a man." Now as all men grow naturally in body, reason, mind, and wisdom, which is a universal experience, Luke agrees with Paul when he says that Christ grew in the same manner, yet being an extraordinary child that developed more rapidly than others. For his bodily constitution was nobler, and the gifts and graces of God were bestowed upon him more abundantly than upon others. Thus the sense of Luke's words is easily understood, perspicacious and simple, if only these wiseacres would leave out their subtleties.—So much on this Gospel.

3. John Calvin

AND HIS FATHER AND MOTHER WERE WONDERING. Luke does not say that they were astonished at it as a new thing, but that they contemplated with reverence, and embraced with becoming admiration, this prediction of the Spirit uttered by the lips of Simeon, so that they continued to make progress in the knowledge of Christ. We learn from this example that, when we have once come to possess a right faith, we ought to collect, on every hand, whatever may aid in giving to it additional strength. That man has made great proficiency in the word of God who does not fail to admire whatever he reads or hears every day, that contributes to his unceasing progress in faith.

AND SIMEON BLESSED THEM. If you confine this to Joseph and Mary, there will be no difficulty. But, as Luke appears to include Christ at the same time, it might be asked, "What right had Simeon to take upon him the office of blessing Christ?" "Without all contradiction," says Paul, "the less is blessed of the greater" (Hebrews 7:7). Besides, it has the appearance of absurdity, that any mortal man should offer prayers in behalf of the Son of God. I answer that the Apostle does not speak there of every kind of blessing, but only of the priestly blessing; for, in other respects, it is highly proper in men to pray for each other. Now, it is more probable that Simeon blessed them as a private man and as one of the people than that he did so in a public character, for, as we have already said, we nowhere read that he was a priest. But there would be no absurdity in saying that he prayed for the prosperity and advancement of Christ's kingdom, for in the Book of Psalms the Spirit prescribes such a blessing of this nature to all the godly. "Blessed is he that cometh in the name of the Lord; we have blessed you in the name of the Lord" (Psalm 118:26).

LO, THIS HAS BEEN SET. This discourse was, no doubt, directly addressed by Simeon to Mary; but it has a general reference to all the godly. The holy Virgin needed this admonition that she might not (as usually happens) be lifted up by afflictive events. But she needed it on another account, that she might not expect Christ to be received by the people with universal applause, but that her mind, on the contrary, might be fortified by unshaken courage against all hostile attacks. It was the design, at the same time, of the Spirit of God to lay down a general instruction for all the godly. When they see the world opposing Christ with wicked obstinacy they must be prepared to meet that opposition, and to contend against it undismayed. The unbelief of the world is—we know it—a great and serious hindrance; but it must be conquered, if we wish to believe in Christ. There never was a state of human society so happily constituted that the greater part followed Christ. Those who will enlist in the cause of Christ must learn this as one of their earliest lessons, and must "put on" this "armor" (Ephesians 6:11), that they may be steadfast in believing on Him.

It was by far the heaviest temptation, that Christ was not acknowledged by his own countrymen and was even ignominiously rejected by that nation which boasted that it was the Church of God, and, particularly, that the priests and scribes, who held in their hands the government of the Church, were His most determined enemies. For who would have thought that he was the King of those who not only rejected him, but treated him with such contempt and outrage?

We see, then, that a good purpose was served by Simeon's prediction, that Christ was "set for the ruin of many in Israel." The meaning is that He was divinely appointed to cast down and destroy many. But it must be observed that the ruin of unbelievers results from their striking against

Him. This is immediately afterward expressed when Simeon says that Christ is "a sign, which is spoken against." Because unbelievers are rebels against Christ, they dash themselves against Him, and hence comes their ruin. This metaphor is taken from a mark shot at by archers, as if Simeon had said, "Hence we perceive the malice of men, and even the depravity of the whole human race, that all, as if they had made a conspiracy, rise in murmurs and rebellion against the Son of God." The world would not display such harmony in opposing the Gospel if there were not a natural enmity between the Son of God and those men. The ambition or fury of the enemies of the Gospel carries them in various directions, faction splits them into various sects, and a wide variety of superstitions distinguishes idolaters from each other. But while they thus differ among themselves, they all agree in this, to oppose the Son of God. It has been justly observed, that the opposition everywhere made to Christ is too plain an evidence of human depravity. That the world should thus rise against its Creator is a monstrous sight. But Scripture predicted that this would happen, and the reason is very apparent: that men who have once been alienated from God by sin, always fly from Him. Instances of this kind, therefore, ought not to take us by surprise; but, on the contrary, our faith, provided with this armor, ought to be prepared to fight with the contradiction of the world.

As God has now gathered an Israel to Himself from the whole world, and there is no longer a distinction between the Jew and the Greek, the same thing must now happen as, we learn, happened before. Isaiah had said of his own age, "The Lord will be for a stone of stumbling, and for a rock of offense, to both the houses of Israel" (Isaiah 8:14). From that time, the Jews rarely ceased to dash themselves against God, but the rudest shock was against Christ. The same madness is now imitated by those who call themselves Christians; and even those who lay haughty claims to the first rank in the Church frequently employ all the power they possess in oppressing Christ. But let us remember, all that they gain is to be at length crushed and "broken in pieces" (Isaiah 8:9).

Under the word "ruin" the Spirit denounces the punishment of un-believers and thus warns us to keep at the greatest possible distance from them, lest, by associating with them, we become involved in the same destruction. And Christ is not the less worthy of esteem because, when he appears, many are ruined: for the "savour" of the Gospel is not less "sweet" and delightful to God (2 Corinthians 2:15,16), though it is destructive to the ungodly world. Does anyone inquire how Christ occasions the "ruin" of unbelievers, who without Him were already lost? The reply is easy. Those who voluntarily deprive themselves of the salvation God has offered to them perish twice. "Ruin" implies the double punishment that awaits all unbelievers, after they have knowingly and willfully opposed the Son of God.

AND FOR THE RESURRECTION. This consolation is presented as a con-trast with the former clause to make it less painful to our feelings, for, if nothing else were added, it would be melancholy to hear that Christ is "a stone of stumbling," which will break and crush, by its hardness, a great part of men. Scripture therefore reminds us of His office, which is entirely different; for the salvation of men, which is founded on it, is secure; as

Isaiah also says, "Sanctify the Lord of hosts himself; and let him be your fear, and let him be your dread; and he shall be for a sanctuary," or fortress of defence (Isaiah 8:13-14). And Peter speaks more clearly: "To whom coming, as unto a living stone, disallowed indeed of men, but chosen of God and precious, ye also, as lively stones, are built up a spiritual house. Wherefore also it is contained in Scripture, Behold, I lay in Zion the head-stone of the corner, elect, precious, and he that believeth in him shall not be confounded. Unto you, therefore, which believe, he is precious: but unto them who are disobedient, the stone which the builders disallowed, the same is made the head of the corner" (1 Peter 2:4-7; Isaiah 28:16).

That we may not be terrified by the designation bestowed on Christ, "a stone of stumbling," let it be instantly recollected, on the other hand, that He is likewise called the "cornerstone," on which rests the salvation of all the godly. Let it be also taken into account that the former is accidental, while the latter is properly and strictly his office. Besides, it deserves our notice that Christ is not only called the support, but the *resurrection* of the godly; for the condition of men is not one in which it is safe for them to remain. They must *rise from death* before they begin to live.

BUT ALSO A SWORD SHALL PIERCE THY OWN SOUL. This warning must have contributed greatly to fortify the mind of the holy Virgin and to prevent her from being overwhelmed with grief, when she came to those distressing struggles she had to undergo. Though her faith was agitated and tormented by various temptations, yet her sorest battle was with the Cross: for Christ might appear to be utterly destroyed. She was not over-whelmed with grief, but it would have required a heart of stone not to be deeply wounded, for the patience of the saints differs widely from stupidity.

THAT THE THOUGHTS OF MANY HEARTS MAY BE REVEALED. There are some who connect this clause with a part of the former verse, that Christ is "set for the ruin and for the resurrection of many in Israel," and who include in a parenthesis what we have just now explained about the sword: but it is better, I think, to refer it to the whole passage. The particle, "that," in this passage does not strictly denote a cause, but merely a consequence. When the light of the Gospel arises and persecutions immediately spring up there is, at the same time, a disclosure of affections of the heart, which had been hitherto concealed. The lurking places of human dissimulation are so deep that they easily remain hidden till Christ comes. But Christ, by his light, discloses every artifice and unmasks hypocrisy; and to him is properly ascribed the office of laying open the secrets of the heart. But when the Cross is added to doctrine, it tries the hearts more to the quick. For those who have embraced Christ by outward profession often shrink from bearing the Cross and, when they see the Church exposed to numer-ous calamities, easily desert their post.

4. Charles Kingsley

AND JESUS INCREASED IN WISDOM, AND IN STATURE, AND IN FAVOUR BOTH WITH GOD AND MAN. I do not pretend to understand these words. I preach on them because the Church has appointed them for this day—

and most fitly. At Christmas we think of our Lord's birth. What can be more reasonable than that we should go on to think of our Lord's boyhood? To think of this aright, even if we do not altogether understand it, ought to help us to understand rightly the incarnation of our Lord Jesus Christ; the right faith about which is, that He was very man, of the substance of His mother. Now, if He were very and real man, He must have been also very and real babe, very and real boy, very and real youth, and then very and real full-grown man. Now, it is not so easy to believe that as it may seem. It is not so easy to believe.

I have heard many preachers preach (without knowing it) what used to be called the Apollinarian Heresy, which held that our Lord had not a real human soul, but only a human body; and that His Godhead served Him instead of a human soul, and a man's reason, man's feelings.

About that the old fathers had great difficulty, before they could make people understand that our Lord had been a real babe. It seemed to people's unclean fancies something shocking that our Lord should have been born, as other children are born. They stumbled at the stumbling block of the manger in Bethlehem, as they did at the stumbling block of the cross on Calvary; and they wanted to make out that our Lord was born into the world in some strange way—I know not how; I do not choose to talk of it here—but they would fancy and invent anything rather than believe that Jesus was really born of the Virgin Mary, made of the substance of His mother. So that it was hundreds of years before the fathers of the Church set people's minds thoroughly at rest about that.

In the same way, though not so much, people found it very hard to believe that our Lord grew up as a real human child. They would not believe that He went down to Nazareth, and was subject to His father and mother. People believe generally now—the Roman Catholics as well as we—that our Lord worked at His father's trade—that He Himself handled the carpenter's tools. We have no certain proof of it; but it is so beautiful a thought, that one hopes it is true. At least our believing it is a sign that we do believe the incarnation of our Lord Jesus Christ more rightly than most people did fifteen hundred years ago. For then, too many of them would have been shocked at the notion.

They stumbled at the carpenter's shop, even as they did at the manger and at the Cross. And they invented false gospels—one of which, especially, had strange and fanciful stories about our Lord's childhood—which tried to make him out. Most of these stories are so childish I do not like to repeat them. One of them may serve as a sample. Our Lord, it says, was playing with other children of His own age, and making little birds out of clay: but those which our Lord made became alive, and moved, and sang like real birds. These were stories put together just to give our Lord some magical power, different from other children, and pretending that He worked signs and wonders—which were just what He refused to work.

But the old fathers rejected these false gospels and their childish tales and commanded Christian men to believe only what the Bible tells us about our Lord's childhood. That is enough for us, and that will help us better than any magical stories and childish fairy tales of man's invention to believe rightly that God was made man, and dwelt among us.

And what does the Bible tell us? Very little indeed. And it tells us very little because we were meant to know very little. Trust your Bibles always, my friends, and be sure, if you were meant to know more, the Bible would tell you more. It tells us that Jesus grew just as a human child grows, in body, soul, and spirit. Then it tells us of one case—only one—in which He seemed to act without His parents' leave. And as the saying is, the exception proves the rule. It is plain that His rule was to obey, except in this case; that He was always subject to His parents, as other children are, except on this one occasion. And even in this case, He went back with them, it is expressly said, and was subject to them. Now, I do not pretend to explain *why* our Lord stayed behind in the Temple. I cannot explain (who can?) the why and wherefore of what I see people do in common daily life. How much less can one explain why our Lord, who was both man and God, did this and that. But one reason, and one that seems to me to be plain, on the very face of St. Luke's words—he stayed behind to learn; to learn all he could from the scribes and Pharisees, the doctors of the law. He told the people after, when grown up, "The scribes and Pharisees sit in Moses' seat. All therefore which they command you, that observe and do." And he was a Jew himself, and came to fulfill all righteousness; and therefore he fulfilled such righteousness as was customary among Jews according to their law and religion.

Therefore I do not like at all a great many of the pictures I see in children's Sunday books, which set the child Jesus in the midst, as on a throne, holding up His hand as if *He* were laying down the law, and the scribes and Pharisees looking angry and confounded. The Bible says not that they heard Him, but that He heard them; that they were astonished at His understanding, not that they were confounded and angry. No, I must believe that even those hard, proud Pharisees looked with wonder and admiration on the glorious Child; that they perhaps felt for the moment that a prophet, another Samuel, had risen up among them. And surely that is much more like the right notion of the child Jesus, full of meekness and humility; of Jesus, who, though "he were a Son, learnt obedience by the things which he suffered"; of Jesus who, while He increased in stature, increased in favor with *man*, as well as with God. And surely no child can increase in favor either with God or man if he sets down his elders, and contradicts and despises the teachers whom God has set over him. No; let us believe that when He said, "Know ye not that I must be about my Father's business?" that a child's way of doing the work of his Father in heaven is to learn all that he can understand from his teachers, spiritual pastors, and masters, whom God the Father has set over him.

Therefore—and do listen to this, children and young people—if you wish really to think what Christ has to do with *you*, you must remember that He was once a real human child—not different outwardly from other children, except in being a perfectly good child, in all things like as you are, but without sin. Then, whatever happens to you, you will have the comfort of feeling—Christ understands this; Christ has been through this.

Child though I am, Christ can be touched with the feeling of my weakness, for He was once a child like me.

And then, if trouble, or sickness, or death come among you—and you all know how sickness and death *have* come among you of late—you may be cheerful and joyful still, if you will only try to be such children as Jesus was. Obey your parents and be subject to them, as He was; try to learn from your teachers, pastors, and masters, as He did; try and pray to increase daily in favor both with God and man, as He did: and then, even if death should come and take you before your time, you need not be afraid, for Jesus Christ is with you.

Your childish faults shall be forgiven you for Jesus' sake; your childish good conduct shall be accepted for Jesus Christ's sake; and if you be trying to be good children, doing your little work well where God has put you, humble, obedient, and teachable, winning love from the people round you, and from God your Father in heaven, then, I say, you need not be afraid of sickness, not even afraid of death, for whenever it takes you, it will find you about your Father's business.

THE SECOND SUNDAY AFTER CHRISTMAS DAY

Text: John 1:14-18

1. John Chrysostom

AND THE WORD WAS MADE FLESH, AND DWELT AMONG US. Having declared that they who received Him were "born of God," and had become "sons of God," he [St. John] adds the cause and reason of this unspeakable honor. It is that "the Word became Flesh," that the Master took on Him the form of a servant. For He became Son of man, who was God's own Son, in order that He might make the sons of men to be children of God. For the high when it associates with the low touches not at all its own honor, while it raises up the other from its excessive lowness; and even thus it was with the Lord. He in nothing diminished His own Nature by this condescension, but raised us, who had always sat in disgrace and darkness, to glory unspeakable. Thus it may be, a king, conversing with interest and kindness with a poor, mean man, does not at all shame himself, yet makes the other observed by all and illustrious. Now if in the case of the adventitious dignity of men, intercourse with the humbler person in nothing injures the more honorable, much less can it do so in the case of that simple and blessed Essence, which has nothing adventitious, or subject to growth or decay, but has all good things immovable, and fixed forever. So that when you hear that "the Word became Flesh" be not disturbed nor cast down. For that Essence did not change to flesh (it is impiety to imagine this), but continuing what it is, It so took upon It the form of a servant.

Wherefore then does he use the expression, "was made"? To stop the mouths of the heretics. For since there are some who say that all the circumstances of the Dispensation were an appearance, a piece of acting, an allegory, at once to remove beforehand their blasphemy he has put "was made," desiring to show thereby not a change of substance (away with the thought), but the assumption of very flesh. For as when Paul says, "Christ hath redeemed us from the curse of the law, being made a curse for us," he does not mean that His essence removing from Its proper glory took upon It the being of an accursed thing (this not even devils could imagine, nor even the very foolish, nor those deprived of their natural understanding, such impiety as well as madness does it contain), as St. Paul does not say this, but that He, taking upon Himself the curse pronounced against us, leaves us no more under the curse; so also here he [St. John] says that He "was made flesh," not by changing His Essence to flesh, but by taking flesh to Himself, His Essence remained untouched.

If they say that being God, He is Omnipotent, so that He could lower Himself to the substance of flesh, we will reply to them that He is Omnipotent as long as He continues to be God. But if He admit of change, change for the worse, how could He be God? For change is far from that simple Nature. Wherefore the Prophet saith, "They all shall wax old as doth a garment, and as a vesture shalt thou roll them up, and they shall be changed; but thou art the same, and thy years shall not fail" (Psalm 102:27 LXX). For that Essence is superior to all change. There is nothing better than He, to which He might advance and reach. Better do I say? No, nor equal to, nor the least approaching Him. It remains, therefore, that if He change, He must admit a change for the worse; and this would not be God. But let the blasphemy return upon the heads of those who utter it. Nay, to show that he uses the expression, "was made," only that you should not suppose a mere appearance, hear from what follows how he clears the argument and overthrows that wicked suggestion. For what does he add? "And dwelt among us." All but saying, "Imagine nothing improper from the word 'was made'; I spoke not of any change of that unchangeable Nature, but of Its dwelling and inhabiting. But that which dwells cannot be the same with that in which it dwells, but different; one thing dwells in a different thing, otherwise it would not be dwelling; for nothing can inhabit itself. I mean, different as to essence; for by an Union and Conjoining God the Word and the Flesh are One, not by any confusion or obliteration of substances, but by a certain union ineffable, and past understanding. Ask not how; for It *was made*, so as He knoweth."

What then was the tabernacle in which He dwelt? Hear the Prophet say, "I will raise up the tabernacle of David that is fallen" (Amos 9:11). It was fallen indeed; our nature had fallen an incurable fall, and needed only that mighty Hand. There was no possibility of raising it again had not He who fashioned it at first stretched forth to it His Hand, and stamped it anew with His Image, by the regeneration of water and the Spirit. And observe, I pray you, the awful and ineffable nature of the mystery. He inhabits this tabernacle forever, for He clothed Himself with our flesh, not as again to leave it, but always to have it with Him. Had not this been the case, He would not have deemed it worthy of the royal throne, nor would He while wearing it have been worshiped by all the host of heaven, angels, archangels, thrones, principalities, dominions, powers. What word, what thought can represent such great honor done to our race, so truly marvelous and awful? What angel, what archangel? Not one in any place, whether in heaven or upon earth. For such are the mighty works of God, so great and marvelous are His benefits, that a right description of them exceeds not only the tongue of men, but even the power of angels.

Wherefore we will for a while close our discourse, and be silent, only delivering to you this charge, that you repay this our so great Benefactor by a return which again shall bring round to us all profit. The return is, that we look with all carefulness to the state of our souls. For this too is the work of His lovingkindness, that He who stands in no need of anything of ours says that He is repaid when we take care of our own souls. It is therefore an act of extremest folly, and one deserving ten thousand chastisements, if we, when such honor has been lavished upon us, will not even contribute what we can, and that too when profit comes round to us again by these means, and ten thousand blessings are laid before us on these conditions. For all these things let us return glory to our merciful God, not by words only, but much more by works, that we may obtain the good things hereafter, which may it be that we all attain to, through the grace and lovingkindness of our Lord Jesus Christ, by whom and with whom, to the Father and the Holy Ghost, be glory forever and ever. Amen.

2. Martin Luther

AND THE WORD BECAME FLESH. The Evangelist states: "The same Word of which I declared that it was in the beginning, through which all things were made, which was the Life and Light of man, became flesh." In Scriptural parlance "flesh" denotes a complete human being, as in John 3:6, where we read: "That which is born of the body is flesh." It goes without saying that of a woman both body and soul are born, not an inanimate mass of flesh, a physical being of flesh and blood, designated by Scripture with that one word "flesh." Similarly, fleshly wisdom, glory, power, and strength are the equivalent of what we in the German tongue call human wisdom, glory, power, and whatever may be great and glorious in the world.

Thus the most precious treasure and the strongest consolation we Christians have is this: that the Word, the true and natural Son of God, became man, with flesh and blood like that of any other human; that He became incarnate for our sakes in order that we might enter into great glory, that our flesh and blood, skin and hair, hands and feet, stomach and back might reside in heaven as God does, and in order that we might boldly defy the devil and whatever else assails us. We are convinced that all our members belong in heaven as heirs of heaven's realm.

We have already heard how Arius, Cerinthus, and other heretics impugned the article concerning the deity of Christ. Heretics also arose to call His humanity into question. They asserted that Christ, the true Son of God, was without a soul, inferring this from the fact that the Evangelist failed to make mention of a soul but merely said: "And the Word became flesh." Thus the Apollinarists alleged that Christ adopted only a human body, but not both body and soul; they declared that His divinity replaced the soul. They were stupid asses. It would be just as logical to say that Christ had no body either; for "flesh" and "body" are not identical. But we cannot be mistaken, because we follow Scripture, which says in the story of the creation of Adam and Eve: "They will become one flesh" (Genesis 2:24). Into our language we translate this: "Adam and Eve will become one body." In Scriptural usage the word "flesh" embraces both body and soul, for without the soul the body is dead.

In spite of the fact that throughout Scripture body and soul, together with all their capacities, are called flesh, those stupid asses take the word to mean the kind of flesh dogs and wolves have. Those people have no understanding of Scripture. The text "the Word became flesh" supports our position. "The Word," that is, the eternal Son of God, "became flesh," that is, became man, born of the Virgin Mary. In the German language the word "body" does not denote a corpse; it denotes a living person in possession of body and soul. Therefore the view referred to is rank heresy and is easily detected. And we should gladly hear sermons on this article of faith, accept it in true faith and with a happy heart, and praise and thank God for inviting us to this blessed proclamation.

It is true, the Evangelist might have said: "The Word became man." However, he adapts himself to Scriptural parlance and says: "He became flesh." He does so to point out its weakness and its mortality. For Christ took on the human nature, which was mortal and subject to the terrible wrath and judgment of God because of the sins of the human race. And this anger was felt by the weak and mortal flesh of Christ.

With that word "flesh" the Evangelist wanted to indicate this inexpressible humiliation. Isaiah says (53:10): "When you make his soul," that is, His life, "an offering for sin, he shall see his seed; he shall prolong his days." And St. Paul writes to the Galatians (3:13): "Christ redeemed us from the curse of the law, having become a curse for us."

But we are not to assume that the Evangelist used the word "flesh" lightly. Human reason cannot comprehend the magnitude of God's anger over sin. Therefore it does not fathom Paul's full meaning when he says that God had made Christ a sin and curse for our sakes (2 Corinthians 5:21; Galatians 3:13). But the dear Lord was fully aware of this; He felt and endured the great and terrible wrath of God so that "his sweat became like great drops of blood" and an angel from heaven appeared to strengthen Him (Luke 22:43-44).

AND DWELT AMONG US. The same Word, which became man, Mary suckled and carried in her arms as any other mother does her child. He came to men, lived and dwelt among them. Thus it was no ghost but a true man, "taking the form of a servant," as St. Paul says (Philippians 2:7), "being born in the likeness of man" with regard to seeing, hearing, speaking, eating, drinking, sleeping, and waking, so that all who saw and heard Him were constrained to confess and say that He was a true and natural man. He did not withdraw from people, retire into some shelter, escape into the desert, where no one could hear, see, or touch Him. But He appeared publicly, preaching and performing miracles, thereby enabling all the people who were about Him, among whom He moved and lived, to hear and touch Him. Thus John says in the beginning of his epistle: "That which was from the beginning, which we have heard, which we have seen with our eyes, which we have looked upon and touched with our hands" (1 John 1:1). And at the same time He was the Word of life and the Creator of all creatures. All this is what the Evangelist wants to convey with the words, "and dwelt among us." He was no ghost; He was a true man. Saint Paul bears this out in Philippians 2:6, where he says: "Though he was in the form of God, he did not think it robbery to be equal with God but took upon himself the form of a servant and was like any other man."

The heretical Manichaeans, knaves that they were, took offense at the assertion that the Son of God had become man. To embellish their error, they feigned great saintliness and profound wisdom, saying that it was an insult to the divine majesty to claim that He had been born from poor and sin-corrupted, impure, and mortal flesh, and from the flesh of a woman at that. They protested that it was impossible that the divine purity, which exceeds the brightness of the sun, should submerge itself into this vile slime. Therefore they averred that Mary was not the true, natural, and physical mother of Christ. They used the analogy of a piece of red glass, which casts a red shadow on the wall, where it can be clearly seen although the wall is, in fact, not red in color; or of a sunbeam, which shines through a piece of blue glass and casts a blue reflection. Thus, they claimed, a shadow or phantom passed through Mary, like a ghost that has no real body or soul. They claimed that Christ had only resembled a man, but, in reality, was no true human. Thus they reduced Him to a ghost; this implies, of course, that the Jews crucified an incorporeal phantom.

In this way they tried to make their heresy palatable. And, in fact, they did succeed in seducing many good people; for this is a glittering and glistening heresy. Saint Augustine lay ensnared in it for nine whole years, and he would have remained there had not the assiduous praying of his mother Monica liberated him. It sounds shocking when these people claim that Christ neither ate nor drank and that the Jews crucified a phantom, not the real Christ. By their denial of Christ's humanity, at which they took offense, they wished to pay homage to God.

But we believe the Scriptures and confess with holy Christendom, which existed at all times and will endure till the end of the world, that this article of our holy Christian creed, together with all others, is firmly and solidly established by the testimony of the holy prophets and apostles, the spokesmen of the Holy Spirit: that Christ, our Lord and God, assumed true human nature, not the nature of an immaterial phantom, and that He became a natural man like any other man of flesh and blood. He did not flutter about like a spirit, but He dwelt among men. He had eyes, ears, mouth, nose, chest, stomach, hands, and feet, just as you and I do. He took the breast. His mother nursed Him as any other child is nursed. He acted as any other human does. He was born as a true man from the Virgin Mary; the one difference, however, was that He was not born in sin as we are, that "he committed no sin, and no guile was found on his lips" (Isaiah 53:9; 1 Peter 2:22).

When the Evangelist declared that Christ dwelt among us, he meant to say: "He did not appear like the angel Gabriel, who came to Mary with God's command and then soon departed from her; for angels do not tarry long in visible form among mankind. Christ, however, remained with us according to His human nature, which was inseparably united with the divine since His incarnation. Into His thirty-fourth year He ate and drank with us; He was angry and sad, He prayed, and He wept. He executed His Father's mission, suffered persecution and death in the end at the hands of His own people. And thus the Jews crucified the true Son of God, the Lord of Glory (1 Corinthians 2:8); and we saw His blood oozing forth and flowing to the ground."

This is the article of faith we Christians believe, which is our greatest consolation, and by means of which we become children of God. We should not engage in lengthy debates about whether the fact that God became man redounds to God's glory or to His disgrace; but we should accept it gladly and with all our hearts as something for our welfare and comfort, and we should thank God for it sincerely.

3. Friedrich Schleiermacher

We assert first then, that it belongs to the deepest foundations of our Christian faith (as this very festival bears witness), that we regard Christ as endowed, from the moment of His appearing in this world, with all that was necessary for Him as the Saviour of the world. We are to believe that already He was in Himself the eternal Word, though as yet silent; the Light sent to shine in the darkness, though as yet concealed; distinguished from all sinners by that saving power that dwelt in Him; and separated from the fellowship of sin. This, I admit, is a hard saying. It is so because of the difficulty we find in doing in connection with spiritual things what we are constantly doing in material and natural things—fully believing in what we cannot clearly imagine and picture to ourselves in all its bearings; and that is what is required of us here. Our own experience contributes to this difficulty. For while there is no question that we know something of an inward union of a divine power with the human soul, because all of us who can glory in belonging to Christ know that in becoming partakers of the Holy Spirit, we become partakers of a divine Being, thus being made one with God. We know also that we could not actually receive this divine gift until full human consciousness had begun in us, and all the mental powers which the Spirit of God should directly and specially control were awakened, so that He could begin this control, and with it His sanctifying work; otherwise than thus we have never become conscious of Him. But in the case of the Saviour, if we are to think of the divine power being in Him while He was still in man's most imperfect state—that of the new-born babe, in whom all the faculties, through which the presence of the higher divine power could be manifested and proved, were still dormant—we must conceive of it as having been present without being in any way brought into exercise; and it is just this that we find it difficult to imagine, and therefore hard to believe.

Hence it comes that there have always been Christians who hold an opinion such as I have referred to—that not only in the years of the Saviour's childhood, but up to the time when His human faculties attained maturity, He was in no way different and bore within Him nothing different from other children; and that not until He was to enter on the great work to which He was appointed did the power of God come upon Him and pervade His whole being. And hence it is also that many Christians, though they do not hold this opinion, yet cannot quite heartily join in the childlike devotion which, going back to the very beginning of Christ's life, with the full reverence that binds the grateful soul to the Saviour, recognizes in the new-born Babe, even in His unconsciousness, the Son of God, in such a sense that He needed to receive nothing new from above, but would become, by the ordinary development of His human soul, the Saviour who, by word and deed, by His life and by His death would both merit and produce that faith which those doubtful Christians themselves cherish; that He was, in short, the Son of the living God, He through whom God would in these last days speak for the last time to men, and after whom we need expect no other. But if these fellow Christians will only look at things clearly, if they are really in earnest in that faith which brings us here together, then must they not grant that it would be at least as hard for us to give up this faith, on which the festival of today is founded, merely because we can no more understand the beginning of the second creation than that of the first or any other beginning? For if in Christ the divine Word did not become flesh so soon as His human eyes opened, what follows? This much is certain, that it is the experience of all without exception that in everyone who has appeared on earth, endowed only as the children of men, sin has sooner or later developed. There will be differences; but these, great as they may seem to us, are really slight when we take into account the differences in mental capacity and strength of will; but that the development of sin should ever be wholly wanting is entirely contradicted by the testimony of our consciousness. And therefore we cannot but believe that so it would have been with the Redeemer Himself if He had been from His birth like other children. Whatever promise the angel had left laid up in the humble soul of Mary, however thoughtfully she might have prepared herself, in childlike and fervent fear of God, to be the mother and nurse of One who was to be called the Son of the Highest, still, if He was only to become this in the future, however faithfully and wisely she might have watched over the tender mind and kept far from Him the widespread poison that, alas, is breathed by every child of man, she would not have been able entirely to guard Him from it; for here we recognize the limit of all, even the most perfect human love and faithfulness and wisdom. And if Christ had been a sinner even in the least degree, could He have been our Saviour? God might have spoken through Him, as through the prophets of the Old Covenant who were, like ourselves, sinful men. But would we call ourselves after the name of a prophet —would we gather together in the name of a prophet, whose work was only a continuation of what had gone before? And indeed, as there can never be *little* sin anywhere, however little it were thought to be in Him, we could never be sure that this continuation of the old way was the last. And though God might speak more fully by Him, and manifest Himself more clearly through His life than ever before, still all this would come only under the head of law. And whether an external law, written on tables of stone or brass, comes directly down from heaven, or is a human law and given through a man, such a law can never redeem the human race. Even when spoken by the holiest lips and written with the finger of God it can only produce a consciousness of sin, from which it provides no deliverance— a consciousness that, the more fully we recognize our sin, constrains us the more to cry, "Who shall deliver me from the body of this death?" Salvation must consist, before everything, just in this, that we are freed from the consciousness of sin. We must have sinlessness clearly set forth to us. And the Redeemer is this living sinlessness. Only as we make this our own by the most intimate friendship and fellowship with Him (as all things are common with friends), only so can we partake of the peace and blessedness which are the fruits of redemption.

Could this sinlessness, then, have been manifested to us in the Saviour and have claimed so entire a self-devotion on our part, if He was only at some future time to be filled, in some mysterious way, with the Holy Spirit and with divine power, even though it should be without measure and quite different from those former prophets? If after this change He was still a man, and the very same man, and had not become a weird, spectral vision whose history would constantly give us a feeling of repulsion, in spite of our reverence for His nature, still the remembrance of His former life and position could not be effaced, even supposing that after this wonderful, sanctifying change, He were incapable of ever again committing sin. And if He retained the memory of His former sinful state—well, let us see, from our own and the most common experience of men, what would follow from that. We feel that it is a sorrowful experience, one which in many respects we would rather leave hidden in silence than communicate, that even the most remote remembrance of former sin which our soul retains never remains there only as a dead letter, a mere piece of knowledge, as of things that exist and go on apart from us. It remains as something alive, and often casts a stain on our holiest thoughts and actions, even on those in the beginnings of which we were most distinctly conscious of the power of the Holy Spirit. It lives in us to teach us that so long as man walks as sinful man on earth, richly as the grace of God may be poured out on him, his soul can never become so perfectly pure a mirror for that grace as it might have been if its depths had never been penetrated by anything of that poison. Then, if the Saviour was like us in having such memories, His after experience must also have been similar to ours. And do we not know that every sin of which even the slightest stirring remains in the soul will inevitably have the effect, in particular instances, which a besetting sin has habitually, of darkening our understanding, blinding our judgment and swaying it to false conclusions, and making dim and impure our view of the divine Will? If, then, the Saviour had retained in His soul the faintest shadow of sin, how could we hope that the words in which He declares to us the will of His and our Father and unfolds our whole relationship to Him were such perfect truth, and rested on so clear and complete an understanding, that men might safely be guided by them forever? How could we suppose that His whole being was in harmony, His human nature being entirely pervaded by and made one with the Spirit, so that He is the model after which all are to form themselves, the guide in whose footsteps all are to walk, without feeling at the same time that we could never exhaust His truth, even by our most earnest appropriation of it; never, even by the truest obedience, quite attain to His likeness? And yet it was just such a Saviour we needed if we were to feel entirely satisfied and have no wish for any other to come after Him.

EPIPHANY

Text: Matthew 2:1-12

1. Leo the Great

WHEN WE WERE YET SINNERS, CHRIST CAME TO SAVE. Although I know, dearly beloved, that you are fully aware of the purpose of today's festival, and that the words of the Gospel have according to use unfolded it to you, yet, that nothing may be omitted on our part, I shall venture to say on the subject what the Lord has put in my mouth; so that in our common joy the devotion of our hearts may be so much the more sincere as the reason of our keeping the feast is better understood. The providential Mercy of God, having determined to succor the perishing world in these latter times, fore-ordained the salvation of all nations in the Person of Christ; in order that, because all nations had long been turned aside from the worship of the true God by wicked error, and even God's peculiar people Israel had well-nigh entirely fallen away from the enactments of the Law, now that all were shut up under sin, He might have mercy upon us all.

For as justice was everywhere failing and the whole world was given over to vanity and wickedness, if the Divine Power had not deferred its judgment the whole of mankind would have received the sentence of damnation. But wrath was changed to forgiveness and, that the greatness of the Grace to be displayed might be the more conspicuous, it pleased God to apply the mystery of remission to the abolishing of men's sins at a time when no one could boast of his own merits.

THE WISE MEN FROM THE EAST ARE TYPICAL FULFILLMENTS OF GOD'S PROMISE TO ABRAHAM. Now the manifestation of this unspeakable Mercy, dearly beloved, came to pass when Herod held the royal power in Judea, where the legitimate succession of kings having failed and the power of the high priests having been overthrown, an alien-born had gained the sovereignty: that the rising of the true King might be attested by the voice of prophecy which had said: "A prince shall not fail from Juda, nor a leader from his loins, until he come for whom it is reserved, and he shall be the expectation of the nations." Concerning which an innumerable succession was once promised to the most blessed patriarch Abraham to be begotten not by fleshly seed but by fertile faith; and therefore it was compared to the stars in multitude that as father of all the nations he might hope not for an earthly but for a heavenly progeny. And therefore, for the creating of the promised posterity, the heirs designated under the figure of the stars are awakened by the rising of a new star, that the ministrations of the heaven might do service in that wherein the witness of the heaven had been adduced. A star more brilliant than the other stars arouses wise men that dwell in the far East, and from the brightness of the wondrous light these men, not unskilled in observing such things, appreciate the importance of the sign. This doubtless was brought about in their hearts by divine Inspiration, in order that the mystery of so great a sight might not be hid from them and what was an unusual appearance to their eyes might not be obscure to their minds. In a word they scrupulously set about their duty and provided themselves with such gifts that in worshiping the One they may at the same time show their belief in His threefold function: with gold they honor the Person of a King, with myrrh that of Man, with incense that of God.

THE CHOSEN RACE IS NO LONGER THE JEWS, BUT BELIEVERS OF EVERY NATION. And so they enter the chief city of the kingdom of Judea, and in the royal city ask that He should be shown them Whom they had learnt was begotten to be King. Herod is perturbed; he fears for his safety, he trembles for his power, he asks of the priests and teachers of the Law what the Scripture has predicted about the birth of Christ, he ascertains what had been prophesied. Truth enlightens the wise men, unbelief binds the experts; carnal Israel understands not what it reads, sees not what it points out, refers to the pages whose utterances it does not believe. Where is thy boasting, Oh Jew? where thy noble birth drawn from the stem of Abraham? is not thy circumcision become uncircumcision? Behold thou, the greater servest the less and, by the reading of that covenant which thou keepest in the letter only, thou becomest the slave of strangers born, who enter into the lot of thy heritage. Let the fullness of the nations enter into the family of the patriarchs, yea let it enter, and let the sons of promise receive in Abraham's seed the blessing to which his sons, according to the flesh, renounce their claim. In the three Magi let all people worship the Author of the universe; and let God be known not in Judea alone, but in all the world, so that everywhere "His name" may be "great in Israel." For while the dignity of the chosen race is proved to be degenerate by unbelief in its descendants, it is made common to all alike by our belief.

THE MASSACRE OF THE INNOCENTS THROUGH THE CONSEQUENT FLIGHT OF CHRIST, BRINGS THE TRUTH INTO EGYPT. Now when the wise men had worshiped the Lord and finished all their devotions, according to the warning of a dream, they returned not by the same route by which they had come. For it behooved them now that they believed in Christ not to walk in the paths of their old line of life, but having entered in a new way to keep away from the errors they had left: and it was also to baffle Herod's design, who, under the cloke of homage, was planning a wicked plot against the infant Jesus. Hence when his crafty hopes were overthrown, the king's wrath rose in a greater fury. Reckoning up the time which the wise men had indicated, he poured out his cruel rage on all the men-children of Bethlehem, and in a general massacre of the whole of that city slew the infants, who thus passed to their eternal glory, thinking that, if every single babe was slain there, Christ too would be slain. But He Who was postponing the shedding of His blood for the world's redemption till another time was carried and brought into Egypt by His parents' aid, and thus sought the ancient cradle of the Hebrew race, and in the power of a greater providence dispensing the princely office of the true Joseph, in that He, the Bread of Life and the Food of Reason that came down from heaven, removed that worse than all famines under which the Egyptians' minds were laboring, the lack of truth, nor without that sojourn would the symbolism of that One Victim have been complete; for there first by the slaying of the lamb was foreshadowed the health-bringing sign of the Cross and the Lord's Passover.

We must keep this festival as thankful sons of light. Taught then, dearly beloved, by these mysteries of divine Grace, let us with reasonable joy celebrate the day of our first fruits and the commencement of the nations' calling, "giving thanks to" the merciful God "who made us worthy," as the Apostle says, "to be partakers of the lot of the saints in light: who delivered us from the power of darkness and translated us into the kingdom of the Son of his love"; since as Isaiah prophesied, "the people of the nations that sat in darkness, have seen a great light, and they that dwelt in the land of the shadow of death, upon them hath the light shined." Of whom he also said to the Lord, "nations which knew not thee, shall call on thee: and peoples which were ignorant of thee, shall run together unto thee." This day "Abraham saw and was glad," when he understood that the sons of his faith would be blessed in his seed that is in Christ, and foresaw that by believing he should be the father of all nations, "giving glory to God and being fully assured that what he had promised, he was able also to perform." This day David sang of in psalms, saying: "All nations that thou hast made shall come and worship before Thee, O Lord: and they shall glorify Thy name"; and again: "The Lord hath made known his salvation: his righteousness hath he openly showed in the sight of the nations." This in good truth we know to have taken place ever since the three wise men aroused in their far-off land were led by a star to recognize and worship the King of heaven and earth (which to those who gaze aright ceases not daily to appear. And if it could make Christ known when concealed in infancy, how much more able was it to reveal Him when reigning in majesty). And surely their worship of Him exhorts us to imitation, that, as far as we can, we should serve our gracious God who invites us all to Christ. For whosoever lives religiously and chastely in the Church and "sets his mind on the things which are above, not on the things that are upon the earth," is in some measure like the heavenly light; and whilst he himself keeps the brightness of a holy life, he points out to many the way to the Lord like a star. In which regard, dearly beloved, ye ought all to help one another in turn, that in the kingdom of God, which is reached by right faith and good works, ye may shine as the sons of light: through our Lord Jesus Christ, Who with God the Father and the Holy Spirit, lives and reigns forever and ever. Amen.

2. Bernard of Clairvaux

The First Manifestation: To the Magi. Today the Magi came from the sun-rising to seek the risen Sun of Righteousness, even the Same of Whom the Scripture says, "Behold the Man Whose name is Dawn."

Today, at a new star's leading, they worshiped Him Whom the Virgin had newly born; they called Him God, not with their lips but by their deeds. Whatever are you doing, you Magi? You worship a baby at the breast, in a poor shed, in common swaddling clothes! Is He then *God*? God is in His holy temple, surely; the Lord's seat is in heaven; yet you are looking for Him in a wretched stable and on His mother's lap! What do you mean by offering Him gold? Is He a king? If so, where is His palace, where His throne, and where the many members of the royal court? Is the stable a palace? Is the manger a throne? Do Joseph and Mary constitute the court? How have wise men become such fools as to adore a child, whose age and whose relations' poverty alike deserve contempt?

They have become fools, that they may be wise. The Spirit has taught them in advance what later the Apostle preached, "Let him who would be wise become as a fool, that so he may be wise. For because through wisdom the world in its wisdom could not have knowledge of God, it pleased God by the foolishness of preaching to save them that believe." Might we not well have been afraid, my brethren, lest seeing such unworthy sights should be a stumbling block to those wise men and make them think that they had been deceived? From the royal city, where they reckoned the king should be sought, they are directed to Bethlehem, an insignificant village; they enter a stable, and find a tiny infant wrapped in swaddling clothes. But the stable does not seem mean to them, they find no cause of stumbling in the swaddling bands, nor does the suckling's speechlessness offend them. They fall on their faces, they revere Him as King, they worship Him as God. Of a truth He, Who led them hither, has instructed them too; He, Who urged them on by means of the star without, has Himself taught them in their inmost heart. Wherefore this manifestation of the Lord has glorified this day, and the sages' faithful act of worship has rendered it a day to be observed with reverence and love.

3. *Martin Luther*

AND THEY HAVING HEARD THE KING, WENT THEIR WAY. It is not said here that the wise men promised the king to return, but that they heard his request to bring him word again. Yet it appears from the warning they received in a dream that, in the simplicity of their hearts, they were willing to return to Herod, not knowing his depravity nor his purpose and thinking him to be an artless honest man. We learn from this that the children of God may be so misled by the pleasing manners and false pretensions of unbelieving saints that they take that to be good which is not. But they do not always remain in deception, for they are directed and delivered, if need be, from heaven. Their hearing of the king, as mentioned by the Evangelist, may also be understood to mean that they listened to the words of the prophet, that in Bethlehem was to be born the new King for whom they inquired and Who was the object of their search.

This is an illustration of how the enemies of Christ may at times be of service and teach others rightly, as Caiaphas teaches (John 11:50), that it was expedient that one man should die for the people, and as Balaam (Numbers 24) utters many beautiful words concerning Christ, although they do it sometimes unintentionally and in ignorance. So Christ instructs the people (Matthew 23:2-3) that they should listen to the scribes and Pharisees and follow them when they sit in Moses' seat, but forbids them to do after their works. These wise men were right, therefore, and give us a good example by listening to Herod, not for Herod's sake, neither as said by him, but for the sake of the Scriptures, which he taught them; and they followed this and not Herod's works. From this is derived the good rule that we should hear the evil bishops and priests, as well as the good ones, and should follow, not their lives, but their teachings, provided their teaching is Scripture and not idle talk. For, as we are to listen to the teachings of Holy Writ, even when spoken by Herod, though he also committed murder, so we are not to listen to human doctrine, even if spoken by St. Peter, Paul, or an angel, and accompanied by many wondrous signs.

God uses Herod when he may be used to advantage as God's creature, and offers him to the wise men for their service. Hence they did not look upon or listen to Herod but to the king. It did not concern them that he was wicked within himself—they took hold of what was good in him, as the bee sucks the honey from the flower and leaves the poison to the spider. They listened to him when he told them to go to Bethlehem and search diligently for the child, as the prophet had foretold (which intelligence he had not from himself but from the priests). They could not, however, know his wicked counsel and purpose, nor his evil life. Thus we are to learn to hate the vices of men, but love the men; we are to distinguish the honey from the poison.

AND THEY CAME INTO THE HOUSE AND SAW THE YOUNG CHILD WITH MARY HIS MOTHER. It was diligently prevented that the wise men should find Christ through themselves, or men. On the contrary, they found him alone through the Scriptures of the prophet and by the aid of the stars of heaven that there might be put to naught all natural ability, all human reason, all light outside of the spirit and of grace, which now boasts and pretends to teach the truth and lead people aright, as was said above is done in the universities. Here it is concluded that Christ, the Knowledge of salvation, is not taught or acquired by human teaching or assistance, but the Scriptures and divine light must reveal Him, as He says (Matthew 16:17), "Blessed art thou, Simon Bar-Jonah: for flesh and blood hath not revealed it unto thee, but my Father who is in heaven." With this Christ distinctly casts aside flesh and blood with its revelation, that is, man and all human wisdom, which, being nothing but darkness, cannot reveal Christ.

Christ says (John 6:44): "No man can come to me, except the Father that hath sent me draw him." By this all boasting of human reason is condemned, since it cannot guide aright and all who follow it must go astray. So strongly does God everywhere resist our natural haughtiness and will that we may know we are blind, despair of our own light, put ourselves into His hands, and be led by Him into the ways which reason cannot know or follow.

OF THE FAITH OF THE WISE MEN. The wise men here teach us the true faith. After they heard the sermon and the word of the prophet they were not slow to believe, in spite of obstacles and difficulties. First they came to Jerusalem, the capital, and did not find Him, the star also disappearing. Do you not think they would have said within themselves, if they had followed human reason alone: "Alas, we have traveled so far in vain, the star has misled us, it was a phantom. If a King were born He should of course be found in the capital and lie in the royal chamber. But when we arrived the star disappeared and no one knew anything about Him. We strangers are the first to speak of Him in His own country and royal city! Indeed, it must be all false!"

Besides, His own people are troubled and do not care to hear of Him, and direct us from the royal city to a little village. Who knows what we shall find? The people act so coldly and strangely, no one accompanies us to show us the Child; they themselves do not believe that a King is born to them, and we come from afar and expect to find Him. Oh how odd and unusual everything appears at the birth of a king! If a young pup were born, there would be a little noise. A King is born here, and there is no stir. Should not they sing and dance, light candles and torches, and pave the streets with branches and roses? Oh the poor King whom we seek! Fools we are to permit ourselves to be deceived so shamefully.

Having been flesh and blood, doubtless they were not free from such thoughts and views, and they had to battle for their faith. Natural reason could here not have held its own; if they had not found the King as they had expected, they would have murmured and complained and said: "The devil must have led us here. A king cannot have been born since everything is so quiet and nothing is going on. There is more noise when a child is born to our shepherd, and a calving cow is more talked about than this King."

Reason and nature never proceed any further than they can see and feel. When they cease to feel, they at once deny God's existence and say as Psalm 14:1 says, "There is no God," therefore the devil must be here. This is the light of the universities which is to lead men to God, but rather leads to the abyss of hell. The light of nature and the light of grace cannot be friends. Nature wants to feel and be certain before she believes, grace believes before she perceives. For this reason, nature does not go further than her own light. Grace joyfully steps out into the darkness, follows the mere word of Scripture, no matter how it appears. Whether nature holds it true or false, she clings to the Word.

For the sake of this very strife and struggle, by which the wise men accepted the word of the prophet and followed it into such wild, unnatural appearance of a royal birth, God comforted and strengthened them by this star which went before them more friendly than before. Now they see it near, it is their guide, and they have an assurance that needs no further question. Before, it was far from them, and they were not certain where they would find the King.

So it is always with the Christian; after affliction has been endured God becomes more dear to him and is so near and so distinctly seen that man not only forgets anxiety and affliction, but has a desire for greater affliction. He gradually becomes so strong that he does not take offense at the insignificant, unattractive life of Christ. For now he experiences and realizes that to find Christ it must appear as though he found nothing but disgrace.

4. *John Keble*

WE HAVE SEEN HIS STAR IN THE EAST, AND ARE COME TO WORSHIP HIM. In all the history of our Lord's manifestation on earth, and especially in the account of His childhood, there is a wonderful mixture of openness and reserve. There is a veil over the brightness of His Presence, through which He allows Himself to be seen only occasionally, and not by all sorts of persons, but by a few only of a particular class and character.

Thus, in His birth, how was the unspeakable dignity of the Son of God hidden and clouded over! His mother, the wife of a poor carpenter of Nazareth; the chamber, a stable; the cradle, a manger: yet how wonderful the manifestation of His glory! Angels coming in brightness from the heavens to announce Him—a thing that had never been known or thought of before, since, on the birthday of the world itself, "the morning stars sang together, and all the sons of God shouted for joy."

Again, when He was circumcised, He seemed like one among many sinners, having need to be admitted into the Lord's earthly family; but great indeed was the token of His majesty, in having His name twice brought by an angel from heaven; and that, the name JESUS, which declared Him the Saviour of the world. Then He was brought to the Temple, in the usual way, with simple offerings, as any poor man's child might be; but He was received with an outpouring of the Holy Spirit of prophecy, so many hundred years silent in that place. Still, however, the Spirit was vouchsafed only to quiet and meek persons, and His message spoken of only to those who looked for redemption; even as before, His birth was made known only to the shepherds, watchfully doing their duty; and the secret of the name JESUS, brought from heaven, was known, as far as we can tell, only to St. Joseph and the blessed Virgin.

The next event in our Lord's childhood is the Epiphany, or visit of the wise men, which we commemorate this day. And here, surely, we may plainly perceive the same rule or law to have been kept. On the one hand, how clear and glorious the token from heaven! A new and wonderful star, appearing so far away, and inviting even Gentiles to so great a distance, not merely to see, but even to worship Him. On the other hand, when He is found, He is a meek and lowly Babe, resting on His mother's knees, as any other child might do, in a poor cottage of a humble village. And the immediate consequence of their visit is that He is forced to fly for His life; or rather His mother and Joseph are forced to remove Him by night, as if He were helpless, like all infants, and could do nothing for Himself. They worship Him, owning His Godhead: He flies, confessing Himself a true child of man, as we are.

Thus the Epiphany, like the other manifestations of our Lord, partly veils and partly discloses His glory.

As in those other instances also, the disclosure is made to persons of a certain character, and to those only. It is not hard to see what sort of mind these wise men were in, how earnest, not only in obtaining what heavenly knowledge they could, but also in obeying what they knew. They lived in a country, and most likely belonged to a profession, in which the observation of the stars was a great part of their daily business. And as the shepherds, when the angel was sent to them, were watching over their flocks by night, that is, in the honest exercise of their daily calling, so this star was ordered to meet the eyes of these men, so learned in the signs of the heavens. It seems in both cases to signify that God loves to visit, with His heavenly and spiritual blessings, those whom He sees diligent and conscientious in their daily duty.

Such were the persons who were honored by our Lord to be the second set of chosen witnesses, invited by miraculous guidance to see Him in His childhood. Are we not, so far, all of us like them in that, when children, we too have a sort of Star in the East, to guide us toward the cradle of our Lord? We are carried to Church, we are taught to pray, we learn more or less of Scripture words and histories; God gives us notice, in various ways, of that wonderful Child, Who was born at Bethlehem to be King of the Jews. Various things happen, from time to time, that give us a sort of blind indistinct feeling, that there is within our reach, we know not how near us, a great and heavenly Being, could we but feel after Him and find Him.

Now these notices and feelings, if they are indeed sent by the Most High, as the star was sent to the wise men, will guide us, more or less directly, to Jerusalem, that is, to the Holy Church of God, the city set on a hill which cannot be hid. We indeed are in that Church already, by the Almighty's especial favor, ever since the moment of our Baptism. And still as we search after the truth our thoughts are brought back to the same Church; and Providence teaches us, as the star guided the wise men, to go to Jerusalem, the Church and city of God, and ask where the Truth, that is, Christ, is to be found.

And the Church, like a gracious mother, will be ready at our need. She will guide us, as herself is guided, by Holy Scripture. She will send us to Bethlehem, because it is so written in the Prophets: Bethlehem, which is, being interpreted, the House of Bread, and which therefore is an apt figure of the place where He gives Himself to us, Who is "the true bread which cometh down from heaven, the bread of God which giveth life unto the world." The Church, in short, being guided by the Scriptures, will send us to the Holy Communion, there to worship and receive Jesus Christ. What have we to do in this world but to prepare ourselves, and follow that heavenly guidance? And we are so far rightly preparing ourselves as we really from our heart are endeavoring to copy the wise men in their search for the new-born Saviour.

The wise men were ready to follow wherever God's providence might lead them, however slight and even doubtful the notices of His will might be. They follow the star, not knowing whither it would take them, much as Abraham had done, from nearly the same country, two thousand years before. So ought it to be enough for us to know the next step in our journey, the next thing God would have us do, with something like tolerable certainty. One step before them is as much as sinners in a troublous world should expect to see.

The wise men did not mind the trouble of their journey to find our Lord. Day after day they went on, and still the star, as it may appear, or at least some providential sign, showed them they had still further to go; and they did not grow weary, nor turn back, nor say, "Why could not we as well have honored the young Child at a distance, in the sight of God Who knows our hearts?"

This surely may reprove our indolence and want of faith; we, who are so seldom willing to leave our homes, and go ever so little way, there, where we are sure the young Child is to be found, but rather put up with idle excuses, the more profane because they make a show of respect, of God being in one place as much as in another, and of our being able to serve Him at home as acceptably as in Church.

Neither, again, did those wise men shrink from their long journey, nor fear to ask about our Lord, nor to go where they heard He was, nor to worship when they had found Him, lest they should be wondered at, and thought strange, and pointed to, as willfully and fancifully making themselves unlike other people. No such thought, it would appear, came at all into their minds: they just followed the star and the Prophet, whether those who looked on derided them or no. Will it not be a good token of our faith, when we too make up our minds to obey the Church and serve God as we best may, not regarding what kind of talk people may at first make about it?

I say, "at first," because in no long time, if we let them alone, they will let us alone. It is but exercising a little courage and perseverance at first, and taking care not to disgrace our profession by willful sin; and we shall quickly find leave from the world to serve God regularly in spite of her scorn.

Further, the wise men were not ashamed to acknowledge and honor Christ as especially present in a poor cottage, and as a young Child: neither let us doubt, but take Him at His word when He says, "Inasmuch as ye have done it unto one of the least of these, ye have done it unto me"; and again, "Whosoever shall receive one such little child in my name, receiveth me." As ever we desire to find Christ truly in His Sacraments and His Scriptures, be it our care never to forget Him in His poor, if we can relieve them, or in His little ones, if we can help them to continue His way, at least by not doing anything to corrupt them in the way of bad example.

The wise men, being bidden by an angel not to return to Herod, obeyed and went back as they might, some other way. They did not stumble at the command, though it might seem strange to find so sacred a Person in danger and His life made to depend on anything they could do. They did not say, "How is this, that He should be the Son of God, and yet we must go out of our way to save His life from the tyrant?" But being bidden, at once, without objection, they obey the bidding. It will be a good sign when Christian persons, having found truth, show themselves worthy of it by the like obedience to plain commands, without asking questions.

Lastly, the wise men grudged not the Holy Child the best and most expensive gifts they could offer, though it were hard to see how some of them, at least, could be of any use to Him. But they were full of adoring love, and a heart where love dwells cannot stop to consider the use of things. Does not this tell us something about our way of serving and honoring Christ in His Churches, and in all that appertains to them, especially in whatever belongs to the services of the Holy Communion? Ought it not to be all as handsome as we can make it? Ought we nicely to count the cost, or measure the good done, when we are bringing our offerings for such purposes? Are we used to do so, when we are bringing tokens of affection to those whom we most love and honor on earth? Did David so behave? or Mary Magdalene? or these wise men? or any of those whom the Bible mentions as honoring God and being honored by Him?

For indeed these wise men were greatly honored by Him, especially if, as was of old believed, they became afterward disciples of His Apostle, ministers and stewards of His mysteries. Think what a glorious ending, from a beginning in appearance so slight and seemingly accidental, as their observing a particular star, religiously taking it to be from God, and with all perseverance inquiring its import and following after its course.

Let any Christian child, or poor person as ignorant as a child, only go on doing his best in silence, and God for His part will most surely keep and perform His part of the promise. Let the star, the lesser light you have, guide you to Christ here, that you may after this life have the fruition of His glorious Godhead.

THE FIRST SUNDAY AFTER THE EPIPHANY

Text: Luke 2:41-52

1. St. Augustine

When the Lord Jesus, as to His human nature, was twelve years old (for as to His divine nature He is before all times, and without time), He tarried behind in the Temple and disputed with the elders, and they wondered at His doctrine. And His parents who were returning from Jerusalem sought Him among their company, among those, that is, who were journeying with them, and when they found Him not, they returned in trouble to Jerusalem and found Him disputing in the Temple with the elders—when He was, as I said, twelve years old. But what wonder? The Word of God is never silent, though it is not always heard. He is found then in the Temple, and His mother saith to Him, "Why hast thou thus dealt with us? Thy father and I have sought thee sorrowing"; and He said, "Wist ye not that I must be about my Father's service?" This He said for that the Son of God was in the Temple of God, for that Temple was not Joseph's, but God's. See, says someone, "He did not allow that He was the Son of Joseph." Wait, brethren, with a little patience, because of the press of time, that it may be long enough for what I have to say. When Mary had said, "Thy father and I have sought thee sorrowing," He answered, "Wist ye not that I must be about my Father's service?" for He would not be their Son in such a sense, as not to be understood to be also the Son of God. For the Son of God He was—ever the Son of God—Creator even of themselves who spake to Him; but the Son of Man in time; born of a Virgin without the operation of her husband, yet the Son of both parents. Whence prove we this? Already have we proved it by the words of Mary, "Thy father and I have sought thee sorrowing."

Now in the first place for the instruction of the women, our sisters, such saintly modesty of the Virgin Mary must not be passed over, brethren. She had given birth to Christ—the angel had come to her and said, "Behold, thou shalt conceive in thy womb, and bring forth a Son, and shalt call his name Jesus. He shall be great and shall be called the Son of the Highest." Yet was she most humble; nor did she put herself before her husband, even in the order of naming him, so as to say, "I and thy father," but she saith, "Thy father and I." She regarded not the high honor of her womb, but the order of wedlock did she regard, for Christ the humble would not have taught His mother to be proud. "Thy father and I have sought thee sorrowing." Thy father and I, she saith, "for the husband is the head of the woman." How much less then ought other women to be proud! For Mary herself also is called a woman, not from the loss of virginity, but by a form

105

of expression peculiar to her country; for of the Lord Jesus the Apostle also said, "made of a woman," yet there is no interruption hence to the order and connection of our Creed wherein we confess "that He was born of the Holy Ghost and the Virgin Mary." For as a virgin she conceived Him, as a virgin brought Him forth, and a virgin she continued; but all females they called "women" by a peculiarity of the Hebrew tongue. Hear a most plain example of this. The first woman whom God made, having taken her out of the side of a man, was called a woman before she "knew her husband," which we are told was not till after they went out of Paradise, for the Scripture saith, "He made her a woman."

The answer then of the Lord Jesus Christ, "I must be about my Father's service," does not in such sense declare God to be His Father, as to deny that Joseph was His father also. And whence prove we this? By the Scripture, which saith on this wise, "And he said unto them, Wist ye not that I must be about my Father's service; but they understood not what he spake to them: and when He went down with them, he came to Nazareth, and was subject to them." It did not say, "He was subject to His mother," or was "subject to her," but "He was subject to them." To whom was He subject? Was it not to His parents? It was to both His parents that He was subject, by the same condescension by which He was the Son of Man. A little way back women received their precepts. Now let children receive theirs—to obey their parents and to be subject to them. The world was subject unto Christ, and Christ was subject to His parents.

You see then, brethren, that He did not say, "I must needs be about My Father's service," in any such sense as that we should understand Him thereby to have said, "You are not My parents." They were His parents in time, God was His Father eternally. They were the parents of the Son of Man—"He," the Father of His Word, and Wisdom, and Power, by whom He made all things. But if all things were made by that Wisdom "which reacheth from one end to another mightily, and sweetly ordereth all things," then were they also made by the Son of God to whom He Himself as Son of Man was afterward to be subject; and the Apostle says that He is the Son of David, "who was made of the seed of David according to the flesh." But yet the Lord Himself proposes a question to the Jews, which the Apostle solves in these very words; for when he said, "who was made of the seed of David," he added, "according to the flesh," that it might be understood that He is not the Son of David according to His Divinity, but that the Son of God is David's Lord. For thus in another place, when He is setting forth the privileges of the Jewish people, the Apostle saith, "Whose are the fathers, of whom as concerning the flesh Christ came, who is over all, God blessed for ever." As "according to the flesh" He is David's son; but as being "God over all, blessed for ever," He is David's Lord. The Lord then saith to the Jews, "Whose son say ye that Christ is?" They answered, "The son of David." For this they knew, as they had learnt it easily from the preaching of the Prophets; and, in truth, He was of the seed of David, "but according to the flesh," by the Virgin Mary, who was espoused to Joseph. When they answered then that Christ was David's son, Jesus said to them, "How then doth David in spirit call Him Lord, saying, The Lord said unto my Lord, Sit thou on my right hand, till I put thine enemies under thy feet. If David then in spirit call Him Lord, how is he his son?" And the Jews could not answer Him. So we have it in the Gospel. He did not deny that He was David's son, so that they could not understand that He was also David's Lord. For they acknowledged in Christ that which He became in time, but they did not understand in Him what He was in all eternity. Wherefore wishing to teach them His divinity, He proposed a question touching His humanity; as though He would say, "You know that Christ is David's son, answer me, how is he also David's Lord?" And that they might not say, "He is *not* David's Lord," He introduced the testimony of David himself. And what doth he say? He saith indeed the truth. For you find God in the Psalms saying to David, "Of the fruit of thy body will I set upon thy seat." Here then He is the son of David. But how is He the Lord of David, who is David's son? "The Lord said unto my Lord, Sit thou on my right hand." Can you wonder that David's son is his Lord, when you see that Mary was the mother of her Lord? He is David's Lord then as being God. David's Lord, as being Lord of all; and David's son, as being the Son of Man. At once Lord and son. David's Lord, "who, being in the form of God, thought it not robbery to be equal with God"; and David's son in that "he emptied himself, taking the form of a servant."

Joseph then was not the less His father because he knew not the mother of our Lord, as though concupiscence and not conjugal affection constituted the marriage bond. Attend, holy brethren: Christ's Apostle was some time after this to say in the Church, "It remaineth that they that have wives be as though they had none." And we know many of our brethren bringing forth fruit through grace who, for the Name of Christ, practice an entire restraint by mutual consent, yet who suffer no restraint of true conjugal affection. Yea, the more the former is repressed, the more is the other strengthened and confirmed. Are they then not married people who thus live, not requiring from each other any carnal gratification or exacting the satisfaction of any bodily desire? And yet the wife is subject to the husband because it is fitting that she should be, and so much the more in subjection is she in proportion to her greater chastity; and the husband for his part loveth his wife truly, as it is written, "In honor and sanctification," as a co-heir of grace: as "Christ," saith the Apostle, "loveth the Church." If then this be a union, and a marriage, if it be not the less a marriage because nothing of that kind passes between them which even with unmarried persons may take place, but then unlawfully (Oh that all could live so, but many have not the power!), let them at least not separate those who have the power and deny that the man is a husband or the woman a wife because there is no fleshly intercourse, but only the union of hearts between them.

2. *Martin Luther*

Behold, here is the precious doctrine of this Gospel, namely, how rightly to seek Christ and how He may be found; and it points out the real comfort that can satisfy troubled consciences, take away all terror and anxiety and again rejoice the heart and at the same time give it a new life. But the heart must become heavy before it can attain and lay hold of this truth; it must first run and experience that everything else is lost and useless in the search for Christ, and finally no counsel is to be had unless you give yourself, without your own and all human comfort, to the Word alone. In bodily mishaps and straits you may seek comfort in gold, possessions, friends, and acquaintances; but in these matters you must have something that is not human but divine, namely, the Word, through which alone Christ deals with us and we can deal with Him.

THEY UNDERSTOOD NOT THE SAYING, WHICH HE SPAKE UNTO THEM. This should shut the mouths of vain babblers who exalt the holy Virgin Mary and other saints as if they knew everything and could not err; for you can see here how they err and falter, not only in that they seek Christ and know not where to find Him until they accidentally come to the Temple, but also that they could not understand these words with which He censured their ignorance and is compelled to say to them: "Knew ye not, that I must be in the things of my Father?" The Evangelist has pointed this out with great diligence in order that men should not give credence to such falsehoods as ignorant, inexperienced, and conceited teachers of work-righteousness present in exalting the saints, even setting them up as idols.

The holy Virgin is not in need of such falsely invented praise. God led her in such a way that He concealed much from her and daily permitted many things to happen which she had not known beforehand, in order that He might keep her humble, so that she should not regard herself better than others. And this is praise and honor enough for her, that He guided and sustained her by His grace, although He had endowed her with many far greater gifts than others; yet so that she, like others, was compelled, through manifold temptations and sorrows, to learn daily and grow in grace.

Examples like this are useful and necessary to show us that even the saints, who are the children of God and highly favored above others, still have weaknesses so that they frequently err and blunder, yea, retain many faults, at times even commit great sins; yet not intentionally and willfully, but from weakness and ignorance, as we see again and again in the lives of the Apostles. This happens in order that we may learn neither to build nor depend on any man, but, as this Gospel teaches, to cling to the Word of God only; and in order that we may find comfort in such examples and be not led to despair, although we may be weak and ignorant; and yet that we should not become bold and carnally secure on account of such grace as the haughty and pretended saints are wont to do.

In a word, you have in this Gospel a strong example with which to overthrow the common cry both of the false saints and the great critics, which they still keep up, in order that contrary to the Word of God they may continue in their trifling; to wit, that they may reproach us with the writings and teachings of the fathers and the decrees of the Church and councils; for, they say, these had the Holy Spirit, therefore they could not err, and so on. In this way they desire to mislead us concerning the Scriptures and the true place to which Christ Himself points and where He can surely be found; in order that what happened to Mary the Mother and to Joseph may happen also to us, namely, that we seek Christ everywhere and yet find him nowhere except at the place where He is to be found. The same thing has been carried on with great power in Christendom through the cursed government of the pope, who has striven both by his teachings and actions, threats and punishments, to cause men to fail in seeking or finding Christ in the Scriptures.

3. John Calvin

AND HIS PARENTS WENT EVERY YEAR TO JERUSALEM. It is mentioned in commendation of the piety of Mary and Joseph that they gave diligent attendance to the outward worship of God. It was not of their own accord, but by a divine command, that they undertook this annual journey. The law enjoins the "males" only to "appear before the Lord" (Exodus 23:17). This arrangement does not entirely exclude females, but spares them by an exercise of kindness. This mark distinguishes the true religion from vain and wicked superstitions. The former confines itself within the limits of obedience to God, and of compliance with the enactments of His law. The latter wander, at their own pleasure, beyond the limits of God's word, without any fixed rule. The worship of the Temple was, no doubt, infected with many corruptions, the priesthood was sold for money, and doctrine was involved in many errors. Yet, as legal ceremonies were still in force, and the outward rite of sacrifice was observed as it is laid down in the Law, believers were bound to perform such exercises in testimony of their faith. The name "father" is here given to Joseph, not with strict accuracy, but according to the opinion generally entertained respecting him.

AND THINKING THAT HE WAS IN THE COMPANY. Many passages of Scripture show plainly that those who came from a distance, at the festivals and to worship in the Temple, were accustomed to travel in companies. There is no reason, therefore, to wonder that, on the first day, Joseph and Mary were less anxious about the Child; and their subsequent conduct shows that this was not owing to indolence or carelessness.

SITTING IN THE MIDST OF THE DOCTORS. Rays of divine brightness must have evidently shone in this Child; otherwise those haughty men would not have permitted Him to sit along with them. Though it is probable that He occupied a lower seat and not the rank of the doctors, yet such disdainful men would not have condescended to give Him an audience in a public assembly if some divine power had not constrained them. This was a sort of prelude to His public calling, the full time of which had not yet arrived. In this way, however, He intended to give nothing more than a taste, which would immediately have faded from the recollection of men, had not Mary "kept" it for us "laid up in her heart" (Luke 2:19,51), to bring it out afterward, along with other treasures, for the use of all the godly.

AND ALL WHO HEARD HIM. Two things here claim our attention. "All who heard him were astonished" for they reckoned it a miracle that a child should frame his questions with such correctness and propriety. Again, they "heard" Christ, and thus acted the part rather of scholars than of teachers. He had not yet been called by the Father, to avow Himself a public teacher of the Church, and therefore satisfied Himself with putting modest questions to the doctors. Yet there is no room to doubt that, in this first attempt, He already began to tax their perverse way of teaching: for what Luke afterward says about "answers," I consider as denoting, agreeably to the Hebrew idiom, any kind of discourse.

AND HIS MOTHER SAID TO HIM. Those who think that the holy Virgin spake in this manner for the purpose of showing her authority are, in my opinion, mistaken. It is even possible that it was not till they were apart, and the witnesses had withdrawn, that she began to expostulate with her son, after they had left the assembly. However that may be, this complaint was not the result of ambition, but was the expression of grief, which had lasted three days. Yet the manner of her complaint, as if she had received an injury, shows how ready we are by nature to defend our own rights, even without paying regard to God. The holy Virgin would a thousand times rather have died than deliberately preferred herself to God: but, in the indulgence of a mother's grief, she falls into it through inadvertency. And undoubtedly this example warns us how jealous we ought to be of all the affections of the flesh, and what care we ought to exercise, lest, by being too tenacious of our rights and following our own desires, we defraud God of his honor.

DID YE NOT KNOW? Our Lord justly blames His mother, though He does it in a gentle and indirect manner. The amount of what He says is that the duty which He owes to God His Father ought to be immeasurably preferred to all human duties; and that, consequently, earthly parents do wrong in taking it amiss that they have been neglected in comparison of God. And hence we may infer the general doctrine that whatever we owe to men must yield to the first table of the Law, that God's authority over us may remain untouched. Thus we ought to obey kings, and parents, and masters, but only in subjection to God: that is, we must not, for the sake of men, lessen or take away anything from God. And, indeed, a regard to the superior claims of God does not imply a violation of the duties that we owe to men.

IN THOSE THINGS WHICH BELONG TO MY FATHER. This expression intimates that there is something about Him greater than man. It points out also the chief design of His being sent into the world, which was that he might discharge the office enjoined upon Him by His heavenly Father. But is it not astonishing that Joseph and Mary, "did not understand" this answer, for they had been instructed by many proofs that Jesus is the Son of God? I reply: Though they were not wholly unacquainted with Christ's heavenly origin, yet they did not comprehend, in every respect, how He was intent on executing His heavenly Father's commands: for His calling had not yet been expressly revealed to them. Mary "kept in her heart" those things she did not fully understand. Let us learn from this to receive with reverence, and "to lay up" in our minds (like the seed, which is allowed to remain for some time under ground), those mysteries of God that exceed our capacity.

AND HE WAS SUBJECT TO THEM. It was for our salvation that Christ took upon Him this low estate—that the Lord and head of angels voluntarily became "subject to" mortal creatures. Such was the purpose of God, that Christ should remain for some time under a shadow, bearing the name of Joseph. Though this subjection, on the part of Christ, arose from no necessity which He could not have avoided, yet, as He had taken upon Him human nature on the condition of being subject to parents and had assumed the character both of a man and of a servant, with respect to the office of Redeemer this was His lawful condition. The more cheerfully, on this account, ought every one to bear the yoke which the Lord has been pleased to lay upon him.

4. Phillips Brooks

The mother of Jesus is the speaker, and it is of Jesus that she asks her question. On the way home from the Temple at Jerusalem where they had gone to worship, you remember, they missed the child Jesus from their company. On going back they found Him in the Temple, "sitting in the midst of the doctors, both hearing them and asking them questions." Then it was that His mother said unto him, "Son, why hast thou thus dealt with us? Behold, thy father and I have sought thee sorrowing. And he said unto them, How is it that ye sought me? wist ye not that I must be about my Father's business?"

WHY HAST THOU DEALT THUS WITH US? It is a puzzled question. The Boy, Who had been an obedient Child in her household, whom she had cared for in her own way and found always docile to her guidance, had suddenly passed beyond her and done a thing which she could not understand. It seemed as if she had lost Him. Her tone is full of love, but there is something almost like jealousy about it. He has taken Himself into His own keeping, and this one act seems to foretell the time when He will take His whole life into His own hands and leave her outside altogether. The time is past when she could hold Him as a babe upon her bosom as she carried Him down into Egypt. The time is prophesied already when He should go in His solitude up to the Cross and only leave His mother weeping at the foot. She is bidden to stand by and see her Son do His work and live His life, which thus far has been all of her shaping, in ways she cannot understand. No wonder that it is a clear, critical moment in her life. No wonder that her question still rings with the pain that she put into it. No wonder that when she went home, although He was still "subject unto her," her life with her Son was all changed, and she "kept all these sayings in her heart."

I think that this question of the mother of Jesus reveals an experience of the human heart that is very common, that is most common in the best hearts and in those who feel their responsibility the most. It is an experience that well deserves our study, and I ask you this morning to think about it with me in some of its examples. The Virgin Mary is the perpetual type of people who, intrusted with any great and sacred interest, identify their own lives with that interest and care for it conscientiously, but who, by-and-by, when the interest begins to manifest its own vitality and shape its own methods, are filled with perplexity. They cannot keep the causes for which they labor under their own care. As His mother asked of Jesus, so are they always asking of the objects for which they live, "Why hast thou thus dealt with us?" Such people are people who have realized responsibility more than they have realized God. Just as Mary felt, at the moment when she asked this question, that Jesus was her son more than that He was God's Son, so there is a constant tendency among the most earnest and conscientious people to feel that the causes for which they live and work are their causes more than they are God's causes, and so to experience something which is almost like jealousy when they see those causes pass beyond their power and fulfill themselves in larger ways than theirs. For such people, often the most devoted and faithful souls among us, it seems to me that there must be some help and light in this story of Jesus and His mother.

The first and simplest case of the experience that I want to speak of is that which comes nearest to the circumstances of our story. It comes in every childhood. It comes whenever a boy grows up to the time at which he passes beyond the merely parental government of his earliest years. It comes with all assertion of individual character and purpose in a boy's life. A boy has had his career all identified with his home where he was cradled. What he was and did, he was and did as a member of that household. But by-and-by there comes some sudden outbreak of a personal energy. He shows some disposition and attempts some task distinctively his own. It is a puzzling moment alike for the child and for the father. The child is perplexed with pleasure which is almost pain to find himself for the first time doing an act that is genuinely his own. The father is filled with a pain which yet has pride and pleasure in it to see his boy doing something original, something that he never bade him do, something that perhaps he could not do himself. The real understanding of that moment, both to child and father, depends upon one thing—upon whether they can see in it the larger truth that this child is not merely the son of his father, but also is the son of God. If they both understand that, then the child, as he undertakes his personal life, passes not into a looser, but into a stronger, responsibility. And the father is satisfied to see his first authority over his son grow less because he cannot be jealous of God. It is a noble progress and expansion of life when the first independent venture of a young man on a career of his own is not the willful claim of the prodigal: "Give me the portion of goods that falleth to me," but the reverent appeal of Jesus: "Wist ye not that I must be about my Father's business?"

Let this serve for an illustration. It is the scene that, recurring in every household as a boy claims his own life, is constantly repeating the experience of the household of Nazareth. And now all responsible life, all life entrusted with the care of any of God's causes, has this same sort of correspondence with the life of the mother of Jesus. There can be no higher specimen of responsibility than she exhibits. She is entrusted with the care of Him who is to be the Saviour of the world. And that responsibility she accepts entirely. She is willing to give up everything else in life, to be absorbed and worn out in the task of supreme privilege which God has given her. There comes no trouble or lack in the degree of her readiness for labor or for pain. But the quality of her self-sacrifice shows its defect elsewhere. She is not able to see where the limits of her work must be. She is not able to stop short in her devout responsibility when the task passes beyond her power, and her son begins to deal directly with His Father.

Compare with her, in the first place, that person with whom we are familiar in all the history of Christianity, whom we see about us constantly —the champion of the faith, the man who counts it his work in life to maintain and protect the purity of the belief in Christ. It is a noble task for a man to accept. It is filled with anxiety. The faith for which the man cares is beset with many dangers. It costs him sleepless nights and weary days. He incurs dislike; he excites hostility by his eager zeal. To all this he is fully equal. The danger of many a stout champion of truth comes quite at the other end. There comes a time when God, as it were, takes back into His own keeping that faith over which He has bidden His disciples to stand guard. The truth begins to show a vitality upon which the believer has not counted. It puts itself into new forms. It develops new associations. No wonder that he is troubled. No wonder that, unless he is a large and thoughtful man, thoroughly reverent of truth as well as thoroughly devoted to the truths which he has held, he grudges truth in some way the larger freedom that it is claiming for itself, and almost opposes its development.

Once more return to the story that has given us our suggestions for today. As Mary went back with her Son, realizing, out of His own mouth, that He was not only her Son, but God's, as she settled down with Him to their Nazareth life again, must not one single strong question have been upon her heart, "What does God want this Son of His to be? Oh, let me find that out, that I may work with Him." And as you go into the house where you are to train your soul, realizing, through some revelation that has come to it, that it is God's soul as well as yours, one strong and single question must be pressing on you too. "What does God want this soul of mine to be? Oh, let me find out that I may work with Him." And how can you find that out? Only by finding Him out. Only by understanding what He is, can you understand what He wants you to do. And understanding comes by love. And love to God comes by faith in Jesus Christ. See then, what is the divine progress of self-culture. You let Christ give you His blessings. Through gratitude to Him you come to the love of God. By loving God you understand God. By understanding God you come to see what He wants you to be, and so you are ready to work with Him for your own soul. From the first touch of Christ's hand in blessing, on to the eternal work of laboring with God for our own sanctification, that is the progress of the Christian life.

The Son of Mary was a revelation to the mother in whose care He lived. So a man's soul, his spiritual nature which is entrusted to his care, is a perpetual revelation to him. If you can only know that your soul is God's child, that He is caring for it and training it, then it may become to you the source of deep divine communications. God will speak to you through your own mysterious life. He will show you His wisdom and goodness, not in the heaven above you, but in the soul within you. He will make you His fellow worker in that which is the most divine work of His of which we can have any knowledge, the training and perfecting of a soul. That is the privilege of every man who knows, and finds his life and joy in knowing, that the soul which lives within him, the soul which he calls his soul, is the child of God.

THE SECOND SUNDAY AFTER THE EPIPHANY

Text: John 2:1-11

1. St. Augustine

The miracle of our Lord Jesus Christ whereby He made the water into wine is not marvellous to those who know that it was God's doing. For He who made wine on that day at the marriage feast, in those six water-pots, which He commanded to be filled with water, the self-same does this every year in vines. For even as that which the servants put into the water-pots was turned into wine by the doing of the Lord, so in like manner also is what the clouds pour forth changed into wine by the doing of the same Lord. But we do not wonder at the latter because it happens every year: it has lost its marvellousness by its constant recurrence. And yet it suggests a greater consideration than that which was done in the water-pots. For who is there that considers the works of God, whereby this whole world is governed and regulated, who is not amazed and overwhelmed with miracles? If he considers the vigorous power of a single grain of any seed whatever, it is a mighty thing, it inspires him with awe. But since men, intent on a different matter, have lost the consideration of the works of God by which they should daily praise Him as the Creator, God has, as it were, reserved to Himself the doing of certain extraordinary actions that, by striking them with wonder, He might rouse men as from sleep to worship Him. A dead man has risen again; men marvel: so many are born daily, and none marvels. If we reflect more considerately, it is a matter of greater wonder for one to be who was not before, than for one who was, to come to life again. Yet the same God, the Father of our Lord Jesus Christ, doeth by His word all these things; and it is He who created that governs also. The former miracles He did by His Word, God with Himself; the latter miracles He did by the same Word incarnate, and for us made man. As we wonder at the things that were done by the man Jesus, so let us wonder at the things that were done by Jesus God. By Jesus God were made heaven, and earth, and the sea, all the garniture of heaven, the abounding riches of the earth, and the fruitfulness of the sea—all these things which lie within the reach of our eyes were made by Jesus God. And we look at these things, and if His own spirit is in us they in such manner please us that we praise Him that contrived them; not in such manner that turning ourselves to the works we turn away from the Maker and, in a manner, turning our face to the things made and our backs to Him that made them.

And these things indeed we see; they lie before our eyes. But what of those we do not see, as angels, virtues, powers, dominions, and every in-

115

habitant of this fabric which is above the heavens, and beyond the reach of our eyes? Yet angels, too, when necessary, often showed themselves to men. Has not God made all these too by His Word, that is, by His only Son, our Lord Jesus Christ? What of the human soul itself, which is not seen and yet by its works shown in the flesh excites great admiration in those that duly reflect on them—by whom was it made, unless by God? And through whom was it made, unless through the Son of God? Not to speak as yet of the soul of man: the soul of any brute whatever, see how it regulates the huge body, puts forth the senses, the eyes to see, the ears to hear, the nostrils to smell, the taste to discern flavors—the members, in short, to execute their respective functions! Is it the body, not the soul, namely the inhabitant of the body, that doeth these things? The soul is not apparent to the eyes, nevertheless it excites admiration by these its actions.

Direct now thy consideration to the soul of man, on which God has bestowed understanding to know its Creator, to discern and distinguish between good and evil, that is, between right and wrong: see how many things it does through the body! Observe this whole world arranged in the same human commonwealth, with what administrations, with what orderly degrees of authority, with what conditions of citizenship, with what laws, manners, arts! The whole of this is brought about by the soul, and yet this power of the soul is not visible. When withdrawn from the body, the latter is a mere carcase: first, it in a manner preserves it from rottenness. For all flesh is corruptible and falls off into putridity unless preserved by the soul as by a kind of seasoning. But the human soul has this quality in common with the soul of the brute; those qualities rather are to be admired which I have stated, such as belong to the mind and intellect, wherein also it is renewed after the image of its Creator, after Whose image man was formed. What will this power of the soul be when this body shall have put on incorruption and this mortal shall have put on immortality? If such is its power, acting through corruptible flesh, what shall be its power through a spiritual body after the resurrection of the dead? Yet this soul, as I have said, of admirable nature and substance, is a thing invisible, intellectual; this soul also was made by God Jesus, for He is the Word of God. "All things were made by him, and without him was nothing made."

When we see, therefore, such deeds wrought by Jesus God, why should we wonder at water being turned into wine by the man Jesus? For He was not made man in such manner that He lost His being God. Man was added to Him, God not lost to Him. This miracle was brought by the same who made all those things. Let us not therefore wonder that God did it, but love Him because He did it in our midst and for the purpose of our restoration. For He gives us certain intimations by the very circumstances of the case. I suppose that it was not without cause He came to the marriage. The miracle apart, there lies something mysterious and sacramental in the very fact. Let us knock, that He may open to us, and fill us with the invisible wine: for we were water, and He made us wine, made us wise; for He gave us the wisdom of His faith, whilst before we were foolish. And it appertains, it may be, to this wisdom, together with the honor of God, and with the praise of His majesty, and with the charity of His most powerful mercy, to understand what was done in this miracle.

The Lord, on being invited, came to the marriage. What wonder if He came to that house to a marriage, having come into this world to a marriage? For, indeed, if He came not to a marriage, He has not here a bride. But what says the Apostle? "I have espoused you to one husband, to present you a chaste virgin to Christ." Why does he fear lest the virginity of Christ's bride should be corrupted by the subtilty of the devil? "I fear," saith he, "lest as the serpent beguiled Eve by his subtilty, so also your minds should be corrupted from the simplicity and chastity which is in Christ." Thus has He here a bride whom He has redeemed by His blood, and to whom He has given the Holy Spirit as a pledge. He has freed her from the bondage of the devil: He died for her sins and is risen again for her justification. Who will make such offerings to his bride? Men may offer to a bride every sort of earthly ornament—gold, silver, precious stones, houses, slaves, estates, farms—but will any give his own blood? For if one should give his own blood to his bride, he would not live to take her for his wife. But the Lord, dying without fear, gave His own blood for her, whom rising again He was to have, whom He had already united to Himself in the Virgin's womb. For the Word was the Bridegroom, and human flesh the bride; and both one, the Son of God, the same also being Son of man. The womb of the Virgin Mary, in which He became head of the Church, was His bridal chamber; thence He came forth, as a bridegroom from his chamber, as the Scripture foretold, "And rejoiced as a giant to run his way." From His chamber He came forth as a bridegroom; and being invited, came to the marriage.

It is because of an indubitable mystery that He appears not to acknowledge His mother, from whom as the Bridegroom He came forth, when He says to her, "Woman, what have I to do with thee? mine hour is not yet come." What is this? Did He come to the marriage for the purpose of teaching men to treat their mothers with contempt? Surely he to whose marriage He had come was taking a wife with the view of having children, and surely he wished to be honored by those children he would beget: had Jesus then come to the marriage in order to dishonor His mother, when marriages are celebrated and wives married with the view of having children, whom God commands to honor their parents?

Why, then, said the Son to the mother, "Woman, what have I to do with thee? mine hour is not yet come"? Our Lord Jesus Christ was both God and man. According as He was God, He had not a mother; according as He was man, He had. She was the mother, then, of His flesh, of His humanity, of the weakness which for our sakes He took upon Him. But the miracle which He was about to do, He was about to do according to His divine nature, not according to His weakness; according to that wherein He was God, not according to that wherein He was born weak. But the weakness of God is stronger than men. His mother then demanded a miracle of Him; but He, about to perform divine works, so far did not recognize a human womb; saying in effect, "That in Me which works a miracle was not born of thee, thou gavest not birth to My divine nature; but because My weakness was born of thee, I will recognize thee at the time when that same weakness shall hang upon the cross." This, indeed, is the meaning of "mine hour is not yet come." For then it was that He recognized, who, in truth, always did know. He knew His mother in predestination, even before He was born of her; even before, as God, He created her of whom, as man, He was to be created, He knew her as His mother: but at a certain hour in a mystery He did not recognize her; and at a certain hour which had not yet come, again in a mystery, He does recognize her. For then did He recognize her, when that to which she gave birth was a-dying. That by which Mary was made did not die, but that which was made of Mary; not the eternity of the divine nature, but the weakness of the flesh, was dying. He made that answer therefore, making a distinction in the faith of believers, between the *who*, and the *how*, He came. For awhile He was God and the Lord of heaven and earth, He came by a mother who was a woman. In that He was Lord of the world, Lord of heaven and earth, He was, of course, the Lord of Mary also; but in that wherein it is said, "Made of a woman, made under the law," He was Mary's son. The same both the Lord of Mary and the son of Mary; the same both the Creator of Mary and created from Mary. Marvel not that He was both son and Lord. For just as He is called the son of Mary, so likewise is He called the son of David; and son of David because son of Mary. Hear the Apostle openly declaring, "Who was made of the seed of David according to the flesh." Hear Him also declared the Lord of David; let David himself declare this: "The Lord said to my Lord, Sit thou on my right hand." And this passage Jesus Himself brought forward to the Jews and refuted them from it. How then was He both David's son and David's Lord? David's son according to the flesh, David's Lord according to His divinity; so also Mary's son after the flesh, and Mary's Lord after His majesty. Now as she was not the mother of His divine nature, whilst it was by His divinity the miracle she asked for would be wrought, therefore He answered her, "Woman, what have I to do with thee?" But think not that I deny thee to be my mother: "Mine hour is not yet come"; for in that hour I will acknowledge thee, when the weakness of which thou art the mother comes to hang on the Cross. Let us prove the truth of this. When the Lord suffered, the same Evangelist tells us, who knew the mother of the Lord, and who has given us to know about her in this marriage feast— the same, I say, tells us, "There was there near the cross the mother of Jesus; and Jesus saith to his mother, Woman, behold thy son! and to the disciple, Behold thy mother!" He commends His mother to the care of the disciple; commends His mother, as about to die before her and to rise again before her death. The man commends her, a human being, to man's care. This humanity had Mary given birth to. That hour had now come, the hour of which He had then said, "Mine hour is not yet come."

In my opinion, brethren, we have answered the heretics. Let us now answer the astrologers. And how do they attempt to prove that Jesus was under fate? Because, say they, Himself said, "Mine hour is not yet come." Therefore we believe Him; and if He had said, "I have no hour," He would have excluded the astrologers: but behold, say they, He said, "Mine hour is not yet come." If then He had said, "I have no hour," the astrologers would have been shut out and would have no ground for their slander; but now that He said, "Mine hour is not yet come," how can we contradict His own words? 'Tis wonderful that the astrologers, by believing Christ's words, endeavor to convince Christians that Christ lived under an hour of fate. Well, let them believe Christ when He saith, "I have power to lay down my life and to take it up again." Is this power then under fate? Let them show us a man who has it in his power when to die, how long to live: this they can never do. Let them, therefore, believe God when He says, "I have power to lay down my life, and to take it up again"; and let them inquire why it was said, "Mine hour is not yet come"; and let them not, because of these words, be imposing fate on the Maker of heaven, the Creator and Ruler of the stars. For even if fate were from the stars, the Maker of the stars could not be subject to their destiny. Moreover, not only Christ had not what thou callest fate, but not even hast thou, or I, or he there, or any human being whatsoever.

Nevertheless, being deceived, they deceive others, and propound fallacies to men. They lay snares to catch men, and that, too, in the open streets. They who spread nets to catch wild beasts do it in woods and desert places: how miserably vain are men, for catching whom the net is spread in the forum! When men sell themselves to men, they receive money; but these give money in order to sell themselves to vanities. For they go in to an astrologer to buy themselves masters, such as the astrologer is pleased to give them: be it Saturn, Jupiter, Mercury, or any other named profanity. The man went in free that, having given his money, he might come out a slave. Nay, rather, had he been free he would not have gone in; but he entered whither his master Error and his mistress Avarice dragged him. Whence also the truth says, "Every one that doeth sin is the slave of sin."

Why then did He say, "Mine hour is not yet come"? Rather because, having it in His power when to die, He did not yet see it fit to use that power. Just as we, brethren, say, for example, "Now is the appointed hour for us to go out to celebrate the sacraments." If we go out before it is necessary, do not we act perversely and absurdly? And because we act only at the proper time, do we therefore in this action regard fate when we so express ourselves? What means then, "Mine hour is not yet come"? When I know that it is the fitting time for me to suffer, when my suffering will be profitable, then I will willingly suffer. That hour is not yet: that thou mayest preserve both, this, "Mine hour is not yet come"; and that, "I have power to lay down my life, and power to take it up again." He had come, then, having it in His power when to die. And surely it would not have been right were He to die before He had chosen disciples. Had He been a man who had not his hour in his own power, he might have died before he had chosen disciples; and if haply he had died when his disciples were now chosen and instructed, it would be something conferred on him, not his own doing. But, on the contrary, He who had come having in His power when to go, when to return, how far to advance, and for whom the regions of the grave were open, not only when dying but when rising again; He, I say, in order to show us His Church's hope of immortality, showed in the head what it behooved the members to expect. For He who has risen again in the head will also rise again in all His members. The hour then had not yet come; the fit time was not yet. Disciples had to be called, the kingdom of heaven to be proclaimed, the Lord's divinity to be shown forth in miracles, and His humanity in His very sympathy with mortal men. For He who hungered because He was man, fed so many thousands with five loaves because He was God; He who slept because He was man, commanded the winds and the waves because He was God. All these things had first to be set forth, that the evangelists might have whereof to write, that there might be what should be preached to the Church. But when He had done as much as He judged to be sufficient, then His hour came, not of necessity, but of will—not of condition, but of power.

What then, brethren? Because we have replied to these and those, shall we say nothing as to what the water-pots signify? what the water turned into wine? what the master of the feast? what the bridegroom? what in mystery the mother of Jesus? what the marriage itself? We must speak of all these, but we must not burden you. I would have preached to you in Christ's name yesterday also, when the usual sermon was due to you, my beloved, but I was hindered by certain necessities. If you please then, holy brethren, let us defer until tomorrow what pertains to the hidden meaning of this translation, and not burden both your and our own weakness. There are many of you, perhaps, who have today come together on account of the solemnity of the day, not to hear the sermon. Let those who come tomorrow come to hear, so that we may not defraud those who are eager to learn nor burden those who are fastidious.

2. Bernard of Clairvaux

THE MEANING OF THE MIRACLE. Souls of less capacity are fed by looking at the Lord's works superficially, but those with more developed faculties find solider and sweeter food within, like the rich kernel in a grain of corn. His works are lovely outwardly indeed, but in their inward force they are much lovelier; even as He Himself is fairer than the sons of men without, but is the Splendor of eternal light within. To outward eyes He appeared as a Man devoid of fault, Flesh without sin, a spotless Lamb. Lovely to look upon was He in Whom there was no sin, and blessed were the eyes that looked on Him; but much more blessed are the pure in heart, for they see God. And as He appears in Himself, so also will you find Him in His works. Their outward appearance is beautiful indeed; but anyone who cracks the nut will find something far sweeter and more enjoyable inside. With the Old Testament Fathers this is not so; often the mystical meaning of what they do is beautiful, whereas their deeds considered in themselves are much less worthy. This is the case with things that Jacob did, for instance, and with David's adultery and many like events.

You will have guessed why I have said all this. You have heard read today the miracle that took place at the wedding, the first of the Lord's signs; and the story of that is marvellous enough, but its meaning is lovelier still. For though it was a great disclosure of God's majesty that water should be turned to wine at the Lord's nod, the transformation wrought by the Right Hand of the Most High, prefigured by this sign, is a far better one. For we have all been called to a spiritual wedding, in which the Lord Christ is the Bridegroom; that is why we sing in the Psalm, "He cometh forth as a bridegroom out of his chamber." And we, if you can believe it, are the Bride; so is the heart of everyone of us a bride. When will our weakness grasp the fact that God, our God, loves us with the same love as that with which a bridegroom loves his bride? This Bride is far below her Spouse in race, in kind, in worth; and yet the Son of the eternal King came from afar in order to betroth this Ethiopian woman to Himself, and He was even not afraid to die for her. Moses in truth married an Ethiopian wife, but could not change her color; Christ, on the other hand, having loved the Church so deeply while she is still degraded and befouled, will present her to Himself a glorious Church, having neither spot nor wrinkle. So then let Aaron murmur if he likes, let Mary murmur too—the old one, Moses's sister, not the new one, our Mary, mother of the Lord; for she is only anxious lest at the wedding anything should fail!

Whence then is this to thee, Oh human soul? Whence such inestimable glory, that thou shouldest be found fit to be the bride of Him on Whom the very angels yearn to look? What reward will you give Him for all the benefits that He has given you, sharing His table with you, and His kingdom, and bringing you at last to share His bridal chamber? Consider how the love of Him, Who set such store by you and indeed made you such a precious thing, should be returned. Out of His own side He refashioned you, when for your sake He slumbered on the Cross and underwent the sleep of death. He came forth from the Father for your sake, and left the Synagogue His mother, that cleaving to Him only you might be made one spirit with Himself. Hearken, Oh daughter, and see how great is the condescension of God in your regard.

3. Phillips Brooks

Through the mists of long and devout tradition that have obscured her character and made her very person almost mythical we are surprised sometimes in reading the Gospels at the clearness and simplicity with which Mary the mother of our Lord stands out before us there. She speaks only on three occasions, but when she speaks her words have such a directness and transparency about them, they come so short and true, they are so perfectly the words that an earnest and unselfish woman would have spoken that they leave us the clearest and most satisfactory idea of what manner of woman she must have been. Those three utterances of hers are like three clear notes of a bell, that show how solid and rich its metal is. Think what they were. In the presence of the messenger who comes to tell her of her great privilege she bows her head and says, "Behold the handmaid of the

Lord. Be it unto me according to thy word." When she finds her son in the Temple she cries out to Him, "Son, why hast thou thus dealt with us? Thy father and I have sought thee sorrowing." When she stands with Him before the puzzled guests at Cana she turns to the servants and says, "Whatsoever he saith unto you, do it." The young soul's consecration! The mother's overrunning love! The disciple's perfect loyalty! What can be clearer than the simple, true, brave, loving woman that those words reveal? How all the poor tawdry mythology which has clustered about her, and called her the Queen of Heaven, disappears before the vastly deeper beauty of this true woman of the earth, who wins our confidence and love.

I want to speak today of the last of those three words, and some of its suggestions. You remember the circumstances, but let me repeat them once more in the words of the ever fresh and beautiful old story. "And the third day there was a marriage in Cana of Galilee, and the mother of Jesus was there. And both Jesus was called and his disciples to the marriage. And when they wanted wine the mother of Jesus saith unto him, They have no wine. Jesus saith unto her, Woman what have I to do with thee, my hour is not come. His mother saith unto the servants, Whatsoever he saith unto you, do it." It is a moment of bewilderment. The impatient guests are asking for what the host has not to give them. The mother of Jesus turns to Him, but He seems to put her suggestion back. There is an air of embarrassment about it all. She and the guests are puzzled, and then she says to them, as if that were the only outlet and escape from their perplexity, "Do what he bids you to do." It is as if she said, "I do not understand Him, I do not know what He means or why He speaks as you have heard Him speak, but the only way for Him to interpret Himself is to say what He wants done, and you and I in doing it will see exactly what He means. Therefore, whatever He saith unto you, do it."

We ask ourselves at once, where had she learned this of her son? And we remember that since the last glimpse the Gospel gave us of them, they have been quietly living together, mother and son, at Nazareth. There she had studied Him with a love that must have been more and more filled with reverence. There she had realized the mystery of His nature. And one of the things which her experience of Him had taught her must have been just this: that often there were meanings and ideas which He intended to convey which could not be set forth in words, but which must be displayed in action—in the completely sympathetic action of two beings working together with a common will. Can we not picture many a time in the intercourse of their quiet home in which this must have come to her—times when some deep mysterious word fell from His lips which awed and fascinated her, perhaps, but of which she could make no clear meaning, and when, as she watched His actions and helped them, doing all that He wanted her to do, there gradually came out from His action the meaning which was in His words, but which they could not perfectly express? I think their life together must have been full of such experiences.

There is something like it in the relation that all thoughtful and watchful parents hold to their little children. How often you have watched their actions and quietly helped them out, and learned from them what they were wholly powerless to put in words! There are always some child-like people of whom we feel that the only true expression must be in the working out of their activity. They cannot tell their meaning except in deeds. We feel something of the same kind in our intercourse with Nature. We try to catch her messages, to put ourselves into sympathy with the vague spirit which breathes through all her life; but at the last we learn that it is only by obedience, only by helping her works to their completest by our service and by attentive study of the things she does, that we come really to know this mysterious life of Nature on whose bosom we are living. Whatsoever she saith unto you, do it. Obey Nature and she will reveal herself to your obedience—is not that the real watchword of our modern science?

And like that, only more deep and holy, was the law which the mother of Jesus had learned in the treatment of her Son. That only by doing His will, even when it was darkest, could she truly come to the light which she knew was in Him.

It sounds perhaps at first as if the words of Mary were a mere utter-ance of despair; as if she said, "I cannot make Him out. He is far away above us. It is not for us to try to make Him out. Such as we are cannot understand such as He is. All we can do is just to take His commandments in the dark, and do them in the dark, and be content." But if what I have just said is true, the tone of the words is not despair but hope. She does not say, "We cannot know Him"; she only says, "He must take His own way to make us know Him, to make Himself known to us. We cannot understand His words. Let us see what He does. Let us put ourselves into His action by obedience, and we shall understand Him." Surely she struck there the note of all the best Christian experience that has come since, through all the ages. How familiar has become the grand and simple way in which the soul which has been puzzled with the words of Jesus may stand still and say, "Lord, reveal Thyself to me in dealing with me. I will not hinder Thee. I will obey Thee. Whatsoever Thou sayest unto me I will do it, and so I shall reach the true knowledge of Thee which my soul craves."

A man has studied Christ in all the books. He has sat still and medi-tated, and tried to see through His meditation into the very face of Christ whom he has longed to understand; and he has not succeeded. Christ has seemed to elude him. He would not show Himself. He has almost seemed to lay His hand upon the eyes of the inquiring man as if He said, "What have I to do? Mine hour is not yet come." But then the man looks up and sees a duty—a very hard one it may be—or sees a burden which is very heavy. It is evidently coming toward him. He cannot escape it. Suppose that he is lifted up to such a knowledge of it all that he is ready with all his heart to say, "I do not want to escape it. If God sends it, God is in it. God sends nothing, God brings everything. Whatever comes from God has the God Whom it comes from in its heart. This, then, is He that is coming to me. What He could not tell me in words about Himself, I shall learn in this touch—what men call this blow—of His hand which I see approach-ing." Oh, it is possible so to look forward to a great, an awful experience, with something that is truly triumph filling all the pain and drowning all the dread, so to look to disaster, to sickness, to bereavement, to death, saying, "Now I shall know! In submissive acceptance of God's will I shall understand that which no study of His words could teach me."

But yet our verse does not allow us to forget that all true waiting for Christ's self-revelation is of an active and not merely of a passive sort. "Whatsoever he saith unto you, do it," says Mary. There is something to be done in order that Jesus may show out completely what He is trying to make manifest. And here, I think, is where a human action mounts to its highest dignity and puts on its fullest meaning. There are two views of human actions. One looks on them as they are in themselves, seeing only the force and friction which is involved in the specific thing that is done, and in the will of the immediate doer; the other regards them as setting free for expression and effect some higher force and purpose—the force and purpose of God which are waiting behind. One is the purely human, the other is the divine view of human action. It is as when you turn a screw in some great engine. A child who sees it turned thinks only of the hand which he sees turning it, and sees only the twisting of that bit of brass; but to the man who knows the engine the turning of that screw is the setting free of the imprisoned steam to do its work.

And so with human actions. Take any one. You engage tomorrow, it may be, in a new business, take a new partner, and begin to sell new goods in a new store. To one man that may mean the setting forth by your own will in search of fortune—nothing more than that; to another man it may mean what we can reverently call the opening up to God of chances to show Himself, and to work effects which have been seemingly impos-sible before. New combinations, new contacts, will result out of that act of yours, new needs of divine illumination, of divine guidance, are sure to come; and if man's need is indeed God's opportunity, then this new enterprise of yours will surely open some new chink through which the everlasting light can shine, or build some wall against which the everlasting and all-loving voice can echo. And so it is with everything you do. You make a friend, you read a book, you take a journey, you buy a house, you write a letter, and so full is the great world of God, so is He waiting every-where to make Himself known and to give himself away, that through this act of yours, to men who are looking and listening, there comes some revelation of His nature and some working of His power. Acts become little or great only according to the degree in which God manifests Him-self and works through them. To call acts insignificant or important in themselves is as if a child looked into an engine room and judged of the importance of different parts of the machinery by the size of the handles that moved them. The slightest handle may set free the great power of the steam. To one who listens wisely, the click of a delicate needle may sound as awful as the thunder of the walking-beam. For acts have their true meanings in the points of manifestation and operation which they give to God. It was not because she knew that somehow they would have wine or something better, it was because her son would surely show Himself through their obedience, if they obeyed Him, that Mary cared what these servants did. It is strange to think what a dignity and interest our own actions might have for us if we constantly recognized this capacity in them which they have not now. We play with bits of glass, finding great pleasure in their pleasant shapes, but never knowing what glorious things they would be if we held them up and let the sun shine through them.

THE THIRD SUNDAY AFTER THE EPIPHANY

Text: Matthew 8:1-13

1. John Chrysostom

The leper came unto Him "when he was come down from the mountain," but this centurion, "when he was entered into Capernaum." Wherefore then did neither the one nor the other go up into the mountain? Not out of remissness, for indeed the faith of them both was fervent, but in order not to interrupt His teaching.

But having come unto Him, he saith, "My servant lieth at home sick of the palsy, grievously tormented." Now some say, that by way of excuse he mentioned also the cause, why he had not brought him. "For neither was it possible," saith he, "paralyzed as he was, and tormented, and at his last gasp, to lift and convey him." For that he was at the point of expiring, Luke saith; "He was even ready to die." But I say, this is a sign of his having great faith, even much greater than theirs, who let one down through the roof. For because he knew for certain that even a mere command was enough for the raising up of the patient, he thought it superfluous to bring him.

What then doth Jesus? What He had in no case done before, here He doeth. For whereas on every occasion He was used to follow the wish of His supplicants, here He rather springs toward it and offers not only to heal him, but also to come to the house. And this He doth that we might learn the virtue of the centurion. For if He had not made this offer, but had said, "Go thy way, let thy servant be healed"; we should have known none of these things.

This at least He did, in an opposite way, in the case also of the Phoenician woman. For here, when not summoned to the house, of His own accord He saith He will come, that thou mightest learn the centurion's faith and great humility; but in the case of the Phoenician woman, He both refuses the grant and drives her, persevering therein, to great perplexity.

For being a wise physician and full of resources, He knows how to bring about contraries the one by the other. And as here by His freely offered coming, so there by His peremptory putting off and denial, He unfolds the woman's faith. So likewise He doth in Abraham's case, saying, "I will by no means hide from Abraham my servant"; to make thee know that man's kindly affection and his care for Sodom. And in the instance of Lot, they that were sent refuse to enter into his house, to make thee know the greatness of that righteous man's hospitality.

What then saith the centurion? "I am not worthy that thou shouldest come under my roof." Let us hearken, as many as are to receive Christ:

127

for it is possible to receive Him even now. Let us hearken, and emulate, and receive Him with as great zeal; for indeed, when thou receivest a poor man who is hungry and naked, thou hast received and cherished Him.

BUT SAY IN A WORD ONLY, AND MY SERVANT SHALL BE HEALED. See this man also, how, like the leper, he hath the right opinion touching Him. For neither did this one say "entreat," nor did he say "pray, and beseech," but "command only." And then from fear lest out of modesty He refuse, He saith, "For I also am a man under authority, having under me soldiers; and I say to this man, go, and he goeth; and to another, come, and he cometh; and to my servant, do this, and he doeth it."

"And what of that," saith one, "if the centurion did suspect it to be so? For the question is, whether Christ affirmed and ratified as much." Thou speakest well, and very sensibly. Let us then look to this very thing; and we shall find what happened in the case of the leper, and the same happening here likewise. For even as the leper said, "If thou wilt" (and not from the leper only are we positive about His authority, but also from the voice of Christ; in that, so far from putting an end to the suspicion, He did even confirm it more, by adding what were else superfluous to say, in the phrase, "I will, be thou cleansed," in order to establish that man's doctrine): so here too, it is right to see whether any such thing occurred. In fact, we shall find this same thing again taking place. For when the centurion had spoken such words and had testified His so great prerogative, so far from blaming, He did even approve it, and did somewhat more than approve it. For neither hath the Evangelist said that He praised the saying only, but declaring a certain earnestness in His praise, that He even "marveled" and neither did He simply marvel, but in the presence also of the whole people, and set him as an example to the rest, that they should emulate him.

Seest thou how each of them that bore witness of His authority is "marveled at"? And the multitudes were astonished at His doctrine because "He taught as one having authority"; and so far from blaming them, He both took them with Him when He came down and, by His words of cleansing to the leper, confirmed their judgment. Again, that leper said, "if thou wilt, thou canst make me clean"; and so far from rebuking, He on the contrary cleansed him by such treatment as He had said. Again, this centurion saith, "Speak the word only, and my servant shall be healed": and "marveling" at him, He said, "I have not found so great faith, no, not in Israel."

Now, to convince thee of this by the opposite also; Martha having said nothing of this sort, but on the contrary, "Whatsoever thou wilt ask of God, he will give thee"; so far from being praised—although an acquaintance, and dear to Him, and one of them that had shown great zeal toward Him—she was rather rebuked and corrected by Him, as not having spoken well; in that He said to her, "Said I not unto thee, that if thou wouldest believe, thou shouldest see the glory of God?" blaming her, as though she did not even yet believe. And again, because she had said, "Whatsoever thou wilt ask of God, he will give thee"; to lead her away from such a surmise, and to teach her that He needs not to receive from another, but is Himself the fountain of all good things, He saith, "I am the resurrection and the life"; that is to say, "I wait not to receive active power, but work all of Myself."

Wherefore at the centurion He both marvels and prefers him to all the people, and honors him with the gift of the kingdom, and provokes the rest to the same zeal. And to show thee that for this end He so spake, namely, for the instructing of the rest to believe in like manner, listen to the exactness of the Evangelist, how he hath intimated it. For, "Jesus," saith he, "turned him about and said to them that followed him, I have not found so great faith, no, not in Israel."

It follows, that to have high imaginations concerning Him, this especially is of faith and tends to procure the kingdom and His other blessings. For neither did His praise reach to words only, but He both restored the sick man whole, in recompense of his faith, and weaves for him a glorious crown, and promises great gifts, saying on this wise, "Many shall come from the east and west, and shall sit down in the bosoms of Abraham, and Isaac, and Jacob; but the children of the kingdom shall be cast out."

Thus, since He had shown many miracles, He proceeds to talk with them more unreservedly. Then, that no one might suppose His words to come of flattery, but that all might be aware that such was the mind of the centurion, He saith, "Go thy way; as thou hast believed, so be it done unto thee." And straightway the work followed, bearing witness to his character. "And his servant was healed from that hour."

But nevertheless, though having such great faith, he still accounted himself to be unworthy. Christ, however, signifying that he was worthy to have Him enter into his house, did much greater things, marveling at him, and proclaiming him, and giving more than he had asked. For he came indeed seeking for his servant health of body, but went away, having received a kingdom. Seest thou how the saying had been already fulfilled, "Seek ye the kingdom of heaven, and all these things shall be added unto you." For, because he evinced great faith and lowliness of mind, He both gave him heaven and added unto him health.

And not by this alone did He honor him, but also by signifying upon whose casting out he is brought in. For now from this time forth He proceeds to make known to all that salvation is by faith, not by works of the law. And this is why not to Jews only, but to Gentiles also the gift so given shall be proffered, and to the latter rather than to the former. For "think not," saith He, "by any means, that so it hath come to pass in regard of this man alone; nay, so it shall be in regard of the whole world." And this he said, prophesying of the Gentiles, and suggesting to them good hopes. For in fact there were some following Him from Galilee of the Gentiles. And this He said, on the one hand, not letting the Gentiles despair; on the other, putting down the proud spirits of the Jews.

But that His saying might not affront the hearers, nor afford them any handle; He neither brings forward prominently what He hath to say of the Gentiles, but upon occasion taken from the centurion; nor doth He use nakedly the term, Gentiles: not saying, "many of the Gentiles," but "many from east and west": which was the language of one pointing out the

Gentiles, but did not so much affront the hearers, because His meaning was under a shadow.

Neither in this way only doth He soften the apparent novelty of His doctrine, but also by speaking of "Abraham's bosom" instead of "the kingdom." For neither was that term familiar to them: moreover, the introduction of Abraham would be a sharper sting to them. Wherefore John also spake nothing at first concerning hell but, what was most apt to grieve them, He saith, "Think not to say, we are children of Abraham."

He is providing for another point also; not to seem in any sense opposed to the ancient polity. For he that admires the patriarchs, and speaks of their bosom as an inheritance of blessings, doth much more than sufficiently remove also this suspicion.

Let no man therefore suppose that the threat is one only, for both the punishment of the one and the joy of the other is double: of the one, not only that they fell away, but that they fell away from their own; of the other, not only that they attained, but that they attained what they had no expectation of: and there is a third together with these, that the one received what pertained to the other. And he calls them "children of the kingdom," for whom the kingdom had been prepared: which also more than all was apt to gall them; in that having pointed to them as being in their bosom by His offer and promise, after all He puts them out.

2. Martin Luther

Two examples of faith and love are taught in this Gospel: one by the leper, the other by the centurion. Let us first consider the leper. This leper would not have been so bold as to go to the Lord and ask to be cleansed if he had not trusted and expected with his whole heart that Christ would be kind and gracious and would cleanse him. Because he was a leper, he had reason to be timid. Moreover the law forbids lepers to mingle with the people. Nevertheless he approaches, regardless of law and people, and of how pure and holy Christ is.

Here behold the attitude of faith toward Christ: it sets before itself absolutely nothing but the pure goodness and free grace of Christ, without seeking and bringing any merit. For here it certainly cannot be said that the leper merited by His purity to approach Christ, to speak to Him and to invoke His help. Nay, just because he feels his impurity and unworthiness, he approaches all the more and looks only upon the goodness of Christ. This is true faith, a living confidence in the goodness of God. The heart that does this has true faith; the heart that does it not has not true faith; as they do who keep not the goodness of God and that alone in sight, but first look around for their own good works in order to be worthy of God's grace and to merit it. These never become bold to call upon God earnestly or to draw near to Him.

Now this confidence of faith or knowledge of the goodness of Christ would never have originated in this leper by virtue of his own reason, if he had not first heard a good report about Christ, namely, how kind, gracious and merciful He is, ready to help and befriend, comfort and counsel every-one that comes to Him. Such a report must undoubtedly have come to his ears, and from this fame he derived courage and turned and interpreted the report to his own advantage. He applied this goodness to his own need and concluded with all confidence: To me also He will be as kind as His fame and good report declare. His faith therefore did not grow out of his reason, but out of the report he heard of Christ, as St. Paul says: "Belief cometh of hearing, and hearing by the Word (or report) of Christ" (Romans 10:17).

This is the Gospel that is the beginning, middle, and end of every-thing good and of all salvation. For we have often heard that we must first hear the Gospel, and after that believe and love and do good works; not first do good works and so reverse the order, as the teachers of works do. But the Gospel is a good report, saying, or fame of Christ, how He is all goodness, love, and grace, as can be said of no other man or saint. For even if other saints have a good report and reputation, it is nevertheless not the Gospel, unless it tells alone of the goodness and grace of Christ; and if it should include other saints also, it is no longer the Gospel. For the Gospel builds faith and confidence alone upon the rock, Jesus Christ.

You see therefore that this example of the leper fights for faith against works. For as Christ helps him out of pure grace through faith without any works or merits of his own, so He does for every man, and would have all to think thus of Him and expect from Him like aid. And if this leper had said: "Behold, Lord, I have prayed and fasted so much; I beg you to look upon this and on account of it make me clean"—if he had come in this manner, Christ would never have cleansed him. For such a person does not rest upon God's grace, but upon his own merit. In this way God's grace is not praised, loved, magnified, nor desired; but one's own works deprive God of His honor and rob Him of that which is His. This is to kiss the hand and to deny God, as Job 31:27-28 says: "If my mouth hath kissed my hand; this also were an iniquity to be punished by the judges; for I should have denied God that is above"; and Isaiah 2:8: "They worship the work of their own hands," that is, the honor and confidence they ought to give to God, they attribute to their own work.

Furthermore the example of love is presented here in the love of Christ to the leper. For you see here, how love makes a servant of Christ, so that He helps the poor man freely without any reward, and seeks neither advan-tage, favor, nor honor thereby, but only the good of the poor man and the honor of God the Father. For this reason He also forbids him to tell any-one, in order that it may be a pure, sincere work of free and gracious love.

This is what I have often said, that faith makes of us lords, and love makes of us servants. Indeed, by faith we become gods and partakers of the divine nature and name, as is said in Psalm 82:6: "I said, Ye are gods, and all of you sons of the Most High." But through love we become equal to the poorest. According to faith we are in need of nothing, and have an abundance; according to love we are servants of all. By faith we receive blessings from above, from God; through love we give them out below, to our neighbor. Even as Christ in His divinity stood in need of nothing, but in His humanity served everybody who had need of Him. Of this we have spoken enough, namely, that we also must by faith be born God's sons and gods, lords and kings, even as Christ is born true God of the Father in eternity; and again, come out of ourselves by love and help our neighbors with kind deeds, even as Christ became man to help us all. And as Christ is not God, because He first merited divinity by His works or attained to it through His incarnation, but has it by birth, without any works, even before He became man; so we also have not merited by works or love sonship with God, so that our sins are forgiven, and death and hell cannot injure us; but without works and before our love, we have received it in the Gospel by grace through faith. And as Christ first became man to serve us after being God from eternity; so we also do good and exercise love to our neighbor, after we have become pious, free from sin, alive, saved, and sons of God by faith. Let this suffice concerning the first example, the leper.

The other example is like it in respect to faith and love. For this centurion also has a heartfelt confidence in Christ, and sets before his eyes nothing but the goodness and grace of Christ; otherwise he would not have come to Him, or he would not have sent to Him, as Luke 7:3 says. Likewise he would not have had this bold confidence, if he had not first heard of the goodness and grace of Christ. In this instance also the Gospel is the beginning and incentive of his confidence and faith.

Here we learn again, that we must begin with the Gospel and believe it and not look upon any merit or work of our own as this centurion also advanced no merit or work, but only his confidence in the goodness of Christ. So we see that all the works of Christ exhibit examples of the Gospel, of faith, and of love.

We also observe the example of love, how Christ freely shows him kindness, without any request or reward, as was said above. Moreover, the centurion also shows an example of love, in that he took pity upon his servant, as Luke 7:2 says, he did it because the servant was dear to him; just as if he said: The love and affection, which he bore to him, impelled him to consider his need and to do this. Let us also do likewise, and see to it that we do not deceive ourselves and rest satisfied in that we now have the Gospel, and yet have no regard for our neighbor in his need.

3. John Keble

Still it is Epiphany, my brethren, and again the Church tells us of a special manifestation of the Lord Jesus, God made Man to redeem and save us. Last Sunday you heard how He changes all good things for the better: the Law for the Gospel, earth for Heaven. Now you have heard, how He changes the worst of evils for the greatest good. To change water into wine, our earthly good things into heavenly, the Law into the Gospel, that indeed was an astonishing miracle: but to change and renew man's nature, utterly poisoned and corrupted by sin, back again into the Image of God; that, as you perceive at once, was a still greater wonder, a work of more amazing mercy; and of this work, my brethren, our Lord gave a token, as often as He cleansed any of the lepers who then abounded among the Jews. And the first instance, related in the Gospels, of His cleansing any leper is that which is related in the Gospel for today. Our Lord was in one of the cities of Galilee, in His first progress through that country, the first year of His ministry; "and behold there came a leper." It was a very bad case, "a man *full* of leprosy." He was in the very greatest of distress, he besought our Lord, and kneeled down to Him, and fell upon his face; and this was his prayer; though in words it was not a prayer—"Lord, if thou wilt, thou canst make me clean." In sound, as you perceive, it was no prayer; it was merely a confession of faith, faith in the power of our Lord Jesus Christ to cleanse him. But here a man may ask two questions. If the leper so earnestly longed for cleansing, as he plainly did by the whole of his behavior, why did he not at once ask for it in so many words? Why did he not distinctly say, "Heal me, O Lord, and I shall be healed"; "cleanse me and I shall be cleansed"? Instead of saying, "If thou wilt, thou canst make me clean," why did he not say, "O Lord, speak the word, and make me clean"? It was no want of faith in Christ's power, for his word if, "If thou wilt, thou canst." It must have been because his heart told him, it was but too likely that our Lord might not have the *will* to cleanse him. Here then comes in the other question, Why did he doubt our Saviour's will? For he knew by what he heard, perhaps by what he saw, how good Jesus of Nazareth was, how He went about doing good, and "healing all manner of sickness and all manner of disease among the people." Why should He not heal this leper, as well as Peter's wife's mother, or the nobleman's son, or the man possessed with a devil in the synagogue of Capernaum, or any others whom the leper might likely enough have heard of? Well, the reason perhaps might be this. It does not appear as if our Lord had as yet healed any leper; this poor man is the first mentioned as coming to Him under that particular distemper. Now there is no doubt that the children of Israel considered leprosy as an especial punishment of sin, more than they did most other diseases: and it would seem from the Old Testament, from the case of Miriam the sister of Moses, and of king Uzziah, that there was enough to lead their thoughts that way. We may well believe therefore that this poor man regarded his leprosy as a just judgment for the sins, of which his conscience was afraid; and went about so humbled and ashamed that he hardly dared pray for deliverance; the rather if, as is very likely, he had heard something of the high and heavenly commandments which Christ had been uttering on the Mount, with all authority. The very echo of that Voice might have brought him down prostrate on the knees of his heart, as it has thousands of sinners since; thinking, "If the law is so holy, whatever shall I do, who am nothing but sin all over?" Moreover he might think to himself (for so the Jews commonly thought, and perhaps this also was true in their days) that there was no healing of leprosy except by mira-cle; by the immediate act of God Almighty Himself; and this again would make his request seem bolder; and altogether, not in unbelief but in humility, he might naturally not feel sure whether He Who can cure all would see fit to make him clean; and so, instead of praying, he merely casts himself down and says, "If thou wilt, thou canst." Not another word does he add.

And what says the Blessed Jesus to this? Oh my brethren, may the words sink deep into every one of our hearts, yours and mine, and every sinner on earth; and He cause us to hear them again and again, as often as our poor souls need it! But then we must come to Him as the leper did, "trusting not in our own worthiness, but in His manifold and great mercies." The words, as you know, are, "I will; be thou clean." "I will," because the poor man had said, "If thou wilt"; "be thou clean," because he had said, "Thou canst make me clean." Oh divine, almighty words! Who could have ventured to utter such, but He Who spake the like words, and the world was created, "Let there be light, and there was light"? Did not the angels standing by know the Voice, and wonder and adore? And shall not we do the like when, in a moment, we see the miserable disease cured, and the most foul cleansed, and he who, a few moments before, lay on the ground, in his own eyes and the eyes of his friends a miserable and most impure outcast, when we see him lifted up in a moment by the touch and voice of the Great Physician, cured wonderfully, cured forever, free to worship among God's people, and to return thanks in His house, his whole heart full of Christ, full of Him Who has wrought such a wonder on him, so that he *cannot* be silent, he *must* in some way tell everyone, that it is Jesus that hath made him whole? Oh my brethren, will you not praise God for this? Yes indeed, you must; you cannot but praise Him unless you are altogether false, vain, hypocritical Christians, unless all your hope of Eternal life in our Lord Jesus Christ is come to be a mere dream. For, my brethren, it is your own case, it is your own cure, that you have been hearing of. You are, each one of you, this leper: and well is it for those who felt it in their very hearts, when the Church began speaking of him in the day's Gospel. God grant that you may have said to yourselves, "That leper is I: his cure is God's mercy to me"; and that so you may have joined as earnestly as ever you could in the good words of joy and thanksgiving with which, according to old custom, we acknowledge God's mercy in giving us His saving message by His own Son, and not by another; "Thanks be to God for His Gospel."

THE FOURTH SUNDAY AFTER THE EPIPHANY

Text: Matthew 8:23-27

1. John Chrysostom

Now Luke, to free himself from having the order of time required of Christ, saith thus, "And it came to pass on a certain day that he went into a ship with his disciples"; and Mark in like manner. But this Evangelist not so, but he maintains the order in this place also. For they did not all of them write all things in this way. And these things I have mentioned before, lest anyone from the omission should suppose there was a discordance.

The multitudes then He sent on, but the disciples He took with Himself: for the others mention this too. And He took them with Him, not for nought, nor at hazard, but in order to make them spectators of the miracle that was to take place. For like a most excellent trainer, He was anointing them with a view to both objects; as well to be undismayed in dangers, as to be modest in honors. Thus, that they might not be highminded, because having sent away the rest, He retained them. He suffers them to be tossed with the tempest; at once correcting this, and disciplining them to bear trials nobly.

For great indeed were the former miracles too, but this contained also in it a kind of discipline, and that no inconsiderable one, and was a sign akin to that of old. For this cause He takes the disciples only with Himself. For as, when there was a display of miracles, He suffers the people also to be present; so when trials and terrors were rising up against Him, then He takes with Him none but the champions of the whole world, whom He was to discipline.

And while Matthew merely mentioned that He "was asleep," Luke saith that it was "on a pillow"; signifying both His freedom from pride and to teach us hereby a high degree of austerity.

The tempest therefore being thoroughly excited, and the sea raging, "They awake him, saying, Lord, save us: we perish." But He rebuked them before He rebuked the sea. Because, as I said, for discipline these things were permitted, and they were a type of the temptations that were to overtake them. Yea, for after these things again, He often suffered them to fall into more grievous tempests of fortune, and bare long with them. Wherefore Paul also said, "I would not, brethren, have you ignorant, that we were pressed out of measure beyond strength, insomuch that we despaired even of life"; and after this again, "Who delivered us from so great deaths." Signifying therefore hereby that they ought to be confident, though the waves rise high, and that He orders all things for good, He first of all reproves them. For indeed their very alarm was a profitable occurrence, that the miracle might appear greater, and their remembrance of the event be rendered lasting. Since when anything strange is about to happen, there are prepared beforehand many things to cause remembrance lest, after the miracle hath passed by, men should sink into forgetfulness.

Thus Moses also first is in fear of the serpent, and not merely in fear, but even with much distress; and then he sees that strange thing come to pass. So these too, having first looked to perish, were then saved, that having confessed the danger, they might learn the greatness of the miracle.

Therefore also He sleeps: for had He been awake when it happened, either they would not have feared, or they would not have besought Him, or they would not so much have thought of His being able to do any such thing. Therefore He sleeps, to give occasion for their timidity and to make their perception of what was happening more distinct. For a man looks not with the same eyes on what happens in the persons of others, as in his own. Therefore since they had seen all benefited, while themselves had enjoyed no benefit, and were supine (for neither were they lame, nor had they any other such infirmity); and it was meet they should enjoy His benefits by their own perception: He permits the storm that by their deliverance they might attain to a clearer perception of the benefit.

Therefore neither doth He this in the presence of the multitudes that they might not be condemned for little faith, but He has them apart, and corrects them, and before the tempest of the waters He puts an end to the tempests of their soul, rebuking them, and saying, "Why are ye fearful, O ye of little faith?" instructing them also that men's fear is wrought not by the approach of the temptation, but by the weakness of their mind.

But should anyone say that it was not fearfulness, or little faith, to come near and awaken Him; I would say this, that that very thing was an especial sign of their wanting the right opinion concerning Him. That is, His power to rebuke when awakened they knew, but that He could do so even sleeping, they knew not as yet.

And why at all marvel that it was so now, when even after many other miracles their impressions were still rather imperfect? Wherefore also they are often rebuked, as when He saith, "Are ye also yet without understanding?" Marvel not then if, when the disciples were in such imperfect dispositions, the multitudes had no exalted imagination of Him. For "They marveled, saying, What manner of man is this, that even the sea and the winds obey Him?"

But Christ chode not with them for calling Him a man, but waited to teach them by His signs that their supposition was mistaken. But from what did they think Him a man? First from His appearance, then from His sleeping, and His making use of a ship. So on this account they were cast into perplexity, saying, "What manner of man is this?" since, while the sleep and the outward appearance showed man, the sea and the calm declared Him God.

For because Moses had once done some such thing, in this regard also doth He signify His own superiority, and that the one works miracles as a slave, the other as Lord. Thus, He put forth no rod, as Moses did, neither did He need any prayer but, as was meet for a master commanding his handmaid, or a creator his creature, so did He quiet and curb it by word and command only; and all the surge was straightway at an end, and not one trace of the disturbance remained. For this the Evangelist declared, saying, "And there was a great calm." And that which had been spoken of the Father as a great thing, this He showed forth again by His works. And what had been said concerning Him? "He spake," it saith, "and the stormy wind ceased." So here, likewise, He spake and "there was a great calm." And for this most of all did the multitudes marvel at him, who would not have marveled had He done it in such manner as did Moses.

2. Martin Luther

This Gospel, as a narrative, gives us an example of faith and unbelief, in order that we may learn how mighty the power of faith is, and that it of necessity has to do with great and terrible things, and that it accomplishes nothing but wonders; and that on the other hand unbelief is so faint-hearted, shamefaced, and trembling with fear that it can do nothing whatever. An illustration of this we see in this experience of the disciples, which shows the real state of their hearts. First, as they in company with Christ entered the ship, all was calm and they experienced nothing unusual, and had anyone asked them then if they believed, they would have answered, Yes. But they were not conscious of how their hearts trusted in the calm sea and the signs for fair weather, and that thus their faith was founded upon what their natural eyes saw. But when the tempest comes and the waves fill the boat, their faith vanishes; because the calm and peace in which they trusted took wings and flew away, therefore they fly with the calm and peace, and nothing is left but unbelief.

But what is this unbelief able to do? It sees nothing but what it experiences. It does not experience life, salvation, and safety; but instead the waves coming into the boat and the sea threatening them with death and every danger. And because they experience these things and give heed to them and turn not their fear from them, trembling and despair cannot be suppressed. Yea, the more they see and experience it the harder death and despair torment them and every moment threatens to devour them. But unbelief cannot avoid such experiences and cannot think otherwise even for a second. For it has nothing besides to which it can hold and comfort itself, and therefore it has no peace or rest for a single moment. And thus will it also be in perdition, where there will be nothing but despair, trembling, and fear, and that without end.

But had they had faith, it would have driven the wind and the waves of the sea out of their minds and pictured before their eyes in place of the wind and tempest the power and grace of God, promised in his Word; and it would have relied upon that Word, as though anchored to an immovable rock, and would not float on the water, and as though the sun shined brightly and all was calm and no storm was raging. For it is the great characteristic and power of faith to see what is not visible, and not to see what is visible, yea, that which at the time drives and oppresses us; just as unbelief can see only what is visible and cannot in the least cleave to what is invisible.

Therefore God bestows faith to the end that it should deal not with ordinary things, but with things no human being can master as death, sin, the world, and Satan. For the whole world united is unable to stand before death, but flees from and is terrified by it, and is also conquered by it; but faith stands firm, opposes death that devours everything, and triumphs over it, and even swallows the insatiable devourer of life. In like manner no one can control or subdue the flesh, but it reigns everywhere in the world, and what it wills must be done, so that the whole world thereby is carnal; but faith lays hold of the flesh and subdues and bridles it, so that it must become a servant. And in like manner no one can endure the rage, persecution, and blasphemy, infamy, hatred, and envy of the world; everyone retreats and falls back exhausted before it; it gets the upper hand over all and triumphs; and if they are without faith it mocks them besides and treads all under its feet, and takes pleasure and delight in doing so.

Further, who could conquer Satan with his innumerable, subtle suggestions and temptations, by which he hinders the truth and God's Word, faith and hope, and starts so many false doctrines, sects, seductions, heresies, doubts, superstitions, and innumerable abominations? The whole world compared with him is like a spark of fire compared with a fountain of water. All must be here subject to him; as we also see, hear, and understand. But it is faith that keeps him busy, and it not only stands before him invulnerable, but also reveals his roguery and puts him to shame, so that his deception fails and he faints and falls; as now takes place with his indulgences and his papacy. Just so no one can allay and quiet the least sin, but it bites and devours the conscience, so that nothing avails even if the whole world were to comfort and support such a person, he must be cast down into perdition. Here faith is a hero, it appeases all sins, even if they were as many as the world had committed.

Is there now not something almighty and inexpressible about faith that it can withstand all our powerful enemies and gain the victory, so that St. John says in his first Epistle 5:4: "This is the victory that hath overcome the world, even our faith"? Not that this is done in peace and by quietly resting; for it is a battle that is carried on not without wounds and shedding of blood. Yea, the heart so severely experiences in this battle sin and death, the flesh, Satan, and the world, that it has no other thought than that it is lost, that sin and death have triumphed, and that Satan holds the field of battle. The power of faith, however, experiences but little of that. This is set forth in our narrative, when the waves not only dashed into the boat, but even covered it, so that it was about to go under and sink, and Christ was lying asleep. Just then there was no hope of life, death had the upper hand and had triumphed; life was lying prostrate and was lost.

As it went here, so it goes and must go in all other temptations of sin, Satan, and so forth. We must experience how sin has taken captive the conscience and nothing but wrath and perdition wish to reign, and how we must be eternally lost. Satan must start so many things by his error and false teaching that it appears God's Word must fall to the ground and the world must glory in falsehood. Likewise the world must rage and persecute to such an extent that it appears no one can stand or be saved, or even confess his faith; but Cain will rule alone and will not rest until his brother is dead, so that he may never be in his way. But we must not judge and act according to appearance and our experience, but according to our faith.

Therefore this Gospel is a comforting example and doctrine, how we should conduct ourselves, so that we may not despair in the agony of sin, in the peril of death, and in the tumult of the world; but be assured that we are not lost, although the waves at once overwhelm our little boat; that we will not perish, although we experience in our evil conscience sin, wrath, and the lack of grace; that we will not die, although the whole world hates and persecutes us, although it opens its jaws as wide as the rosy dawn of the morning. These are all waves that fall over your little bark, cause to despair, and force you to cry out: "Save, Lord; we perish." Thus you have here the first part of this Gospel, faith, how it should thrive and succeed, and besides, how incapable and faint-hearted unbelief is.

The second part of our text, treating of love, shows forth Christ in that He rises, breaks His sleep for their sake, takes to heart their need as though it were His own, and ministers to them help out of free love without any merit on their part. He neither receives nor seeks any reward for His help, but permits them to enjoy and use His power and resources. For as we have often heard, it is characteristic of Christian love to do all freely and gratuitously, to the praise and honor of God, that a Christian lives upon the earth for the sake of such love, just as Christ lived solely for the purpose of doing good; as He Himself says: "The Son of man came not to be ministered unto, but to minister" (Matthew 20:28).

3. John Calvin

AND WHEN HE HAD ENTERED INTO A SHIP. Mark says that "other little ships" crossed "along with him," but that Christ entered into His own ship "with his disciples." Luke too quotes his words; Matthew is more concise. They agree, however, as to the leading fact, that Christ laid Himself down to rest, and that, while He was asleep, a tempest suddenly arose. First, it is certain that the storm which agitated the lake was not accidental: for how would God have permitted His Son to be driven about at random by the violence of the waves? But on this occasion He intended to make known to the apostles how weak and inconsiderable their faith still was. Though Christ's sleep was natural, yet it served the additional purpose of making the disciples better acquainted with their weakness. I will not say, as many do, that Christ pretended sleep, in order to try them. On the contrary, I think that He was asleep in such a manner as the condition and necessity of human nature required.

And yet His divinity watched over Him, so that the apostles had no reason to fear that consolation would not be immediately provided or that assistance would not be obtained from heaven. Let us therefore conclude that all this was arranged by the secret providence of God—that Christ was asleep, that a violent tempest arose, and that the waves covered the ship, which was in imminent danger of perishing. And let us learn hence that, whenever any adverse occurrence takes place, the Lord tries our faith. If the distresses grow to such a height as almost to overwhelm us, let us believe that God does it with the same design of exercising our patience, or of bringing to light in this way our hidden weakness; as we see that, when the apostles were covered by the billows, their weakness, which formerly lay concealed, was discovered.

LORD, SAVE US. A pious prayer, one would think: for what else had they to do when they were lost than to implore safety from Christ? But as Christ charges them with unbelief, we must inquire in what respect they sinned. Certainly, I have no doubt that they attached too much importance to the bodily presence of their Master, for, according to Mark, they do not merely pray, but expostulate with Him, "Master, hast thou no care that we perish?" Luke describes also confusion and trembling: "Master, Master, we perish." They ought to have believed that the Divinity of Christ was not oppressed by carnal sleep, and to His Divinity they ought to have had recourse. But they do nothing till they are urged by extreme danger; and then they are overwhelmed with such unreasonable fear that they do not think they will be safe till Christ is awakened. This is the reason why He accuses them of unbelief: for their entreaty that He would assist them was rather a proof of their faith if, in confident reliance on His divine power, they had calmly, and without so much alarm, expected the assistance which they asked.

And here we obtain an answer to a question which might be put, and which arises out of His reproof. Is every kind of fear sinful and contrary to faith? First, He does not blame them simply because they fear, but because they are "timid." Mark adds the word "so"—"Why are you so timid?" and by this term indicates that their alarm goes beyond proper bounds. Besides, he contrasts faith with their fear, and thus shows that He is speaking about immoderate dread, the tendency of which is not to exercise their faith, but to banish it from their minds. It is not every kind of fear that is opposed to faith. This is evident from the consideration that, if we fear nothing, an indolent and carnal security steals upon us; and thus faith languishes, the desire to pray becomes sluggish, and the remembrance of God is at length extinguished. Besides, those who are not affected by a sense of calamities, so as to *fear*, are rather insensible than firm.

Thus we see that fear, which awakens faith, is not in itself faulty till it goes beyond bounds. Its excess lies in disturbing or weakening the composure of faith, which ought to rest on the word of God. But as it never happens that believers exercise such restraint on themselves as to keep their faith from being injured, their fear is almost always attended by sin. Yet we ought to be aware that it is not every kind of fear which indicates a want of faith, but only that dread which disturbs the peace of the conscience in such a manner that it does not rest on the promise of God.

HE REBUKED THE WINDS. Mark relates also the words of Christ by which, addressing the sea, He enjoins "silence," that is, "stillness": not that the lake had any perception, but to show that the power of His voice reached the elements, which were devoid of feeling. And not only "the sea and the winds," which are without feeling, but wicked men also, with all their obstinacy, obey the commands of God. For when God is pleased to allay the tumults of war, He does not always soften the fierce minds of men, and mould them to obedience, but, even while their rage continues, makes the arms to drop from their hands: and thus is fulfilled that declaration, "He maketh wars to cease to the ends of the earth; he breaketh the bow, and cutteth the spear in pieces, and burneth the chariots in the fire" (Psalm 46:10).

BUT THE MEN WONDERED. Mark and Luke appear to say this in reference to the apostles; for, after having stated that Christ reproved them, they add that they cried out with fear, "Who is this?" It applies, however, more properly to others, who had not yet known Christ. Whether we take the one or the other of these views, the result of the miracle appears in the display of the glory of Christ. If anyone shall suppose that it is the apostles who speak, the meaning of the words will be that His divine power was sufficiently proved by the fact that "the wind and the sea obey him." But as it is more probable that these words were spoken by others, the Evangelists show that the miracle made such an impression on their minds as to produce a certain reverence for Christ which prepared them for believing on Him.

4. Phillips Brooks

The beauty of the story is in the way in which the change all comes from and belongs to Jesus. When He rises, the storm stops. The calm that comes is from the power of His presence. As if a strong, quiet man stepped in majestically among a crowd of noisy brawlers, and his very appearance made them ashamed and hushed their noise. So Jesus steps in among the elements, and they are still in a moment. It is a picture of the peace that He bestows. However feebly we understand it, the story at least is luminous to every loving eye with this—the majesty and beauty of Christ and the way in which peace flows out abundantly wherever He is truly present. A thousand thousand saints have felt that. These stories of the Bible, these stories of Jesus, are so full of His spirit that they scatter it everywhere, and the calm that fell upon the waters of Gennesaret has been renewed in the peacefulness and rest that have fallen upon multitudes of hearts that have read or listened to the narrative.

And how the same words tell the story of some point or crisis in a life. A period of tumult comes and passes. The storm of feeling is excited, and when it has fought itself out in its fury, it goes down and there is peace. A struggle for life, for bread, is pressing for a while and then the life sails out into smoother water; peace comes where there used to be suspense. There is a great calm. It is what the most eager and excited experiences are always looking forward to—not to be forever distressed and harassed, but someday to feel things growing smooth and easy, to find a calmness and repose. Some men do find it far more easily than others—indeed, some lives are placid by their very make and nature—but I think that it comes to us all, at least in vague misgivings, that there must be a calmness and repose consistent with the fullest life and the most faithful duty and the most earnest thought, which almost all men almost entirely miss. As we are whirled about in our maelstrom we are aware, or at least we picture to ourselves, that there is quiet water close beside us. Our ship grazes its placid surface and then is swept back into the tumult and the storm. Is it a reality which we see, or only a picture which our fancy draws? I should like to try to speak this morning of the calmness that God really gives to people's lives. It seems to me to be something that we are all so vaguely desiring and seeking that it cannot but be well worth while to try to understand a little of what it is and how it comes.

In the first place, then, the quality of which we speak is not a matter of original temperament. We know how different men are. We know how serenely some men bear, by the very constitution of their nature, experiences that overwhelm the sensitive brethren beside them. It is an open question which life is best. No man can say whether the passionless serenity of the calm man's life loses more in the lack of strong enjoyment than it escapes in the absence of keen suffering. But, at any rate, that is not the difference we refer to. Nor is it the mere placidity of outward circumstances—the even flow of life that slips without a ripple on from experience to experience, from year to year. That is so often merely external, so apt to be deceptive. There is the chafing and restlessness that goes on in the quietest lives, and now and then we are taken by surprise when we are able to look down through some break in the most restless and excited career and see in what perfect repose of soul the man is living underneath it all. Men try sometimes to calm the tumult of the inner life for themselves, or for one another, by merely making the outward circumstances calm and peaceful, but it does no good. It is only dressing the maniac in a quaker's clothes. They may hush and awe him for a moment with their serene composure, but after the moment's hush is over he will be as wild as ever, and tear his uncongenial dress to tatters.

Neither the calmness of temperament nor the calmness of circumstances, then, is what we mean. Both of these, of course, are gifts of God. No hand but our Father's tunes and disposes the subtle adaptations of His children's characters, or arranges with the fitnesses of harmony or contrast the scenery in the midst of which they are to pass their lives. It is God who lays His hand upon a new life just going out from His creative presence and gives it a peacefulness and calm which it brings back to Him when it returns for judgment. But it is striking to see how much more easily we think of what comes to us by education and experience than of that which comes to us in our original constitution as the gift of God. It seems to be in some higher sense appreciable as a gift when it enters in through our consciousness by His discipline than when He sows it among the seeds of our unconscious being before we are born. And so it is the calmness that comes from our own thoughtful, fruitful experience of life that we want most to consider and be thankful for.

I am assuming all along that calmness is a blessing. Are we ready to assume that absolutely? It is strange what two ideas are current, and how imperfectly we reconcile them with one another. One idea is that tumult and excitement is bad, the other is that nothing can be worse for a man than absolute calmness and serenity. We hold to both ideas by turns. We cannot settle down to either. As soon as our life begins to attain its longed-for peace we begin to fear it and to reach back after the disturbance which we tried so hard to escape from. All this seems strange, but it is not to be disregarded. It is not unaccountable. It shows us clearly enough that mere calmness, indiscriminately, will not do. It must be of the right sort. It must come from the right source. It must be lively and not deadly. It must keep and not lose the best blessings that belong to tumultuous life. It must be the calmness of perfect action and not of mere stagnation.

Indeed it is evident enough what a difference there is in different men's composure. Two men are waiting for their execution. Compare the stolidity of one with the quiet, patient faith of the other. Paul and Silas are in prison at Philippi, "And at midnight they prayed and sang praises unto God." How different from the dreary silence of despair with which perhaps some poor wretch in the next cell waited for his doom. Yet both were calm. See two men as they lie upon their death beds. One like a brute, one like a saint, they both are calmly waiting for the end. Such scenes as these show us plainly enough that there is a higher peace and a lower, a good calmness and a bad. Do they not throw abundant light upon those words of Jesus, "Peace I leave with you. My peace I give unto you. Not as the world giveth give I unto you"?

And now let us come and consider what the calmness is which, brought out by the discipline of life, may be really accepted as God's gift. The truth seems to me to be this: that the calmness to which God is always leading us consists in a perfect poise of tasks and powers. And this idea is valuable because as we follow it out it explains both the attainment of calmness and the loss of calmness which occur in every growing life, and shows how they are consistent with one another. Let us look into this. Take the lowest life, the life of the vegetable. We easily attribute to it a perfectly calm existence. Its tasks and its powers are in perfect poise. Its work is to grow, and the power of growth is present in the plant. But just as soon as life advances another stage, as soon as you come up to the brutes, little as we know of their existence, we have a misgiving that the repose is lost. The poise is not so perfect. Here are desires that the powers cannot gratify. We have entered into a world of passion and unrest. Then come to man, and you have all the higher range of tasks, each calling for its power, each making clamor and disturbance till its power comes to match it. Now see what the course is. Here is a life at low rest (as we may say). It acknowledges few responsibilities and finds in itself the powers to fulfil them all. Now let a new duty press itself upon that life, a new emotion, a new experience of any kind, before untried. The first result is a disturbance. The demands and the powers are thrown out of poise. But by and by the power comes up to meet the new task. The two are harmonized upon a higher level. There is a loftier calm attained. But still it is not the highest—

another need appears. Once more the balance is disturbed; and only when the nature equals this new demand is it restored. So it goes on. So it goes up. Each higher calm provokes a new disturbance, and only so a calm a little higher is reached. Each in its turn is the healthy condition of the growing soul. Before us all, as the consummation, far off is seen the perfect rest in God when task and power shall be eternally equal to one another; but, for the imperfect being seeking perfection, it is in this constantly alternating attainment and dislodgment, this calm and tumult following each other, that the happy and healthy life consists.

THE SUNDAY CALLED SEPTUAGESIMA

Text: Matthew 20:1-16

1. St. Augustine

How is it that he began to pay at the last? Are not all, as we read, to receive together? For we read in another place of the Gospel that He will say to those whom He shall set on the right hand, "Come, ye blessed of my Father, receive the kingdom prepared for you from the beginning of the world." If all then are to receive together, how do we understand in this place that they received first who began to work at the eleventh hour, and they last who were hired at the first hour? If I shall be able so to speak, as to reach your understanding, God be thanked. For to Him ought ye to render thanks, who distributeth to you by me; for nought of my own do I distribute. If ye ask me, for example, which of the two has received first, he who has received after one hour, or he who after twelve hours, every man would answer that he who has received after one hour has received before him who received after twelve hours. So then though they all received at the same hour, yet because some received after one hour, others after twelve hours, they who received after so short a time are said to have received first. The first righteous men, as Abel and Noah, called as it were at the first hour, will receive together with us the blessedness of the Resurrection. Other righteous men after them, Abraham, Isaac, Jacob, and all of their age, called as it were at the third hour, will receive together with us the blessedness of the Resurrection. Other righteous men, as Moses and Aaron, and whosoever with them were called as it were at the sixth hour, will receive together with us the blessedness of the Resurrection. After them the Holy Prophets, called as it were at the ninth hour, will receive together with us the same blessedness. In the end of the world all Christians, called as it were at the eleventh hour, will receive with the rest the blessedness of that Resurrection. All will receive together; but consider those first men, after how long a time do they receive it? If then those first receive after a long time, we after a short time; though we all receive together, yet we seem to have received first, because our hire will not tarry long in coming.

In that hire then shall we be all equal, and the first as the last, and the last as the first; because that denarius is life eternal, and in the life eternal all will be equal. For although through diversity of attainments the saints will shine, some more, some less; yet as to this respect, the gift of eternal life, it will be equal to all. For that will not be longer to one, and shorter to another, which is alike everlasting; that which hath no end will have no end either for thee or me. After one sort in that life will be wedded chastity, after another virgin purity; in one sort there will be the fruit of good works, in another sort the crown of martyrdom. One in one sort, and another in another; yet in respect to the living forever, this man will not live more than that, nor that than this. For alike without end will they live, though each shall live in his own brightness: and the denarius in the parable is that life eternal. Let not him then who has received after a long time murmur against him who has received after a short time. To the first, it is a payment; to the other, a free gift; yet the same thing is given alike to both.

There is also something like this in this present life, and besides that solution of the parable, by which they who were called at the first hour are understood of Abel and the righteous men of his age, and they at the third, of Abraham and the righteous men of his age, and they at the sixth, of Moses and Aaron and the righteous men of their age, and they at the eleventh, as in the end of the world, of all Christians; besides this solution of the parable, the parable may be seen to have an explanation in respect even of this present life. For they are as it were called at the first hour, who begin to be Christians fresh from their mother's womb; boys are called as it were at the third, young men at the sixth, they who are verging toward old age at the ninth hour, and they who are called as if at the eleventh hour are they who are altogether decrepit; yet all these are to receive the one and the same denarius of eternal life.

But, brethren, hearken ye and understand, lest any put off to come into the vineyard because he is sure that, come when he will, he shall receive this denarius. And sure indeed he is that the denarius is promised him; but this is no injunction to put off. For did they who were hired into the vineyard, when the householder came out to them to hire whom he might find, at the third hour for instance, and did hire them, did they say to him, "Wait, we are not going thither till the sixth hour"? or they whom he found at the sixth hour, did they say, "We are not going till the ninth"? or they whom he found at the ninth hour, did they say, "We are not going till the eleventh? For he will give to all alike; why should we fatigue ourselves more than we need?" What He was to give, and what He was to do, was in the secret of His own counsel: do thou come when thou art called. For an equal reward is promised to all; but as to this appointed hour of working, there is an important question. For if, for instance, they who are called at the sixth hour, at that age of life in which, as in the full heat of noon, is felt the glow of manhood's years, if they, called thus in manhood, were to say, "Wait, for we have heard in the Gospel that all are to receive the same reward, we will come at the eleventh hour, when we shall have grown old, and shall still receive the same. Why should we add to our labor?" it would be answered them thus, "Art not thou willing to labor now, who dost not know whether thou shalt live to old age? Thou art called at the sixth hour; come. The Householder hath it is true promised thee a denarius, if thou come at the eleventh hour, but whether thou shalt live even to the seventh, no one hath promised thee. I say not to the eleventh, but even to the seventh hour. Why then dost thou put off Him that calleth thee, certain as thou art of the reward, but uncertain of the day? Take heed then lest peradventure what He is to give thee by promise, thou take from thyself by delay." Now if this may rightly be said of infants as belonging to the first hour, if it may be rightly said of boys as belonging to the third, if it may be rightly said of men in the vigor of life, as in the full-day heat of the sixth hour; how much more rightly may it be said of the decrepit? Lo, already is it the eleventh hour, and dost thou yet stand still, and art thou yet slow to come?

It is plain then, my brethren, it is plain to all; do ye hold it fast, and be sure of it, that whensoever any one turns himself to the faith of our Lord Jesus Christ, from a useless or abandoned way of life, all that is past is forgiven him, and as though all his debts were canceled, a new account is entered into with him. All is entirely forgiven. Let no one be anxious in the thought that there remains anything which is not forgiven him. But on the other hand, let no one rest in a perverse security. For these two things are the death of souls—despair and perverse hope. For as a good and right hope saveth, so doth a perverse hope deceive. First, consider how despair deceiveth. There are men who, when they begin to reflect on the evils they have done, think they cannot be forgiven; and whilst they think they cannot be forgiven, forthwith they give up their souls to ruin, and perish through despair, saying in their thoughts, "Now there is no hope for us; for such great sins as we have committed cannot be remitted or pardoned us; why then should we not satisfy our lusts? Let us at least fill up the pleasure of the time present, seeing we have no reward in that which is to come. Let us do what we list, though it be not lawful; that we may at least have a temporal enjoyment, because we cannot attain to the receiving an eternal." In saying such things they perish through despair, either before they believe at all or when, Christians already, they have fallen by evil living into any sins and wickednesses. The Lord of the vineyard goeth forth to them, and by the Prophet Ezekiel knocketh, and calleth to them in their despair, and as they turn their backs to Him that calleth them, "In whatsoever day a man shall turn from his most wicked way, I will forget all his iniquities." If they hear and believe this voice, they are recovered from despair, and rise up again from that very deep and bottomless gulf, wherein they had been sunk.

2. Martin Luther

Some Church fathers applied this Gospel to all the preachers from the beginning to the end of the world, and taught the first hour was the time of Adam, the third that of Noah, the sixth that of Abraham, the ninth that of Moses, and the eleventh hour that of Christ and His apostles. Such talk is all right for pastime, if there is nothing else to preach. For it does not harmonize with Scripture to say that the shilling signifies eternal life, with which the first, or Adam and the holy patriarchs, were dissatisfied, and that such holy characters should murmur in the kingdom of heaven, and be rebuked by the Householder and made the last, that is, be condemned.

Therefore we will let such fables pass and abide by the simple teaching and meaning of Christ, who wishes to show by this parable how it actually is in the kingdom of heaven, or in Christendom upon the earth;

that God here directs and works wonderfully by making the first last and the last first. And all is spoken to humble those who are great that they should trust in nothing but the goodness and mercy of God. And on the other hand that those who are nothing should not despair, but trust in the goodness of God just as the others do.

Therefore we must not consider this parable in every detail, but confine ourselves to the leading thought, that which Christ designs to teach by it. We should not consider what the penny or shilling means, not what the first or the last hour signifies; but what the Householder had in mind and what He aims to teach, how He desires to have His goodness esteemed higher than all human works and merit, yea, that His mercy alone must have all the praise. As in the parable of the unrighteous steward (Luke 16:5f), the whole parable in its details is not held before our eyes, that we should also defraud our Lord; but it sets forth the wisdom of the steward in that he provided so well and wisely for himself and planned in the very best way, although at the injury of his Lord. Now whoever would investigate and preach long on that parable about the doctors, what the book of accounts, the oil, the wheat, and the measure signify, would miss the true meaning and be led by his own ideas which would never be of any benefit to anyone. For such parables are never spoken for the purpose of being interpreted in all their minutiae. For Paul compared Christ to Adam in Romans 5:18, and says that Adam was a figure of Christ; this Paul did because we inherited from Adam sin and death, and from Christ life and righteousness. But the lesson of the parable does not consist in the inheritance, but in the consequence of the inheritance. That just as sin and death cling to those who are born of Adam and descend by heredity, so do life and righteousness cling to those who are born of Christ, they are inherited. Just as one might take an unchaste woman who adorns herself to please the world and commit sin as a figure of a Christian soul that adorns itself also to please God, but not to commit sin as the woman does.

Hence the substance of the parable in today's Gospel consists not in the penny, what it is, nor in the different hours; but in earning and acquiring, or how one can earn the penny; that as here the first presumed to obtain the penny and even more by their own merit, and yet the last received the same amount because of the goodness of the householder. Thus God will show it is nothing but mercy that He gives and no one is to arrogate to himself more than another. Therefore He says, "I do thee no wrong; is not the money mine and not thine; if I had given away thy property, then thou wouldest have reason to murmur; is it not lawful for me to do what I will with mine own?"

Now in this way Christ strikes a blow first against the presumption (as He also does in today's Epistle) of those who would storm their way into heaven by their good works; as the Jews did and wished to be next to God; as hitherto our own clergy have also done. These all labor for definite wages, that is, they take the law of God in no other sense than that they should fulfil it by certain defined works for a specified reward, and they never understand it correctly, and know not that before God all is pure grace. This signifies that they hire themselves out for wages, and agree with the householder for a penny a day; consequently their lives are bitter and they lead a career that is indeed hard.

Now when the Gospel comes and makes all alike, as Paul teaches in Romans 3:23, so that they who have done great works are no more than public sinners, and must also become sinners and tolerate the saying: "All have sinned" (Romans 3:23), and that no one is justified before God by his works; then they look around and despise those who have done nothing at all, while their great worry and labor avail no more than such idleness and reckless living. Then they murmur against the householder, they imagine it is not right; they blaspheme the Gospel, and become hardened in their ways; then they lose the favor and grace of God, and are obliged to take their temporal reward and trot from him with their penny and be condemned; for they served not for the sake of mercy but for the sake of reward, and they will receive that and nothing more, the others however must confess that they have merited neither the penny nor the grace, but more is given to them than they had ever thought was promised to them. These remained in grace and besides were saved, and besides this, here in time they had enough; for all depended upon the good pleasure of the householder.

Therefore if one were to interpret it critically, the penny would have to signify temporal good, and the favor of the householder, eternal life. But the day and the heat we transfer from temporal things to the conscience, so that work-righteous persons do labor long and hard, that is, they do all with a heavy conscience and an unwilling heart, forced and coerced by the law; but the short time or last hours are the light consciences that live blessed lives, led by grace, and that willingly and without being driven by the law.

Thus they have now each a penny, that is, a temporal reward is given to both. But the last did not seek it, it was added to them because they sought first the kingdom of heaven (Matthew 6:33), and consequently they have the grace to everlasting life and are happy. The first, however, seek the temporal reward, bargain for it, and serve for it; and hence they fail to secure grace and by means of a hard life they merit perdition. For the last do not think of earning the penny, nor do they thus blunder, but they receive all. When the first saw this, by a miscalculation they thought they would receive more, and lost all. Therefore we clearly see, if we look into their hearts, that the last had no regard for their own merit, but enjoyed the goodness of the householder. The first, however, did not esteem the goodness of the householder, but looked to their own merits, and thought it was theirs by right and murmured about it.

We must now look at these two words "last" and "first," from two viewpoints. Let us see what they mean before God, then what they mean before men. Thus, those who are the first in the eyes of man, that is, those who consider themselves or let themselves be considered as the nearest to or the first before God, they are the last in His eyes and the farthest from Him. On the other hand, those who are the last in the eyes of man, those who consider themselves or let themselves be considered the farthest from God and the last before Him, they also are just the opposite, in that they are the nearest and the first before God. Now whoever desires to be secure, let him conduct himself according to the saying: "Whosoever exalteth himself, shall be humbled." For it is here written: The first before men are the last before God; the last in the eyes of men are first in the eyes of God. On the other hand, the first before God are the last before men; and those God esteems as the last are considered by men to be the first.

But since this Gospel does not speak of first and last in a common, ordinary sense, as the exalted of the world are nothing before God, like heathen who know nothing of God; but it means those who imagine they are the first or the last in the eyes of God, the words ascend very high and apply to the better classes of people; yea, they terrify the greatest of the saints. Therefore it holds up Christ before the apostles themselves. For here it happens that one who in the eyes of the world is truly poor, weak, despised, yea, who indeed suffers for God's sake, in whom there is no sign that he is anything, and yet in his heart he is so discouraged and bashful as to think he is the last, is secretly full of his own pleasure and delight, so that he thinks he is the first before God, and just because of that he is the last. On the contrary one should indeed be so discouraged and bashful as to think he is the last before God, although he at the time has money, honor, and property in the eyes of the world, he is just because of this the first.

One sees here also how the greatest saints have feared, how many also have fallen from high spiritual callings. David complains in Psalm 131:2: "Surely I have stilled and quieted my soul; like a weaned child with his mother." Likewise in another place (Psalm 36:11): "Let not the foot of pride come against me." How often he chastises the impudent and haughty (Psalm 119:21). So Paul in 2 Corinthians 12:7 says: "That I should not be exalted overmuch there was given to me a thorn in the flesh." And as we have heard in today's Epistle what honorable men have fallen. To all of whom without doubt the sad, secret ill-turn came because they became secure and thought, we are now near to God, there is no need, we know God, we have done this and that; they did not see how they made themselves the first before God. Behold, how Saul fell! How God permitted David to fall! How Peter had to fall! How some disciples of Paul fell!

Therefore it is indeed necessary to preach this Gospel in our times to those who now know the Gospel as myself and those like me, who imagine they can teach and govern the whole world, and therefore imagine they are the nearest to God and have devoured the Holy Spirit, bones and feathers. For why is it that so many sects have already gone forth, this one making a hobby of one thing in the Gospel and that one of another? No doubt, because none of them considered that the saying, "the first are last," meant and concerned them; or if applied to them, they were secure and without fear, considering themselves as the first. Therefore according to this saying, it must come to pass that they be the last, and hence rush ahead and spread shameful doctrines and blasphemies against God and His Word.

3. Phillips Brooks

First the master of the vineyard sends the men to do their work, and second he agrees with them for "a penny a day." We will look at these two ideas in relation to the great new starts or beginnings that come in every full human life.

First the idea of mission. "He sent them in his vineyard." "He," in the parable, means God in human life. See what a personality steps at once into the story and see how, when it once is there, it cannot be left out again. The whole story lives and moves and has its being in that central person, by whose sending the laborers start out on their day's work. Suppose at first that you did not see the householder. Suppose you only saw a host of workmen with their tools streaming in through an open vineyard gate. "What are they going for?" you ask. The answer must be one of two. Either it is the mere pleasure of the exercise they love, as when a company of boys go hurrying to a fruitless, profitless game of ball, for the pure pleasure of the game, or else it is the desire for something that they are to get, some profits, some reward that lies waiting for them in the vineyard. Both of these are conceivable, both are legitimate motives. And motives that correspond to both of them come in legitimately at every beginning in our lives. Any new undertaking of ours may properly be inspired by the pleasure we find in its execution and by the advantage it will bring to us when it is finished. But now put in the householder. Set him in your picture beside the vineyard gate. Make every laborer who enters in pass under his inspection, go in by his commission, and then have you not put another motive in which does not exclude the others but surrounds and comprehends them? Now you ask any laborer why he is there, and pointing back to the master at the gate, he says, "He sent me." No matter how much any laborer might love the work or want the profits, he would have no right to be there unless the householder had sent him in. Do you not see the parable? Whenever any man believes that God has given him a work to do, that belief becomes the great motive of his labor. It does not exclude the others, but it overshadows and, as it were, includes them. Still the man may find the work delightful and may expect from it a great result, but when you ask him why he does it, he rises from his happy toil and points back to where God stands beside the gate and says, "He sent me." However he might love the work, whatever advantage he might look for from it, he would have no right to be doing it if God had not sent him.

Every work ought to begin simply and with one clear simple motive. It is not pleasant to hear the beginner in any work talk too far-looking talk, anticipate the gain that lies for him far away when his work shall have been successful. Prophecies are too doubtful, and this anticipative spirit is too apt to be discouraged. Some cloud comes between the beginner and his vision of the end, and his impulse is all gone. Nor is it pleasant to hear the new worker congratulating himself that his work is pleasant, that he loves it, and trusting to that love for his energy and his persistence. There will surely come times when the love will grow dull, when the enthusiasm will flicker. What then? There must be some authority that impels as well as some attraction that invites. Not merely a bright vineyard but a majestic master there must be. All serious men have craved a master as well as a task. Some workers call their master duty. Others wiser and devouter call him "God," but all have done their best work only when they were not merely called by the thing that was to be done but sent by him for whom they were to do it. It is like the going of the arrow out of the bow. The starting arrow is only conscious of the string, not yet has it any perception of the target. You question it as it goes flying past you, and ask it why it takes that track, and its reply is not "Because the target stands this way," but "Because this way the bow-string sent me." It is only in going where the bow-string sent it that the arrow finds first the joy of the rushing air and then at last the satisfaction as it buries itself into the very center of the target.

The second beginning of which I spoke was the start of a new occupation, the deliberate entrance by a young man upon what is to be the profession of his life. With regard to that time I think that all of us who have seen many men will bear witness that it is just there that very many men grow narrow and, from being broad in sympathies, large, generous, humane, before, even in all the crudity of their boyhood, the moment of the choice of their profession seems to make them limited and special, shuts them up between narrow walls, makes them uninteresting to all the world outside their little work, and makes all the world outside their little work uninteresting to them. It is not strange. The works that men must do to live become more and more special and absorbing. Anybody who thinks about it sees that the escape must be not in the worker refusing to do one work and undertaking to do all things. It must be in his doing his one thing in a larger spirit. Where shall that larger spirit come from? The spirit of an act comes from its motive. There must be a larger motive then. And the largest of all motives is the sending of God, the commission of Him Who is the Father of us all. When the young lawyer dares to believe beyond the pleasure he finds in the practice of the law, beyond the fortune or the fame he hopes to make out of it, that God sent him there, that the fitness for it which he has found in his character and circumstances is something more than a lucky accident, is a true sign of the intention concerning him of the dear, wise God; when a young lawyer dares to believe this, two great blessings come to him out of so high a faith: first he is armed against the lower temptations of his profession, and second, he is kept in cordial sympathy with all other children of God who are trying to find and follow the same Father's intentions concerning them, though in works utterly different from his. The true salvation from the sordidness and narrowness of professional life comes only with a profound faith that God sent us to be the thing we are, to do the work we are doing.

And then with regard to the third great beginning which comes in every man's life who lives completely, the beginning of conscious religion, of the deliberate consecration to God and culture of the soul. It begins in every kind of way, suddenly with one man, gradually with another. With one man like the swift illumination of a flash of lightning, with another man like the slow brightening of the dawn; but to all men who come to their full life it surely comes by that unchangeable necessity which is in the words of Jesus, "Except a man be born again he cannot see the kingdom of God"; and no man truly lives who does not see that kingdom. But of this deeper life, the life of spiritual struggle, of prayer, of search after divine communion, the life that sacrifices the body for the soul, that hopes for heaven and overcomes the world by faith, of this life so misty and vague to many men, so much realer than all realities besides to every man who lives it, what is the motive power? Why do the best souls undertake it? The simplest answer is the truest, I believe. Because God calls them into it. Ask me why I am a Christian and I may say, "Because the Christian life is satisfactory and full of daily sweetness," or I may say, "Because in the certain distance hangs the prize of everlasting life." Both are good answers. But suppose I say, "Because God bade me be." That is a better answer. It includes both the others. The soul that makes it is sure of happiness and reward not by its own direct perception of them but because they are involved in the very nature of God, in obedience to whose authority it gives itself to Him. It makes the persistence of the Christian life depend not on the constancy of our emotions but on the unremitting sense of the divine authority. The best and noblest Christians, I am sure, have always most loved to give this simplest account of their experience. "Why are you in the vineyard?" "Because He sent me," that is all. Afterward the perception of the sweetness of the work, but first of all because He sent me. Oh my young friends to whom the soul's life with its vast hopes and mysterious joys is just opening, I beg you to set at the gate through which you enter into it the simple authority of your master. Come to your Lord because He calls you. As John and James came off the lake where they were fishing; as Matthew came out of the shop where he was gathering taxes; for only to the soul that first gives itself to Him in unquestioning obedience can Christ give himself in unhindered love.

THE SUNDAY CALLED SEXAGESIMA

Text: Luke 8:4-15

1. John Chrysostom

We have good cause to admire the disciples, how, longing as they do to learn, they know when they ought to ask. For they do it not before all: and this Matthew shows by saying, "And they came." And, as to this assertion not being conjecture, Mark hath expressed it more distinctly by saying, that "they came to him privately." This then His brethren and His mother should also have done, and not have called Him out, and made a display.

But mark their kindly affection also, how they have much regard for the others and seek their good first, and then their own. "For why," it is said, "speakest thou unto them in parables?" They did not say, "why speakest thou unto us in parables?" Yea, and on other occasions also their kindliness toward men appears in many ways; as when they say, "Send the multitude away"; and, "Knowest thou that they were offended?" What then saith Christ? "Because it is given unto you," so He speaks, "to know the mysteries of the kingdom of heaven, but to them it is not given." But this He said, not bringing in necessity, or any allotment made causelessly and at random, but implying them to be the authors of all their own evils, and wishing to represent that the thing is a gift, and a grace bestowed from above.

It by no means follows, however, because it is a gift, that therefore free will is taken away; and this is evident from what comes after. To this purpose, in order that neither the one sort may despair, nor the other grow careless, upon being told that "it is given," He signifies the beginning to be with ourselves. "For whosoever hath, to him shall be given, and he shall have more abundance; but whosoever hath not, from him shall be taken away, even that which he seemeth to have." And although the saying be full of much obscurity, yet it indicates unspeakable justice. For what He saith is like this: "When any one hath forwardness and zeal, there shall be given unto him all things on God's part also: but if he be void of these, and contribute not his own share, neither are God's gifts bestowed." For even "what he seemeth to have," so He saith, "shall be taken away from him"; God not so much taking it away, as counting him unworthy of His gifts. This we also do; when we see anyone listening carelessly, and when with much entreaty we cannot persuade him to attend, it remains for us to be silent. For if we are still to go on, his carelessness is aggravated. But him that is striving to learn, we lead on, and pour in much.

And well said He, "Even that which he seemeth to have." For he

155

hath not really even this. Then He also made what He had said more distinct, pointing out the meaning of "To him that hath, shall be given, but from him that hath not, even that which he seemeth to have, shall be taken away." "Therefore," saith He, "speak I to them in parables; because they seeing see not."

"It were meet then," one may say, "to have opened their eyes, if they see not." Nay, if the blindness were natural, it were meet to open them; but because it was a voluntary and self-chosen blindness, therefore He said not simply, "They see not," but, "seeing, they see not"; so that the blindness is of their own wickedness. For they saw even devils cast out and said, "By Beelzebub, prince of the devils, he casteth out the devils." They heard Him guiding them unto God, and evincing His great unanimity with Him, and they say, "This man is not of God." Since then the judgment they pronounced was contrary both to their sight and hearing, therefore, saith He, the very hearing do I take away from them. For they derive thence no advantage, but rather greater condemnation. For they not only disbelieved, but found fault also, and accused, and laid snares. However, He saith not this, for it is not His will to give disgust in accusing them. Therefore neither at the beginning did He so discourse to them, but with much plainness; but because they perverted themselves, thenceforth He speaks in parables.

After this, lest anyone should suppose His words to be a mere accusation, and lest men should say, "Being our enemy He is bringing these charges and calumnies against us"; He introduces the prophet also, pronouncing the same judgment as Himself. "For in them is fulfilled," saith He, "the prophecy of Esaias, which saith, 'By hearing ye shall hear, and shall not understand, and seeing ye shall see, and shall not perceive.'"

Seest thou the prophet likewise, accusing them with this same accuracy? For neither did He say, "Ye see not," but "Ye shall see and not perceive"; nor again, "Ye shall not hear," but "Ye shall hear and not understand." So that they first inflicted the loss on themselves, by stopping their ears, by closing their eyes, by making their heart fat. For they not only failed to hear, but also "heard heavily," and they did this, He saith, "Lest at any time they should be converted, and I should heal them"; describing their aggravated wickedness, and their determined defection from Him. And this He saith to draw them unto Him, and to provoke them, and to signify that if they would convert He would heal them: much as if one should say, "He would not look at me, and I thank him; for if he had vouchsafed me this, I should straightway have given in": and this He saith, to signify how He would have been reconciled. Even so then here too it is said, "Lest at any time they should convert, and I should heal them"; implying both that their conversion was possible and that upon their repentance they might be saved, and that not for His own glory, but for their salvation, He was doing all things.

For if it had not been His will that they should hear and be saved, He ought to have been silent, not to have spoken in parables; but now by this very thing He stirs them up, even by speaking under a veil. "For God willeth not the death of the sinner, but that he should turn unto Him and live."

For in proof that our sin belongs not to nature, nor to necessity and compulsion, hear what He saith to the apostles, "But blessed are your eyes, for they see, and your ears, for they hear"; not meaning this kind of sight or hearing, but that of the mind. For indeed these too were Jews, and brought up in the same circumstances; but nevertheless they took no hurt from the prophecy because they had the root of His blessings well settled in them, their principle of choice, I mean, and their judgment.

Seest thou that "unto you it is given" was not of necessity? For neither would they have been blessed, unless the well-doing had been their own. For tell me not this, that it was spoken obscurely; for they might have come and asked Him, as the disciples did: but they would not, being careless and supine. Why say I, they would not? Nay, they were doing the very opposite, not only disbelieving, not only not hearkening, but even waging war, and disposed to be very bitter against all He said: which He brings in the prophet laying to their charge, in the words, "They heard heavily."

But not such were these; wherefore He also blessed them. And in another way too He assures them again, saying, "For verily I say unto you, many prophets and righteous men have desired to see those things which ye see, and have not seen them, and to hear those things which ye hear, and have not heard them"; My coming, He means; My very miracles, My voice, My teaching. For here He prefers them not to these depraved only, but even to such as have done virtuously; yea, and He affirms them to be more blessed even than they. Why can this be? Because not only do these see what the Jews saw not, but even what those of old desired to see. For they indeed beheld by faith only: but these by sight too, and much more distinctly.

Seest thou how again He connects the old dispensation with the new, signifying that those of old not only knew the things to come, but also greatly desired them? But had they pertained to some strange and opposing God, they would never have desired them.

2. Martin Luther

The first class of disciples are those who hear the Word but neither understand nor esteem it. And these are not the mean people in the world, but the greatest, wisest, and the most saintly; in short, they are the greatest part of mankind. For Christ does not speak here of those who persecute the Word nor of those who fail to give their ear to it, but of those who hear it and are students of it, who also wish to be called true Christians and to live in Christian fellowship with Christians and are partakers of baptism and the Lord's Supper. But they are of a carnal heart, and remain so, failing to appropriate the Word of God to themselves; it goes in one ear and out the other. Just as the seed along the wayside did not fall into the earth, but remained lying on the ground in the wayside, because the road was tramped hard by the feet of man and beast and it could not take root.

Therefore Christ says the devil cometh and taketh away the Word from their heart, that they may not believe and be saved. What power of

Satan this alone reveals, that hearts, hardened through a worldly mind and life, lose the Word and let it go, so that they never understand or confess it; but instead of the Word of God Satan sends false teachers to tread it under foot by the doctrines of men. For it stands here written both that it was trodden under foot, and the birds of the heaven devoured it. The birds Christ Himself interprets as the messengers of the devil, who snatch away the Word and devour it, which is done when he turns and blinds their hearts so that they neither understand nor esteem it, as St. Paul says in 2 Timothy 4:4: "They will turn away their ears from the truth, and turn aside unto fables." By the treading under foot of men Christ means the teachings of men, that rule in our hearts, as he says in Matthew 5:13 also of the salt that has lost its savor, it is cast out and trodden under foot of men; that is, as St. Paul says in 2 Thessalonians 2:11, they must believe a lie because they have not been obedient to the truth.

Thus all heretics, fanatics, and sects belong to this number who understand the Gospel in a carnal way and explain it as they please, to suit their own ideas, all of whom hear the Gospel and yet they bear no fruit, yea, more, they are governed by Satan and are harder oppressed by human institutions than they were before they heard the Word. For it is a dreadful utterance that Christ here gives that the devil taketh away the Word from their hearts, by which he clearly proves that the devil rules mightily in their hearts, notwithstanding they are called Christians and hear the Word. Likewise it sounds terrible that they are to be trodden under foot, and must be subject unto men and to their ruinous teachings, by which under the appearance and name of the Gospel the devil takes the Word from them so that they may never believe and be saved, but must be lost forever; as the fanatical spirits of our day do in all lands. For where this Word is not, there is no salvation, and great works or holy lives avail nothing, for with this, that He says: "They shall not be saved," since they have not the Word, He shows forcibly enough, that not their works but their faith in the Word alone saves, as Paul says to the Romans: "It is the power of God unto salvation to every one that believeth" (Romans 1:16).

The second class of hearers are those who receive the Word with joy, but they do not persevere. These are also a large multitude who understand the Word correctly and lay hold of it in its purity without any spirit of sect, division, or fanaticism; they rejoice also in that they know the real truth and are able to know how they may be saved without works through faith. They also know that they are free from the bondage of the law, of their conscience, and of human teachings; but when it comes to the test that they must suffer harm, disgrace, and loss of life or property, then they fall and deny it; for they have not root enough, and are not planted deep enough in the soil. Hence they are like the growth on a rock, which springs forth fresh and green, that it is a pleasure to behold it and it awakens bright hopes. But when the sun shines hot it withers because it has no soil and moisture, and only rock is there. So these do; in times of persecution they deny or keep silence about the Word, and work, speak, and suffer all that their persecutors mention or wish, who formerly went forth and spoke, and confessed with a fresh and joyful spirit the same, while there was still peace and no heat, so that there was hope they would bear much fruit and serve the people. For these fruits are not only the works, but more the confession, preaching and spreading of the Word, so that many others may thereby be converted and the kingdom of God be developed.

The third class are those who hear and understand the Word, but still it falls on the other side of the road, among the pleasures and cares of this life, so that they also do nothing with the Word. And there is quite a large multitude of these; for although they do not start heresies, like the first, but always possess the absolutely pure Word, they are also not attacked on the left as the others with opposition and persecution; yet they fall on the right side, and it is their ruin that they enjoy peace and good days. Therefore they do not earnestly give themselves to the Word, but become indifferent and sink in the cares, riches and pleasures of this life, so that they are of no benefit to anyone. Therefore they are like the seed that fell among the thorns. Although it is not rocky but good soil; not wayside but deeply plowed soil; yet, the thorns will not let it spring up, they choke it. Thus these have all in the Word that is needed for their salvation, but they do not make any use of it, and they rot in this life in carnal pleasures. To these belong those who hear the Word but do not bring under subjugation their flesh. They know their duty but do it not, they teach but do not practice what they teach, and they are this year as they were last.

The fourth class are those who lay hold of and keep the Word in a good and honest heart, and bring forth fruit with patience, those who hear the Word and steadfastly retain it, meditate upon it, and act in harmony with it. The devil does not snatch it away, nor are they thereby led astray, moreover the heat of persecution does not rob them of it, and the thorns of pleasure and the avarice of the times do not hinder its growth; but they bear fruit by teaching others and by developing the kingdom of God, hence they also do good to their neighbor in love; and therefore Christ adds, "they bring forth fruit with patience." For these must suffer much on account of the Word, shame and disgrace from fanatics and heretics, hatred and jealousy with injury to body and property from their persecutors, not to mention what the thorns and the temptations of their own flesh do, so that it may well be called the Word of the cross; for he who would keep it must bear the cross and misfortune, and triumph.

He says, "In honest and good hearts." As a field that is without a thorn or brush, cleared and spacious, is a beautiful clean place: so a heart is also cleared and clean, broad and spacious that is without cares and avarice as to temporal needs, so that the Word of God truly finds lodgment there. But the field is good, not only when it lies there cleared and level, but when it is also rich and fruitful, possesses soil and is productive, and not like a stony and gravelly field. Just so is the heart that has good soil and with a full spirit is strong, fertile, and good to keep the Word and bring forth fruit with patience.

Here we see why it is no wonder there are so few true Christians, for all the seed does not fall into good ground, but only the fourth and small part; and that they are not to be trusted who boast they are Christians and praise the teaching of the Gospel; like Demas, a disciple of St. Paul, who forsook him at last (2 Timothy 4:10); like the disciples of Jesus, who turned their backs to him (John 6:66). For Christ Himself cries out here: "He that hath ears to hear, let him hear," as if he should say: "Oh, how few true Christians there are; one dare not believe all to be Christians who are called Christians and hear the Gospel; more is required than that."

All this is spoken for our instruction, that we may not go astray, since so many misuse the Gospel and few lay hold of it aright. True it is unpleasant to preach to those who treat the Gospel so shamefully and even oppose it. For preaching is become so universal that the Gospel is to be proclaimed to all creatures, as Christ says in Mark 16:15: "Preach the Gospel to the whole creation"; and Psalm 19:4: "Their line is gone out through all the earth, and their words to the end of the world." What business is it of mine that many do not esteem it? It must be that many are called but few are chosen. For the sake of the good ground that brings forth fruit with patience, the seed must also fall fruitless by the wayside, on the rock and among the thorns; inasmuch as' we are assured that the Word of God does not go forth without bearing some fruit, but it always finds also good ground; as Christ says here, some seed of the sower falls also into good ground, and not only by the wayside, among the thorns, and on stony ground. For wherever the Gospel goes you will find Christians. "My word shall not return unto me void" (Isaiah 55:11).

3. John Keble

HEARKEN: BEHOLD, A SOWER WENT FORTH TO SOW. The Holy Gospel here tells us of the beginning of one of our Blessed Lord's sermons. "Much people were gathered together, and were come to Him out of every city"; and when they were all in expectation, thus He began, "Hearken." You may imagine how they listened, how every eye, ear, and mind, in that great multitude was fastened on Him, wondering what He might be going to say. And can you not also imagine that when He went on and just told them, "A sower went forth to sow," they might for a moment or two be surprised, and begin to say in their hearts, What is this? What has this to do with faith and religion and the service of God? "A sower went forth to sow!" Well, that is no new thing; of course the sower goes out at the usual time of year to get the crop into the ground; and if he did not, we all know that we must do without bread; but the kingdom of God which this Jesus of Nazareth is preaching, we have always understood to be something new and strange, and we cannot imagine why He begins speaking of such an ordinary thing as sowing seed. They might say among themselves what was once said by the hearers of the prophet Ezekiel, "Wilt thou not tell us what these things are to us, that thou sayest so?"

Our Lord we know expounded it all to His disciples. But without going on now to that explanation, which you heard in the Gospel of the day, I wish you to consider only those simple words, "Behold, a sower went forth to sow." You will find a great deal more in them than you might at first think; deep knowledge, warning of heavenly truth.

In the first place, the mere act of putting the seed into the ground is a lesson from Almighty God, to put us in mind of the fall of our first parents, and our sad condition in consequence of it. Before Adam fell, as you know, the Lord God Himself planted the trees upon the fruit whereof Adam was to live; no need for Adam to sow or set them in the ground, God caused them to grow there (as men speak) of their own accord: "Every tree that was pleasant to the sight and good for food." Adam had indeed to dress and keep the garden, but it was not in the way of toil or hard work: it was rather, as we may believe, in the way of service done to Almighty God the Owner of the garden; it was pleasurable exercise, not wearisome trouble; and having so done, he had but to put forth his hand, and take of all trees but one, and freely eat. But when they had unhappily listened to the enemy—when lust had brought sin, and sin death—all this as you know was changed; the sentence went out immediately, "Cursed is the ground": and ever since the rule of this world has been, "In the sweat of thy face shalt thou eat bread." The ground, left to itself, as we all know, brings forth only thorns and thistles, nettles and all manner of weeds and rubbish. If you want good food out of it, "Wine that maketh glad the heart of man, and oil to make his face to shine, and bread which strengtheneth man's heart," there must be plowing, raking and harrowing, planting and sowing, fencing and weeding, and all the hard and anxious work of the farm and garden. And why should it be so? What reason is there in the nature of things why a piece of ground left to itself should not bear wheat and barley, vines or good fruits, as well as nettles and brambles and all manner of weeds? You never can find any reason but this one, that it so pleased God. It pleased God that the ground so left to itself without any sort of cultivation, should not ordinarily bring forth the food that is needed for man's life. And why? For a remembrance of His curse laid upon the earth for the sinner's sake. That curse is not worn out. This world indeed appears to grow on the whole, outwardly and bodily, more and more comfortable to live in, as fresh contrivances are found out, and civilization, as it is called, goes on: but still each new generation finds, as the former generation had done, that the old sentence remains, man's life must be labor and sorrow. Earth, left to itself, will not feed him.

And thus you perceive that so common a sight as a sower going out to sow his seed is, as I said, a lesson from God, to make you aware how He hates sin, and how surely the words which He has spoken against sinners will sooner or later come to pass.

But the same thing, the sight of a man sowing, is in another way a token of His great mercy. For by this parable He has taught us that this our ordinary sowing is just a type and parable of Jesus Christ the great Husbandman coming to amend this wicked and unfruitful soil—man's fallen and corrupt heart and life—whose end otherwise is to be burned. "He that soweth the good seed is the Son of Man": He soweth, that we may reap, and then so merciful and condescending is He, that He looks forward to the harvest as to a time of joy for Himself as well as for us:

"that both he that soweth and he that reapeth," the Saviour and those who are saved by Him, "may rejoice together." That is, at the last day, when He will see us again, His joy, which He took in us when He first made us His children, remaining in us, and our joy made full by our entering into His joy: entering for ever into the joy of our Lord.

That will be the harvest; but now it is the seed-time: and Christ, as you have heard from Himself, is the Sower: "He that soweth the good seed is the Son of Man." Christ is the Sower: now consider what is the seed. First, the seed is the Word of God: He tells us so Himself. The Sower went forth to sow when Jesus Christ began to go about in Galilee, preaching the Gospel of the kingdom, shewing forth the glad tidings of the kingdom of God. His Sermon on the Mount, and the rest of His holy sayings, were the good seed of the Gospel, scattered here and there, like bread cast on the waters, to be found after many days. It was sown broadcast over the whole country, sometimes among the multitude, sometimes among His disciples only. And when He was gone away from us into heaven, still the same Word continued to be sown, and He to be the Sower of it. No longer indeed in His own Person, but by His Blessed Spirit coming down upon His Apostles, He filled their bosom with good seed, "pressed down and shaken together, and running over"; and what they had freely received they were freely to give. And they did so in all peoples, nations, and languages: "Their sound went out into all lands, and their words into the ends of the world." And so He has done ever since, by the same His apostles and their successors, with whom He has promised to be always, even unto the end of the world. So He does to each one of you, my brethren, as often as you come into this Church and hear the Bible read and the meaning of it preached. At every such time it is as if God's providence spake to your inward ear and conscience, saying, "Hearken: behold, the sower is going forth to sow." Nay, and this is true also as often as any one of you, rich or poor, man or woman, opens his Bible in faith and humility and reads the holy Word which the Blessed Spirit has caused to be written for his learning, whether he read it in silence to himself, or in fatherly care to his family, or in quiet friendliness to some other who cannot perhaps read it for himself. Such moments are very serious, and by God's help may be very blessed. For then it is indeed the divine and gracious Saviour, sowing the very word of life, as He has been doing, publicly and from house to house, now for these 1,800 years: as it is written, "He hath dispersed," that is, hath sown His seed, "abroad, and given to the poor" (for "to the poor the Gospel is preached"). "His righteousness endureth for ever."

But the good seed which the Son of Man sows has yet another and a still more gracious meaning. It signifies not only the Word and doctrine, but the living souls also which hear the Word and believe the doctrine: for so we learn in another parable: "He that soweth the good seed is the Son of Man: the good seed are the children of the kingdom." So that the heavenly and divine Sower is always, night and day, sowing not only the Word but the Church upon earth. The Word He sows by preaching and teaching; the Church by holy baptism; as the Holy Ghost tells us by St.

Peter, "Ye are born again, not of corruptible seed, but of incorruptible, by the Word of God which abideth for ever": i.e., Christ Who is the Word of the Father, Himself living and enduring forever, gives you a new birth of incorruptible seed by making you members of Himself, which we all know He does in our baptism. Christians then, baptized persons, wherever they are found, in whatever way they are behaving, are or have been the crop and the harvest of Christ. As such He sowed them in His field, the world; as such He is ready to cherish, to water, to protect, to fence them in by all the means of grace in His holy Church.

You, my brethren, e.g., you who are gathered together in this congregation are as a field of standing corn which the careful and wise Husbandman has planted in His own ground, has anxiously provided for in every way: a field on which the eyes of the great Owner of all are continually fixed as on Israel of old, from the beginning of the year to the end of the year. You one with another make up the standing corn in this field, each one a separate plant, and from each one according to his growth the Husbandman looks for fruit in due time. Only He is not like an earthly husbandman, in that He knows each seed separately, what fruit it ought to have borne, and what it really does bear. His eye detects every weed, every tare, which has intruded itself among the wheat. For the present indeed He seems to take no notice, for the harvest is not yet come: but it *will* come, and that speedily: and then you will know and feel, if you would not before, that His Eye has all the while been upon you; and what if you should also feel that you have been all the while forgetting Him?

Christ then is the Sower, and His Word and His Church are the Seed. Now you know how a man who goes out to sow feels as concerning the crop which he sows. What if he sees anyone disturbing the seed on purpose? pulling up the young plants? trampling them down as they grow? turning in mischievous animals? sowing or planting weeds, to choke the good corn? How should you like this, brethren, were anyone to deal in this way with your field, or your garden, and that perhaps regularly year after year? Of course you would say as it is in the parable, "an enemy hath done this." You would count that person your enemy, and one of the most spiteful of enemies, who should so deal with the crop on which you had set your heart; on which you had spent your labor, your time, your care. Much more if the person so wronging you should prove to be one most deeply obliged to you; one whose life you had saved; one who owed to you all he has in the world. You would say, and all your neighbors would agree with you, "How would *he* like it if anyone used him so?" Well, my brethren, do as you would be done by. Behold, here is your best friend, your only Saviour, the good and holy Jesus Who bought you with His own Blood; behold, He has been here sowing His seed, the seed of eternal life, in your hearts, and in the hearts of all these your fellow Christians on every side of you. This parish, this congregation, is one of His fields. His corn is growing here; He will come bye and bye at the harvest to gather it in; and He would fain save it all. Not one grain would He have spoiled or lost; it is a thing which He has so much at heart, that He even died the death of a malefactor that He might bring it about. If then you love Him at all, if you have the least wish to please Him, must you not be very careful not to damage this crop of His? You would think it very unkind if anyone came into your garden, and rode or walked carelessly about among your choice herbs and flowers, for which you had paid a large sum: but you think very little of dealing carelessly with the souls for whom Christ died. You will utter your oaths and curses or other bad words in the hearing of young Christian children, or you will even come here and keep a sort of school for teaching the little ones to behave amiss in the very house of God. Is this doing as you would be done by? Do you think your Saviour cares less for the souls of these little ones than you do for your plants and flowers? Nay, He will not endure them to be trampled on: He is even now preparing the millstone to be tied round your neck and to drown you, not in the depth of the sea but in the bottomless pit of fire, whoever you are that take a wicked pleasure in teaching these little ones to sin.

And as His anger is toward those who damage His crop, such is His tender love and favor toward those who take an interest in it. The least little token that you really care for instruction; your coming here when you can on Festivals and other week-days; your listening at lessons and sermons; your turning away from those who would disturb you at Church; your making a rule to read in your Bible, if it be but a few verses, regularly at home; your sparing, if it be but a few pence, as often as you can for Church Missions: every one of these things, even the least little prayer and endeavor to promote the working of God's Word on your own and other men's hearts, our dear Lord will take kindly; He will not forget it: in its way it will bring you a blessing. It is said to such, ye "are laborers together with God." What an honor is that, my brethren, and at the same time what a great thing to answer for! Think of it in this way! Most of you are laboring men; you work for this master and that: but remember that after all there are but two masters. Under which are you now working? Whose wages are you now earning? Do not sleep this night, until you have tried to answer this question in your own secret heart and conscience, lest you should find yourself, waking, where those must go who die scorning God's Word.

THE SUNDAY CALLED QUINQUAGESIMA

Text: Luke 18:31-43

1. John Chrysostom

See whence He passed unto Jerusalem, and where He abode before this, with regard to which it seems to me especially worthy of inquiry, wherefore He went not away even long before this from thence unto Galilee, but through Samaria. But this we will leave to them that are fond of learning. For if anyone were disposed to search the matter out carefully, he will find that John intimates it well and hath expressed the cause.

But let us keep to the things set before us, and let us listen to these blind men, who were better than many that see. For neither having a guide, nor being able to see Him when come near to them, nevertheless they strove to come unto Him, and began to cry with a loud voice, and when rebuked for speaking, they cried the more. For such is the nature of an enduring soul, by the very things that hinder, it is borne up.

But Christ suffered them to be rebuked, that their earnestness might the more appear, and that thou mightest learn that worthily they enjoy the benefits of their cure. Therefore He doth not so much as ask, "Do ye believe?" as He doth with many; for their cry, and their coming unto Him, sufficed to make their faith manifest.

Hence learn, Oh beloved, that though we be very vile and outcast, but yet approach God with earnestness, even by ourselves we shall be able to effect whatsoever we ask. See, for instance, these men, how, having none of the apostles to plead with them but rather many to stop their mouths, they were able to pass over the hindrances and to come unto Jesus Himself. And yet the Evangelist bears witness to no confidence of life in them, but earnestness sufficed them instead of all.

These then let us also emulate. Though God defer the gift, though there be many withdrawing us, let us not desist from asking. For in this way most of all shall we win God to us. See at least even here, how not poverty, not blindness, not their being unheard, nor their being rebuked by the multitude, not anything else, impeded their exceeding earnestness. Such is the nature of a fervent and toiling soul.

What then saith Christ? "He called them, and said, What will ye that I should do unto you? They say unto Him, Lord, that our eyes may be opened." Wherefore doth He ask them? Lest anyone should think that when they wish to receive one thing, He giveth them another thing. For indeed it is usual with Him on every occasion, first to make manifest and discover to all the virtue of those He is healing, and then to apply the cure, for one reason, that He might lead on the others likewise to emulation, and for another, that He might show that they were enjoying the gift worthily. This, for instance, He did with respect to the Canaanitish woman also, this too in the case of the centurion, this again as to her that had the issue of blood, or rather that marvellous woman even anticipated the Lord's inquiry; but not so did He pass her by, but even after the cure makes her manifest. Such earnest care had He on every occasion to proclaim the good deeds of them that come to Him, and to show them to be much greater than they are, which He doth here also.

Then, when they said what they wished, He had compassion on them, and touched them. For this alone is the cause of their cure, for which also He came into the world. But nevertheless, although it be mercy and grace, it seeks for the worthy.

But that they were worthy is manifest, both from what they cried out, and from the fact that, when they had received, they did not hasten away, as many do, being ungrateful after the benefits. Nay, they were not like this, but were both persevering before the gift, and after the gift grateful, for "they followed him."

2. Martin Luther

The second part of our Gospel treats of the blind man, in which we see beautifully and clearly illustrated both the love in Christ to the blind man and the faith of the blind man in Christ. At present we will briefly consider the faith of the blind man.

First, he hears that Christ was passing by; he had also heard of Him before, that Jesus of Nazareth was a kind man, and that He helps everyone who only calls upon Him. His faith and confidence in Christ grew out of his hearing; so he did not doubt but that Christ would also help him. But such faith in his heart he would not have been able to possess had he not heard and known of Christ; for faith does not come except by hearing.

Secondly, he firmly believes and doubts not but that it was true what he heard of Christ, as the following proves. Although he does not yet see nor know Christ, and although he at once knew Him, yet he is not able to see or know whether Christ had a heart and will to help him; but he immediately believed, when he heard of Him; upon such a noise and report he founded his confidence, and therefore he did not make a mistake.

Thirdly, in harmony with his faith, he calls on Christ and prays, as St. Paul in Romans 10:13-14 wrote: "How then shall they call on him in whom they have not believed." Also, "Whoever shall call upon the name of the Lord shall be saved."

Fourthly, he also freely confesses Christ and fears no one; his need constrains him to the point that he inquires for no one else. For it is the nature of true faith to confess Christ to be the only One who can and will help, while others are ashamed and afraid to do this before the world.

Fifthly, he struggles not only with his conscience, which doubtless moves him to think he is not worthy of such favor, but he also struggles with those who threatened him and urged him to keep quiet. They wished thereby to terrify his conscience and make him bashful, so that he should see his own unworthiness, and then despair. For wherever faith begins, there begin also war and conflict.

Sixthly, the blind man stands firm, presses through all obstacles and triumphs; he would not let the whole world sever him from his confidence, and not even his own conscience to do it. Therefore he obtained the answer of his prayer and received Christ, so that Christ stood and commanded him to be brought unto Him, and He offered to do for him whatever he wished. So it goes with all who hold firmly only to the Word of God, close their eyes and ears against the devil, the world, and themselves, and act just as if they and God were the only ones in heaven and on earth.

Seventhly, he follows Christ; that is, he enters upon the road of love and of the cross where Christ is walking, does righteous works, and is of a good character and calling, refrains from going about with foolish works as work-righteous persons do.

Eighthly, he thanks and praises God, and offers a true sacrifice that is pleasing to God (Psalm 50:23): "Whoso offereth the sacrifice of thanks-giving glorifieth me; and to him that ordereth his way aright will I show the salvation of God."

Ninthly, he was the occasion that many others praised God, in that they saw what he did, for every Christian is helpful and a blessing to everybody, and besides he praises and honors God upon earth.

Finally, we see here how Christ encourages us both by His works and words. In the first place by His works, in that He sympathizes so strongly with the blind man and makes it clear how pleasing faith is to him, so that Christ is at once absorbed with interest in the man, stops and does what the blind man desires in his faith. In the second place, that Christ praises his faith in words, and says: "Thy faith hath made thee whole"; he casts the honor of the miracle from Himself and attributes it to the faith of the blind man. The summary is: To faith is vouchsafed what it asks, and it is moreover our great honor before God.

This blind man represents the spiritually blind, the state of every man born of Adam, who neither sees nor knows the kingdom of God; but it is of grace that he feels and knows his blindness and would gladly be delivered from it. They are saintly sinners who feel their faults and sigh for grace. But he sits by the wayside and begs; that is, he sits among the teachers of the law and desires help; but it is begging, with works he must appear blue and help himself. The people pass him by and let him sit; that is, the people of the law make a great noise and are heard among the teachers of good works, they go before Christ and Christ follows them. But when he heard Christ, that is, when a heart hears the Gospel of faith, it calls and cries, and has no rest until it comes to Christ. Those, however, who would silence and scold him are the teachers of works, who wish to quiet and suppress the doctrine and cry of faith; but they stir the heart the more. For the nature of the Gospel is, the more it is restrained the more progress it makes. Afterward he received his sight, all his work and life are nothing but the praise and honor of God, and he follows Christ with joy, so that the whole world wonders and is thereby made better.

3. John Calvin

Though the apostles had been previously informed what kind of death awaited our Lord, yet as they had not sufficiently profited by it, He now repeats anew what He had frequently said. He sees that the day of His death is at hand; nay more, He is already in a state of readiness to offer Himself to be sacrificed; and, on the other hand, He sees the disciples not only afraid, but overwhelmed by blind alarm. He therefore exhorts them to steadiness, that they may not immediately yield to temptation. Now there are two methods by which He confirms them; for, by foretelling what would happen, He not only fortifies them, that they may not give way when a calamity, which has arisen suddenly and contrary to expectation, takes them by surprise, but meets the offence of the cross by a proof of His Divinity, that they may not lose courage at beholding His short abasement when they are convinced that He is the Son of God and therefore will be victorious over death. The second method of confirmation is taken from His approaching resurrection.

But it will be proper to look more closely at the words. Mark states—what is omitted by the other two Evangelists—that, before our Lord explained to His disciples in private that He was going straight to the sacrifice of death, not only they, but also the rest of His followers, were sorrowful and "trembling." Now why they were seized with this fear it is not easy to say, if it was not because they had already learned that they had dangerous adversaries at "Jerusalem," and would therefore have wished that Christ should remain in some quiet retreat beyond the reach of the darts, rather than voluntarily expose Himself to such inveterate enemies. Although this fear was in many respects improper, yet the circumstance of their following Christ is a proof of no ordinary respect and obedience. It would indeed have been far better to hasten cheerfully and without regret wheresoever the Son of God chose to lead them; but commendation is due to their reverence for His person, which appears in choosing to do violence to their own feelings rather than to forsake Him.

TOOK THE TWELVE DISCIPLES APART IN THE WAY. It may appear surprising that He makes "the twelve" alone acquainted with His secret, since all have need of consolation, for all had been alike seized with fear. I consider the reason why He did not publish His death to have been that the report might not spread too widely before the time. Besides, as He did not expect that the warning would be of immediate advantage, He reckoned it enough to entrust it to a few, who were afterward to be His witnesses. For, as the seed thrown into the earth does not immediately spring up, so we know that Christ said many things to the apostles which did not immediately yield fruit. And if He had admitted all indiscriminately to this discourse, it was possible that many persons, seized with alarm, might flee and fill the ears of the public with this report; and thus the death of Christ would have lost its glory, because He would have appeared to have rashly brought it on Himself. Secretly, therefore, He addresses the apostles, and does not even select them as qualified to receive profit by it, but, as I lately hinted, that they may afterward be witnesses.

On this subject Luke is more full than the other; for he relates not only that Christ predicted the events which were near at hand, but also that He added the doctrine, that "those things which had been written by the prophets would be accomplished in the Son of man." It was an excellent remedy for overcoming temptation, to perceive in the very ignominy of the cross the marks by which the Prophets had pointed out the promised Author of salvation. There can be no doubt that our Lord pointed out also from the Prophets what kind of fruit they ought to expect from His death; for the Prophets do not only teach that Christ must suffer, but add the reason, that He may reconcile the world to God.

Lo, WE GO UP TO JERUSALEM. Hence we perceive that Christ was endued with divine fortitude for overcoming the terrors of death, for He knowingly and willingly hastens to undergo it. For why does He, without any constraint, march forward to suffer a shocking murder, but because the invincible power of the Spirit enabled Him to subdue fear and raised Him above all human feelings? By a minute detail of the circumstances, He gives a still more evident proof of His divinity. For He could not—as man—have foreseen that, after having been "condemned by the chief priests and scribes," He would be "delivered up to the Gentiles," and "spat on," and "mocked" in various ways, and "scourged," and at length dragged to the punishment of the cross. Yet it must be observed that, though our Lord was fully acquainted with the weakness of His disciples, He does not conceal from them a very grievous offence. For—as we have said on a former occasion—nothing could at that time have happened more powerfully calculated to shake the minds of the godly than to see the whole of the sacred order of the Church opposed to Christ. And yet He does not spare their weakness by deceiving them but, candidly declaring the whole matter, points out the way to overcome temptation; namely, by looking forward with certainty to His resurrection. But as it was necessary that His death should go before, He makes their triumph, in the meantime, to consist in hope.

AND THEY UNDERSTOOD NONE OF THESE THINGS. What stupidity was this, not to understand what Christ said to them in a plain and familiar manner, on a subject not too lofty or intricate, but of which they had, at their own suggestion, entertained some suspicion! But it is proper also to bear in mind—what I have formerly observed—the reason why they were held in such gross ignorance, which was that they had formed the expectation of a joyful and prosperous advancement, and therefore reckoned it to be in the highest degree absurd, that Christ should be ignominiously crucified. Hence we infer with what madness the minds of men are seized through a false imagination; and therefore we ought to be the more careful not to yield to any foolish thoughts and shut our eyes against the light.

HAVE MERCY ON ME, O LORD. I stated, a little ago, that there was at first but *one* who "cried out," but the other was induced by a similar necessity to join him. They confer on Christ no ordinary honor, when they request Him to "have mercy," and relieve them, for they must have been convinced that He had in His power the assistance or remedy which they needed. But their faith is still more clearly exhibited by their acknowledgment of Him as Messiah, to whom we know that the Jews gave this designation, "Son of David." They therefore apply to Christ, not only as some Prophet, but as that Person whom God had promised to be the only Author of salvation. The "cry" proved the ardor of the desire; for, though they knew that what they said exposed them to the hatred of many who were highly displeased with the honor done to Christ, their fear was overcome by the ardor of desire, so that they did not refrain, on this account, from raising their voice aloud.

AND THE MULTITUDE REPROVED THEM. It is surprising that the disciples of Christ, who follow Him through a sense of duty and of respect, should wish to drive wretched men from the favor of Christ and, so far as lies in them, to prevent the exercise of His power. But it frequently happens that the greater part of those who profess the name of Christ, instead of inviting us to Him, rather hinder or delay our approach. If Satan endeavored to throw obstacles, by means of pious and simple persons, in the way of "two blind men" who were induced by some sentiments of religion to follow Christ, how much more will he succeed in accomplishing it by means of hypocrites and traitors, if we be not strictly on our guard. Perseverance is therefore necessary to overcome every difficulty, and the more numerous the obstacles are which Satan throws in the way, the more powerfully ought we to be excited to earnestness in prayer, as we see that the blind men redoubled their cry.

WHAT DO YOU WISH THAT I SHOULD DO TO YOU? He gently and kindly asks what they desire; for He had determined to grant their requests. There is no reason to doubt that they prayed by a special movement of the Holy Spirit; for, as the Lord does not intend to grant to all persons deliverance from bodily diseases, so neither does He permit them simply to pray for it. A rule has been prescribed for us what we ought to ask, and in what manner, and to what extent; and we are not at liberty to depart from that rule unless the Lord, by a secret movement of the Spirit, suggests to us some special prayer, which rarely happens. Christ puts the question to them, not for their sake as individuals, but for the sake of all the people; for we know how the world swallows God's benefits without perceiving them, unless they are stimulated and aroused. Christ, therefore, by His voice, awakens the assembled crowd to observe the miracle, as He awakens them shortly afterward by a visible sign, when He opens their eyes by touching them.

AND JESUS, MOVED WITH COMPASSION. "Moved with compassion" is not the participle of the same verb which Matthew had just now employed in reference to the "blind man,"—"have mercy." They implored the mercy of Christ, that He might relieve their wretchedness; but now the Evangelist expresses that Christ was induced to cure them, not only by undeserved goodness, but because He pitied their distress. For the metaphor is taken from "the bowels," in which dwells that kindness and mutual compassion which prompts us to assist our neighbors.

THY FAITH HATH SAVED THEE. By the word faith is meant not only a confident hope of recovering sight, but a loftier conviction, which was, that this blind man had acknowledged Jesus to be the Messiah whom God had promised. Nor must we imagine that it was only some confused knowledge; for we have already seen that this confession was taken from the Law and the Prophets. For the blind man did not at random bestow on Christ the name of "Son of David," but embraced Him as that Person whose coming He had been taught by the divine predictions to expect. Now Christ attributes it to faith that "the blind man received sight"; for, though the power and grace of God sometimes extend even to unbelievers, yet no man enjoys His benefits in a right and profitable manner, unless he receives them by faith; nay, the use of the gifts of God is so far from being advantageous to unbelievers that it is even hurtful. And therefore, when Christ says, "thy faith hath saved thee," the word "saved" is not limited to an outward *cure*, but includes also the *health* and *safety* of the soul; as if Christ had said, that by *faith* the blind man obtained that God was gracious to him, and granted his wish. And if it was in regard to faith that God bestowed his favor on the blind man, it follows that he was justified by faith.

4. Charles Kingsley

This is a solemn text, a solemn Gospel; but it is not its solemnity which I wish to speak of this morning, but this— What has it to do with the Epistle, and with the Collect? The Epistle speaks of Charity; the Collect bids us pray for the Holy Spirit of Charity. What have they to do with the Gospel? Let me try to show you.

The Epistle speaks of God's eternal charity. The Gospel tells us how that eternal charity was revealed, and shown plainly in flesh and blood on earth, in the life and death of Jesus Christ our Lord.

But you may ask, How does the Epistle talk of God's charity? It bids men be charitable; but the name of God is never mentioned in it. Not so, my friends. Look again at the Epistle, and you will see one word which shows us that this charity, which St. Paul says we must have, is God's charity. For, he says, Charity never faileth; that though prophecies shall fail, tongues cease, knowledge vanish away, charity shall never fail. Now, if a thing never fail, it must be eternal. And if it be eternal, it must be in God. For, as I have reminded you before about other things, the Athanasian Creed tells us (and never was truer or wiser word written) there is but one eternal.

But if charity be not in God, there must be two eternals; God must be one eternal, and charity another eternal; which cannot be. Therefore charity must be in God, and of God, part of God's essence and being; and not only God's saints, but God himself—suffereth long, and is kind; envieth not, is not puffed up, seeketh not his own, is not easily provoked, thinketh no evil, rejoiceth not in iniquity, but in the truth; beareth all things, believeth all things, hopeth all things, endureth all things.

So St. Augustine believed, and the greatest fathers of old time. They believed, and they have taught us to believe, that before all things, above all things, beneath all things, is the divine charity, the love of God, infinite as God is infinite, everlasting as God is everlasting; the charity by which God made all worlds, all men, and all things, that they might be blest as he is blest, perfect as he is perfect, useful as he is useful; the charity which is God's essence and Holy Spirit, which might be content in itself, because it is perfectly at peace in itself, and yet *cannot* be content in itself, just because it is charity and love, and therefore must be going forth and proceeding everlastingly from the Father and the Son, upon errands of charity, love, and mercy, rewarding those whom it finds doing their work in their proper place, and seeking and saving those who are lost and out of their proper place.

But what has this to do with the Gospel? Surely, my friends, it is not difficult to see. In Jesus Christ our Lord, the eternal charity of God was fully revealed. The veil was taken off it once for all, that men might see the glory of God in the face of Jesus Christ, and know that the glory of God is charity, and the Spirit of God is love.

There was a veil over that in old times; and the veil comes over it often enough now. It was difficult in old times to believe that God was charity; it is difficult sometimes now. Sad and terrible things happen— plague and famine, earthquake and war. All these things have happened in our times. Not two months ago, in Italy, an earthquake destroyed many thousands of people; and in India, this summer, things have happened of which I dare not speak, which have turned the hearts of women to water, and the hearts of men to fire: and when such things happen, it is difficult for the moment to believe that God is love, and that He is full of eternal, boundless, untiring charity toward the creatures whom He has made, and who yet perish so terribly, suddenly, strangely.

Well, then, we must fall back on the Gospel. We must not be afraid of the terror of such awful events, but sanctify the Lord God in our hearts and say, Whatever may happen I know that God is love; I know that His glory is charity; I know that His mercy is over all His works; for I know that Jesus Christ, Who was full of perfect charity, is the express image of His Father's person, and the brightness of His Father's glory. I know (for the Gospel tells me), that He dared all things, endured all things, in the depth of His great love, for the sake of sinful men. I know that when He knew what was going to happen to Him, when He knew that He should be mocked, scourged, crucified, He deliberately, calmly faced all that shame, horror, agony, and went up willingly to Jerusalem to suffer and die there; because He was full of the Spirit of God, the spirit of charity and love. I know that He was *so* full of it that as He went up on his fatal journey, with a horrible death staring Him in the face, still, instead of thinking of Himself, He was thinking of others, and could find time to stop and heal the poor blind man by the wayside, who called "Jesus, thou Son of David, have mercy on me." And in Him and His love will I trust, when there seems nothing else left to trust on earth.

Oh, my friends, believe this with your whole heart. Whatever happens to you or to your friends, happens out of the eternal charity of God, Who cannot change, Who cannot hate, Who can be nothing but what He is and was, and ever will be—love.

And when St. Paul tells you, as he told you in the Epistle today, to have charity, to try for charity, because it is the most excellent way to please God; and the eternal virtue, which will abide forever in heaven, when all wisdom and learning, even about spiritual things, which men have had on earth shall seem to us, when we look back, such as a child's lessons to a grown man—when, I say St. Paul tells you to try after charity, he tells you to be like God himself; to be perfect even as your Father in heaven is perfect; to bear and forbear because God does so; to give and forgive because God does so; to love all because God loves all, and willeth that none should perish, but that all should come to the knowledge of the truth.

How He will fulfil that; how He fulfilled it last summer with those poor souls in India, we know not, and never shall know in this life. Let it be enough for us that known unto God are all His works from the foundation of the world, and that His charity embraces the whole universe.

ASH WEDNESDAY

Text: Matthew 6:16-21

1. St. Augustine

TAKE HEED, THEREFORE, THAT YE DO NOT YOUR RIGHTEOUSNESS BEFORE MEN, TO BE SEEN OF THEM. Take heed that ye do not live righteously with this intent, and that ye do not place your happiness in this, that men may see you. "Otherwise ye have no reward of your Father who is in heaven": not if ye should be seen by men; but if ye should live righteously with the intent of being seen by men. For (were it the former), what would become of the statement made in the beginning of this sermon, "Ye are the light of the world. A city that is set on an hill cannot be hid. Neither do men light a candle, and put it under a bushel, but on a candlestick; and it giveth light unto all that are in the house. Let your light so shine before men, that they may see your good works"? But He did not set up this as the end; for He has added, "and glorify your Father who is in heaven." But here, because he is finding fault with this, if the end of our right actions is there, that is, if we act rightly with this design, only of being seen of men; after He has said, "Take heed that ye do not your righteousness before men," He has added nothing. And hereby it is evident that He has said this, not to prevent us from acting rightly before men, but lest perchance we should act rightly before men for the purpose of being seen by them, that is, should fix our eye on this and make it the end of what we have set before us.

For the apostle also says, "If I yet pleased men, I should not be the servant of Christ"; while he says in another place, "Please all men in all things, even as I also please all men in all things." And they who do not understand this think it a contradiction; while the explanation is, that he has said he does not please men, because he was accustomed to act rightly, not with the express design of pleasing men, but of pleasing God, to the love of whom he wished to turn men's hearts by that very thing in which he was pleasing men. Therefore he was both right in saying that he did not please men, because in that very thing he aimed at pleasing God: and right in authoritatively teaching that we ought to please men, not in order that this should be sought for as the reward of our good deeds; but because the man who would not offer himself for imitation to those whom he wished to be saved could not please God; but no man possibly can imitate one who has not pleased him. As, therefore, that man would not speak absurdly who should say, "In this work of seeking a ship, it is not a ship, but my native country, that I seek": so the apostle also might fitly say, "In this work of pleasing men, it is not men, but God that I please; because

175

I do not aim at pleasing men, but have it as my object, that those whom I wish to be saved may imitate me." Just as he says of an offering that is made for the saints, "Not because I desire a gift, but I desire fruit"; that is, "In seeking your gift, I seek not it, but your fruit." For by this proof it could appear how far they had advanced Godward, when they offered that willingly which was sought from them not for the sake of his own joy over their gifts, but for the sake of the fellowship of love.

Although when He also goes on to say, "Otherwise ye have no reward of your Father who is in heaven," He points out nothing else but that we ought to be on our guard against seeking man's praise as the reward of our deeds, that is, against thinking we thereby attain to blessedness.

THEREFORE, WHEN THOU DOEST THINE ALMS, DO NOT SOUND A TRUM-PET BEFORE THEE, AS THE HYPOCRITES DO IN THE SYNAGOGUES AND IN THE STREETS, THAT THEY MAY HAVE GLORY OF MEN. Do not, says He, desire to become known in the same way as the hypocrites. Now it is manifest that hypocrites have not that in their heart also which they hold forth before the eyes of men. For hypocrites are pretenders, as it were setters forth of other characters, just as in the plays of the theater. For he who acts the part of Agamemnon in tragedy, for example, or of any other person belonging to the history or legend which is acted, is not really the person himself, but personates him, and is called a hypocrite. In like manner, in the Church, or in any phase of human life, whoever wishes to seem what he is not is a hypocrite. For he pretends, but does not show himself, to be a righteous man; because he places the whole fruit (of his acting) in the praise of men, which even pretenders may receive, while they deceive those to whom they seem good, and are praised by them. But such do not receive a reward from God the Searcher of the heart, unless it be the punishment of their deceit: from men, however, says He, "They have received their reward"; and most righteously will it be said to them, "Depart from me, ye workers of deceit; ye had my name, but ye did not my works." Hence they have received their reward, who do their alms for no other reason than that they may have glory of men; not if they have glory of men, but if they do them for the express purpose of having this glory, as has been discussed above. For the praise of men ought not to be sought by him who acts rightly, but ought to follow him who acts rightly, so that they may profit who can also imitate what they praise, not that he whom they praise may think that they are profiting him anything.

BUT WHEN THOU DOEST ALMS, LET NOT THY LEFT HAND KNOW WHAT THY RIGHT HAND DOETH. If you should understand unbelievers to be meant by the left hand, then it will seem to be no fault to wish to please believers; while nevertheless we are altogether prohibited from placing the fruit and end of our good deed in the praise of any men whatever. But as regards this point, that those who have been pleased with your good deeds should imitate you, we are to act before the eyes not only of believers, but also of unbelievers, so that by our good works, which are to be praised, they may honor God and may come to salvation. But if you should be of opinion that the left hand means an enemy, so that your enemy is not to know when you do alms, why did the Lord Himself, when His enemies the Jews were standing round, mercifully heal men? Why did the

Apostle Peter, by healing the lame man whom he pitied at the gate Beautiful, bring also the wrath of the enemy upon himself, and upon the other disciples of Christ? Then, further, if it is necessary that the enemy should not know when we do our alms, how shall we do with the enemy himself so as to fulfil that precept, "If thine enemy be hungry, give him bread to eat; and if he be thirsty, give him water to drink"?

A third opinion is wont to be held by carnal people, so absurd and ridiculous, that I would not mention it had I not found that not a few are entangled in that error, who say that by the expression *left hand* a wife is meant; so that, inasmuch in family affairs women are wont to be more tenacious of money, it is to be kept hid from them when their husbands compassionately spend anything upon the needy, for fear of domestic quarrels. As if, forsooth, men alone were Christians, and this precept were not addressed to women also! From what left hand, then, is a woman enjoined to conceal her deed of mercy? Is a husband also the left hand of his wife? A statement most absurd. Or if anyone thinks that they are left hands to each other; if any part of the family property be expended by the one party in such a way as to be contrary to the will of the other party, such a marriage will not be a Christian one; but whichever of them should choose to do alms according to the command of God, whomsoever he should find opposed, would inevitably be an enemy to the command of God, and therefore reckoned among unbelievers—the command with respect to such parties being, that a believing husband should win his wife, and a believing wife her husband, by their good conversation and conduct; and therefore they ought not to conceal their good works from each other, by which they are to be mutually attracted, so that the one may be able to attract the other to communion in the Christian faith. Nor are thefts to be perpetrated in order that God may be rendered propitious. But if anything is to be concealed as long as the infirmity of the other party is unable to bear with equanimity what nevertheless is not done unjustly and unlawfully; yet, that the left hand is not meant in such a sense on the present occasion, readily appears from a consideration of the whole section, whereby it will at the same time be discovered what He calls the left hand.

TAKE HEED THAT YE DO NOT YOUR RIGHTEOUSNESS BEFORE MEN, TO BE SEEN OF THEM; OTHERWISE YE HAVE NO REWARD OF YOUR FATHER WHICH IS IN HEAVEN. Here He has mentioned righteousness generally, then He follows it up in detail. For a deed that is done in the way of alms is a certain part of righteousness, and therefore He connects the two by saying, "Therefore, when thou doest thine alms, do not sound a trumpet before thee, as the hypocrites do in the synagogues and in the streets, that they may have glory of men." In this there is a reference to what He says before, "Take heed that ye do not your righteousness before men, to be seen of them." But what follows, "Verily I say unto you, They have received their reward," refers to that other statement which He has made above, "Otherwise ye have no reward of your Father which is in heaven." Then follows, "But when thou doest alms." When He says, "But thou," what else does He mean but "Not in the same manner as they"? What, then, does He bid me do? "But when thou doest alms," says He, "let not thy left hand know what thy right hand doeth." What, therefore, is blamed in them, this thou art forbidden to do. But this is what is blamed in them, that they act in such a way as to seek the praises of men. And therefore the left hand seems to have no more suitable meaning than just this delight in praise. But the right hand means the intention of fulfilling the divine commands. When, therefore, with the consciousness of him who does alms is mixed up the desire of man's praise, the left hand becomes conscious of the work of the right hand: "Let not, therefore, thy left hand know what thy right hand doeth"; that is, let not there be mixed up in thy consciousness the desire of man's praise, when in doing alms thou art striving to fulfill a divine command.

THAT THY ALMS MAY BE IN SECRET. What else is meant by "in secret," but just in a good conscience, which cannot be shown to human eyes nor revealed by words, since, indeed, the mass of men tell many lies? And therefore, if the right hand acts inwardly in secret, all outward things, which are visible and temporal, belong to the left hand. Let thine alms, therefore, be in thine own consciousness, where many do alms by their good intention, even if they have no money or anything else which is to be bestowed on one who is needy. But many give alms outwardly, and not inwardly, who either from ambition, or for the sake of some temporal object, wish to appear merciful, in whom the left hand only is to be reckoned as working. Others again hold, as it were, a middle place between the two; so that, with a design which is directed Godward, they do their alms, and yet there insinuates itself into this excellent wish also some desire after praise, or after a perishable and temporal object of some sort or other. But our Lord much more strongly prohibits the left hand alone being at work in us, when He even forbids its being mixed up with the works of the right hand: that is to say, that we are not only to beware of doing alms from the desire of temporal objects alone, but that in this work we are not even to have regard to God in such a way as that there should be mingled up or united therewith the grasping after outward advantages. For the question under discussion is the cleansing of the heart, which, unless it be single, will not be clean. But how will it be single, if it serves two masters and does not purge its vision by the striving after eternal things alone, but clouds it by the love of mortal and perishable things as well? "Let thine alms," therefore, "be in secret; and thy Father, who seeth in secret, shall reward thee." Altogether most righteously and most truly. For if you expect a reward from Him who is the only Searcher of the conscience, let conscience itself suffice thee for meriting a reward. Many Latin copies have it thus, "And thy Father who seeth in secret shall reward thee openly"; but because we have not found the word "openly" in the Greek copies, which are earlier, we have not thought that anything was to be said about it.

2. John Calvin

Christ again returns to the former doctrine: for, having begun to rebuke vain ostentation in alms and prayer, He laid down, before proceeding further, the rule for praying in a right manner. The same injunction is now given to his disciples about "fasting," which he had formerly given about "prayers" and "alms," not to be too solicitous to obtain the applause of spectators, but to have God as the witness of their actions. When he bids them "anoint your head and wash your face," his language is hyperbolical: for Christ does not withdraw us from one kind of hypocrisy, to lead us into another. He does not enjoin us to counterfeit splendor or exhort us to temperance in food in such a manner as to encourage the luxuries of ointments and of dress, but merely exhorts us to preserve moderation, without anything new or affected—in short, that the fastings in which we engage should make no change in our accustomed way of living.

THY FATHER WILL REWARD THEE. When He promises a reward from God to "fastings," this mode of expression, as we said a little before with respect to prayer, is not strictly accurate. There is a wide difference, indeed, between prayer and fastings. Prayer holds the first rank among the duties of piety: but fasting is a doubtful operation, and does not, like alms, belong to the class of those actions which God requires and approves. It is pleasing to God, only so far as it is directed to another object: and that is, to train us to abstinence, to subdue the lust of the flesh, to excite us to earnestness in prayer, and to testify our repentance when we are affected by the view of the tribunal of God. The meaning of Christ's words is: "God will one day show that He was pleased with those good works, which appeared to be lost, because they were concealed from the eyes of men."

LAY NOT UP. This deadly plague reigns everywhere throughout the world. Men are grown mad with an insatiable desire of gain. Christ charges them with folly in collecting wealth with great care and then giving up their happiness to "moths" and to "rust," or exposing it as a prey to thieves. What is more unreasonable than to place their property where it may perish of itself or be carried off by men? Covetous men, indeed, take no thought of this. They lock up their riches in well-secured chests, but cannot prevent them from being exposed to "thieves" or to "moths." They are blind and destitute of sound judgment, who give themselves so much toil and uneasiness in amassing wealth which is liable to putrefaction, or robbery, or a thousand other accidents: particularly, when God allows us a place "in heaven for laying up a treasure," and kindly invites us to enjoy riches which never perish.

BUT LAY UP FOR YOURSELVES TREASURES IN HEAVEN. They are said to do so, who, instead of entangling themselves in the snares of this world, make it their care and their business to meditate on the heavenly life. In Luke's narrative no mention is made of the contrast between "laying up treasures on the earth" and "laying up treasures in heaven"; and he refers to a different occasion for the command of Christ "to prepare bags, which do not grow old": for he had previously said, "Sell what you possess, and give alms." It is a harsh and unpleasant thing for men to strip themselves of their own wealth; and, with the view of alleviating their uneasiness, he holds out a large and magnificent hope of remuneration. Those who assist their poor brethren "on the earth lay up for themselves treasures in heaven," according to the saying of Solomon, "He that hath pity upon the poor lendeth to the Lord, and that which he hath given will he pay him again" (Proverbs 19:17). The command to "sell possessions" must not be literally interpreted, as if a Christian were not at liberty to retain anything for himself. He only intended to show that we must not be satisfied with bestowing on the poor what we can easily spare, but that we must not refuse to part with our estates if their revenue does not supply the wants of the poor. His meaning is, "Let your liberality go so far as to lessen your patrimony, and dispose of your lands."

WHERE YOUR TREASURE SHALL BE. By this statement Christ proves that they are unhappy men who have their treasures laid up on the earth: because their happiness is uncertain and of short duration. Covetous men cannot be prevented from breathing in their hearts a wish for heaven: but Christ lays down an opposite principle, that wherever men imagine the greatest happiness to be, there they are surrounded and confined. Hence it follows that they who desire to be happy in the world renounce heaven. We know how carefully the philosophers conducted their inquiries respecting the supreme good. It was the chief point on which they bestowed their labor, and justly: for it is the principle on which the regulation of our life entirely depends, and the object to which all our senses are directed. If honor is reckoned the supreme good, the minds of men must be wholly occupied with ambition: if money, covetousness will immediately predominate: if pleasure, it will be impossible to prevent men from sinking into brutal indulgence. We have all a natural desire to pursue happiness; and the consequence is that false imaginations carry us away in every direction. But if we were honestly and firmly convinced that our happiness is in heaven, it would be easy for us to trample upon the world, to despise earthly blessings (by the deceitful attractions of which the greater part of men are fascinated), and to rise toward heaven. For this reason Paul, with the view of exciting believers to look upwards, and of exhorting them to meditate on the heavenly life (Colossians 3:1), presents to them Christ, in whom alone they ought to seek perfect happiness; thus declaring that to allow their souls to grovel on the earth would be inconsistent and unworthy of those whose "treasure is in heaven."

3. John Wesley

The most plausible of these, I come now to consider. And first, it has been frequently said, "Let a Christian fast from sin and not from food; this is what God requires at his hands." So He does; but He requires the other also. Therefore this ought to be done and that not left undone.

View your argument in its full dimensions; and you will easily judge of the strength of it.

"If a Christian ought to abstain from sin, then he ought not to abstain from food:

"But a Christian ought to abstain from sin:

"Therefore he ought not to abstain from food."

That a Christian ought to abstain from sin, is most true; but how does it follow from hence that he ought not to abstain from food? Yea, let him do both the one and the other. Let him, by the grace of God, always abstain from sin; and let him often abstain from food, for such reasons and ends as experience and Scripture plainly show to be answered thereby.

"But is it not better" (as it has, secondly, been objected) "to abstain from pride and vanity, from foolish and hurtful desires, from peevishness and anger, and discontent, than from food?" Without question it is. But here again we have need to remind you of our Lord's words: "These things ought ye to have done, and not to leave the other undone." And, indeed, the latter is only in order to the former; it is a means to that great end. We abstain from food with this view, that, by the grace of God conveyed into our souls through this outward means, in conjunction with all the other channels of His grace which He hath appointed, we may be enabled to abstain from every passion and temper which is not pleasing in His sight. We refrain from the one that, being endued with power from on high, we may be able to refrain from the other. So that your argument proves just the contrary to what you designed. It proves that we ought to fast. For if we ought to abstain from evil tempers, and desires, then we ought thus to abstain from food; since these little instances of self-denial are the ways God hath chosen, wherein to bestow that great salvation.

"But we do not find it so in fact" (this is a third objection): "we have fasted much and often; but what did it avail? We were not a whit better; we found no blessing therein. Nay, we have found it a hindrance rather than a help. Instead of preventing anger, for instance, or fretfulness, it has been a means of increasing them to such a height that we could neither bear others nor ourselves." This may very possibly be the case. It is possible, either to fast or pray in such a manner as to make you much worse than before; more unhappy, and more unholy. Yet the fault does not lie in the means itself, but in the manner of using it. Use it still, but use it in a different manner. Do what God commands, as He commands it; and then, doubtless, His promise shall not fail: His blessing shall be withheld no longer; but, when thou fastest in secret, "He that seeth in secret shall reward thee openly."

"But is it not mere superstition" (so it has been, fourthly, objected) "to imagine that God regards such little things as these?" If you say it is, you condemn all the generations of God's children. But will you say these were all weak, superstitious men? Can you be so hardy as to affirm this, both of Moses and Joshua, of Samuel and David, of Jehoshaphat, Ezra, Nehemiah, and all the prophets? Yea, of a greater than all, the Son of God Himself? It is certain, both our Master, and all these His servants, did imagine that fasting is not a little thing, and that He who is higher than the highest doth regard it. Of the same judgment, it is plain, were all His apostles, after they were "filled with the Holy Ghost, and with wisdom." When they had the "unction of the Holy One, teaching them all things," they still approved themselves the ministers of God "by fastings" as well as "by the armour of righteousness on the right hand and on the left." After "the bridegroom was taken from them, then did they fast in those days." Nor would they attempt anything (as we have seen above) wherein the glory of God was nearly concerned, such as the sending forth laborers into the harvest, without solemn fasting as well as prayer.

"But if fasting be indeed of so great importance, and attended with such a blessing, is it not best," say some, fifthly, "to fast always? Not to do it now and then, but to keep a continual fast? To use as much abstinence, at all times, as bodily strength will bear?" Let none be discouraged from doing this. By all means use as little and plain food, exercise as much self-denial herein at all times, as your bodily strength will bear. And this may conduce, by the blessing of God, to several of the great ends above mentioned. It may be a considerable help, not only to chastity, but also to heavenly mindedness; to the weaning your affections from things below, and setting them on things above. But this is not fasting, scriptural fasting; it is never termed so in all the Bible. It, in some measure, answers some of the ends thereof; but still it is another thing. Practise it by all means; but not so as thereby to set aside a command of God, and an instituted means of averting His judgments, and obtaining the blessings of His children.

Use continually then as much abstinence as you please; which, taken thus, is no other than Christian temperance; but this need not at all interfere with your observing solemn times of fasting and prayer. For instance, your habitual abstinence or temperance would not prevent your fasting in secret, if you were suddenly overwhelmed with huge sorrow and remorse, and with horrible fear and dismay. Such a situation of mind would almost constrain you to fast; you would loathe your daily food; you would scarce endure even to take such supplies as were needful for the body, till God "lifted you up out of the horrible pit, and set your feet upon a rock, and ordered your goings." The same would be the case if you were in agony of desire, vehemently wrestling with God for His blessing. You would need none to instruct you not to eat bread till you had obtained the request of your lips.

Again, had you been at Nineveh when it was proclaimed throughout the city, "Let neither man nor beast, herd nor flock, taste any thing; let them not feed or drink water, but let them cry mightily unto God"—would your continual fast have been any reason for not bearing part in that general humiliation? Doubtless it would not. You would have been as much concerned as any other not to taste food on that day.

No more would abstinence, or the observing of a continual fast, have excused any of the children of Israel from fasting on the tenth day of the seventh month, the great annual day of atonement. There was no exception for these in that solemn decree, "Whatsoever soul it shall be, that shall not be afflicted (shall not fast) in that day, he shall be cut off from among his people."

Lastly, had you been with the brethren in Antioch, at the time when they fasted and prayed, before the sending forth of Barnabas and Saul, can you possibly imagine that your temperance or abstinence would have been a sufficient cause for not joining therein? Without doubt, if you had not, you would soon have been cut off from the Christian community. You would have deservedly been cast out from among them, as bringing confusion into the church of God.

I am, in the last place, to show in what manner we are to fast, that it may be an acceptable service unto the Lord. And, first, let it be done unto the Lord, with our eye singly fixed on Him. Let our intention herein be this, and this alone, to glorify our Father which is in heaven; to express our sorrow and shame for our manifold transgressions of His holy law; to wait for an increase of purifying grace, drawing our affections to things above; to add seriousness and earnestness to our prayers; to avert the wrath of God, and to obtain all the great and precious promises, which He hath made to us in Jesus Christ.

Let us beware of mocking God, or turning our fast as well as our prayers into an abomination unto the Lord by the mixture of any temporal view, particularly by seeking the praise of men. Against this our blessed Lord more peculiarly guards us in the words of the text. "Moreover, when ye fast, be ye not as the hypocrites"—such were too many who were called the people of God; "of a sad countenance"—sour, affectedly sad, putting their looks into a peculiar form. "For they disfigure their faces," not only by unnatural distortions, but also by covering them with dust and ashes; "that they may appear unto men to fast," their chief, if not only, design. "Verily I say unto you, They have their reward," even the admiration and praise of men. "But thou, when thou fastest, anoint thy head, and wash thy face"—do as thou art accustomed to do at other times; "that thou appear not unto men to fast"—let this be no part of thy intention; if they know it without any desire of thine, it matters not, thou art neither the better nor the worse—"but unto thy Father which is in secret and thy Father, which seeth in secret, shall reward thee openly."

But if we desire this reward, let us beware, secondly, of fancying we *merit* anything of God by our fasting. We cannot be too often warned of this; inasmuch as a desire to "establish our own righteousness," to procure salvation of debt and not of grace, is so deeply rooted in all our hearts. Fasting is only a way which God hath ordained wherein we wait for His unmerited mercy; and wherein, without any desert of ours, He hath promised freely to give us His blessing.

Not that we are to imagine that performing the bare outward act will receive any blessing from God. "Is it such a fast that I have chosen, saith the Lord; a day for a man to afflict his soul: Is it to bow down his head as a bulrush, and to spread sackcloth and ashes under him?" Are these outward acts, however strictly performed, all that is meant by a man's "afflicting his soul"?—"Wilt thou call this a fast, and an acceptable day to the Lord?" No surely: if it be a mere external service, it is all but lost labor. Such a performance may possibly afflict the body; but as to the soul, it profiteth nothing.

Yea, the body may sometimes be afflicted too much, so as to be unfit for the works of our calling. This also we are diligently to guard against; for we ought to preserve our health as a good gift of God. Therefore care is to be taken, whenever we fast, to proportion the fast to our strength. For we may not offer God murder for sacrifice, or destroy our bodies to help our souls.

But at these solemn seasons we may, even in great weakness of body, avoid that other extreme for which God condemns those who of old expostulated with Him for not accepting their fasts. "Wherefore have we fasted, say they, and thou seest not?—Behold, in the day of your fast you find pleasure, saith the Lord." If we cannot wholly abstain from food, we may, at least, abstain from pleasant food; and then we shall not seek His face in vain.

But let us take care to afflict our souls, as well as our bodies. Let every season, either of public or private fasting, be a season of exercising all those holy affections that are implied in a broken and contrite heart. Let it be a season of devout mourning, of godly sorrow for sin; such a sorrow as that of the Corinthians, concerning which the apostle saith, "I rejoice, not that ye were made sorry, but that ye sorrowed to repentance. For ye were made sorry after a godly manner, that ye might receive damage by us in nothing. For godly sorrow"—the sorrow which is according to God, which is a precious gift of His Spirit, lifting the soul to God from whom it flows—"worketh repentance to salvation, not to be repented of." Yea, and let our sorrowing after a godly sort work in us the same inward and outward *repentance*; the same entire change of heart, renewed after the image of God, in righteousness and true holiness; and the same change of life, till we are holy as He is holy, in all manner of conversation. Let it work in us the same *carefulness* to be found in Him, without spot and blameless; the same *clearing of ourselves*, by our lives rather than words, by our abstaining from all appearance of evil; the same *indignation*, vehement abhorrence of every sin; the same *fear* of our own deceitful hearts; the same *desire* to be in all things conformed to the holy and acceptable will of God; the same *zeal* for whatever may be a means of His glory, and of our growth in the knowledge of our Lord Jesus Christ; and the same *revenge* against Satan and all his works, against all filthiness of flesh and spirit (2 Corinthians 7:9ff).

And with fasting let us always join fervent prayer, pouring out our whole souls before God, confessing our sins with all their aggravations, humbling ourselves under His mighty hand, laying open before Him all our wants, all our guiltiness and helplessness. This is a season for enlarging our prayers, both in behalf of ourselves and of our brethren. Let us now bewail the sins of our people; and cry aloud for the city of our God, that the Lord may build up Zion, and cause His face to shine on her desolations. Thus, we may observe, the men of God in ancient times always joined prayer and fasting together; thus the apostles, in all the instances cited above; and thus our Lord joins them in the discourse before us.

It remains only, in order to our observing such a fast as is acceptable to the Lord, that we add alms thereto; works of mercy, after our power, both to the bodies and souls of men: "With such sacrifices (also) God is well pleased." Thus the angel declares to Cornelius, fasting and praying in his house, "Thy prayers and thine alms are come up for a memorial before God" (Acts 10:4). And this God Himself expressly and largely declares: "Is not this the fast that I have chosen? To loose the bands of wickedness, to undo the heavy burdens, and to let the oppressed go free, and that ye break every yoke? Is it not to deal thy bread to the hungry, and that thou bring the poor that are cast out to thy house? When thou seest the naked, that thou cover him; and that thou hide not thyself from thine own flesh? Then shall thy light break forth as the morning, and thine health shall spring forth speedily; and thy righteousness shall go before thee; the glory of the Lord shall be thy reward. Then shalt thou call, and the Lord shall answer: thou shalt cry, and he shall say, Here I am—If (when thou fastest) thou draw out thy soul to the hungry, and satisfy the afflicted soul; then shall thy light rise in obscurity, and thy darkness be as the noon day. And the Lord shall guide thee continually, and satisfy thy soul in drought, and make fat thy bones: and thou shalt be like a watered garden, and like a spring of water, whose waters fail not" (Isaiah 58:6ff).

THE FIRST SUNDAY IN LENT

Text: Matthew 4:1-11

1. Leo the Great

THE BENEFITS OF ABSTINENCE SHOWN BY THE EXAMPLE OF THE HEBREWS. In former days, when the people of the Hebrews and all the tribes of Israel were oppressed for their scandalous sins by the grievous tyranny of the Philistines, in order that they might be able to overcome their enemies, as the sacred story declares, they restored their powers of mind and body by the injunction of a fast. For they understood that they had deserved that hard and wretched subjection for their neglect of God's commands, and for their evil ways, and that it was in vain for them to strive with arms unless they had first withstood their sin. Therefore abstaining from food and drink, they applied the discipline of strict correction to themselves, and in order to conquer their foes, first conquered the allurements of the palate in themselves. And thus it came about that their fierce enemies and cruel taskmasters yielded to them when fasting, whom they had held in subjection when full. And so we too, dearly beloved, who are set in the midst of many oppositions and conflicts, may be cured by a little carefulness if only we will use the same means. For our case is almost the same as theirs, seeing that, as they were attacked by foes in the flesh, so are we chiefly by spiritual enemies. And if we can conquer them by God's grace enabling us to correct our ways, the strength of our bodily enemies also will give way before us, and by our self-amendment we shall weaken those who are rendered formidable to us, not by their own merits but by our shortcomings.

USE LENT TO VANQUISH THE ENEMY, AND BE THUS PREPARING FOR EASTERTIDE. Accordingly, dearly beloved, that we may be able to overcome all our enemies, let us seek Divine aid by the observance of the heavenly bidding, knowing that we cannot otherwise prevail against our adversaries unless we prevail against our own selves. For we have many encounters with our own selves: the flesh desires one thing against the spirit, and the spirit another thing against the flesh. And in this disagreement, if the desires of the body be stronger, the mind will disgracefully lose its proper dignity, and it will be most disastrous for that to serve which ought to have ruled. But if the mind, being subject to its Ruler, and delighting in gifts from above, shall have trampled under foot the allurements of earthly pleasure, and shall not have allowed sin to reign in its mortal body, reason will maintain a well-ordered supremacy, and its strongholds no strategy of spiritual wickedness will cast down, because man has then only true peace and true freedom when the flesh is ruled by the judgment of the mind, and the mind is directed by the will of God. And although this state of preparedness, dearly beloved, should always be maintained that our ever-watchful foes may be overcome by unceasing diligence, yet now it must be the more anxiously sought for and the more zealously cultivated when the designs of our subtle foes themselves are conducted with keener craft than ever. For knowing that the most hallowed days of Lent are now at hand, in the keeping of which all past slothfulnesses are chastised, all negligences atoned for, they direct all the force of their spite on this one thing, that they who intend to celebrate the Lord's holy Passover may be found unclean in some matter, and that cause of offense may arise where propitiation ought to have been obtained.

FIGHTS ARE NECESSARY TO PROVE OUR FAITH. As we approach, then, dearly beloved, the beginning of Lent, which is a time for the more careful serving of the Lord because we are, as it were, entering on a kind of contest in good works, let us prepare our souls for fighting with temptations, and understand that the more zealous we are for our salvation, the more determined must be the assaults of our opponents. But "stronger is He that is in us than He that is against us," and through Him are we powerful in whose strength we rely: because it was for this that the Lord allowed Himself to be tempted by the tempter, that we might be taught by His example as well as fortified by His aid. For He conquered the adversary, as ye have heard, by quotations from the Law, not by actual strength, that by this very thing He might do greater honor to man and inflict a greater punishment on the adversary by conquering the enemy of the human race not now as God but as Man. He fought then, therefore, that we too might fight thereafter; He conquered that we too might likewise conquer. For there are no works of power, dearly beloved, without the trials of temptations, there is no faith without proof, no contest without a foe, no victory without conflict. This life of ours is in the midst of snares, in the midst of battles; if we do not wish to be deceived, we must watch: if we want to overcome, we must fight. And therefore the most wise Solomon says, "My son, in approaching the service of God prepare thy soul for temptation." For he being a man full of the wisdom of God, and knowing that the pursuit of religion involves laborious struggles, foreseeing too the danger of the fight, forewarned the intending combatant, lest haply, if the tempter came upon him in his ignorance, he might find him unready and wound him unawares.

THE CHRISTIAN'S ARMOR IS BOTH FOR DEFENSE AND FOR ATTACK. So, dearly beloved, let us who instructed in divine learning come wittingly to the present contest and strife, hear the Apostle when he says, "for our struggle is not against flesh and blood, but against principalities and powers, against the rulers of this dark world, against spiritual wickedness in heavenly things," and let us not forget that these our enemies feel it is against them that all is done which we strive to do for our salvation, and that by the very fact of our seeking after some good thing we are challenging our foes. For this is an old-standing quarrel between us and them fostered by the devil's ill-will, so that they are tortured by our being justified, because they have fallen from those good things to which we, God helping us, are advancing. If, therefore, we are raised, they are prostrated: if we are strengthened, they are weakened. Our cures are their blows, because they are wounded by our wounds' cure. "Stand, therefore," dearly beloved, as the Apostle says, "having the loins of your mind girt in truth, and your feet shod in the preparation of the gospel of peace, in all things taking the shield of faith in which ye may be able to extinguish all the fiery darts of the evil one, and put on the helmet of salvation and the sword of the Spirit, which is the Word of God." See, dearly beloved, with what mighty weapons, with what impregnable defenses, we are armed by our Leader, who is famous for His many triumphs, the unconquered Master of the Christian warfare. He has girt our loins with the belt of chastity, He has shod our feet with the bonds of peace: because the unbelted soldier is quickly vanquished by the suggester of immodesty, and he that is unshod is easily bitten by the serpent. He has given the shield of faith for the protection of our whole body; on our head has He set the helmet of salvation; our right hand has He furnished with a sword, that is with the word of Truth: that the spiritual warrior may not only be safe from wounds, but also may have strength to wound his assailant.

ABSTINENCE NOT ONLY FROM FOOD BUT FROM OTHER EVIL DESIRES, ESPECIALLY FROM WRATH, IS REQUIRED IN LENT. Relying, therefore, dearly beloved, on these arms, let us enter actively and fearlessly on the contest set before us: so that in this fasting struggle we may not rest satisfied with only this end, that we should think abstinence from food alone desirable. For it is not enough that the substance of our flesh should be reduced, if the strength of the soul be not also developed. When the outer man is somewhat subdued, let the inner man be somewhat refreshed; and when bodily excess is denied to our flesh, let our mind be invigorated by spiritual delights. Let every Christian scrutinize himself, and search severely into his inmost heart: let him see that no discord cling there, no wrong desire be harbored. Let chasteness drive incontinence far away; let the light of truth dispel the shades of deception; let the swellings of pride subside; let wrath yield to reason; let the darts of ill-treatment be shattered, and the chidings of the tongue be bridled; let thoughts of revenge fall through, and injuries be given over to oblivion. In fine, let "every plant which the heavenly Father hath not planted be removed by the roots." For then only are the seeds of virtue well nourished in us, when every foreign germ is uprooted from the field of wheat. If anyone, therefore, has been fired by the desire for vengeance against another, so that he has given him up to prison or bound him with chains, let him make haste to forgive not only the innocent but also one who seems worthy of punishment, that he may with confidence make use of the clause in the Lord's Prayer and say, "Forgive us our debts, as we also forgive our debtors." Which petition the Lord marks with peculiar emphasis, as if the efficacy of the whole rested on this condition, by saying, "For if ye forgive men their sins, your Father which is in heaven also will forgive you: but if ye forgive not men, neither will your Father forgive you your sins."

THE RIGHT USE OF LENT WILL LEAD TO A HAPPY PARTICIPATION IN EASTER. Accordingly, dearly beloved, being mindful of our weakness, because we easily fall into all kinds of faults, let us by no means neglect this special remedy and most effectual healing of our wounds. Let us remit, that we may have remission; let us grant the pardon which we crave; let us not be eager to be revenged when we pray to be forgiven. Let us not pass over the groans of the poor with deaf ear, but with prompt kindness bestow our mercy on the needy, that we may deserve to find mercy in the judgment. And he that, aided by God's grace, shall strain every nerve after this perfection, will keep this holy fast faithfully; free from the leaven of the old wickedness, in the unleavened bread of sincerity and truth, he will reach the blessed Passover, and by newness of life will worthily rejoice in the mystery of man's reformation through Christ our Lord, Who with the Father and the Holy Spirit lives and reigns for ever and ever. Amen.

2. Martin Luther

But as to how temptation takes place, and how it is overcome, is all very beautifully pictured to us here in Christ. First, that He is led up into the wilderness, that is, He is left solitary and alone by God, angels and men, by all creatures. What kind of a temptation would it be if we were not forsaken and stood not alone? It is, however, painful when we do not feel anything that presents its back to us; as for example, that I should support myself and have not a nickel, not a thread, not a twig, and I experience no help from others, and no advice is offered. That means to be led into the desert and to be left alone. There I am in the true school, and I learn what I am, how weak my faith is, how great and rare true faith is, and how deeply unbelief is entrenched in the hearts of all men. But whoever has his purse, cellar, and fields full is not yet led into the desert, neither is he left alone; therefore he is not conscious of temptation.

Secondly, the tempter came forward and attacked Christ with these very same cares of food for the body and with the unbelief in the goodness of God, and said: "If thou art the Son of God, command that these stones become bread," as if he should say: "Yes, trust thou in God and bake and cook nothing; only wait patiently until a roasted fowl flies into your mouth; do you now say that you have a God Who cares for you; where is now your heavenly Father, Who has charge of you? Yea, it seems to me He lets you in a fine condition; eat now and drink from your faith, let us see how you will satisfy your hunger; yea, when you have stones for bread. What a fine Son of God you are! How fatherly He is disposed toward you in that He fails to send you a slice of bread and permits you to be so poor and needy; do you now continue to believe that you are His Son and He is your Father?" With like thoughts he truly attacks all the children of God. And Christ surely felt this temptation, for He was no stick nor stone; although He was and remained pure and without sin, as we cannot do.

That Satan attacked Christ with the cares for daily food or with unbelief and avarice, Christ's answer proves in that He says: "Man shall not live by bread alone"; that sounds as if He said: "thou wilt direct Me by bread alone and dost treat Me as though I thought of nothing but the sustenance of My body." This temptation is very common also among pious people, and they especially feel it keenly who have children and a family and have nothing to eat. Therefore St. Paul says in 1 Timothy 6:10 that avarice is a root of all kind of evil; for it is a fruit of unbelief. Do you not think that unbelief, care, and avarice are the reasons people are afraid to enter married life? Why do people avoid it and live in unchastity, unless it be the fear that they must die of hunger and suffer want? But here we should consider Christ's work and example, Who suffered want forty days and nights and finally was not forsaken, but was ministered to even by angels.

Thirdly, behold how Christ resists this temptation of bread, and overcomes; He sees nothing but stones and what is uneatable, then He approaches and clings to the Word of God, strengthens Himself by it and strikes the devil to the ground with it. This saying all Christians should lay hold of when they see that there is lack and want and everything has become stones, so that courage trembles, and they should say: "What were it if the whole world were full of bread, still man does not live by bread alone, but more belongs to life, namely, the Word of God." The words, however, are so beautiful and powerful that we must not pass over them lightly, but carefully explain them.

These words Christ quotes from Deuteronomy 8:3, where Moses says: "Thy God humbled thee, and suffered thee to hunger, and fed thee with manna, which thou knewest not, neither did thy fathers know; that he might make thee know that man doth not live by bread only, but by everything that proceedeth out of the mouth of Jehovah doth man live." That is as much as to say: "Since God permits you to hunger and you still continue to live, you ought indeed to grasp the thought that God nourishes you without bread through His Word; for if you should live and sustain yourself by bread alone then you must continually be full of bread. But the Word, that nourishes us, is that He promises us and causes it to be published that He is our God and desires to be our God."

Thus now the meaning of Moses and of Christ is: Whoever has here God's Word and believes, has both blessings; the first, where he is in want and has nothing, but must suffer hunger, that Word will sustain him, so that he will not die of hunger nor perish, just as well as if he had abundance to eat; for the Word he has in his heart nourishes and sustains him without eating and drinking. But has he little to eat, then a bite or slice of bread will feed and nourish him like a kingly meal; for not only bread but the Word of God also nourishes the body naturally, as it creates and upholds all things (Hebrews 1:3). The other blessing he will also enjoy, namely, that finally bread will surely be at hand, come whence it will, and should it rain from heaven like manna where none grows and none can grow. In these two thoughts every person can freely trust, namely, that he must in time of hunger receive bread or something to eat, or if not, then his hunger must become so moderate and bearable that it will nourish him even as well as bread does.

Christ's second temptation is opposed to the first and is repugnant to common sense. Its substance is that the devil teaches us to tempt God; as he here calls to Christ to cast Himself down from the pinnacle of the temple, which was not at all necessary, since there were surely good steps upon which He could descend. And that this temptation was for the purpose of tempting or making trial of God, the answer of Christ also clearly proves, when He says: "Thou shalt not make trial of the Lord thy God." By this He shows that the devil wished to lead Him into temptation.

And this very appropriately follows the first temptation. For where the devil feels a heart trusts God in times of want and need, he soon ceases his temptation of bread and avarice and thinks: Wait, wilt thou be very spiritual and believing, I will assist you: He approaches and attacks on the other side, that we might believe where God has not commanded us to believe, nor wills that we should believe. For example, if God gave you bread in your homes, as He does yearly everywhere in the world, and you would not use it, but instead you would cause need and want yourselves, and say: Why, we are to believe God: I will not eat the bread, but will patiently wait until God sends me manna from heaven. See, that would be tempting God; for that is not believing where all is at hand that we need and should have. How can one believe that he will receive what he already has?

Thus you see here that Satan held before Christ want and need where there was neither want nor need; but where there was already good means by which to descend from the temple without such a newly devised and unnecessary way of descending. For this purpose Satan led Christ to the top of the temple, in the holy city, says the Evangelist, and placed Him in a holy place. For he creates such precious thoughts in man that he thinks he is filled with faith and is on the true way of holiness; and yet he does not stand in the temple, but is only on the outside of the temple, that is, he is not in the true holy mind or life of faith; and yet he is in the holy city; that is, such persons are found only in Christendom and among true Christians, who hear a great deal of preaching about faith. To these persons he applies the sayings of Scripture. For such persons learn Scripture also by daily hearing it; but not farther than they can apply it to their erroneous opinions and their false faith. For Satan here quotes from the Psalter (Psalm 91:11-12), that God commanded the angels that they should protect the children of God and carry them on their hands. But Satan like a rogue and cheat fails to quote what follows, namely, that the angels shall protect the children of God in all their ways. For the Psalm reads thus: "For he will give his angels charge over thee to keep thee in all thy ways. They shall bear thee up in their hands, lest thou dash thy foot against a stone"; hence the protection of the angels does not reach farther, according to the command of God, than the ways in which God has commanded us to walk. When we walk in these ways of God, His angels take care of us. But the devil omits to quote "the ways of God" and interprets and applies the protection of the angels to all things, also to that which God has not commanded; then it fails and we tempt God.

Now, this temptation seldom takes place in outward material things as bread, clothing, house, and so forth. For we find many foolhardy people who risk and endanger their body and life, their property and honor, without any need of doing so; as those do who willfully enter into battle or jump into the water, or gamble for money, or in other ways venture into danger, of whom the wise man says in Sirach 3:27: "Whoever takes pleasure in danger, will thereby be overcome"; for in the degree one struggles to get a thing, will he succeed in obtaining it; and good swimmers are likely to drown and good climbers likely to fall. Yet it is seldom that those of false faith in God abstain from bread, clothing, and other necessities of life when they are at hand. As we read of two hermits who would not accept bread from the people, but thought God should send it to them directly from heaven; so the consequence was that one died and went to his father, the devil, who taught him such faith and left him to fall from the pinnacle.

But in spiritual matters this temptation is powerful when one has to do with the nourishment not of the body but of the soul. Here God has held before us the person and way, by which the soul can be forever nourished in the richest manner possible without any want, namely Christ, our Saviour. But this way, this treasure, this provision no one desires. Everybody seeks another way, other provisions to help their souls. The real guilty ones are those who would be saved through their own works; these the devil sets conspicuously on the top of the temple. They follow him and go down where there is no stairway; they believe and trust in their own work where there is no faith nor trust, no way nor bridge, and break their necks. But Satan makes use of and persuades them through the Scriptures to believe that the angels will protect them, and that their way, works, and faith are pleasing to God, who called them through the Scriptures to do good works; but they do not care how falsely they explain the Scriptures.

Christ's third temptation consists in temporal honor and power; as the words of the devil clearly teach, when Satan shows and offers Christ all the kingdoms of the world if He would worship him. To this class belong those who fall from their faith for the sake of honor and power, that they may enjoy good days, or not believe further than their honor and power extend. Such are also the heretics who start sects and factions in matters of faith among Christians, that they may make a great parade before the world and soar aloft in their own honor. Hence one may place this third temptation on the right, and the first on the left side. The first is the temptation of misfortune, by which man is stirred to anger, impatience, and unbelief; the third and last, the temptation of prosperity, by which man is enticed to lust, honor, joy, and whatever is high. The second or middle temptation is spiritual and deals with the blind tricks and errors that mislead reason from faith.

For whom the devil cannot overcome with poverty, want, need, and misery, he attacks with riches, favor, honor, pleasure, power, and the like, and contends on both sides against us; yea, "he walketh about," says St. Peter in 1 Peter 5:8, so that if he cannot overthrow us either with suffering or love, that is, with the first temptation on the left or the third on the right, he retires to a higher and different method and attacks us with error, blindness, and a false understanding of the Scripture. If he wins there, we fare ill on all sides and in all things; and whether one suffers poverty or has abundance, whether he fights or surrenders, all is lost. For when one is in error, neither patience in misfortune nor firmness in prosperity helps him; seeing that in both heretics are often powerful and the devil deliberately acts as if he were overcome in the first and last temptation, although he is not, if he has only won in the middle or second temptation. For he lets his own children suffer much and be patient, even at times to spurn the world; but never with a true and honest heart.

Now these three temptations taken together are heavy and hard, but the middle one is the greatest, for it attacks the doctrine of faith itself in the soul, and is spiritual and in spiritual matters. The other two attack faith in outward things, in fortune and misfortune, in pleasure and pain, and so forth, although both severely try us. For it is sad that one should lay hold of heaven and ever be in want and eat stones where there is no bread. Again, it is sad to despise favors, honor and possessions, friends and associates, and let go what one already has. But faith, rooted in God's Word, is able to do all things; is faith strong, then it is also easy for the believer to do this.

At last angels approached and served Him. This must have taken place in a literal sense, that they appeared in a bodily form and gave Him to eat and drink and, just as at a table, they ministered to all his wants. For the service is offered outwardly to His body just as, no doubt, the devil, His tempter, also appeared in a bodily form, perhaps like an angel. For, seeing that he places Him on the pinnacle of the temple and shows Him all the kingdoms of the world in a moment, he must have been a higher being than a man, since he represents himself as a higher being, in that he offers Him all the kingdoms of the world and permits himself to be worshiped. But he surely did not bear the form of the devil, for he desires to be beautiful when he lies and deceives, as St. Paul says of him in 2 Corinthians 11:14: "For even Satan fashioneth himself into an angel of light."

This however is written for our comfort, that we may know that many angels minister also to us, where one devil attacks us; if we fight with a knightly spirit and firmly stand, God will not let us suffer want, the angels of heaven would sooner appear and be our bakers, waiters, and cooks and minister to all our wants. This is not written for Christ's sake for He does not need it. Did the angels serve Him, then they may also serve us.

3. Charles Kingsley

Let me say a few words today about a solemn subject, namely, Temptation. I do not mean the temptation of the flesh—the temptations that all men have to yield to the low animal nature in them and behave like brutes. I mean those deeper and more terrible temptations, which our Lord conquered in that great struggle with evil which is commonly called His temptation in the wilderness. These were temptations of an evil spirit—the temptations that entice some men, at least, to behave like devils.

Now these temptations specially beset religious men—men who are, or fancy themselves, superior to their fellow men, more favored by God, and with nobler powers, and grander work to do, than the common average of mankind. But specially, I say, they beset those who are, or fancy themselves, the children of God. And, therefore, I humbly suppose our Lord had to endure and to conquer these very temptations because He was not merely a child of God, but the Son of God—the perfect Man, made in the perfect likeness of His Father. He had to endure these temptations, and to conquer them, that He might be able to succor us when we are tempted, seeing that He was tempted in like manner as we are, yet without sin.

Now it has been said, and, I think, well said, that what proves our Lord's three temptations to have been very subtle and dangerous and terrible is this—that we cannot see at first sight that they were temptations at all. The first two do not look to us to be wrong. If our Lord could make stones into bread to satisfy His hunger, why should He not do so? If He could prove to the Jews that He was the Son of God, their divine King and Saviour, by casting Himself down from the pinnacle of the temple, and being miraculously supported in the air by angels—if He could do that, why should He not do it? And lastly, the third temptation looks at first sight so preposterous that it seems silly of the evil spirit to have hinted at it. To ask any man of piety, much less the Son of God Himself, to fall down and worship the devil, seems perfectly absurd—a request not to be listened to for a moment, but put aside with contempt.

Well, my friends, the very danger of these spiritual temptations is—that they do not look like temptations. They do not look ugly, absurd, wrong; they look pleasant, reasonable, right.

"The devil," says the apostle, "transforms himself at times into an angel of light." If so, then he is certainly far more dangerous than if he came as an angel of darkness and horror. If you met some venomous snake, with loathsome spots upon his scales, his eyes full of rage and cunning, his head raised to strike at you, hissing and showing his fangs, there would be no temptation to have to do with him. You would know that you had to deal with an evil beast, and must either kill him or escape from him at once. But if, again, you met, as you may meet in the tropics, a lovely little coral snake, braided with red and white, its mouth so small that it seems impossible that it can bite, so gentle that children may take it up and play with it, then you might be tempted, as many a poor child has been ere now, to admire it, fondle it, wreathe it round the neck for a necklace or round the arm for a bracelet, till the play goes one step too far, the snake loses its temper, gives one tiny scratch upon the lip or finger, and that scratch is certain death. That would be a temptation indeed; one all the more dangerous because there is, I am told, another sort of coral snake perfectly harmless, which is so exactly like the deadly one, that no child, and few grown people, can know them apart.

Even so it is with our worst temptations. They look sometimes so exactly like what is good and noble and useful and religious, that we mistake the evil for the good, and play with it till it stings us, and we find out too late that the wages of sin are death. Thus religious people, just because they are religious, are apt to be specially tempted to mistake evil for good, and to do something specially wrong when they think they are doing something specially right, and so give occasion to the enemies of the Lord to blaspheme; till, as a hard and experienced man of the world once said: "Whenever I hear a man talking of his conscience, I know that he is going to do something particularly foolish; whenever I hear of a man talking of his duty, I know that he is going to do something particularly cruel."

Do I say this to frighten you away from being religious? God forbid. Better to be religious and to fear and love God, though you were tempted by all the devils out of the pit, than to be irreligious and a mere animal, and be tempted only by your own carnal nature, as the animals are. Better to be tempted, like the hermits of old, and even to fall and rise again, singing, "Rejoice not against me, O mine enemy, when I fall I shall arise"; than to live the life of the flesh, "like a beast with lower pains." It is the price a man must pay for hungering and thirsting after righteousness, for longing to be a child of God in spirit and in truth. "The devil," says a wise man of old, "does not tempt bad men, because he has got them already; he tempts good men, because he has *not* got them and wants to get them."

But how shall we know these temptations? God knows, my friends, better than I; and I trust that He will teach you to know, according to what each of you needs to know. But as far as my small experience goes, the root of them all is pride and self-conceit. Whatsoever thoughts or feelings tempt us to pride and self-conceit are of the devil, not of God. The devil is specially the spirit of pride; and, therefore, whatever tempts you to fancy yourself something different from your fellow men, superior to your fellow men, safer than they, more favored by God than they, that is a temptation of the spirit of pride. Whatever tempts you to think that you can do without God's help and God's providence; whatever tempts you to do anything extraordinary, and show yourself off, that you may make a figure in the world; and above all, whatever tempts you to antinomianism, that is, to fancy that God will overlook sins in you which He will not overlook in other men—all these are temptations from the spirit of pride. They are temptations like our Lord's temptations. These temptations came on our Lord more terribly than they ever can on you and me, just because He was the Son of Man, the perfect Man and, therefore, had more real reason for being proud (if such a thing could be) than any man, or than all men put together. But He conquered the temptations because He was perfect Man, led by the Spirit of God; and, therefore, He knew that the only way to be a perfect man was not to be proud, however powerful, wise, and glorious He might be, but to submit Himself humbly and utterly, as every man should do, to the will of His Father in heaven, from whom alone His greatness came.

Now the spirit of pride cannot understand the beauty of humility, and the spirit of self-will cannot understand the beauty of obedience; and, therefore, it is reasonable to suppose the devil could not understand our Lord. If He be the Son of God, so might Satan argue, He has all the more reason to be proud; and, therefore, it is all the more easy to tempt Him into showing His pride, into proving Himself a conceited, self-willed, rebellious being—in one word, an evil spirit.

And therefore (as you will see at first sight) the first two temptations were clearly meant to tempt our Lord to pride; for would they not tempt you and me to pride? If we could feed ourselves by making bread of stones, would not that make us proud enough? So proud, I fear, that we should soon fancy that we could do without God and His providence, and were masters of nature and all her secrets. If you and I could make the whole city worship and obey us, by casting ourselves off this cathedral unhurt, would not that make us proud enough? So proud, I fear, that we should end in committing some great folly or great crime in our conceit and vainglory.

Now, whether our Lord could or could not have done these wonderful deeds, one thing is plain—that He would not do them; and, therefore, we may presume that He ought not to have done them. It seems as if He did not wish to be a wonderful man: but only a perfectly good man, and He would do nothing to help Himself but what any other man could do. He answered the evil spirit simply out of Scripture, as any other pious man might have done. When He was bidden to make the stones into bread, He answers not as the Eternal Son of God, but simply as a man. "It is written" (it is the belief of Moses and the old prophets of my people): "that man doth not live by bread alone, but by every word that proceedeth out of the mouth of God"—as much as to say, If I am to be delivered out of this need, God will deliver me by some means or other, just as He delivers other men out of their needs. When He was bidden cast Himself from the temple, and so save Himself, probably from sorrow, poverty, persecution, and the death on the cross, He answers out of Scripture as any other Jew would have done. "It is written again, Thou shalt not tempt the Lord thy God." He says nothing—this is most important—of His being the eternal Son of God. He keeps that in the background. There the fact was; but He veiled the glory of His godhead, that He might assert the rights of His manhood, and show that mere man, by the help of the Spirit of God, could obey God, and keep His commandments.

I say these last words with all diffidence and humility, and trusting that the Lord will pardon any mistake which I may make about His divine Words. I only say them because wiser men than I have often taken the same view already. Of course there is more, far more, in this wonderful saying than we can understand, or ever will understand. But this I think is plain—that our Lord determined to behave as any and every other man ought to have done in His place, in order to show all God's children the example of perfect humility and perfect obedience to God.

But again, the devil asked our Lord to fall down and worship him. Now how could that be a temptation to pride? Surely that was asking our Lord to do anything but a proud action, rather, the most humiliating and most base of all actions. My friends, it seems to me that if our Lord had fallen down and worshiped the evil spirit, He would have given way to the spirit of pride utterly and boundlessly; and I will tell you why.

The devil wanted our Lord to do evil that good might come. It would have been a blessing, that all the kingdoms of the world and the glory of man should be our Lord's,—the very blessing for this poor earth which He came to buy, and which He bought with His own precious blood. And here the devil offered Him the very prize for which He came down on earth, without struggle or difficulty, if He would but do, for one moment, one wrong thing. What temptation that would be to our Lord as God, I dare not say. But that to our Lord as Man, it must have been the most terrible of all temptations, I can well believe: because history shows us, and, alas! our own experience in modern times shows us, persons yielding to that temptation perpetually—pious people, benevolent people, people who long to spread the Bible, to convert sinners, to found charities, to amend laws, to set the world right in some way or other, and who fancy that therefore, in carrying out their fine projects, they have a right to do evil that good may come.

This is a very painful subject; all the more painful just now, because I sometimes think it is the special sin of this country and this generation, and that God will bring on us some heavy punishment for it. But all who know the world in its various phases, and especially what are called the religious world, and the philanthropic world, and the political world, know too well that men, not otherwise bad men, will do things and say things, to carry out some favorite project or movement, or to support some party, religious or other, which they would (I hope) be ashamed to say and do for their own private gain. Now what is this but worshiping the evil spirit, in order to get power over this world, that they may (as they fancy) amend it? And what is this but self-conceit—ruinous, I had almost said, blasphemous? These people think themselves so certainly in the right, and their plans so absolutely necessary to the good of the world, that God has given them a special license to do what they like in carrying them out; that He will excuse in them falsehoods and meannesses, even tyranny and violences which He will excuse in no one else.

Now, is not this self-conceit? What would you think of a servant who disobeyed you, cheated you, and yet said to himself—"No matter, my master dare not turn me off: I am so useful that he cannot do without me." Even so in all ages, and now as much as, or more than ever, have men said, "We are so necessary to God and God's cause that He cannot do without us; and therefore though He hates sin in everyone else, He will excuse sin in us, as long as we are about His business."

Therefore, my dear friends, whenever we are tempted to do or say anything rash, or vain, or mean, because we are the children of God; whenever we are inclined to be puffed up with spiritual pride, and to fancy that we may take liberties which other men must not take, because we are the children of God; let us remember the words of the text, and answer the tempter, when he says, "If thou be the Son of God, do this and that," as our Lord answered him—"If I be the Child of God, what then? This—that I must behave as if God were my Father. I must trust my God utterly, and I must obey Him utterly. I must do no rash or vain thing to tempt God, even though it looks as if I should have a great success, and do much good thereby. I must do no mean or base thing, nor give way for a moment to the wicked ways of this wicked world, even though again it looks as if I should have a great success, and do much good thereby. In one word, I must worship my Father in heaven, and Him only must I serve. If He wants me, He will use me. If He does not want me, He will use some one else. Who am I, that God cannot govern the world without my help? My business is to refrain my soul, and keep it low, even as a weaned child, and not to meddle with matters too high for me. My business is to do the little, simple, everyday duties which lie nearest me, and be faithful in a few things, and I shall enter into the joy of my Lord, which is the joy of doing good to my fellow men. But I shall never enter into that by thrusting myself into Christ's way, with grand schemes and hasty projects, as if I knew better than He how to make His kingdom come. If I do, my pride will have a fall. Because I would not be faithful over a few things, I shall be tempted to be unfaithful over many things; and instead of entering into the joy of my Lord, I shall be in danger of the awful judgment pronounced on those who do evil that good may come, who shall say in that day, Lord, Lord, have we not prophesied in thy name? and in thy name cast out devils? and in thy name done many wonderful works? And then will He protest unto them—I never knew you. Depart from me, ye that work iniquity."

Oh, my friends, in all your projects for good, as in all other matters which come before you in your mortal life, keep innocence and take heed to the thing that is right. For that, and that alone, shall bring a man peace at the last.

To which, may God in His mercy bring us all. Amen.

THE SECOND SUNDAY IN LENT

Text: Matthew 15:21-28

1. St. Augustine

This woman of Canaan, who has just now been brought before us in the lesson of the Gospel, shows us an example of humility and the way of godliness; shows us how to rise from humility unto exaltation. Now she was, as it appears, not of the people of Israel, of whom came the Patriarchs, and Prophets, and the parents of the Lord Jesus Christ according to the flesh; of whom the Virgin Mary herself was, who was the Mother of Christ. This woman then was not of this people, but of the Gentiles. For, as we have heard, the Lord "departed into the coasts of Tyre and Sidon, and behold, a woman of Canaan came out of the same coasts," and with the greatest earnestness begged of Him the mercy to heal her daughter, "who was grievously vexed with a devil." Tyre and Sidon were not cities of the people of Israel, but of the Gentiles; though they bordered on that people. So then, as being eager to obtain mercy, she cried out and boldly knocked; and He made as though He heard her not, not to the end that mercy might be refused her, but that her desire might be enkindled; and not only that her desire might be enkindled, but that, as I have said before, her humility might be set forth. Therefore did she cry, while the Lord was as though He heard her not, but was ordering in silence what He was about to do. The disciples besought the Lord for her, and said, "Send her away, for she crieth after us." And He said, "I am not sent, but unto the lost sheep of the house of Israel."

The Lord was not sent but "unto the lost sheep of the house of Israel." But because a "people whom he had not known, was also to serve him, and to obey him in the hearing of the ear," He made mention of them too when He was among the others. For the same Lord said in a certain place, "Other sheep I have which are not of this fold; them also I must bring, that there may be one fold and one shepherd."

Of these was this woman; therefore she was not refused, but only put off. "I am not sent," saith He, "but unto the lost sheep of the house of Israel." And she was instant in her cries: she persevered, she knocked, as if she had already heard, "Ask, and receive; seek, and thou shalt find; knock, and it shall be opened unto thee." She kept on, she knocked. For so the Lord when He spake these words, "Ask, and ye shall receive; seek, and ye shall find; knock, and it shall be opened unto you"; had also said before, "Give not that which is holy unto the dogs, neither cast ye your pearls before swine, lest they trample them under their feet, and turn again

201

and rend you"; that is, lest after despising your pearls, they should even ill use you. Cast not therefore before them what they despise.

And how distinguish we (as might be answered) who are "swine," and who are "dogs"? This has been shown in the case of this woman. For He only answered to her entreaties, "It is not meet to take the children's bread, and to cast it to dogs." Thou art a dog, thou art one of the Gentiles, thou worshipest idols. But for dogs what is so proper as to lick stones? "It is not" therefore "meet to take the children's bread, and to cast it to dogs." Had she retired after these words, she had gone away as she had come, a dog; but by knocking she was made of a dog one of human kind. For she persevered in asking, and from that reproach as it were she manifested her humility and obtained mercy. For she was not excited, nor incensed, because she was called a dog as she asked the blessing and prayed for mercy, but she said, "Truth, Lord"; "Thou hast called me a dog, and truly a dog I am, I acknowledge my name: it is the truth that speaks: but I ought not on that account to be refused this blessing. Verily I am a dog; 'yet the dogs eat of the crumbs which fall from their masters' table.' It is but a moderate and a small blessing I desire; I do not press to the table, I only seek for the crumbs."

See, brethren, how the value of humility is set before us! The Lord had called her a dog; but she did not say, "I am not," but she said, "I am." And because she acknowledged herself to be a dog, immediately the Lord said, "Woman, great is thy faith; be it unto thee even as thou hast asked." Thou hast acknowledged thyself to be a dog, I now acknowledge thee to be of human kind. "Oh woman, great is thy faith"; thou hast asked, and sought, and knocked; receive, find, be it opened unto thee. See, brethren, how in this woman who was a Canaanite, that is, who came from among the Gentiles, and was a type, that is a figure, of the Church, the grace of humility has been eminently set before us. For the Jewish nation, to the end that it might be deprived of the grace of the Gospel, was puffed up with pride because to them it had been vouchsafed to receive the Law, because out of this nation the Patriarchs had proceeded, the Prophets had sprung, Moses, the servant of God, had done the great miracles in Egypt which we have heard of in the Psalm, had led the people through the Red Sea when the waters retired, and had received the Law, which he gave to this people. This was that whereupon the Jewish nation was lifted up, and through this very pride it happened that they were not willing to humble themselves to Christ the Author of humility, and the Restrainer of proud swelling, to God the Physician, who, being God, for this cause became Man, that man might know himself to be but man. Oh mighty remedy! If this remedy cure not pride, I know not what can cure it. He is God, and is made Man; He lays aside His divinity, that is, in a manner sequestrates, hides, what was His Own, and appears only in that He had taken to Him. Being God He is made man: and man will not acknowledge himself to be man, will not acknowledge himself to be mortal, will not acknowledge himself to be frail, will not acknowledge himself to be a sinner, will not acknowledge himself to be sick, at least so sick as to seek the Physician; but what is more perilous still, he fancies himself in sound health.

So then for this reason people did not come to Him, by reason of pride; and the natural branches are said to be broken off from the olive tree, that is from that people founded by the Patriarchs; in other words, the Jews are for their punishment justly barren through the spirit of pride; and the wild olive is grafted into that olive tree. The wild olive tree is the people of the Gentiles. So says the Apostle, "that the wild olive tree is grafted into the good olive tree, but the natural branches are broken off." Because of pride they were broken off: and the wild olive tree grafted in because of humility. This humility did the woman show forth when she said, "Truth, Lord," "I am a dog, I desire only the crumbs." In this humility also did the centurion please Him; who when he desired that his servant might be healed by the Lord, and the Lord said, "I will come and heal him," answered, "Lord, I am not worthy that thou shouldest come under my roof, but speak the word only, and my servant shall be healed. I am not worthy that thou shouldest come under my roof." He did not receive Him into his house, but he had received Him already in his heart. The more humble, the more capacious, and the more full. For the hills drive back the water, but the valleys are filled by it. And what then, what said the Lord to those who followed Him after that he had said, "I am not worthy that thou shouldest come under my roof"? "Verily I say unto you, I have not found so great faith, no, not in Israel"; that is, in that people to whom I came, "I have not found so great faith." And whence great? Great from being the least, that is, great from humility. "I have not found so great faith"; like a grain of mustard seed, which by how much smaller it is, by so much the more burning is it. Therefore did the Lord at once graft the wild olive into the good olive tree. He did it then when He said, "Verily I say unto you, I have not found so great faith, no, not in Israel."

Lastly, mark what follows. "Therefore"—because "I have not found so great faith in Israel," that is, so great humility with faith—"Therefore I say unto you, that many shall come from the east and west, and shall sit down with Abraham and Isaac and Jacob in the kingdom of heaven." "Shall sit," that is, "shall rest." For we must not form notions of carnal banquets there or desire any such thing in that kingdom, as to change not vices for virtues, but only to make an exchange of vices. For it is one thing to desire the kingdom of heaven for the sake of wisdom and life eternal; another, for the sake of earthly felicity, as though there we should have it in more abundant and greater measure. If thou think to be rich in that kingdom, thou dost not cut off, but only changest desire; and yet rich thou wilt really be, and in none other place but there wilt thou be rich; for here thy want gathers together the abundance of things. Why have rich men much? Because they want much. A greater want heaps together as it were greater means; there want itself shall die. Then thou shalt be truly rich, when thou shalt be in want of nothing. For now thou art not surely rich, and an angel poor, who has not horses, and carriages, and servants. Why? Because he does not want any of these: because in proportion to his greater strength, is his want the less. Therefore in that kingdom there are riches, and the true riches. Figure not to yourselves then banquets of this earth in that place. For the banquets of this world are daily medicines; they are necessary for a kind of sickness we have, wherewith we are born. This sickness everyone is sensible of, when the hour for refreshment is passed. Wouldest thou see how great a sickness this is, that as an acute fever would be fatal in seven days? Do not fancy thyself then to be in health. Immortality will be health. For this present is only one long sickness. Because thou dost support thy disease by daily medicines, thou fanciest thyself in health; take away the medicines, and then see what thou canst do.

For from the moment we are born, we must needs be dying. This disease must needs bring us to death. This, indeed, physicians say when they examine their patients. For instance, "This man has the dropsy, he is dying; this disease cannot be cured. This man has the leprosy: this disease too cannot be cured. He is in a consumption. Who can cure this? He must needs die, he must perish." See, the physician has now pronounced that he is in a consumption, that he cannot but die; and yet sometimes the dropsical patient does not die of his disease, and the leprous does not die of his, nor the consumptive patient of his; but now it is absolutely necessary that everyone who is born should die of this. He dies of it, he cannot do otherwise. This the physician and the unskilled both pronounce upon; and though he die somewhat more slowly, does he on that account not die? Where then is there true health, except where there is true immortality? But if it be true immortality, and no corruption, no wasting, what need will there be there of nourishment? Therefore, when you hear it said, "They shall sit down with Abraham, Isaac, and Jacob"; get not your body, but your soul in order. There shalt thou be filled; and this inner man has its proper food. In relation to this is it said, "Blessed are they which do hunger and thirst after righteousness, for they shall be filled." And so truly filled shall they be that they shall hunger no more.

Therefore did the Lord graft in at once the wild olive tree when He said, "Many shall come from the east and west, and shall sit down with Abraham, and Isaac, and Jacob, in the kingdom of heaven"; that is, they shall be grafted into the good olive tree. For Abraham, and Isaac, and Jacob are the roots of this olive tree; "but the children of the kingdom," that is, the unbelieving Jews, "shall go away into outer darkness." The "natural branches shall be broken off," that the "wild olive tree may be grafted in." Now why did the natural branches deserve to be cut off, except for pride? Why the wild olive tree to be grafted in, except for humility? Whence also that woman said, "Truth, Lord, yet the dogs eat of the crumbs which fall from their masters' table." And thereupon she hears, "O woman, great is thy faith." And so again that centurion, "I am not worthy that thou shouldest come under my roof." "Verily I say unto you, I have not found so great faith, no, not in Israel." Let us then learn, or let us hold fast, humility. If we have it not yet, let us learn it; if we have it, let us not lose it. If we have it not yet, let us have it, that we may be grafted in; if we have it already, let us hold it fast, that we may not be cut off.

2. Martin Luther

This Gospel presents to us a true example of firm and perfect faith. For this woman endures and overcomes in three great and hard battles, and teaches us in a beautiful manner the true way and virtue of faith, namely, that it is a hearty trust in the grace and goodness of God as experienced and revealed through His Word. For St. Mark says she heard some news about Jesus (Mark 7:25). What kind of news? Without doubt good news, and the good report that Christ was a pious man and cheerfully helped everybody. Such news about God is a true Gospel and a word of grace, out of which sprang the faith of this woman; for had she not believed, she would not have thus run after Christ. In like manner we have often heard how St. Paul in Romans 10:17 says that faith cometh by hearing, that the Word must go in advance and be the beginning of our salvation.

But how is it that many more have heard this good news concerning Christ, who have not followed Him and did not esteem it as good news? Answer? The physician is helpful and welcome to the sick; the healthy have no use for him. But this woman felt her need, hence she followed the sweet scent, as is written in the Song of Solomon 1:3. In like manner Moses must precede and teach people to feel their sins in order that grace may be sweet and welcome to them. Therefore all is in vain, however friendly and lovely Christ may be pictured, if man is not first humbled by a knowledge of himself and he possesses not longing for Christ, as Mary's Song says, "The hungry he hath filled with good things; and the rich he hath sent empty away" (Luke 1:53). All this is spoken and written for the comfort of the distressed, the poor, the needy, the sinful, the despised, so that they may know in all times of need to whom to flee and where to seek comfort and help.

But see in this example how Christ, like a hunter, exercises and chases faith in His followers in order that it may become strong and firm. First when the woman follows Him upon hearing of His fame and cries with assured confidence that He would, according to His reputation, deal mercifully with her, Christ certainly acts differently, as if to let her faith and good confidence be in vain and turn His good reputation into a lie, so that she could have thought: Is this the gracious, friendly man? or: Are these the good words that I have heard spoken about him, upon which I have depended? It must not be true; He is my enemy and will not receive me; nevertheless He might speak a word and tell me that He will have nothing to do with me. Now He is as silent as a stone. Behold, this is a very hard rebuff, when God appears so earnest and angry and conceals His grace so high and deep; as those know so well, who feel and experience it in their hearts. Therefore she imagines He will not fulfil what He has spoken and will let His Word be false, as it happened to the children of Israel at the Red Sea and to many other saints.

Now, what does the poor woman do? She turns her eyes from all this unfriendly treatment of Christ; all this does not lead her astray, neither does she take it to heart, but she continues immediately and firmly to cling in her confidence to the good news she had heard and embraced concerning Him, and never gives up. We must also do the same and learn firmly to cling to the Word, even though God with all His creatures appears different than His Word teaches. But, oh, how painful it is to nature and reason that this woman should strip herself of self and forsake all that she experienced, and cling alone to God's bare Word, until she experienced the contrary. May God help us in time of need and of death to possess like courage and faith!

Secondly, since her cry and faith avail nothing, the disciples approach with their faith, and pray for her, and imagine they will surely be heard. But while they thought He should be more tenderhearted, He became only the more indifferent, as we see and think. For now He is silent no more nor leaves them in doubt; He declines their prayer and says: "I was not sent but unto the lost sheep of the house of Israel." This rebuff is still harder since not only our own person is rejected, but the only comfort that remains to us—namely, the comfort and prayers of pious and holy persons—is rejected. For our last resort, when we feel that God is ungracious, or we are in need, is that we go to pious, spiritual persons and there seek counsel and help, and they are willing to help as love demands; and yet that may amount to nothing, even they may not be heard and our condition becomes only worse.

Here one might upbraid Christ with all the words in which He promised to hear His saints, as Matthew 18:19: "If two of you shall agree on earth as touching anything that they shall ask, it shall be done for them." Likewise, Mark 11:24: "All things whatsoever ye pray and ask for, believe that ye receive them, and ye shall have them"; and many more like passages. What becomes of such promises in this woman's case? Christ, however, promptly answers and says: "Yes, it is true, I hear all prayers, but I gave these promises only to the house of Israel." What do you think? Is not that a thunderbolt that dashes both heart and faith into a thousand pieces, when one feels that God's Word, upon which one trusts, was not spoken for him, but applies only to others? Here all saints and prayers must be speechless, yea, here the heart must let go of the Word, to which it would gladly hold, if it would consult its own feelings.

But what does the poor woman do? She does not give up, she clings to the Word although it be torn out of her heart by force, she is not turned away by this stern answer, still firmly believing His goodness is yet concealed in that answer, and still she will not pass judgment that Christ is or may be ungracious. That is persevering steadfastness.

Thirdly, she follows Christ into the house, as Mark 7:24-25 informs us, perseveres, falls down at His feet, and says: "Lord, help me!" There she received her last mortal blow, in that Christ said in her face, as the words tell, that she was a dog and not worthy to partake of the children's bread. What will she say to this? Here He presents her in a bad light; she is a condemned and an outcast person who is not to be reckoned among God's chosen ones.

That is an eternally unanswerable reply, to which no one can give a satisfactory answer. Yet she does not despair, but agrees with His judgment and concedes she is a dog, and desires also no more than a dog is entitled to, namely, that she may eat the crumbs that fall from the table of the Lord. Is not that a masterly stroke as a reply? She catches Christ with His own words. He compares her to a dog, she concedes it, and asks nothing more than that He let her be a dog, as He Himself judged her to be. Where will Christ now take refuge? He is caught. Truly, people let the dog have the crumbs under the table; it is entitled to that. Therefore Christ now completely opens His heart to her and yields to her will, so that she is now no dog, but even a child of Israel.

All this, however, is written for our comfort and instruction, that we may know how deeply God conceals His grace before our face, and that we may not estimate Him according to our feelings and thinking, but strictly according to His Word. For here you see, though Christ appears to be even hardhearted, yet He gives no final decision by saying "No." All His answers indeed sound like no, but they are not no, they remain undecided and pending. For He does not say: "I will not hear thee," but is silent and passive and says neither yes nor no. In like manner He does not say she is not of the house of Israel; but He is sent only to the house of Israel; He leaves it undecided and pending between yes and no. So He does not say, "Thou art a dog, one should not give thee of the children's bread," but, "it is not meet to take the children's bread and cast it to the dogs," leaving it undecided whether she is a dog or not. Yet all those trials of her faith sounded more like no than yes; but there was more yea in them than nay; aye, there is only yes in them, but it is very deep and very concealed, while there appears to be nothing but no.

By this is set forth the condition of our heart in times of temptation; Christ here represents how it feels. It thinks there is nothing but no and yet that is not true. Therefore it must turn from this feeling and lay hold of and retain the deep spiritual yes under and above the no with a firm faith in God's Word, as this poor woman does, and say God is right in His judgment which He visits upon us; then we have triumphed and caught Christ in His own words. As, for example, when we feel in our conscience that God rebukes us as sinners and judges us unworthy of the kingdom of heaven, then we experience hell, and we think we are lost forever. Now whoever understands here the actions of this poor woman and catches God in His own judgment, and says: "Lord, it is true, I am a sinner and not worthy of thy grace; but still thou hast promised sinners forgiveness, and thou art come not to call the righteous, but, as St. Paul says in 1 Timothy 1:15 'to save sinners.'" Behold, then must God according to His own judgment have mercy upon us.

3. Phillips Brooks

Through all that I have said today there runs one truth which I cannot state too simply and strongly, as my time draws near its close. I want to make you feel it and know it if I can. It is the necessary power that the weaker has over the stronger, the lower over the higher. It is a power which develops as all life grows higher, and which comes to its completeness when we get up into the region where man has to do with God. The lowest conditions of life hardly know it at all. Think of the masteries that are strongest and most imperative in two communities at the opposite extremes of social life. Into a village of savages comes some ruffian, more big and brutal than any other who is there, stronger in limb, bolder in arrogant courage; and all the savage village owns him as its master; all its people are at his feet in admiration and obedience; what he bids them they will do. Then turn to the other extreme. In some civilized village of England and America there is heard the cry of a suffering infant, the story of some wrong done to a little child comes to men's pitying ears, and all the village is stirred and will not rest until the wrong be righted, and the little child relieved. That little child with its woes is the master of those strong and busy men; his cry of pain summons them from their work as a bugle calls the soldiers to the field.

This power of weakness over strength comes to perfection in Jesus. Could there be a more complete picture of it than shines out in His own story of the shepherd and the sheep. The shepherd has folded his ninety-and-nine; everything is safe and strong and prosperous; he stands with his hand upon the sheepfold gate; and then, just as he seems all wrapped up in the satisfaction and completeness of the sight, there comes, so light that no ear except his can hear it, the cry of one poor lost sheep off in the mountains, and it summons him with an irresistible challenge, and his staff is in his hand instantly, and he turns his back on everything else to be the slave of that one lost sheep till it is found. What a wonderful and everlasting and universal story that parable is!

Oh, my dear friends, we have not entered into Christ's salvation, He has not rescued and redeemed us into His own divine life, until that which was true of Him is also true of us. Do we know as He knew this power of the weakest? Are our ears quick as His were to hear through every tumult the far-away cry of any poor human soul that needs us? Are our ears quick as His was to own the right which that cry has to our instant attention and obedience? If they are not, our life is very poor. For we are fed through our obediences; and he who only knows what it is to obey those who are stronger than himself, he who has never felt the imperiousness of the need which cries up to him out of some depth of want or pain, has missed one-half, the largest and richest half, of the nourishment and enrichment which God provided for his human life.

We may dare to believe that in this service of weakness, this obedience to need, this submission of His power to the demands of His feeblest brethren, Christ our Lord found part of the development of His divine consciousness. Every beggar whom He met was a king to Him. Let us not think for a moment that that was something which belonged only to the days when He was here upon the earth. It is true still. When you and I are weak, Christ in a true sense owns the claim of our weakness and comes to serve us with His love. Behold, how this transfigures life! The times that make us weakest and that force our weakness most upon us, and make us most know how weak we are, those are our coronation times. The days of sickness, days of temptation, days of doubt, days of discouragement, days of bereavement, and of the aching loneliness which comes when the strong voice is silent and the dear face is gone, these are the days when Christ sees most clear the crown of our need upon our foreheads, and comes to serve us with His love.

Faith is the king's knowledge of his own kingship. A weak man who has no faith in Christ is a king who does not know his own royalty. But the soul which in its need cries out and claims its need's dominion—the soul that dares to take the prerogative of its own feebleness and cry aloud, "Come to me, Oh Christ, for I need Thee," finds itself justified. Its bold and humble cry is honored and answered instantly; instantly by its side the answer comes: "Great is thy faith: be it unto thee even as thou wilt. What wilt thou that I should do unto thee?"

THE THIRD SUNDAY IN LENT

Text: Luke 11:14-28

1. John Chrysostom

Even before now they had accused Christ of this, that "by Beelzebub he casteth out the devils." But whereas then He did not rebuke them, allowing them both to know His power by His more numerous miracles, and by His teaching to learn His majesty: now, since they continued saying the same, He proceeds also to rebuke them, showing His Godhead by this first, that He made their secrets public; and secondly, by the very act of casting out the devils with ease.

And indeed the accusation too was very shameless, because, as I have said, envy seeks not what to say, but only that it may say somewhat. Yet for all that, not even so did Christ despise them, but defends Himself with the forbearance proper to Him, teaching us to be meek to our enemies; and though they say such things, as we are neither conscious of, nor have they any the least probability, not to be disturbed, nor troubled, but with all long suffering to render them an account. This then He did most especially on that very occasion, affording the strongest proof that the things were false that were said by them. For neither was it a demoniac's part to exhibit so much meekness; it was not a demoniac's part to know men's secrets.

For, in truth, both because of the exceeding impudence of such a suspicion, and because of the fear of the multitude, they durst not publicly make these charges, but were turning them in their mind. But He, to show them that He knew all that likewise, doth not set down the accusation, nor doth He expose their wickedness; but the refutation He adds, leaving it to the conscience of them that had said it to convict them. For on one thing only was He bent, to do good to them that were sinning, not to expose them.

Yet surely, if He had been minded to extend His speech in length, and to make them ridiculous, and withal to have exacted of them also the most extreme penalty, there was nothing to hinder Him. Nevertheless He put aside all these things and looked to one object only, not to render them more contentious, but more candid, and so to dispose them better toward amendment.

How then doth He plead with them? Not by allegation out of the Scriptures (for they would not so much as attend, but were sure rather to distort their meaning), but by the events of ordinary life. For "every kingdom," saith He, "divided against itself shall not stand; and a city and a house, if it be divided, is soon dissolved." For the wars from without are not so ruinous as the civil ones. Yea, and this is the case in bodies too; it is the

211

case even in all things; but for this time He takes His illustration from those that are more publicly known.

And yet, what is there more powerful on earth than a kingdom? Nothing, but nevertheless it perished if in dissension. And if in that case one throw the blame on the great burden of the affairs thereof, as breaking down by its own weight; what wouldest thou say of a city? and what of a house? Thus, whether it be a small thing, or a great, if at dissension with itself, it perishes. If then I, having a devil, do by him cast out the devils, there is a dissension and fighting among devils, and they take their stand one against another. But if they stand one against another, their strength is wasted and destroyed. "For if Satan cast out Satan" (and He said not "the devils," implying their great unanimity one with another), "he is then divided against himself"; so He speaks. But if he be divided, he is become weaker, and is ruined; and if he be ruined, how can he cast out another?

Seest thou how great the absurdity of the accusation, how great the folly, the inconsistency? Since it is not for the same persons to say, first, that He stands and casts out devils, and then to say that He stands by that, which it was likely would be the cause of His undoing.

This then being the first refutation, the next after it is that which relates to the disciples. For not always in one way only, but also in a second and third, He solves their objections, being minded most abundantly to silence their shamelessness. Which sort of thing He did also with respect to the Sabbath, bringing forward David, the priests, the testimony that saith, "I will have mercy, and not sacrifice," the cause of the Sabbath, for which it was ordained; "for the Sabbath," saith He, "was for man." This then He doth in the present case also, where after the first He proceeds to a second refutation, plainer than the former.

"For if I," saith He, "by Beelzebub cast out devils, by whom do your sons cast them out?" See here, too, His gentleness. For He said not, "my disciples," nor, "the apostles," but "your sons"; to the end that if indeed they were minded to return to the same nobleness with them, they might derive hence a powerful spring that way; but if they were uncandid, and continued in the same course, they might not thenceforth be able to allege any plea, though ever so shameless.

But what He saith is like this, "By whom do the apostles cast them out?" For in fact they were doing so already, because they had received authority from Him, and these men brought no charge against them; their quarrel not being with the acts, but with the person only. As then it was His will to show that their sayings arose only from their envy against Him, He brings forward the apostles, thus: "If I so cast them out, much more those, who have received their authority from me. Nevertheless, no such thing have ye said to them. How then bring ye these charges against Me, the Author of their doings, while acquitting them of the accusations? This, however, will not free you from your punishment, rather it will condemn you the more." Therefore also He added, "They shall be your judges."—"For when persons from among you, and having been practised in these things, both believe Me and obey, it is most clear that they will also condemn those who are against Me both in deed and word."

"But if I cast out devils by the Spirit of God, then the kingdom of God is come unto you." What means "the kingdom"? "My coming." See how again He conciliates and soothes them, and draws them to the knowledge of Himself, and signifies that they are warring with their own good and contentious against their own salvation. "For whereas ye ought to rejoice," saith He, "and leap for joy, that One is come bestowing those great and unutterable blessings, hymned of old by the prophets, and that the time of your prosperity is at hand, ye do the contrary; so far from receiving the blessings, you do even speak ill of them, and frame accusations that have no real being."

Now Matthew indeed saith, "If I by the Spirit of God cast out"; but Luke, "If I by the finger of God cast out the devils," implying that to cast out devils is a work of the greatest power and not of any ordinary grace. And He means indeed that from these things they should infer and say, "If this be so, then the Son of God is come." This, however, He saith not, but in a reserved way, and so as not to be galling to them, He darkly intimates it by saying, "Then the kingdom of God is come unto you."

Seest thou exceeding wisdom? By the very things which they were blaming, He showed His presence shining forth.

Then, to conciliate them, He said not simply, "The kingdom is come," but, "unto you," as though He had said, "To you the good things are come; wherefore then feel displeased at your proper blessings? why war against your own salvation? This is that time, which the prophets long ago foretold: this, the sign of that Advent which was celebrated by them, even these things being wrought by divine power. For the fact, indeed, that they are wrought, yourselves know; but that they are wrought by divine power, the deeds themselves cry out. Yea, and it is impossible that Satan should be stronger now; rather he must of absolute necessity be weak. But it cannot be, that he who is weak should, as though he were strong, cast out the strong devil."

Now thus speaking He signified the power of charity and the weakness of separation and contentiousness. Wherefore He was Himself also continually charging His disciples, on every occasion, concerning charity, and teaching them that the devil, to subvert it, leaves nothing undone.

2. John Calvin

AND OTHERS TEMPTING SOUGHT FROM HIM A SIGN. Something similar to this is afterward related by Matthew (16:4) and by Mark (8:11, 12). Hence it is evident that Christ repeatedly attacked them on this subject, so that there was no end to the wickedness of those men who had once resolved to oppress the truth. There can be no doubt that they ask a sign in order to plead, as a plausible pretense for their unbelief, that Christ's calling has not been duly attested. They do not express such submissiveness as to be prepared to yield to two or three miracles, and still less to be satisfied with a single miracle; but as I hinted a little before, they apologize for not believing the Gospel on this pretense, that Christ shows no sign of it from heaven. He had already performed miracles before their eyes sufficiently numerous and manifest; but as if these were not enough for the confirmation of doctrine, they wish to have something exhibited from heaven, by which God will, as it were, make a visible appearance. They call him *Master*, according to custom; for such was the appellation given at that time to all scribes and expounders of the Law. But they do not acknowledge Him to be a prophet of God till He produce a testimony from heaven. The meaning therefore is: "Since Thou professest to be a teacher and Master, if Thou desirest that we should be Thy disciples, let God declare from heaven that He is the Author of Thy teaching, and let Him confirm Thy calling by a miracle."

BLESSED IS THE WOMB. By this eulogium the woman intended to magnify the excellence of Christ, for she had no reference to Mary, whom, perhaps, she had never seen. And yet it tends in a high degree to illustrate the glory of Christ, that she pronounces "the womb that bore him" to be noble and "blessed." Nor was the blessing inappropriate, but in strict accordance with the manner of Scripture; for we know that offspring, and particularly when endued with distinguished virtues, is declared to be a remarkable gift of God, preferable to all others. It cannot even be denied that God conferred the highest honor on Mary, by choosing and appointing her to be the mother of His Son. And yet Christ's reply is so far from assenting to this female voice, that it contains an indirect reproof.

NAY, RATHER, BLESSED ARE THEY THAT HEAR THE WORD OF GOD. We see that Christ treats almost as a matter of indifference that point on which the woman had set a high value. And undoubtedly what she supposed to be Mary's highest honor was far inferior to the other favors which she had received; for it was of vastly greater importance to be regenerated by the Spirit of God than to conceive Christ, according to the flesh, in her womb; to have Christ living spiritually within her than to suckle Him with her breasts. In a word, the highest happiness and glory of the holy Virgin consisted in her being a member of His Son, so that the heavenly Father reckoned her in the number of new creatures.

In my opinion, however, it was for another reason, and with a view to another object, that Christ now corrected the saying of the woman. It was because men are commonly chargeable with neglecting even those gifts of God on which they gaze with astonishment and bestow the highest praise. This woman, in applauding Christ, had left out what was of the very highest consequence, that in Him salvation is exhibited to all; and, therefore, it was a feeble commendation that made no mention of His grace and power, which is extended to all. Christ justly claims for Himself another kind of praise, not that His mother alone is reckoned "blessed," but that He brings to us all perfect and eternal happiness. We never form a just estimate of the excellence of Christ till we consider for what purpose He was given to us by the Father, and perceive the benefits which He has brought to us, so that we who are wretched in ourselves may become happy in Him. But why does He say nothing about Himself, and mention only the Word of God? It is because in this way He opens to us all His treasures; for without the Word He has no intercourse with us, nor we with Him. Communicating Himself to us by "the word," He rightly and properly calls us to "hear and keep it," that by faith He may become ours.

We now see the difference between Christ's reply and the woman's commendation; for the blessedness, which she had limited to His own relatives, is a favor that He offers freely to all. He shows that we ought to entertain no ordinary esteem for Him, because He has all "the treasures" of life, "blessedness," and glory, "hidden in him" (Colossians 2:3), which He dispenses by the Word, that they may be communicated to those who embrace "the word" by faith; for God's free adoption of us, which we obtain by faith, is the key to the kingdom of heaven. The connection between the two things must also be observed. We must first "hear" and then "keep"; for as "faith cometh by hearing" (Romans 10:17), it is in this way that the spiritual life must be commenced. Now as the simple hearing is like a transitory "looking into a mirror," as James says (1:23), he likewise adds, "the keeping of the word," which means the effectual reception of it, when it strikes its roots deep into our hearts, and yields its fruit. The forgetful hearer, whose ears alone are struck by the outward doctrine, gains no advantage. On the other hand, they who boast that they are satisfied with the secret inspiration, and on this ground disregard the outward preaching, shut themselves out from the heavenly life. What the Son of God "hath joined let not men," with wicked rashness, "put asunder" (Matthew 19:6). The Papists discover amazing stupidity by singing, in honor of Mary, those very words by which their superstition is expressly condemned; and they, in giving thanks, detach the woman's saying and leave out the correction. But it was proper that such a universal stupefaction should come upon those who intentionally profane, at their pleasure, the sacred word of God.

3. John Keble

It is a warfare in which it is utterly impossible for anyone to stand by and be neutral. In all wars and quarrels here we know there are many who take no part at all, but only just look on. But in this war between Christ and the devil, that cannot be the case with anyone. We must all take a part in it, whether we will or no. "He that is not with me is against me, and he that gathereth not with me, scattereth." Even in another place He says, "he that is not against us is on our part." Do you hear this, my brethren? It is a fearful sound, surely, for us all: more fearful than if a trumpet sounded from Heaven for a signal, which we must obey, to range ourselves on the right hand or on the left, on the side of Christ's enemies or of His friends. For such a trumpet would only be an angel's voice, but these are the very words of the Judge, spoken to the very inmost conscience of every one of us. Some of us may find it hard to receive them, just as it is hard, very hard, to bring it home to ourselves that we must all without exception, every single one of us, either go away at last into everlasting punishment with the wicked or with the righteous into life eternal. Oh! if we could indeed realize this, if we could keep it steadily before our mind's eye, how would it help us in the right way! And in like measure, if we could really settle it in our hearts to feel that we are, even now, in one or other of two great armies, if we could by faith constantly discern our King on the one side, and our enemy on the other, and ourselves ranged under this banner or that, would it not make us very serious? Would it be possible for us to go on as if our conduct signified little?

One thing at any rate is clear, if we will take our Lord really at His word, that such as feel quite easy in their minds, such as have no anxiety concerning their duty and their souls, can hardly be on Christ's side, and in the way of salvation. For as on the one hand we read, "happy is the man that feareth always," so on the other hand when the strong man armed keepeth his palace, our Lord tells us his goods are at peace: that is, when the devil has his own way with us most entirely, then we are quite entirely free from spiritual anxiety and misgiving of mind. We say to ourselves, peace, peace, most confidently when there is no peace. I have heard people boast that they let nothing daunt them, that they always kept up a good heart, and I have had reason to fear that their hope was little better than an ignorant deadness to spiritual things; that they were going on at the very time in plain, open, grievous sin. Therefore, I beseech you, let us greatly beware of indulging easy views of our condition; I mean our condition toward God; let us shrink from the thought that all is safe, let us say often in our hearts, What if after all I should be lost? Whatever else is right or wrong, this we are quite sure must be wrong, for a soldier in the midst of the battle to go on as if there was no enemy, no danger at all, for a Christian in the wicked world to feel entirely at ease about his soul and his behavior, as if all would go right of itself. Such an one is surely against Christ, if he did but know it.

So, too, is he (no uncommon sort of person I fear) who thinks he may stand off for a while, and take no part in this warfare, until he is older, or differently circumstanced; then he fully means to be religious, but he thinks he may be otherwise as yet; not irreligious, from such a thought he unfeignedly shrinks; but still not disposed to serve God entirely and always. What shall we say to such a man? That he is like a soldier in sight of the enemy, refusing to put on his armor, and declaring the hour of the battle to be not yet come: as if, when the order was given to charge, some should stand still, and say to themselves and to another, it will be time enough by and by to take up our arms. Nay, who told you that you should be here to take them up? Who told you that they should still be within your reach? Who told you that you shall not by that time be in the other world?

Bear with me, my brethren and sons in the Lord, if I say distinctly that this way of putting off your duties is far too common among you. I will just mention one instance: and many of you will guess beforehand what I am going to say. You all know in your hearts, you have been taught it from your childhood, and you have no doubt of it, that to be a good and thorough soldier of Christ, to be really and truly with Him and against His enemy, you must be one with Christ and Christ with you, and you know also that this is promised to those only who eat His Flesh and drink His Blood, as He bade them, in remembrance of Him. How can you put this duty away from you, and yet hope to be counted on our Saviour's side?

Good intentions I daresay you have. I daresay you think you shall begin to prepare yourselves, and come by and by. But remember that a wise and good man used to say, "hell is paved with good intentions." The greater number of those who go down that miserable road mean to repent at some time: only the time never quite comes. Our Lord did not say, he that does not purpose at some time or other to be with Me, but He said distinctly, he that is not with Me, not with Me now, not fighting now on My side, now at this very time, he, be he who he may, is against Me. He needs a great change, he is still in the snare of the devil.

But some might say, surely we are on Christ's side, the other day we resisted such a temptation, yesterday we performed such and such a good work, and though we have perhaps today fallen under the same temptation, and failed to do the same kind of good work, yet will not one tell against another? Are we not on the whole with Him and not against Him? I would ask you, my brethren one question. Suppose in battle you saw a soldier striking a blow or aiming a shot or a dart now against his own comrades, now against the enemy: on which side should you imagine him really to be, in the purpose and intention of his heart? Should you not judge this of him, that his secret purpose was rather on the side of the enemy, and that what blows he struck at them were rather to save appearances, or for some other selfish reason, than for any loyalty or duty which he had in his heart? In like manner you may be quite sure that as long as you allow yourself in any known willful sin, you cannot be quite sincere in any part of your duty, you are not a faithful soldier and servant, you do not love your King and Master. He Who sees into your heart cannot reckon you to be with Him.

Besides, what is the real consequence, even outwardly and before men, when Christians thus allow themselves to be half on the devil's side? Much the same as it would be in an army, when the soldiers should now and then turn against their own leader, in the very moment of action. There would be no confidence, no one would know on whom he could depend: the end would be confusion and flight, as our Lord goes on to say, "He that gathereth not with me, scattereth." We see and hear and feel daily the like sad effect of our many backslidings and inconsistencies. The unlearned and unbelievers say, behold how these Christians, these men professing godliness, do in their hearts and works deny it. Why then need we care for it? And they are bold to break off from God more and more. Oh! depend on it, it will never do, it is what neither God nor man will endure, for Christ's soldiers willfully to go on striking one blow for Satan and another for Christ. They will find in the end that they have been against their Lord altogether.

Neither again will it answer in this warfare if any man think to be passively on Christ's side, that is, to lie still and merely do nothing against Him. We cannot do so, my brethren if we would. Even if the hands could be idle, the mind, the will, the heart, must be employed, the whole soul must be tending this way or that, upward or downward, toward hell or toward Heaven. I suppose there are not a few who, looking on the sad falls and strange inconsistencies of such as have appeared earnest in religion, are inclined to shrink from being earnest themselves, as though there were some deceit in it: and so they are contented to go on, not only cold and indifferent in their devotions, but careless too, and loose in their rules of life, to their own and others' great danger and harm. I wish they and all of us considered more what the Great Shepherd here assures us, he that is not actively engaged gathering the flock with Me, is really scattering it. It is vain to think of being on Christ's side, and not being earnest and active in His cause. Remember the wicked and slothful servant: what cast him into the outer darkness? Not his ill-using his talent, but his not using it at all. Look round you, my brethren, and see, see what comes of lukewarmness, and ordinary ways, of being or seeming indifferent to the cause of God and His Church. The bad example speaks: one after another says, my neighbor is not particular, why should I be? My friend, my father, my master does not communicate, why should I? My mother, my mistress, my elder sister bears with unwomanly discreditable conduct, why may not I keep company with whom I will? Look into your own hearts, consider how much you are losing of God's grace and blessing. You might be fervent in prayer, you might be full of all good thoughts, holy seasons and communions might be a joy and crown to you: what a pity to lose all this for want of courage and exactness in your doings! Look again toward the enemy, see how you encourage him. Depend upon it, he rejoices in every moment you lose, every opportunity you neglect. Look, above all, to that which you know, or may know, to be written in God's book, as concerning your daily falls and backslidings: the positive sins, of will and temper at least, into which you are continually betrayed, for want of a courageous purpose of being entirely and zealously on God's side. Oh! if we will but turn our minds toward it, we shall see that Heaven and earth all around us, are full of tokens how blessed a thing it is to serve Christ with our whole heart, how fatal to serve Him with half a heart.

THE FOURTH SUNDAY IN LENT

Text: John 6:1-15

1. St. Augustine

It was a great miracle that was wrought, dearly beloved, for five thousand men to be filled with five loaves and two fishes, and the remnants of the fragments to fill twelve baskets. A great miracle; but we shall not wonder much at what was done if we give heed to Him that did it. He multiplied the five loaves in the hands of them that brake them, Who multiplieth the seeds that grow in the earth, so as that a few grains are sown, and whole barns are filled. But, because He doth this every year, no one marvels. Not the inconsiderableness of what is done, but its constancy takes away admiration of it. But when the Lord did these things, He spake to them that had understanding, not by words only, but even by the miracles themselves. The five loaves signified the five books of Moses' Law. The old Law is barley compared to the Gospel wheat. In those books are great mysteries concerning Christ contained. Whence He saith Himself, "If ye had believed Moses, ye would believe me also; for he wrote of me." But as in barley the marrow is hid under the chaff, so in the veil of the mysteries of the Law is Christ hidden. As those mysteries of the Law are developed and unfolded, so too those loaves increased when they were broken. And in this that I have explained to you, I have broken bread unto you. The five thousand men signify the people ordered under the five books of the Law. The twelve baskets are the twelve Apostles, who themselves too were filled with the fragments of the Law. The two fishes are either the two precepts of the love of God and our neighbor, or the two peoples of the circumcision and uncircumcision, or those two sacred personages of the king and the priest. As these things are explained, they are broken; when they are understood, they are eaten.

Let us turn to Him who did these things. He is Himself "the Bread which came down from heaven"; but Bread which refresheth the failing, and doth not fail; Bread which can be tasted, cannot be wasted. This Bread did the manna also figure. Wherefore it is said, "He gave them the Bread of heaven, man ate angels' Bread." Who is the Bread of heaven, but Christ? But in order that man might eat angels' Bread, the Lord of Angels was made Man. For if He had not been made Man, we should not have His Flesh; if we had not His Flesh, we should not eat the Bread of the Altar. Let us hasten to the inheritance, seeing we have hereby received a great earnest of it. My brethren, let us long for the life of Christ, seeing we hold as an earnest the death of Christ. How shall He not give us His good things, who hath suffered our evil things? In this our earth, in this evil

219

world, what abounds, but to be born, to labor, and to die? Examine thoroughly man's estate, convict me if I lie: consider all men whether they are in this world for any other end than to be born, to labor, and to die? This is the merchandise of our country: these things here abound. To such merchandise did that Merchantman descend. And forasmuch as every merchant gives and receives, gives what he has and receives what he has not, when he procures anything, he gives money and receives what he buys: so Christ too in this His traffic gave and received. But what received He? That which aboundeth here, to be born, to labor, and to die. And what did He give? To be born again, to rise again, and to reign forever. Oh good Merchant, buy us. Why should I say buy us, when we ought to give Thee thanks that Thou hast bought us? Thou dost deal out our Price to us, we drink Thy blood; so dost thou deal out to us our Price. And we read the Gospel, our title deed. We are Thy servants, we are Thy creatures: Thou hast made us, Thou hast redeemed us. Anyone can buy his servant, create him he cannot; but the Lord hath both created and redeemed His servants; created them, that they might be; redeemed them, that they might not be captives ever. For we fell into the hands of the prince of this world, who seduced Adam, and made him his servant, and began to possess us as his slaves. But the Redeemer came, and the seducer was overcome. And what did our Redeemer to him who held us captive? For our ransom He held out His cross as a trap; He placed in it as a bait His blood. He indeed had power to shed His blood, he did not attain to drink it. And in that he shed the blood of Him who was no debtor, he was commanded to render up the debtors; he shed the blood of the Innocent, he was commanded to withdraw from the guilty. He verily shed His blood to this end, that He might wipe out our sins. That then whereby he held us fast was effaced by the Redeemer's blood. For he only held us fast by the bonds of our own sins. They were the captive's chains. He came, He bound the strong one with the bonds of His Passion; He entered into his house, into the hearts, that is, of those where he did dwell, and took away his vessels. We are his vessels. He had filled them with his own bitterness. This bitterness too he pledged to our Redeemer in the gall. He had filled us then as his vessels; but our Lord spoiling his vessels, and making them His own, poured out the bitterness, filled them with sweetness.

Let us then love Him, for He is sweet. "Taste and see that the Lord is sweet." He is to be feared, but to be loved still more. He is Man and God; the One Christ is Man and God; as one man is soul and body; but God and Man are not two Persons. In Christ indeed there are two substances, God and Man; but one Person, that the Trinity may remain, and that there be not a quaternity introduced by the addition of the human nature. How then can it be that God should not have mercy upon us, for whose sake God was made Man? Much is that which He hath done already; more wonderful is that which He hath done than what He hath promised. For that which He hath done we should scarcely believe, unless we also saw it. Where do we see it? In the peoples that believe, in the multitude that has been brought unto Him. For that hath been fulfilled which was promised to Abraham; and from these things that we see, we believe what we do not see. Abraham was one single man, and to him was it said, "In thy seed shall all nations be blessed." If he had looked to himself, when would he have believed? He was one single man, and was now old; and he had a barren wife, and one who was so far advanced in age that she could not conceive, even though she had not been barren. There was nothing at all from which any hope could be drawn. But he looked to Him that gave the promise, and believed what he did not see. Lo, what he believed, we see. Therefore from these things that we see, we ought to believe what we see not. He begat Isaac, we saw it not; and Isaac begat Jacob, and this we did not see; and Jacob begat twelve sons, and them we saw not; and his twelve sons begat the people of Israel; this great people we see. I have now begun to mention those things which we do see. Of the people of Israel was born the Virgin Mary, and she gave birth to Christ; and, lo, in Christ all nations are blessed. What more true? more certain? more plain? Together with me, long after the world to come, ye who have been gathered together out of the nations. In this world hath God fulfilled His promise concerning the seed of Abraham. How shall He not give us His eternal promises, whom He hath made to be Abraham's seed? For this the Apostle saith; "But if ye be Christ's" (they are the Apostle's words), "then are ye Abraham's seed."

2. Martin Luther

THE FEEDING OF THE FIVE THOUSAND. In today's Gospel Christ gives us another lesson in faith, that we should not be over-anxious about our daily bread and our temporal existence, and stirs us up by means of a miracle; as though to say by His act what He says by His words in Matthew 6:33: "Seek ye first the kingdom of God, and his righteousness, and all these things shall be added unto you." For here we see, since the people followed Christ for the sake of God's Word and the signs, and thus sought the kingdom of God, he did not forsake them but richly fed them. He hereby also shows that, rather than those who seek the kingdom of God should suffer need, the grass in the desert would become wheat, or a crumb of bread would be turned into a thousand loaves; or a morsel of bread would feed as many people and just as satisfactorily as a thousand loaves; in order that the words in Matthew 4:4 might stand firm, that "Man shall not live by bread alone, but by every word that proceedeth out of the mouth of God." And to confirm these words Christ is the first to be concerned about the people, as to what they should eat, and asks Philip, before they complain or ask Him; so that we may indeed let Him care for us, remembering that He cares more and sooner for us than we do for ourselves.

Secondly, He gives an example of great love, and He does this in many ways. First, in that He lets not only the pious, who followed Him because of the signs and the Word, enjoy the food, but also the slaves of appetite, who only eat and drink and seek in Him temporal honor; as follows later when they disputed with Him at Capernaum about the food, and He said to them in John 6:26: "Ye seek me, not because ye saw signs, but because ye ate of the loaves," also because they desired to make Him king; thus here also He lets His sun shine on the evil and the good (Matthew 5:45). Secondly, in that He bears with the rudeness and weak faith of His disciples in such a friendly manner. For that He tests Philip, who thus comes with his reason, and Andrew, who speaks so childishly on the subject, all is done to bring to light the imperfections of the disciples and, on the contrary, to set forth His love and dealings with them in a more beautiful and loving light, to encourage us to believe in Him, and to give us an example to do likewise; as the members of our body and all God's creatures in their relation to one another teach us. For these are full of love, so that one bears with the other, helps and preserves what God has created.

That He now takes the five loaves and gives thanks, and so forth, teaches that nothing is too small and insignificant for Him to do for His followers, and He can indeed so bless their pittance that they have an abundance, whereas even the rich have not enough with all their riches; as Psalm 34:11 says: "They that seek Jehovah shall not want any good thing; but the rich must suffer hunger." And Mary in her song of praise says: "The hungry he hath filled with good things; and the rich he hath sent empty away" (Luke 1:53).

Again, that He tells them so faithfully to gather up the fragments teaches us to be frugal and to preserve and use His gifts, in order that we may not tempt God. For just as it is God's will that we should believe when we have nothing and be assured that He will provide, so He does not desire to be tempted nor to allow the blessings He has bestowed to be despised, or lie unused and spoil, while we expect other blessings from heaven by means of miracles. Whatever He gives, we should receive and use, and what He does not give, we should believe and expect He will bestow.

3. John Calvin

Let us now sum up the meaning of the whole miracle. It has this in common with the other miracles, that Christ displayed in it His divine power in union with beneficence. It is also a confirmation to us of that statement by which He exhorts us to "seek the kingdom of God," promising that "all other things shall be added to us" (Matthew 6:33). For if He took care of those who were led to Him only by a sudden impulse, how would He desert us if we seek Him with a firm and steady purpose? True, indeed, He will sometimes allow His own people, as I have said, to suffer hunger; but He will never deprive them of His aid; and, in the meantime, He has very good reasons for not assisting us till matters come to an extremity.

Besides, Christ plainly showed that He not only bestows spiritual life on the world, but that His Father commanded Him also to nourish the body. For abundance of all blessings is committed to His hand that, as a channel, He may convey them to us (though I speak incorrectly by calling him "a channel," for He is rather the living Fountain flowing from the eternal Father). Accordingly, Paul prays that all blessings may come to us "from God the Father, and from the Lord Jesus Christ," in common

(1 Corinthians 1:3); and, in another passage, he shows that "in all things we ought to give thanks to God, the Father, through our Lord Jesus Christ" (Ephesians 5:20). And not only does this office belong to His eternal divinity, but even in His human nature, and so far as He has taken upon Him our flesh, the Father has appointed Him to be the Dispenser, that by His hands He may feed us. Now, though we do not every day see miracles before our eyes, yet not less bountifully does God display His power in feeding us. And indeed we do not read that, when he wished to give a supper to His people, He used any new means; and, therefore, it would be an inconsiderate prayer if anyone were to ask that meat and drink might be given to him by some unusual method.

Again, Christ did not provide great delicacies for the people, but they who saw His amazing power displayed in that supper were obliged to rest satisfied with barley-bread and fish without sauce. And though He does not now satisfy "five thousand men" with "five loaves," still He does not cease to feed the whole world in a wonderful manner. It sounds to us, no doubt, like a paradox that "man liveth not by bread alone, but by the word which proceedeth out of the mouth of God" (Deuteronomy 8:3). For we are so strongly attached to outward means that nothing is more difficult than to depend on the providence of God. Hence it arises that we tremble so much as soon as we have not bread at hand. And if we consider everything aright, we shall be compelled to discern the blessing of God in all the creatures which serve for our bodily support; but use and frequency lead us to undervalue the miracles of nature. And yet, in this respect, it is not so much our stupidity as our malignity that hinders us; for where is the man to be found who does not choose to wander astray in his mind, and to encompass heaven and earth a hundred times, rather than look at God Who presents Himself to his view?

AND FILLED TWELVE BASKETS. When "four thousand men" were fed by "seven loaves," Matthew relates that the number of baskets filled with fragments was exactly the same as the number of the loaves (Matthew 15:37). Since, therefore, a smaller quantity is sufficient for a greater number of men, and since the quantity left is nearly double, we see more clearly of what value is that blessing of God against the sight of which we deliberately shut our eyes. We ought also to observe, in passing, that though Christ commands them to "fill the baskets" for illustrating the miracle, yet He likewise exhorts His disciples to frugality when he says, "Gather the fragments which are left, that nothing may be lost"; for the increase of the bounty of God ought not to be an excitement to luxury. Let those, therefore, who have abundance remember that they will one day render an account of their immoderate wealth if they do not carefully and faithfully apply their superfluity to purposes which are good, and of which God approves.

4. Charles Spurgeon

Now I come to the second part of the subject, and that is, that *there was no question with Jesus*. The question was with Philip, but Christ had no question. "This he said to prove him: for he himself knew what he would do."

Let us take these words and pull them to pieces a minute. *"He knew."* He always does know. "Ah," says one, "I am sure I do not know what I shall do." No, dear friend, and yet you have been taking advice, have you not? That is a splendid way of confusing yourself. I hear you cry in bewilderment, "I do not know. I have been to everybody, and I do not know what I shall do." That is a chronic state with us when we puzzle our own poor brains; but Jesus knew what He would do. This is sweet comfort; Jesus knows. He always knows all about it. He knew how many people there were. He knew how much bread it would take. He knew how many fish He would want, and how He meant to feed the crowd, and send them all away refreshed. He knew all before it happened. Tried brother, Jesus knows all about *your* case and how He is going to bring *you* through. Do not think that you can inform Him as to anything. "Your heavenly Father knoweth what ye have need of before ye ask him." Prayer is not meant for the Lord's information. The question is not put to you that you may instruct Him, but that He may instruct you. He made the heavens and the earth without you. With whom took He counsel? Who instructed Him? And He will bring you through this present trial of yours without needing to add your poor wisdom to His infinite knowledge. He knows.

Jesus "knew what he would do." He meant to do something; He was quite ready to do it; and He knew what He was going to do. We embarrass ourselves by saying, "Something must be done, but I do not know who is to do it." The Saviour knew that something must be done, and He knew that He was going to do it Himself. He was not in a hurry, He never is: "He never is before his time, he never is too late." Our blessed Master has glorious leisure, because He is always punctual. Late people are in a hurry; but He, being never late, never hurries. He does everything calmly and serenely because He foresees what He will do. Jesus knows, dear friend, concerning you, not only what you will do, but what *He* will do. That is the point, and He means to do some great thing for you and to help you. He means also to bring this city and this nation to His feet. He means that every knee shall bow to Him, and that the whole earth shall be filled with His glory. He knows what He means to do.

He knew, moreover, *how he meant to do it*. He knew precisely the way and method which He intended to use. He perceived long before Andrew told Him that there was a lad somewhere in the crowd with five barley cakes. When the lad set out that morning, I cannot make out what made him bring five barley loaves and two fishes into that crowd; except the Master had whispered in his heart, "Young lad, take with you a good lunch. Put those barley cakes into the basket, and do not forget the fishes. You do not know how long you may be from home." Nature bade him provide for contingencies, but then nature is God's voice when He chooses to make it so. He was a hungry, growing lad with a fine appetite, and he meant to be well provided for; but had he ever thought in his mind that these strangely providential cakes would multiply so as to feed that mass of people? Where is the man that is to be the universal provider? Where is the chief of the commissariat? It is that youth, and that is the whole of his storehouse. He is carrying a magazine of victuals on his back—in that basket. The Saviour knew that. And He knows exactly, dear friend, where your help is to come from in your hour of trouble. You do not know, but He does. He knows where the ministers are to come from that will stir up this city of London; and He knows in what style and manner they shall come, and how they shall get at the masses. When everybody else is defeated and nonplussed, He is fully prepared. He knew that those loaves and fishes would be fetched out in due time to be the basis of a banquet; He knew that He would bless them, break them, multiply them, and give them to the disciples, and the disciples to the multitude. Everything was arranged in His mind, and as much fixed as the rising of the sun.

Once more, *he did it as one who knew what he was going to do*. How does a man act when he knows what he is going to do? Well, he generally proceeds in the most *natural* way. He knows that he is going to do it; so he just goes and does it. Can you conceive that a miracle was ever performed in a more natural style? If this had been a Roman Catholic miracle, they would have thrown the loaves up in the air, and they would have come down mysteriously transformed and multiplied a million times; all popish miracles, if you observe, have a great deal of the theatrical and showy about them. They are totally distinct from the miracles of Christ. He does this miracle in the most natural way in the world, because it is virtually the same miracle which Christ works every year. We take a certain quantity of wheat, and put it into the ground, and, in the long run, the end of it is that it is multiplied into loaves of bread. Certain fishes are in the sea, and they increase into great shoals. The sown wheat passes through the same operation in the ground in the same hands—in God's hands, but it comes out loaves of bread; and this is precisely what came of our Lord's action. He took a little into His own blessed hands, and brake it, and it kept on multiplying in His hands, and in the hands of His disciples, till they were all filled.

He knew what He was going to do, and so He did it naturally, and did it *orderly*. It is not so when a man does not know what he is to provide for. We have a large meeting, and there is provision made for a tea, and three times as many come as you have provided for. What a hurry! What a scurry! What a running to and fro! Jesus never conducts His matters in that way. He knew what He was going to do, and, therefore, He bade the men sit down on the grass; and they sat down like so many children. Mark tells us that they sat down in rows by fifties and by hundreds; they were arranged as if each one had been specially set to his plate, and found his name laid upon it. Moreover, there was much grass in the place, so that the hall was carpeted in a way that no firm in London could have done it. The feast was conducted as orderly as if there had been notice given seven days beforehand, and a contractor had supplied the provisions. Nothing could have been done in a better way, and all because Jesus knew what He would do.

Moreover, He did it very *joyfully*. He took bread and blessed it. He went about it with great pleasure. I should have liked to have seen His face as He looked on these poor famishing people being fed. Like a good host, He cheered them with His smile, while He blessed them with the food.

And then He did it so *plentifully*, for He knew what He would do; so He did not come half provided, or stint them so that every man should have "a little." No; He knew what He would do, and He measured their appetites exactly, a difficult thing when you have a number of hungry people to feed. He provided all that they wanted, and afterward there was provision left for the head waiters, so that each one should have a basketful for himself; for they took up of the fragments twelve basketfuls—one for each of the head waiters.

Our Lord Jesus Christ, in the matter of bringing in His own elect, is going about it, I am quite certain, knowing what He is going to do; and when you and I see the end of the great festival of mercy we shall say, "Blessed be the Lord! We were in a great worry; we were in sore trouble; but our Lord has done it easily, and thoroughly. There has been no muddle, no crowding, no passing over of anybody. Blessed be His name! He has not done it by chance or through fortunate circumstances; but He knew what He would do, and He has planned it all through from the beginning to the end in such a way that principalities and powers in heaven shall sing forever of the grace and love and wisdom and power and prudence wherein He has abounded toward His people." Oh, but if we could see the end as well as the beginning we should begin even now to exalt the name of Jesus our Saviour, who foreknows all His work, and never deviates from His plan.

I conclude by saying that because there is no question with Christ, though He puts questions to us, THERE OUGHT TO BE NO QUESTION OF A DOUBTFUL CHARACTER ANY LONGER TO US.

THE FIFTH SUNDAY IN LENT

Text: John 8:46-59

1. St. Augustine

In that lesson of the holy Gospel which has been read today, from power we learn patience. For what are we as servants to the Lord, as sinners to the Just One, as creatures to the Creator? Howbeit, just as in what we are evil, we are so of ourselves; so in whatever respects we are good, we are so of Him, and through Him. And nothing does man so seek as he does power. He has great power in the Lord Christ; but let him first imitate His patience, that he may attain to power. Who of us would listen with patience if it were said to him, "Thou hast a devil," as was said to Him, Who was not only bringing men to salvation, but also subjecting devils to His authority?

For when the Jews had said, "Say we not well that thou art a Samaritan, and hast a devil?" of these two charges cast at Him, He denied the one, but not the other. For He answered and said, "I have not a devil." He did not say, I am not a Samaritan; and yet the two charges had been made. Although He returned not cursing with cursing, although He met not slander with slander, yet was it proper for Him to deny the one charge and not to deny the other. And not without a purpose, brethren. For Samaritan means keeper. He knew that He was our keeper. For "He that keepeth Israel neither slumbereth nor sleepeth"; and, "Except the Lord keep the city, they wake in vain who keep it." He then is our Keeper who is our Creator. For did it belong to Him to redeem us, and would it not be His to preserve us? Finally, that you may know more fully the hidden reason why He ought not to have denied that He was a Samaritan, call to mind that well-known parable where a certain man went down from Jerusalem to Jericho and fell among thieves, who wounded him severely and left him half dead on the road. A priest came along and took no notice of him. A Levite came up, and he also passed on his way. A certain Samaritan came up—He who is our Keeper. *He* went up to the wounded man. *He* exercised mercy, and did a neighbor's part to one whom *He* did not account an alien. To this, then, He only replied that He had not a devil, but not that He was not a Samaritan.

And then after such an insult, this was all that He said of His own glory: "But I honor," said He, "my Father, and ye dishonor me." That is, I honor not Myself, that ye may not think Me arrogant. I have One to honor; and did ye recognize Me, just as I honor the Father, so would ye also honor Me. I do what I ought; ye do not what ye ought.

"And I," said He, "seek not mine own glory: there is one that seeketh

227

and judgeth." Whom does He wish to be understood but the Father? How, then, does He say in another place, "The Father judgeth no man, but hath committed all judgment unto the Son," while here He says, "I seek not mine own glory: there is one that seeketh and judgeth"? If, then, the Father judgeth, how is it that He judgeth no man, but hath committed all judgment unto the Son?

In order to solve this point, attend. It may be solved by (quoting) a similar mode of speaking. Thou hast it written, "God tempteth not any man"; and again thou hast it written, "The Lord your God tempteth you, to know whether you love him." Just the point in dispute, you see, For how does God *tempt not any man*, and how does the Lord your God *tempt you, to know whether ye love Him?* It is also written, "There is no fear in love; but perfect love casteth out fear"; and in another place it is written, "The fear of the Lord is clean, enduring for ever." Here also is the point in dispute. For how does *perfect love cast out fear*, if *the fear of the Lord*, which is clean, *endureth for ever?*

We are to understand, then, that there are two kinds of temptation: one, that deceives; the other, that proves. As regards that which deceives, "God tempteth not any man"; as regards that which proves, "the Lord your God tempteth you, that he may know whether ye love him." But here again, also, there arises another question, how He *tempteth that He may know*, from whom, prior to the temptation, nothing can be hid. It is not that God is ignorant; but it is said, *that He may know*, that is, that He may make you to know. Such modes of speaking are found both in our ordinary conversation and in writers of eloquence. Let me say a word on our style of conversation. We speak of a blind ditch, not because it has lost its eyes, but because by lying hid it makes us blind to its existence. One speaks of "bitter," that is, "sour," lupins; not that they themselves are bitter, but because they occasion bitterness to those who taste them. And so there are also expressions of this sort in Scripture. Those who take the trouble to attain a knowledge of such points have no trouble in solving them. And so, "the Lord your God tempts you, that he may know." What is this, "that he may know"? That He may make you to know "if you love him." Job was unknown to himself, but he was not unknown to God. He led the tempter into (Job), and brought him to a knowledge of himself.

What then of the two fears? There is a servile fear, and there is a clean (chaste) fear; there is the fear of suffering punishment, there is another fear of losing righteousness. That fear of suffering punishment is slavish. What great thing is it to fear punishment? The vilest slave and the cruelest robber do so. It is no great thing to fear punishment, but great it is to love righteousness. Has he, then, who loves righteousness no fear? Certainly he has; not of incurring of punishment, but of losing righteousness. My brethren, assure yourselves of it, and draw your inference from that which you love. Some one of you is fond of money. Can I find any one, think you, who is not so? Yet from this very thing which he loves he may understand my meaning. He is afraid of loss: why is he so? Because he loves money. In the same measure that he loves money, is he afraid of losing it. So, then, someone is found to be a lover of righteousness, who at heart is much more afraid of its loss, who dreads more being stripped of his righteousness, than thou of thy money. This is the fear that is clean—this (the fear) that endureth forever. It is not this that love makes away with, or casteth out, but rather embraces it, and keeps it with it, and possesses it as a companion. For we come to the Lord that we may see Him face to face. And there it is this pure fear that preserves us; for such a fear as that does not disturb, but reassure. The adulterous woman fears the coming of her husband, and the chaste one fears her husband's departure.

Therefore, as, according to one kind of temptation, "God tempteth not any man," but according to another, "the Lord your God tempteth you"; and according to one kind of fear, "there is no fear in love; but perfect love casteth out fear," but according to another, "the fear of the Lord is clean, enduring for ever"—so also, in this passage, according to one kind of judgment, "the Father judgeth no man, but hath committed all judgment unto the Son," and according to another, "I," said He, "seek not mine own glory: there is one that seeketh and judgeth."

This point may also be solved from the word itself. Thou hast penal judgment spoken of in the Gospel: "He that believeth not is judged already"; and in another place, "The hour is coming, when those who are in the graves shall hear his voice, and shall come forth; they that have done good, unto the resurrection of life; and they that have done evil, unto the resurrection of judgment." You see how He has put judgment for condemnation and punishment. And yet if judgment were always to be taken for condemnation, should we ever have heard in the Psalm, "Judge me, O God"? In the former place, judgment is used in the sense of inflicting pain; here, it is used in the sense of discernment. How so? Just because so expounded by him who says, "Judge me, O God." For read, and see what follows. What is this "Judge me, O God," but just what he adds, "and discern my cause against an unholy nation"? Because then it was said, "Judge me, O God, and discern (the true merits of) my cause against an unholy nation"; similarly now said the Lord Christ, "I seek not mine own glory: there is One that seeketh and judgeth." How is there "one that seeketh and judgeth"? There is the Father, Who discerns and distinguishes between my glory and yours. For ye glory in the spirit of this present world. Not so do I, who say to the Father, "Father, glorify Thou me with that glory which I had with Thee before the world was." What is "that glory"? One altogether different from human inflation. Thus doth the Father judge. And so to "judge" is to "discern." And what does He discern? The glory of His Son from the glory of mere men; for to that end is it said, "God, Thy God, hath anointed Thee with the oil of gladness above Thy fellows." For not because He became man is He now to be compared with us. We, as men, are sinful, He is sinless; we, as men, inherit from Adam both death and delinquency, He received from the Virgin mortal flesh, but no iniquity. In fine, neither because *we* wish it are we born, nor as long as we wish it do we live, nor in the way that we wish it do we die: but He, before He was born, chose of whom He should be born; at His birth He brought about the adoration of the Magi; He grew as an infant, and showed Himself God by His miracles, and surpassed man in His weakness. Lastly, He chose also the manner of His death, that is, to be hung on the cross, and to fasten the cross itself on the foreheads of believers, so that the Christian may say, "God forbid that I should glory, save in the cross of our Lord Jesus Christ." On the very cross, when He pleased, He made His body be taken down, and departed; in the very sepulchre, as long as it pleased Him, He lay; and, when He pleased, He arose as from a bed. So, then, brethren, in respect to His very form as a servant (for who can speak of that other form as it ought to be spoken of, "In the beginning was the Word, and the Word was with God, and the Word was God"?)— in respect, I say, to His very form as a servant, the difference is great between the glory of Christ and the glory of other men. Of that glory He spoke, when the devil-possessed heard Him say, "I seek not mine own glory: there is One that seeketh and judgeth."

2. *Martin Luther*

This Gospel teaches how hardened persons become the more furious the more one teaches them and lovingly stirs them to do their duty. For Christ asks them here in a very loving way for a reason why they still disbelieve, since they can find fault neither with His life nor with His teaching. His life is blameless, for He defies them and says: "Which of you convicteth me of sin?" His teaching also is blameless, for He adds: "If I say truth, why do ye not believe me?" Thus Christ lives, as He teaches.

And every preacher should prove that he possesses both: first, a blameless life, by which he can defy his enemies and no one may have occasion to slander his teachings; secondly, that he possesses the pure doctrine, so that he may not mislead those who follow him. And thus he will be right and firm on both sides: with his good life against his enemies, who look much more at his life than at his doctrine, and despise the doctrine for the sake of the life; with his doctrine among his friends, who have much more respect for his doctrine than for the kind of life he leads, and will bear with his life for the sake of his teaching.

For it is indeed true that no one lives so perfect a life as to be without sin before God. Therefore it is sufficient that he be blameless in the eyes of the people. But his doctrine must be so good and pure as to stand not only before man but also before God. Therefore every pious pastor may well ask: Who among you can find fault with my life? Among you, I say, who are men; but before God I am a sinner. Thus Moses also boasts in Numbers 16:15 that he took nothing from the people and he did them no injustice. Samuel did likewise in 1 Samuel 12:3; also Jeremiah and Hezekiah, who rightly boasted of their blameless life before the people in order to stop the mouths of blasphemers. But Christ does not speak thus of His doctrine, He says not: "Who among you can find fault with My doctrine"; but "If I tell you the truth." For one must be assured that His doctrine is right before God and that it is the truth, and accordingly care not how it is judged by the people.

Hence the Jews have no ground for their unbelief than that they are not the children of God; therefore He passes judgment upon them and says: "He that is of God heareth the words of God; for this cause ye hear them not, because ye are not of God," that cannot mean anything else than that you are of the devil.

The Jews could not stand this, for they wished to be God's children and people; therefore they are now raging and slander both Christ's life and His doctrine; His doctrine, in that they say: "Thou hast a devil," that is, thou speakest moved by the devil and thy doctrine is his lie; and they slander His life, in that they say, "Thou art a Samaritan," which sounds among the Jews worse than any other crime. In this way Christ teaches us here the fate that awaits us Christians and His Word; both our life and our doctrine must be condemned and reviled, and that by the foremost, wisest, and greatest of earth. Thus one knows the corrupt tree by its fruits, as they, under the pretense of being good, are so bitter, angry, impatient, cruel, and mad as to condemn and pass sentence when one touches them at their tender spot and rejects their ideas and ways.

What does Christ do here? His life He abandons to shame and dishonor, He is silent and suffers them to call Him a Samaritan, while He takes pains to defend His doctrine. For the doctrine is not ours, but God's, and God dare not suffer in the least, here patience is at an end; but I should stake all that I have and suffer, all that they do, in order that the honor of God and of His Word may not be injured. For if I perish, no great harm is done; but if I let God's Word perish, and I remain silent, then I do harm to God and to the whole world. Although I cannot now close their mouth nor prevent their wickedness, I shall nevertheless not keep silent, nor act as if they are right, as I do about my good life, so that they retain their right. Although they do me injustice at the time, yet it remains right before God. Further, Christ excuses Himself, and says: "I have not a demon," that is, My doctrine is not of the devil's lies; "but I honor my Father," that is, I preach in My doctrine the grace of God, through which He is to be praised, loved, and honored by believers. For the evangelical office of the ministry is nothing but glorifying God (Psalm 19:2): "The heavens declare the glory of God." "But you dishonor me," that is, you call Me the devil's liar, who reviles and dishonors God.

Why does He not say: I honor my Father, and ye dishonor him; but says: "Ye dishonor me?" Impliedly He proves by this that the Father's and His honor are alike and the same, as He and the Father are one God; yet along with this He also wishes to teach that if the office of the ministry, which God honors, is to be duly praised, then it must suffer disgrace. In like manner we will also do to our princes and priests; when they attack our manner of life, we should suffer it and show love for hatred, good for evil; but when they attack our doctrine, God's honor is attacked, then love and patience should cease and we should not keep silent, but also say: I honor my Father, and you dishonor me, for I do not seek my own honor. But nevertheless be on your guard, there is One who seeks it and judges, that is, the Father will require it of you, and judge you and never let you go unpunished. He seeks not only His honor, but also mine, because I seek His honor, as he says in 1 Samuel 2:30: "Them that honor me I will honor." And it is our consolation that we are happy; although the whole world reviles and dishonors us, we are assured that God will advance our honor, and therefore will punish, judge, and revenge. If one could only believe it and persevere, He will surely come.

3. *Charles Kingsley*

Let us think a few minutes, with all humility, not rashly intruding ourselves into the things we have not seen, or meddling with divine matters which are too hard for us, but taking our Lord's words simply as they stand, and where we do not understand them, believing them nevertheless.

Now it is clear that the book of Exodus and our Lord's words speak of the same person. The Old Testament tells of a personage who appeared to Moses in the wilderness, and who called Himself "the Lord God of Abraham, Isaac and Jacob." But this personage also calls Himself "I AM." "I AM THAT I AM:" "and He said, Thus shalt thou say unto the children of Israel, I AM hath sent me unto you."

In the New Testament we read of a personage who calls Himself the Son of God, is continually called the Lord, and who tells His disciples to call Him by that name without reproving them, though they and He knew well what it meant—that it meant no less than this, that He, Jesus of Nazareth, poor mortal man as He seemed, was still the Lord, the God of Abraham, Isaac, and Jacob. I do not say that the disciples saw that at first, clearly or fully, till after our Lord's resurrection. But there was one moment shortly before His death, when they could have had no doubt who He assumed Himself to be. For the unbelieving Jews had no doubt and considered Him a blasphemer; and these were His awful and wonderful words—I do not pretend to understand them—I take them simply as I find them, and believe and adore. "Your father Abraham rejoiced to see my day, and he saw it, and was glad. Then said the Jews unto him, Thou art not yet fifty years old, and hast thou seen Abraham?" One cannot blame them for asking that question, for Abraham had been dead then nearly two thousand years. But what is our Lord's solemn answer? "Verily, verily, I say unto you, before Abraham was, I am.

"I AM." The same name by which our Lord God had revealed Himself to Moses in the wilderness, some sixteen hundred years before. If these words were true—and the Lord prefaces them with Verily, verily, Amen, Amen, which was as solemn an asseveration as any oath could be—then the Lord Jesus Christ is none other than the God of Abraham, the God of Moses, the God of the Jews, the God of the whole universe, past, present, and to come.

Let us think awhile over this wonder of all wonders. The more we think over it, we shall find it not only the wonder of all wonders, but the good news of all good news.

The deepest and soundest philosophers will tell us that there must be an "I AM." That is, as they would say, a self-existent Being; neither made nor created, but who has made and created all things; who is without parts and passions, and is incomprehensible, that is, cannot be comprehended, limited, made smaller or weaker, or acted on in any way by any of the things that He has made. So that this self-existing Being whom we call God, would be exactly what He is now if the whole universe, sun, moon, and stars, were destroyed this moment; and would be exactly what He is now, if there had never been any universe at all, or any thing or being except His own perfect and self-existent Self. For He lives and moves and has His being in nothing. But all things live and move and have their being in Him. He was before all things, and by Him all things consist. And this is the Catholic faith; and not only that, this is according to sound and right reason. But more: the soundest philosophers will tell you that God must be not merely a self-existent Being, but the "I AM": that if God is a Spirit, and not merely a name for some powers and laws of brute nature and matter, He must be able to say to Himself, "I AM": that He must know Himself, that He must be conscious of Himself, of who and what He is, as you and I are conscious of ourselves, and more or less of who and what we are. And this, also, I believe to be true, and rational, and necessary to the Catholic faith.

But they will tell you again—and this, too, is surely true—that I AM must be the very name of God, because God alone can say perfectly, "I AM," and no more. You and I dare not, if we think accurately, say of ourselves, "I am." We may say, I am this or that; I am a man; I am an Englishman; but we must not say, "I am"; that is, "I exist of myself." We must say—not I am; but I become, or have become; I was made; I was created; I am growing, changing; I depend for my very existence on God and God's will, and if He willed, I should be nothing and nowhere in a moment. God alone can say, I AM, and there is none beside Me, and never has been, nor can be. I exist, absolutely, and simply; because I choose to exist, and get life from nothing; for I AM the Life, and give life to all things.

But you may say, What is all this to us? It is very difficult to understand, and dreary, and even awful. Why should we care for it, even if it be true? Yes, my friends; philosophy may be true, and yet be dreary, and awful, and have no gospel and good news in it at all. I believe it never can have; that only in Revelation, and in the Revelation of our Lord Jesus Christ, can poor human beings find any gospel and good news at all. And sure I am, that that is an awful thought, a dreary thought, a crushing thought, which makes a man feel as small, and worthless, and helpless, and hopeless, as a grain of dust, or a mote in the sunbeam—that thought of God forever contained in Himself, and saying forever to Himself, "I AM, and there is none beside Me."

But the Gospel, the good news of the Old Testament, the Gospel, the good news of the New Testament, is the Revelation of God and God's ways, which began on Christmas Day, and finished on Ascension Day: and what is that? What but this? That God does not merely say to Himself in Majesty, "I AM," but that He goes out of Himself in Love, and says to men, "I AM." That He is a God who has spoken to poor human beings, and told them who He was; and that He, the I AM, the self-existent One, the Cause of life, of all things, even the Maker and Ruler of the Universe, can stoop to man—and not merely to perfect men, righteous men, holy men, wise men, but to the enslaved, the sinful, the brutish—that He may deliver them, and teach them, and raise them from the death of sin, to His own life of righteousness.

Do you not see the difference, the infinite difference, and the good news in that? Do you not see a whole heaven of new hope and new duty is opened to mankind in that one fact—God has spoken to man. He, the I AM, the Self-Existent, who needs no one, and no thing, has turned aside, as it were, and stooped from the throne of heaven, again and again, during thousands of years, to say to you, and me, and millions of mankind, I AM your God. How do you prosper? what do you need? what are you doing?— for if you are doing justice to yourself and your fellow men, then fear not that I shall be just to you.

And more. When that I AM, the self-existent God, could not set sinful men right by saying this, then did He stoop once more from the throne of the heavens to do that infinite deed of love, of which it is written, that He who called Himself "I am," the God of Abraham, was conceived of the Holy Ghost, born of the Virgin Mary, crucified under Pontius Pilate, rose again the third day, and ascended into heaven—that He might send down the Spirit of the "I AM," the Holy Spirit who proceedeth from the Father and the Son, upon all who ask Him; that they may be holy as God is holy, and perfect as God is perfect. Yes, my dear friends, remember that, and live in the light of that; the gospel of good news of the Incarnation of Jesus Christ, very God of very God begotten. Know that God has spoken to you as He spoke to Abraham, and said—I am the Almighty God, walk before Me, and be thou perfect. Know that He has spoken to you as He spoke to Moses, saying—I am the Lord thy God, who have brought you, and your fathers before you, out of the spiritual Egypt of heathendom, and igno-rance, sin, and wickedness, into the knowledge of the one, true, and right-eous God. But know more, that He has spoken to you by the mouth of Jesus Christ, saying—I am He that died in the form of mortal man upon the cross for you. And, behold, I am alive for evermore; and to Me all power is given in heaven and earth.

PALM SUNDAY

Text: Matthew 21:1-9

1. *Bernard of Clairvaux*

THE PALM PROCESSION AND THE PASSION FOLLOWING. It is not without reason that the Church, inspired by her Bridegroom and her God, has united a procession with today's reading of the Passion, in a new and wonderful association. In the procession there is clapping of hands; beating of breasts accompanies the Passion. Since we are debtors both to the wise and to the unwise, let us consider what this conjunction of the two denotes for each. The worldly soul may learn from it that, on the natural plane, sorrow will always follow on the heels of joy. The Lord, when He appeared in flesh, declared this fact by His example as well as by His words; His own experience fulfilled the prophet's saying that "all flesh is grass and all the glory thereof as the flower of grass"; and to this end He willed to be glorified in the procession, knowing that the day of His most shameful Passion was to follow very soon. And who can thus see Him Who did no sin, Who fashioned times and seasons and made the universe, pass from such exaltation to such great abasement, and himself put any confidence in the uncertainty of temporal glory? In the same city, by the same people, at the same season, He was honored with divine praises one day and, a little later, put on His trial amid insults and torture and reckoned among the transgressors! That is the end to which all passing gladness leads; that is the fruit that temporal glory bears.

But you, beloved, are spiritual; therefore for you the procession represents a spiritual truth, namely, the glory of our heavenly fatherland; and the Passion shows the way that leads thereto. For if, as you take part in our procession today, the thought of the joy that is to be is in your mind, and the surpassing exultation there will be when we are caught up in the clouds to meet Christ in the air; if you desire with your whole heart to see that Day when Christ the Lord, the Head with all His members, shall be received into the heavenly Jerusalem bearing the palm of victory and with angelic powers and the peoples of both Testaments crying on every side "Blessed is he that cometh!" instead of common crowds; if, I say, you consider during the procession whither you must hasten, then in the Passion learn the way that you must take! For this present tribulation is itself the way of life, the way of glory, the way to the heavenly habitation, the way of the Kingdom concerning which the thief cried from the cross, "Remember me, Lord, when thou comest into thy kingdom!" He saw Him going to His kingdom, and asked Him, when He got there, to be mindful of himself. And he, the thief, arrived there too; and you can see how short a road it was, for on that very day he was accounted worthy to be with the Lord in Paradise. Thus the procession's glory makes the travail of the Passion bearable; for when one loves, nothing is difficult.

You need not be surprised at my saying that our procession represents a heavenly one; for the central Figure in each is One and the Same, though He is carried and accompanied in very different ways. Christ sits on an irrational beast of burden in today's procession; in that which is to come He will be mounted too, but on a rational creature, even as it is written, "Thou, Lord, shalt save both man and beast," and, in another place, "I am become before thee as a beast, and I am always with thee." The next words also seem to speak of this procession: "Thou heldest my right hand," it says, "and leddest me according to thy will, and thou receivedst me with glory." And so that the foal might find a place in the future procession too, He, Who Himself was born a little Child and chose the infant Innocents to form the vanguard of His army, does not shut out young children from His grace today, but suffers them to come to Him in baptism. For neither does His love find it unfitting, nor does His majesty account it difficult thus to bestow the gift of grace on those whose nature is most needy.

Again, in the heavenly procession, instead of a crowd of people strewing branches and vile garments in the way, the holy living creatures will drop feathers from their wings and the four-and-twenty elders will cast their crowns before the throne of the Lamb, and all the angelic powers will ascribe and attribute wholly to Him whatever they possess of honor and of glory.

2. Martin Luther

This Gospel encourages and demands faith, for it prefigures Christ coming with grace, whom none may receive or accept save he who believes Him to be the Man, and has the mind, as this Gospel portrays in Christ. Nothing but the mercy, tenderness, and kindness of Christ are here shown, and he who so receives and believes on Him is saved. He sits not upon a proud steed, an animal of war, nor does He come in great pomp and power, but sitting upon an ass, an animal of peace fit only for burdens and labor and a help to man. He indicates by this that He comes not to frighten man, nor to drive or crush him, but to help him and to carry his burden for him. And although it was the custom of the country to ride on asses and to use horses for war, as the Scriptures often tell us, yet here the object is to show that the entrance of this King shall be meek and lowly.

Again it also shows the pomp and conduct of the disciples toward Christ who bring the colt to Christ, set Him thereon, and spread their garments in the way and cut branches from the trees. They manifested no fear nor terror, but only blessed confidence in Him as One for whom they dared to do such things and Who would take it kindly and readily consent to it.

Again, He begins His journey and comes to the Mount of Olives to indicate that He comes out of pure mercy. For olive oil in the Scriptures signifies the grace of God that soothes and strengthens the soul as oil soothes and strengthens the body.

Thirdly, there is no armor present, nor war-cry, but songs and praise, rejoicing and thanksgiving to the Lord.

Fourthly, Christ weeps, as Luke 19:41 writes, weeps over Jerusalem because she does not know nor receive such grace; yet He was so grieved at her loss that He did not deal harshly with her.

Fifthly, His goodness and mercy are best shown when He quotes the words of the Prophets (Isaiah 62:11; Zech. 9:9), and tenderly invites men to believe and accept Christ, for the fulfilling of which prophecies the events of this Gospel took place and the story was written, as the Evangelist himself testifies. Therefore we must look upon this verse as the chief part of this Gospel, for in it Christ is pictured to us and we are told what we are to believe and to expect of Him, what we are to seek in Him, and how we may be benefited by Him.

First he says: *"Tell ye the daughter of Zion."* This is said to the ministry and a new sermon is given them to preach, namely, nothing but what the words following indicate, a right knowledge of Christ. Whoever preaches anything else is a wolf and deceiver. This is one of the verses in which the Gospel is promised, of which Paul writes in Romans 1:2, for the Gospel is a sermon from Christ, as he is here placed before us, calling for faith in Him.

I have often said that there are two kinds of faith. First, a faith in which you indeed believe that Christ is such a Man as He is described and proclaimed here and in all the Gospels, but do not believe that He is such a Man for you, and are in doubt whether you have any part in Him, and think: Yes, He is such a Man to others, to Peter, Paul, and the blessed saints; but who knows that He is such to me and that I may expect the same from Him and may confide in it, as these saints did?

Behold, this faith is nothing, it does not receive Christ nor enjoy Him, neither can it feel any love and affection for Him or from Him. It is a faith about Christ and not in or of Christ, a faith which the devils also have as well as evil men. For who is it that does not believe that Christ is a gracious King to the saints? This vain and wicked faith is now taught by the pernicious synagogues of Satan. The universities (Paris and her sister schools), together with the monasteries and all Papists, say that this faith is sufficient to make Christians. In this way they virtually deny Christian faith, make heathen and Turks out of Christians, as St. Peter in 2 Peter 2:1 had foretold: "There shall be false teachers, who shall privily bring in destructive heresies, denying even the Master that bought them."

In the second place He particularly mentions, "the *daughter* of Zion." In these words He refers to the other, the true faith. For if He commands that the following words concerning Christ be proclaimed, there must be someone to hear, to receive, and to treasure them in firm faith. He does not say: Tell of the daughter of Zion, as if someone were to believe that she has Christ; but to her you are to say that she is to believe it of herself, and not in any wise doubt that it will be fulfilled as the words declare. That alone can be called Christian faith, which believes without wavering that

Christ is the Saviour not only to Peter and to the saints but also to you. Your salvation does not depend on the fact that you believe Christ to be the Saviour of the godly, but that He is a Saviour to you and has become your own.

Such a faith will work in you love for Christ and joy in Him, and good works will naturally follow. If they do not, faith is surely not present; for where faith is, there the Holy Ghost is and must work love and good works.

If you believe in Christ and in His advent, it is the highest praise and thanks to God to be holy. If you recognize, love, and magnify His grace and work in you, and cast aside and condemn self and the works of self, then are you a Christian. We say: "I believe in the holy Christian church, the communion of saints." Do you desire to be a part of the holy Christian church and communion of saints, you must also be holy as she is, yet not of yourself but through Christ alone in whom all are holy.

Thirdly He says: "Behold." With this word He rouses us at once from sleep and unbelief as though He had something great, strange, or remarkable to offer, something we have long wished for and now would receive with joy. Such waking up is necessary for the reason that everything that concerns faith is against reason and nature; for example, how can nature and reason comprehend that such an One should be King of Jerusalem Who enters in such poverty and humility as to ride upon a borrowed ass? How does such an advent become a great king? But faith is of the nature that it does not judge nor reason by what it sees or feels but by what it hears. It depends upon the Word alone and not on vision or sight. For this reason Christ was received as King only by the followers of the word of the prophet, by the believers in Christ, by those who judged and received His kingdom not by sight but by the spirit—these are the true daughters of Zion. For it is not possible for those not to be offended in Christ who walk by sight and feeling and do not adhere firmly to the Word.

Let us receive first and hold fast this picture in which the nature of faith is placed before us. For as the appearance and object of faith as here presented is contrary to nature and reason, so the same ineffectual and unreasonable appearance is to be found in all articles and instances of faith. It would be no faith if it appeared and acted as faith acts and as the words indicate. It is faith because it does not appear and deport itself as faith and as the words declare.

If Christ had entered in splendor like a king of earth, the appearance and the words would have been according to nature and reason and would have seemed to the eye according to the words, but then there would have been no room for faith. He who believes in Christ must find riches in poverty, honor in dishonor, joy in sorrow, life in death, and hold fast to them in that faith which clings to the Word and expects such things.

Fourthly: "Thy king." Here He distinguishes this King from all other kings. It is thy King, He says, Who was promised to you, Whose own you are, Who alone shall direct you, yet in the spirit and not in the body. It is He for whom you have yearned from the beginning, Whom the fathers have desired to see, Who will deliver you from all that has hitherto burdened, troubled, and held you captive. Oh, this is a comforting word to a believing heart, for without Christ, man is subjected to many raging tyrants who are not kings but murderers, at whose hands he suffers great misery and fear. These are the devil, the flesh, the world, sin, also the law and eternal death, by all of which the troubled conscience is burdened, is under bondage, and lives in anguish. For where there is sin there is no clear conscience; where there is no clear conscience, there is a life of uncertainty and an unquenchable fear of death and hell in the presence of which no real joy can exist in the heart, as Leviticus 26:36 says: "The sound of a driven leaf shall chase them."

Where the heart receives the King with a firm faith, it is secure and does not fear sin, death, hell, nor any other evil; for he well knows and in no wise doubts that this King is the Lord of life and death, of sin and grace, of hell and heaven, and that all things are in His hand. For this reason He became our King and came down to us that He might deliver us from these tyrants and rule over us Himself alone. Therefore he who is under this King cannot be harmed either by sin, death, hell, Satan, man, or any other creature. As his King lives without sin and is blessed, so must he be kept forever without sin and death in living blessedness.

See, such great things are contained in these seemingly unimportant words: "Behold, thy king." Such boundless gifts are brought by this poor and despised King. All this reason does not understand, nor nature comprehend, but faith alone does. Therefore He is called thy King; thine, who art vexed and harassed by sin, Satan, death and hell, the flesh and the world, so that thou mayest be governed and directed in the grace, in the spirit, in life, in heaven, in God.

With this word, therefore, He demands faith in order that you may be certain that He is such a King to you, has such a Kingdom, and has come and is proclaimed for this purpose. If you do not believe this of Him, you will never acquire such faith by any work of yours. What you think of Him you will have; what you expect of Him you will find; and as you believe so shall it be to you. He will still remain what He is, the King of life, of grace, and of salvation, whether He is believed on or not.

3. Charles Kingsley

Now, it does not matter in the least whether the prophet, when he spoke these words, knew that they would apply to the Lord Jesus Christ. We have no need whatsoever to suppose that he did: for Scripture gives us no hint or warrant that he did; and if we have any real or honest reverence for Scripture, we shall be careful to let it tell its own story, and believe that it contains all things necessary for salvation, without our patching our own notions into it over and above. Wise men are generally agreed that those old prophets did not, for the most part, comprehend the full meaning of their own words. Not that they were mere puppets and mouthpieces, speaking what to them was nonsense—God forbid!—but that just because they did thoroughly understand what was going on round them, and see things as God saw them, just because they had God's Eternal Spirit with them, therefore they spoke great and eternal words, which will be true forever, and will go on forever fulfilling themselves for more and more. For in proportion as any man's words are true, and wide, and deep, they are truer, and wider, and deeper than that man thinks, and will apply to a thousand matters of which he never dreamt. And so in all true and righteous speech, as in the speeches of the prophets of old, the glory is not man's who speaks them, but God's Who reveals them, and Who fulfills them again and again.

It is true, then, that this text describes what every king should be— gentle and humble, a merciful and righteous lawgiver, not a self-willed and capricious tyrant. But Josiah could not fulfill that. He was a good king, but he could not be a perfect one, for he was but a poor, sinful, weak, and inconsistent man, as we are. But those words being inspired by the Holy Spirit, must be fulfilled. There ought to be a perfect king, perfectly gentle and humble, having a perfect salvation, a perfect lawgiver; and therefore there must be such a king; and therefore St. Matthew tells us there came at last a perfect King—One who fulfilled perfectly the prophet's words—One Who was not made king of Jerusalem, but was her King from the beginning; for that is the full meaning of "thy king cometh to thee." To Jerusalem He came, riding on the ass's colt, like the peaceful and fatherly judges of old time, for a sign to the poor souls round Him, who had no lawgivers but the proud and fierce Scribes and Pharisees, no king but the cruel and godless Caesar and his oppressive and extortionate officers and troops. Meek and lowly He came; and for once the people saw that He was the true Son of David—a man and king, like him, after God's own heart. For once they felt that He had come in the name of the Lord the old Deliverer Who brought them out of the land of Egypt, and made them into a nation, and loved and pitied them still, in spite of all their sins, and remembered His covenant, which they had forgotten. And before that humble Man, the Son of the village maiden, they cried: "Hosanna to the Son of David. Blessed is he that cometh in the name of the Lord. Hosanna in the highest."

And do you think He came, the true and perfect King, only to go away again and leave this world as it was before, without a law, a ruler, a heavenly kingdom? God forbid! Jesus is the same yesterday, today, and forever. What He was then, when He rode in triumph into Jerusalem, that is He now to us this day—a King, meek and lowly, and having salvation; the Head and Founder of a kingdom which can never be moved, a city which has foundations, whose Builder and Maker is God. To that kingdom this land of England now belongs. Into it we, as Englishmen, have been christened. And the unchristened, though they know not of it, belong to it as well. What God's will, what Christ's mercies may be to them, we know not. That He has mercy for them, if their ignorance is not their own fault, we doubt not; perhaps, even if their ignorance be their own fault, we need not doubt that He has mercy for them, considering the mercy which He has shown to us, who deserved no more than they. But His will to us we do know; and His will is this—our holiness. For He came not only to assert His own power, to redeem His own world, but to set His people, the children of men, an example, that they should follow in His steps. Herein, too, He is the perfect king. He leads His subjects, He sets a perfect example to His subjects, and more, He inspires them with the power of following that example, as, if you will think, a perfect ruler ought to be able to do. Josiah set the Jews an example, but he could not make them follow it. They turned to God at the bidding of their good king, with their lips, in their outward conduct; but their hearts were still far from Him. Jeremiah complains bitterly of this in the beginning of his prophecies. He complains that Josiah's reformation was after all empty, hollow, hypocritical, a change on the surface only, while the wicked root was left. They had healed, he said, the hurt of the daughter of his people slightly, crying, "Peace, peace, when there was no peace." But Jesus, the perfect King, is King of men's spirits as well as of their bodies. He can turn the heart, He can renew the soul. None so ignorant, none so sinful, none so crushed down with evil habits, but the Lord will and can forgive him, raise him up, enlighten him, strengthen him, if he will but claim his share in his King's mercy, his citizenship in the heavenly kingdom, and so put himself in tune again with himself, and with heaven, and earth, and all therein.

Keeping in mind these things, that Jesus, because He is our perfect King, is both the example and the inspirer of our souls and characters, we may look without fear at the epistle for the day, where it calls on us to be very different persons from what we are, and declares to us our duty as subjects of Him who is meek and lowly, just, and having salvation. It is no superstitious, slavish message, saying: "You have lost Christ's mercy and Christ's kingdom; you must buy it back again by sacrifices, and tears, and hard penances, or great alms-deeds and works of mercy." No. It simply says: "You belong to Christ already, give up your hearts to Him and follow His example. If He is perfect, His is the example to follow; if He is perfect, His commandments must be perfect, fit for all places, all times, all employments; if He is the King of heaven and earth, His commandments must be in tune with heaven and earth, with the laws of nature, the true laws of society and trade, with the constitution, and business, and duty, and happiness of all mankind. And forever obey Him."

Owe no man anything save love, for He owed no man anything. He gave up all, even His own rights, for a time, for His subjects. Will you pretend to follow Him while you hold back from your brothers and fellow servants their just due? One debt you must always owe; one debt will grow the more you pay it, and become more delightful to owe, the greater and heavier you feel it to be, and that is love; love to all around you, for all around you are your brothers and sisters; all around you are the beloved subjects of your King and Saviour. Love them as you love yourself, and then you cannot harm them, you cannot tyrannize over them, you cannot wish to rise by scrambling upon their shoulders, taking the bread out of their mouths, making your profit out of their weakness and their need. This, St. Paul says, was the duty of men in his time, because the night of heathendom was far spent, the day of Christianity and the Church was at hand. Much more is it our duty now—our duty, who have been born in the full sunshine of Christianity, christened into His church as children, we and our fathers before us, for generations, of the kingdom of God. Aye, my friends, these words, that kingdom, that King, witness this day against this land of England. Not merely against popery, the mote which we are trying to take out of the foreigner's eye, but against Mammon, the beam which we are overlooking in our own. Owe no man anything save love. "Thou shalt love thy neighbor as thyself." That is the law of your King, who loved not Himself or His own profit, His own glory, but gave Himself even to death for those who had forgotten Him and rebelled against Him. That law witnesses against the tradesman who tries to draw away his neighbor's custom. It witnesses against the working man who spends in the alehouse the wages which might support and raise his children, and then falls back recklessly and dishonestly on the parish rates and the alms of the charitable. Against them all this law witnesses. These things are unfit for the kingdom of Christ, contrary to the laws and constitution thereof; and if a nation will not amend these abominations, the King will arise out of His place, and with sore judgments and terrible He will visit His land and purify His temple, saying: "My Father's house should be a house of prayer, and ye have made it a den of thieves." Aye, woe to any soul, or to any nation, which, instead of putting on the Lord Jesus Christ, copying His example, obeying His laws, and living worthy of His kingdom, not only in the church, but in the market, the shop, the senate, or the palace, give themselves up to covetousness, which is idolatry, and care only to make provision for the flesh, to fulfill the lusts thereof. Woe to them; for, let them be what they will, their King cannot change. He is still meek and lowly; He is still just and having salvation; and He will purge out of His kingdom all that is not like Himself, the unchaste and the idle, the unjust and the unmerciful, and the covetous man, who is an idolater, says the Scripture, though he may call himself seven times a Protestant, and rail at the Pope in public meetings, while he justifies greediness and tyranny by glib words about the necessities of business and the laws of trade, and by philosophy falsely so called, which cometh not from above, but is earthly, sensual, devilish. Such a man loves and makes a lie, and the Lord of truth will surely send him to his own place.

EASTER

Text: Mark 16:1-7

1. St. Augustine

According to our custom, during these days the account of the Resurrection of our Lord Jesus Christ is read from all the books of the holy Gospel. In this selection (from Mark) we notice how the Lord Jesus Himself chided His disciples, His first members who remained close to Him, because they did not believe that He, over whom they grieved as dead, was now alive. They were the fathers of the faith, but not yet were they believers. They did not yet believe, although they were made teachers so that the whole world might believe what they were destined to preach and what they were going to die for. They did not yet believe that He, Whom they had seen raising others from the dead, had arisen Himself. Deservedly, then, were they rebuked. They were revealed to themselves so that they might recognize what they were through their own efforts and what they would be through Him. Thus, too, Peter was revealed to himself, in that he manifested presumption when the Passion of the Lord was imminent, but wavered when the actual suffering materialized. In person he saw himself; in person he grieved himself; in person he wept over himself; he turned to Him who had made him. Behold, they still did not believe, although they now saw. What has been His condescension in permitting us to believe what we do not see! We believe the words of those who did not trust their own eyes.

Moreover, the Resurrection of our Lord Jesus Christ is a new life for those who believe in Jesus, and this is the sacrament of His Passion and Resurrection which you ought to know and discuss. For, with good reason, Life came to death; with good reason, He, the Fountain of Life, whence one drinks in order to live, drank this chalice when He was under no obligation to do so. Truly, Christ was under no obligation to die. Let us examine the source from which death arose. Sin is the father of death. If there had been no sin, there would have been no death. The first man received the law of God, that is, the command of God, with this stipulation: that, if he kept the law, he would live; if he violated it, he would die. By not believing that he was going to die, man brought about his own death; and he discovered that He who had given the law had said what was true. Thence (came) death; thence, mortality; thence, fatigue; thence, wretchedness; thence, even after the first death, came a second death, that is, after the death in time came death for all eternity. Therefore, every man is born subject to this condition of death, subject to these laws of the lower world, with the sole exception of that Man who became Man so that

243

man might not perish. For He came, hampered by no laws of death, as the Psalmist says: "Free among the dead." Without concupiscence a virgin conceived Him to whom she, still a virgin, gave birth, remaining a virgin. He lived without sin; He did not die because of His own sin; He shared with us our punishment, but not our sin. Death is the punishment of sin. The Lord Jesus Christ came to die; He did not come to sin. By sharing with us the penalty without the sin, He cancelled both the penalty and the sin. What penalty did He cancel? That which was destined for us after this life. Hence, He was crucified, so that on the Cross He might show the destruction of our old man; and He rose again so that He might point out the newness of our life. For thus the apostolic teaching expresses it: "He was delivered up for our sins, and rose again for our justification." To symbolize this fact, circumcision was imposed upon the ancients, so that on the eighth day every male child was circumcised. The circumcision was performed with stone knives "because Christ was the Rock." That circumcision typified the stripping off of the carnal life on the eighth day through the Resurrection of Christ. For the seventh day of the week is completed by the sabbath. On the sabbath, the seventh day being the day of the sabbath, the Lord lay in the tomb. He arose on the eighth day; and His Resurrection renews us. Therefore, by rising on the eighth day He circumcises us; in this hope we live.

Let us hearken to the Apostle when he says: "If you have risen with Christ." How do we rise when we are not yet dead? What, then, is it that the Apostle intended to say by the words: "If you have risen with Christ"? Would Christ have risen again if He had not first died? Was the Apostle addressing persons who were still living, not yet dying, and yet rising again? What does he mean? Consider what he says: "If you have risen with Christ, seek the things that are above, where Christ is seated at the right hand of God. Mind the things that are above, not the things that are on earth. For you have died." The Apostle himself says that, not I; nevertheless, he tells the truth, and for that reason I, too, say it. Why do I say it? "I have believed, therefore have I spoken." If we are living well, we are dead, and we have risen. Moreover, he who is not yet dead and has not risen is still living badly; and if he is living badly, he is not living; let him die, lest he die. What does that mean, "let him die, lest he die"? Let him change himself, lest he be condemned. "If you have risen with Christ," I repeat the words of the Apostle, "seek the things that are above, where Christ is seated at the right hand of God. Mind the things that are above, not the things that are on earth. For you have died and your life is hidden with Christ in God. When Christ, your life, shall appear, then you too will appear with him in glory." These are the words of the Apostle. I bid him, who is not yet dead, to die; I bid him, who is still living badly, to change himself. For, if he used to live badly and is not now doing so, he has died; if he is now living well, he has risen again.

But what does it mean to live well? It means to seek "the things that are above, not the things that are on earth." How long are you going to be earth and how long are you returning into earth? How long are you going to lick the earth? By loving the earth you certainly lick it, and you become an enemy of Him of whom the Psalmist says: "And his enemies shall lick the ground." What were you? Sons of men. What are you? Sons of God. "O ye sons of men, how long will you be dull of heart? why do you love vanity and seek after lying?" What lying do you seek? Now I shall tell you. I know that you wish to be happy. Show me a robber, a scoundrel, a fornicator, an evil-doer, a lawbreaker, a person stained with all vices, steeped in all crimes or outrages, who does not wish to be happy. I know you all wish to live happily, but you do not wish to find out what it is that makes a man live happily. You seek gold because you think that you will acquire happiness from the possession of gold, but gold does not make men happy. Why do you seek for what is deceptive? Why do you wish to be exalted in this world? Because you think that you will acquire happiness from the honor of men and from worldly display? But worldly display does not make men happy. Why do you seek lying and whatever else you seek here? When you seek in a worldly fashion, when you seek through love of the earth, when you seek by clinging to the earth, you seek for one purpose, that is, to be happy; but no earthly object makes you happy. Why do you not cease to look for what is deceptive? What, then, will make you happy? "O ye sons of men, how long will you be dull of heart?" Do you, who thus weigh down your hearts with earth, not wish to be dull of heart? How long were men dull of heart? Until Christ came, until Christ rose again, men were dull of heart. "How long will you be dull of heart? why do you love vanity, and seek after lying?" Though you wish to be happy, you are seeking things which make you unhappy. What you are seeking is betraying you; what you are seeking is a lie.

Do you wish to be happy? If you wish, I shall show you how you may be happy. Continue to read that passage: "How long will you be dull of heart? why do you love vanity and seek after lying? Know ye . . ." What? . . ." that the Lord hath made his holy one wonderful." Christ came to our miseries. He was hungry and thirsty; He was weary and He slept; He worked wonders and He suffered evils; He was scourged, crowned with thorns, covered with spittle, beaten with cudgels, fixed to a cross, wounded with a lance, placed in a tomb. But He rose again on the third day when His work was finished and death was dead. Lo, keep your eye fixed on His resurrection, because "the Lord hath made his holy one wonderful" to such a degree that He raised Him from the dead, and bestowed upon Him the honor of sitting at His right hand in heaven. He showed you what you ought to attend to, if you wish to be happy, for here on earth you cannot be happy. In this life you cannot be happy; no one can. You seek what is good, but earth is not the source of that which you seek. What are you seeking? A happy life. But it is not available here. If you were looking for gold in a place where it did not exist, would not he who knew that it was not here say to you: "Why are you digging? Why are you plowing up the earth? You are digging a trench to descend into a place where you will find nothing." What are you going to answer the one who proffers you this advice? "I am looking for gold." And he answers: "I do not tell you that what you seek is of no importance, but I do say that it is not in the place where you are looking for it." Likewise, when you say: "I desire to be happy," the answer may be given: "You seek what is good, but it is not in this place." If Christ had happiness here, so also will you. But notice what He found in this land of your death. When He came from another region, what did He find here except what abounds here? With you He ate what is plentiful in the cellar of your wretchedness. He drank vinegar here; He had gall, too. Behold, what He found in your cellar!

However, He has invited you to His own table abounding in all good things, the table of heaven, the table of the angels where He Himself is the bread. Coming, then, and finding these unpalatable viands in your cellar, He did not disdain such a table as yours, but He promised you His own. And what does He say to us? "Believe, just believe that you will come to the good things of My table inasmuch as I did not scorn the poor things of your table." He accepted your evil; will He not give you His good? Certainly He will. He promised His life to us; but what He has done is more unbelievable. He offered His own life to us, as if to say: "I invite you to My life where no one dies, where life is truly blessed, where food is not corrupted, where it refreshes and does not fail. Behold the place to which I invite you, to the abode of the angels, to the friendship of the Father and of the Holy Spirit, to the eternal banquet, to My companionship, finally, to Me Myself and to My life do I invite you. Do you not wish to believe that I will give you My life? Take My death as a pledge." Now, therefore, while we are living in this corruptible flesh, by changing our ways, let us die with Christ; by loving justice, let us live with Christ. We shall not gain the happy life unless we shall have come to Him who came to us and unless we shall have begun to live with Him who died for us.

2. Martin Luther

St. Paul writes in Romans 4:25 as follows: "Christ was delivered up for our trespasses, and was raised for our justification." Paul is indeed the man who extols Christ in a masterly manner, telling us exactly why and for what purpose He suffered and how we should conform ourselves to His sufferings, namely, that He died for our sins. This is a correct interpretation of the sufferings of Christ, by which we may profit. And as it is not sufficient to know and believe that Christ has died, so it will not suffice to know and believe that He rose with a transfigured body and is now in a state of joy and blessedness, no longer subject to mortality, for all this would profit me nothing or very little. But when I come to understand the fact that all the works God does in Christ are done for me, nay, they are bestowed upon and given to me, the effect of His resurrection being that I also will arise and live with Him; that will cause me to rejoice. This must be brought home to our hearts, and we must not merely hear it with the ears of our body nor merely confess it with our mouth.

You have heard in the story of the Passion how Christ is portrayed as our Exemplar and Helper, and that he who follows Him and clings to Him receives the Spirit, who will enable him also to suffer. But the words of Paul are more Christian and should come closer home to our hearts and comfort us more, when he says: "Christ was raised for our justification." Here the Lamb is truly revealed, of whom John the Baptist testifies, when he says in John 1:29: "Behold, the Lamb of God, that taketh away the sin of the world." Here is fulfilled that which was spoken to the serpent: "I will put enmity between thee and the woman, and between thy seed and her seed: he shall bruise thy head," which means that for all those who believe in Him, hell, death, and the devil and sin have been destroyed. In the same manner the promise is fulfilled today which God gave to Abraham, when he said in Genesis 22:18: "In thy seed shall all the nations of the earth be blessed." Here Christ is meant, Who takes away our curse and the power of sin, death, and the devil.

All this is done, I say, by faith. For if you believe that by this Seed the serpent has been slain, then it is slain for you; and if you believe that in this Seed all nations are to be blessed, then you are also blessed. For each one individually should have crushed the serpent under foot and redeemed himself from the curse, which would have been too difficult, nay impossible for us. But now it has been done easily, namely, by Christ, Who has crushed the serpent once, Who alone is given as a blessing and benediction, and Who has caused this Gospel to be published throughout the world, so that he who believes, accepts it and clings to it, is also in possession of it, and is assured that it is as he believes. For in the heart of such a man the Word becomes so powerful that he will conquer death, the devil, sin, and all adversity, as Christ Himself did. So mighty is the Word that God Himself would sooner be vanquished than that His Word would be conquered.

This is the meaning of the words by St. Paul: "Christ was raised for our justification." Here Paul turns my eyes away from my sins and directs them to Christ, for if I look at my sins, they will destroy me. Therefore I must look unto Christ Who has taken my sins upon Himself, crushed the head of the serpent, and become the blessing. Now they no longer burden my conscience, but rest upon Christ, Whom they desire to destroy. Let us see how they treat Him. They hurl Him to the ground and kill him. Oh God; where is now my Christ and my Saviour? But then God appears, delivers Christ and makes Him alive; and not only does He make Him alive, but He translates Him into heaven and lets Him rule over all. What has now become of sin? There it lies under His feet. If I then cling to this, I have a cheerful conscience like Christ, because I am without sin. Now I can defy death, the devil, sin, and hell to do me any harm. As I am a child of Adam, they can indeed accomplish it that I must die. But since Christ has taken my sins upon Himself, has died for them, has suffered Himself to be slain on account of my sins, they can no longer harm me; for Christ is too strong for them, they cannot keep Him, He breaks forth and overpowers them, ascends into heaven (takes sin and sorrow captive, Ed. 1531), and rules there over all throughout eternity. Now I have a clear conscience, am joyful and happy and am no longer afraid of this tyrant, for Christ has taken my sins away from me and made them His own. But they cannot remain upon Him; what then becomes of them? They must disappear and be destroyed. This then is the effect of faith. He who believes that Christ has taken away our sin, is without sin, like Christ Himself, and death, the devil, and hell are vanquished as far as he is concerned and they can no longer harm him.

Here we also refer to the passage in Hosea 13:14, which Paul quotes in reference to the victory that Christ has won by His resurrection and by which He has conquered sin, death, hell, and all our enemies. Paul says that death is swallowed up in this victory, and he defies death with these words: "O death, where is thy victory? O death, where is thy sting?" Just as if Paul would say: "O death, where are thy teeth? Come, bite off one of my fingers. Thou formerly hadst a spear, what has become of it now? Christ has taken it from thee. Death, where is now thy spear, and so forth?" Sin, where is now the edge of thy sword and thy power? Paul says that the power of sin is the Law. The more clearly we understand the Law, the more sin oppresses and stings us. For this reason Paul says that Christ has completely destroyed and annihilated the spear and whetstone of death. Now, this Gospel He has not taken with Him into heaven, but He caused it to be preached throughout the world, so that for him who believes in Christ, spear and whetstone, nay, sin and death, should be destroyed. This is the true Gospel, which bestows life, strength, power, and marrow, and of which all the passages of Scripture speak.

Therefore seek and learn to know Christ aright, for the whole Scriptures confer upon us the righteousness of the true knowledge of Christ. But this must be brought about by the Holy Spirit. Let us therefore pray God that His Gospel may prosper, that we all may truly learn to know Christ and thus rise with Him and be honored by God as He was honored.

The question now arises: If Christ has taken away death and our sins by His resurrection and has justified us, why do we then still feel death and sin within us? For our sins torment us still, we are stung by our conscience, and this evil conscience creates the fear of hell.

To this I reply: I have often said before that feeling and faith are two different things. It is the nature of faith not to feel, to lay aside reason and close the eyes, to submit absolutely to the Word, and follow it in life and death. Feeling, however, does not extend beyond that which may be apprehended by reason and the senses, which may be heard, seen, felt, and known by the outward senses. For this cause feeling is opposed to faith and faith is opposed to feeling. Therefore the author of the Epistle to the Hebrews writes of faith: "Now faith is assurance of things hoped for, a conviction of things not seen." For if we would see Christ visibly in heaven, like the visible sun, we would not need to believe it. But since Christ died for our sins and was raised for our justification, we cannot see it nor feel it, neither can we comprehend it with our reason. Therefore we must disregard our feeling and accept only the Word, write it into our heart and cling to it, even though it seems as if my sins were not taken from me, and even though I still feel them within me. Our feelings must not be considered, but we must constantly insist that death, sin, and hell have been conquered, although I feel that I am still under the power of death, sin, and hell. For although we feel that sin is still in us, it is only permitted that our faith may be developed and strengthened, that in spite of all our feelings we accept the Word, and that we unite our hearts and consciences more and more to Christ. Thus faith leads us quietly, contrary to all feeling and comprehension of reason, through sin, through death, and through hell. Then we shall see salvation before our eyes, and then we shall know perfectly what we have believed, namely, that death and all sorrow have been conquered.

Take as an illustration the fish in the water. When they are caught in the net, you lead it quietly along, so that they imagine they are still in the water; but when you draw them to the shore, they are exposed and begin to struggle, and then they first feel they are caught. Thus it also happens with souls that are caught with the Gospel, which Christ compares with a net (Matthew 13:47). When the heart has been conquered, the Word unites this poor heart to Christ and leads it gently and quietly from hell and from sin, although the soul still feels sin and imagines to be still under its power. Then a conflict begins, the feelings struggling against the Spirit and faith, and the Spirit and faith against our feelings; and the more faith increases, the more our feelings diminish, and vice versa. We have still sins within us, as for instance pride, avarice, anger, and so forth, but only in order to lead us to faith, so that faith may increase from day to day, and the man become finally a thorough Christian and keep the true sabbath, consecrating himself to Christ entirely. Then the conscience must become calm and satisfied and all the surging waves of sin subside. For as upon the sea one billow follows and buffets the other, as though they would destroy the shore, yet they must disappear and destroy themselves, so also our sins strive against us and would fain bring us to despair, but finally they must desist, grow weary, and disappear.

In the second place, death is still at our elbow. It also is to exercise the faith of him who believes that death has been killed and all his power taken away. Now, reason feels that death is still at our elbow and is continually troubling us. He who follows his feelings will perish, but he who clings to the Word with his heart will be delivered. Now, if the heart clings to the Word, reason will also follow; but if reason follows, everything will follow, desire and love and all that is in man. Yea, we desire that all may come to the point when they may consider death to be dead and powerless. But this cannot come to pass until the old man, that is the old Adam, be entirely destroyed, and meanwhile that process has been going on of which Christ speaks in Matthew 13:33, where he compares the kingdom of God to leaven, which a woman took and hid in three measures of meal. For even if the kneading has begun, the meal is not yet thoroughly leavened. So it is here. Although the heart clings to the belief that death and hell are destroyed, yet the leaven has not yet worked through it entirely. For it must penetrate and impregnate all the members of the body, until everything becomes leavened and pure, and there remains nothing but a pure faith. This will not be brought about before the old man is entirely destroyed; then all that is in man is Christlike from center to circumference.

These two things, sin and death, therefore remain with us to the end that we might cultivate and exercise our faith, in order that it may become more perfect in our heart from day to day and finally break forth, and all that we are, body and soul, become more Christlike. For when the heart clings to the Word, feelings and reasoning must fail. Then in the course of time the will also clings to the Word, and with the will everything else, our desire and love, till we surrender ourselves entirely to the Gospel, are renewed and leave the old sin behind. Then there comes a different light, different feelings, different seeing, different hearing, acting, and speaking, and also a different outflow of good works. Now, our scholastics and papists have taught an external piety; they would command the eyes not to see, and the ears not to hear, and would put piety into our hearts from the outside. Ah, how far this is from the truth! But it comes in this way: When the heart and conscience cling to the Word in faith, they overflow in works, so that, when the heart is holy, all the members become holy, and good works follow naturally.

This is signified by the sabbath that was to be hallowed and on which the Lord lay quietly in the grave. It signifies that we should rest from all our works, should not stir, nay, should not allow any sin to stir within us, but we should firmly believe that death, hell, sin, and the devil are destroyed by the death of Christ, and we are righteous, pious, holy, and therefore contented, experiencing no longer any sin. Then all the members are calm and quiet, being convinced that sin and death are vanquished and prostrated. But this cannot be brought about, as I have said, until this impotent, wretched body and the old Adam are destroyed. Therefore it is indeed necessary that we are required to keep this sabbath. For as Christ lies in the grave on the sabbath, never feels or moves, so it must be with us, as we have heard: Our feelings and actions must cease. And I say again that this cannot be accomplished before the old Adam is annihilated. Nevertheless we still experience sin and death within us, wrestle with them and fight against them. You may tie a hog ever so well, but you cannot prevent it from grunting (until it is strangled and killed, Ed. 1531). Thus it is with the sins in our flesh. As they are not yet entirely conquered and killed, they are still active, but when death comes, they must also die, and then we are perfect Christians and pure, but not before. This is the reason why we must die, namely, that we may be entirely freed from sin and death. These words on the fruits of the resurrection of Christ may suffice for the present, and with them we will close. Let us pray God for grace that we may understand them and learn to know Christ aright.

3. John Calvin

We now come to the closing scene of our redemption. For the lively assurance of our reconciliation with God arises from Christ having come from hell as the Conqueror of death, in order to show that He had the power of a new life at His disposal. Justly, therefore, does Paul say that there will be no Gospel, and that the hope of salvation will be vain and fruitless, unless we believe that "Christ is risen from the dead" (1 Corinthians 15:14). For then did Christ obtain righteousness for us, and open up our entrance into heaven, and, in short, then was our adoption ratified, when Christ, by rising from the dead, exerted the power of His Spirit, and proved Himself to be the Son of God. Now, though He manifested His resurrection in a different manner from what the sense of our flesh would have desired, still the method of which He approved ought to be regarded by us also as the best. He went out of the grave without a witness, that the emptiness of the place might be the earliest indication; next, He chose to have it announced to the women by the angels that He was alive; and shortly afterward He appeared to the women and, finally, to the apostles, and on various occasions.

Thus He gradually brought His followers, according to their capacity, to a larger measure of knowledge. He began with "the women," and not only presented Himself to be seen by them, but even gave them a commission to announce the Gospel to the apostles, so as to become their instructors. This was intended, first, to chastise the indifference of the apostles, who were like persons half-dead with fear, while the women ran with alacrity to the sepulcher, and likewise obtained no ordinary reward. For though their design to anoint Christ, as if He were still dead, was not free from blame, still He forgave their weakness and bestowed on them distinguished honor, by taking away from men the apostolic office and committing it to them for a short time. In this manner also He exhibited an instance of what Paul tells us, that He "chooses those things which are foolish and weak in the world" to abase the loftiness of the flesh. And never shall we be duly prepared to learn this article of our faith in any other manner than by laying aside all pride and submitting to receive the testimony of the women. Not that our faith ought to be confined within such narrow limits, but because the Lord, in order to make trial of our faith, determines that we shall become fools before He admits us to a more ample knowledge of His mysteries.

So far as regards the narrative, Matthew says only that "the two Marys came to see the sepulcher"; Mark adds a third, "Salome," and says that they "bought spices to anoint the body"; and from Luke we infer that not two or three only, but many women came. But we know that it is customary with the sacred writers when speaking of a great number, to name but a few of them. It may also be conjectured with probability that "Mary Magdalene," with another companion—whether she was sent before, or ran forward of her own accord—arrived at the grave before the rest of the women. And this appears to be conveyed by the words of Matthew, that those two women "came for the purpose of seeing"; for without *seeing* Christ, they had no means of anointing Him. He says nothing, in the meantime, about the purpose which they had formed of doing honor to Him; for the principal object which he had in view was to testify of the Resurrection.

But it may be asked, How could this zeal of the women, which was mixed with superstition, be acceptable to God? I have no doubt that the custom of anointing the dead, which they had borrowed from the Fathers, was applied by them to its proper object, which was to draw consolation, amidst the mourning of death, from the hope of the life to come. I readily acknowledge that they sinned in not immediately raising their minds to that prediction they had heard from the lips of their Master, when He foretold that He would rise again on the third day. But as they retain the general principle of the final resurrection that defect is forgiven, which would justly have vitiated, as the phrase is, the whole of the action. Thus God frequently accepts, with fatherly kindness, the works of the saints which, without pardon, not only would not have pleased him, but would even have been justly rejected with shame and punishment. It is, therefore, an astonishing display of the goodness of Christ that He kindly and generously presents Himself alive to the women, who did Him wrong in seeking Him among the dead. Now if He did not permit them to come in vain to His grave, we may conclude with certainty that those who now aspire to Him by faith will not be disappointed; for the distance of places does not prevent believers from enjoying Him who fills heaven and earth by the power of His Spirit.

AND THEY SAID AMONG THEMSELVES. Mark alone expresses this doubt, but as the other Evangelists relate that "the stone was rolled away by the angel," it may easily be inferred that they remained in perplexity and doubt as to what they should do, until the entrance was opened up by the hand of God. But let us learn from this that, in consequence of having been carried away by their zeal, they came there without due consideration. They had seen "a stone" placed before the sepulcher, to hinder anyone from entering. Why did not this occur to them, when they were at home and at leisure, but because they were seized with such fear and astonishment that thought and recollection failed them? But as it is a holy zeal that blinds them, God does not charge them with this fault.

THROUGH FEAR THE GUARDS TREMBLED. The Lord struck the guards with terror, as if He had engraved their consciences with a hot iron, so as to constrain them reluctantly to feel His divine power. The terror had, at least, the effect of hindering them from treating with careless mockery the report of the Resurrection which was to be spread abroad shortly afterward. For though they were not ashamed of prostituting their tongues for Him, still they were compelled, whether they would or not, to acknowledge inwardly what they wickedly denied before men. Nor can it be doubted that, when they were at liberty to talk freely among their acquaintances, they frankly admitted what they durst not openly avow, in consequence of having been gained over by money.

We must attend to the distinction between the two kinds of *terror*, between which Matthew draws a comparison. The soldiers, who were accustomed to tumults, were terrified and were so completely overwhelmed by alarm that they fell down like men who were almost dead; but no power was exerted to raise them from that condition. A similar terror seized the women; but their minds, which had nearly given way, were restored by the consolation that immediately followed, so as to begin, at least, to entertain some better hope. And, certainly, it is proper that the majesty of God should strike both terror and fear indiscriminately into the godly, as well as the reprobate, that all flesh may be silent before His face. But when the Lord has humbled and subdued His elect, He immediately mitigates their dread, that they may not sink under its oppressive influence; and not only so, but by the sweetness of His grace heals the wound which He had inflicted. The reprobate, on the other hand, He either overwhelms by sudden dread or suffers to languish in slow torments. As to the soldiers themselves, they were, no doubt, "like dead men," but without any serious impression. Like men in a state of insensibility, they tremble, indeed, for a moment but presently forget that they were afraid, not that the remembrance of their terror was wholly obliterated, but because that lively and powerful apprehension of the power of God, to which they were compelled to yield, soon passed away from them. But we ought chiefly to attend to this point, that though they, as well as the women, were afraid, no medicine was applied to soothe their terror, for to the women only did the angel say: "Fear not." He held out to them a ground of joy and assurance in the resurrection of Christ. Luke adds a reproof, "Why do you seek the living among the dead?" as if the angel pulled their ear, that they might no longer remain in sluggishness and despair.

AND GO QUICKLY, AND TELL HIS DISCIPLES. Here God, by the angel, confers extraordinary honor on the women by enjoining them to proclaim to the apostles themselves the chief point of our salvation. In Mark's account of it, they are expressly enjoined to carry this message to "Peter," not because he was at that time higher in rank than the others, but because his crime, which was so disgraceful, needed peculiar consolation to assure him that Christ had not cast him off, though he had basely and wickedly fallen. He had already entered into the sepulcher, and beheld the traces of the resurrection of Christ; but God denied him the honor, which He shortly afterward conferred on the women, of hearing from the lips of the angel that Christ "was risen." And, indeed, the great insensibility under which he still labored is evident from the fact that he again fled trembling to conceal himself, as if he had seen nothing, while Mary sat down to weep at the grave. It cannot be doubted, therefore, that she and her companions, in beholding the angel, obtained the reward of their patience.

AND, LO, HE GOETH BEFORE YOU INTO GALILEE. When the angel sent the disciples into Galilee, he did so, I think, in order that Christ might make Himself known to a great number of persons, for we know that He had lived a long time in Galilee. He intended also to give His followers greater liberty, that by the very circumstance of their retirement they might gradually acquire courage. Besides, by being accustomed to the places, they were aided in recognizing their Master with greater certainty, for it was proper to adopt every method of confirming them that nothing might be wanting to complete the certainty of their faith.

LO, I HAVE TOLD YOU. By this manner of speaking the angel earnestly assures them that what is said is true. He states this, not as much from himself, as if he had been the first to suggest it, but gives his signature to the promise of Christ; and, therefore, in Mark's account of it, he merely recalls to their remembrance the very words of Christ. Luke carries out the address still farther by saying that the disciples were informed by Christ "that he must be crucified, and rise again on the third day." But the meaning is the same; for along with His resurrection He had foretold His death.

He then adds: "And they remembered his words," by which we are taught that, though they had made little proficiency in the doctrine of Christ, still it was not lost, but was choked up, until in due time it yielded fruit.

4. John Donne

God made this Jesus, Christ, and he made him Lord; He brought him to heaven, in his own person, in his humane nature; so he shall all us; but when we shall be all there, he onely shall be Lord of all. And if there should be no other bodies in heaven, then his, yet, yet now he is Lord of all, as He is Head of the Church. Aske of me, sayes his Father, *and I will give thee the heathen for thine inheritance, and the uttermost parts of the Earth for thy possession* (Psalm 2:8). And, as it is added, ver. 6. *I have set my King upon my holy hill of Sion;* So he hath made him Lord, Head of the Jews, and of the Gentiles too, of Sion, and of the Nations also; Hee hath consecrated his person, raised his humane nature, to the glorious region of blessed Spirits, to Heaven, and he hath dignified him with an office, made him Lord, Head of the Church, not only of Jews, and Gentiles upon earth, but of the Militant and Triumphant Church too.

Our two general parts were *Scientia, & modus,* what we must all know, and by what we must know it. Our knowledge is, this Exaltation of Jesus; and our meanes is implied, in the first word of the Text, *Therefore,* Therefore because he is raised from the Dead; for to that Resurrection, expressed in three, or foure severall phrases before the Text, is this Text, and this Exaltation referred; Christ was delivered for our sins, raised for our justification, and upon that depends all. Christs descending into hell, and his Resurrection, in our Creed, make but one Article, and in our Creed we beleeve them both alike: *Quis nisi Infidelis negaverit, apud inferos fuisse Christum?* saies S. Augustine; Who but an Infidell, will deny Christs descending into hell? And if he beleeve that to be a limme of the article of the Resurrection, His descent into hell, must rather be an inchoation of his triumph, then a consummation of his Exinanition, The first step of his Exaltation there, rather then the last step of his Passion upon the Crosse: But the Declaration, the Manifestation, that which admits no disputation, was his Resurrection. *Factus, id est, declaratus per Resurrectionem,* saies S. Cyrill, He was made Christ, and Lord, that is, declared evidently to be so, by his Resurrection; As there is the like phrase, in S. *Paul, God hath made the wisdome of this world, foolishnesse,* that is, declared it to be so. And therefore it is imputed to be a crucifying of the Lord Jesus againe, *Non credere eum, post mortem, immortalem,* Not to beleeve, that now after his having overcome death in his Resurrection, he is in an immortall, and in a glorious state in heaven. For when the Apostle argues thus, *If Christ be not risen, then is our preaching in vaine, and your faith in vaine,* he implies the contrary too, If you beleeve the Resurrection, we have preached to good purpose: *Mortuum esse Christum, pagani credunt; resurrexisse propria fides Christianorum:* The Heathen confesse Christs death; To beleeve his Resurrection, is the proper character of a Christian: for the first stone of the Christian faith, was laid in this article of the Resurrection; In the Resurrection onely was the first promise performed, *Ipse conteret, He shall bruise the Serpents head*; for, in this, he triumphed over Death, and Hell; And the last stone of our faith, is laid in the same article too, that is, the day of Judgement; of a day of Judgement God hath given an assurance unto all men (saies S. *Paul* at Athens) *In that he hath raised Christ Jesus from the dead*. In this Christ makes up his circle; in this he is truly *Alpha* and *Omega*, His comming in Paradise in a promise, his comming to Judgement in the clouds, are tied together in the Resurrection: And therefore all the Gospell, all our preaching, is contracted to that one text, *To beare witnesse of the Resurrection*; onely for that, was there need of a new Apostle, *There was a necessity of one to be chosen in Judas roome, to be a witnesse of the Resurrection; Non ait caeterorum, sed tantum Resurrectionis*, saies S. *Chrysostome*, He does not say, to beare witnesse of the other articles, but onely of the Resurrection; he charges him with no more instructions, he needs no more, in his Commission, but to preach the Resurrection: for in that, *Trophaeum de morte excitavit, & indubitatum reddidit corruptionem deletam:* Here is a retreat from the whole warfare, here is a Trophee erected upon the last enemy; *The last enemy that shall be destroyed is death,* and here is the death of that enemy, in the Resurrection.

And therefore, to all those who importuned him for a signe, Christ still turnes upon the Resurrection. The Jewes pressed him in generall, *Quod signum, What signe showest thou unto us?* and he answers, *Destroy this Temple,* (this body) *and in three dayes I will raise it.* In another place, the Scribes and the Pharisees joyne, *Master we would see a signe from thee,* and he tels them, *There shall be no signe, but the signe of the Prophet Jonas;* who was a type of the Resurrection. And then the Pharisees, and Sadduces joyn; now they were bitter enemies to one another; but, as *Tertullian* saies, *Semper inter duos latrones crucifixus Christus,* It was alwaies Christs case to be crucified betweene two Thieves; So these, though enemies joyne in this vexation, *They aske a signe,* as the rest, and, as to the rest, Christ gives that answer of *Jonas.* So that Christ himselfe determines all, summes up all in this one Article, the Resurrection.

Now, if the Resurrection of this Jesus, have made him, not onely *Christ*, Anointed and consecrated in Heaven, in his owne person, but made him *Lord*, then he hath Subjects, upon whom that dominion, and that power works, and so we have assurance of a resurrection in him too. That he is made Lord of us by his Resurrection, is rooted in prophecie; *It pleased the Lord to bruise him,* saies the Prophet *Esay; But he shall see his seed, and he shall prolong his daies;* that is, he shall see those that are regenerate in him, live with him, for ever. It is rooted in prophecy, and it spreads forth in the Gospell. To *this end,* saies the Apostle, *Christ died, and rose, that he might be Lord of the dead, and of the living.* Now, what kinde of Lord, if he had no subjects? *Cum videmus caput super aquas,* when the head is above water, will any imagine the body to be drowned? What a perverse consideration were it, to imagine a live head, and dead members? Or, consider our bodies in our selves, and *Our bodies are Temples of the*

Holy Ghost; and shall the Temples of the holy Ghost lye for ever, for ever, buried in their rubbidge? They shall not; for, the day of Judgement, is the day of Regeneration, as it is called in the Gospell; *Quia caro nostra ita generabitur per incorruptionem, sicut anima per fidem*: Because our bodies shall be regenerated by glory there, as our soules are by faith here. Therefore, *Tertullian* cals the Resurrection, *Exemplum spei nostrae*, The Originall, out of which we copy out our hope; and *Clavem sepulchorum nostrorum*, How hard soever my grave be locked, yet with that key, with the application of the Resurrection of Christ Jesus, it will open; And they are all names, which express this well, which *Tertullian* gives Christ, *Vadem, obsidem, fidejussorem resurrectionis nostrae*, That he is the pledge, the hostage, the surety of our Resurrection: So doth that also which is said in the Schoole, *Sicut Adam forma morientium, ita Christus forma resurgentium*; Without *Adam*, there had beene no such thing as death, without Christ, no such thing as a Resurrection: But *ascendit ille effractor*, (as the Prophet speaks) *The breaker is gone up before, and they have passed through the gate*, that is, assuredly, infallibly, they shall passe.

But what needs all this heat, all this animosity, all this vehemence, about the Resurrection? May not man be happy enough in heaven, though his body never come thither? upon what will ye ground the Resurrection? upon the Omnipotence of God? *Asylum haereticorum est Omnipotentia Dei*, (which was well said, and often repeated amongst the Ancients) The Omnipotence of God, hath alwaies been the Sanctuary of Heretiques, that is, alwaies their refuge, in all their incredible doctrines, God is able to do it, can do it. You confesse, the Resurrection is a miracle; And miracles are not to be multiplied, nor imagined without necessity; and what necessity of bodies in Heaven?

Beloved, we make the ground and foundation of the Resurrection, to be, not meerely the Omnipotency of God, for God will not doe all, that he can doe: but the ground is, *Omnipotens voluntas Dei revelata*, The Almighty will of God revealed by him, to us: And therefore Christ joynes both these together, *Erratis, Ye erre, not knowing the Scriptures, nor the power of God*; that is, not considering the power of God, as it revealed in the Scriptures: for there is our foundation of this Doctrine: we know, out of the Omnipotence of God, it may be; and we know out of the Scriptures it must be: That works upon our faith, this upon our reason; That it is man that must be saved, man that must be damned; and to constitute a man, there must be a body, as well as a soule. Nay, the Immortality of the soule, will not so well lie in proofe, without a resuming of the body. For, upon those words of the Apostle, *If there were no Resurrection, we were the miserablest of all men*, the Schoole reasons reasonably; Naturally the soule and body are united, when they are separated by Death, it is contrary to nature, which nature still affects this union; and consequently the soule is the lesse perfect, for this separation; and it is not likely, that the perfect naturall state of the soule, which is, to be united to the body, should last but three or foure score yeares, and, in most, much lesse, and the unpervect state, that in the separation, should last eternally, for ever: so that either the body must be beleeved to live againe, or the soule beleeved to die.

Never therefore dispute against thine own happinesse; never say, God asks the heart, that is, the soule, and therefore rewards the soule, or punishes the soule, and hath no respect to the body; *Nec auferamus cogitationes a collegio carnis, saies Tertullian,* Never go about to separate the thoughts of the heart, from the colledge, from the fellowship of the body; *Siquidem in carne, & cum carne, & per carnem agitur, quicquid ab anima agitur,* All that the soule does, it does in, and with and by the body. And therefore (saies he also) *Caro abluitur, ut anima emaculetur,* The body is washed in baptisme, but it is that the soule might be made cleane; *Caro ungitur, ut anima consecretur,* In all unctions, whether that which was then in use in Baptisme, or that which was in use at our transmigration, and passage out of this world, the body was anointed, that the soule might be armed against tentations; And againe, *Caro de Corpore Christi vescitur, ut anima de Deo saginetur;* My body received the body of Christ, that my soule might partake of his merits. He extends it into many particulars, and summes up all thus, *Non possunt in mercede separari, que opera conjungunt,* These two, Body, and Soule, cannot be separated for ever, which, whilst they are together, concurre in all that either of them doe. Never thinke it presumption, saies *S. Gregory, Sperare in te, quod in se exhibuit Deus homo,* To hope for that in thy selfe, which God admitted, when he tooke thy nature upon him. And God hath made it, saies he, more easie then so, for thee, to beleeve it, because not onely Christ himself, but such men, as thou art, did rise at the Resurrection of Christ. And therefore when our bodies are dissolved and liquefied in the Sea, putrified in the earth, resolv'd to ashes in the fire, macerated in the ayre, *Velut in vasa sua transfunditur caro nostra,* make account that all the world is Gods cabinet, and water, and earth, and fire, and ayre, are the proper boxes, in which God laies up our bodies, for the Resurrection. Curiously to dispute against our owne Resurrection, is seditiously to dispute against the dominion of Jesus; who is not made Lord by the Resurrection, if he have no subjects to follow him in the same way. Wee beleeve him to be Lord, therefore let us Beleeve his, and our Resurrection.

This blessed day, which we celebrate now, he rose; he rose so, as none before did, none after, ever shall rise; He rose; others are but raised: *Destroy this Temple,* saies he, *and I will raise it;* I, without employing any other Architect. *I lay downe my life,* saies he; the Jewes could not have killed him, when he was alive; If he were alive here now, the Jesuits could not kill him here now; except his being made *Christ,* and *Lord,* an anointed King, have made him more open to them. *I have a power to lay it downe,* saies he, *and I have a power to take it up againe.*

This day, we celebrate his Resurrection; this day let us celebrate our owne: Our own, not our one Resurrection, for we need many. Upon those words of our Saviour to *Nicodemus, Oportet denuo nasci,* speaking of the necessity of Baptisme, *Non solum denuo, sed tertio nasci oportet,* saies S. Bernard, He must be born againe, and againe; againe by baptisme, for Originall sin, and for actuall sin, againe by repentance; *Infoelix homo eto, & miserabilis casus,* saies he, *cui non sufficit una regeneratio!* Miserable man that I am, and miserable condition that I am fallen into, whom one regeneration will not serve! So it is a miserable death that hath swallowed us, whom one Resurrection will serve. We need three, but if we have not two, we were as good be without one. There is a Resurrection from worldly calamities, a resurrection from sin, and a resurrection from the grave.

First, from calamities; for, as dangers are called death, (*Pharaoh* cals the plague of Locusts, a death, *Intreat the Lord your God, that he may take from me, this death onely.* And so S. *Paul* saies, in his dangers, *I dye daily*) So is the deliverance from danger called a Resurrection: It is the hope of the wicked upon the godly, *Now that he lieth, he shall rise no more*; that is, Now that he is dead in misery, he shall have no resurrection in this world. Now, this resurrection God does not alwaies give to his servants, neither is this resurrection the measure of Gods love of man, whether he do raise him from worldly calamities or no.

The second is the resurrection from sin; and therefore, this S. John calls *The first Resurrection*, as though the other, whether we rise from worldly calamities, or no, were not to be reckoned. *Anima spiritualiter cadit, & spiritualiter resurget*, saies S. *Augustine*, Since we are sure, there is a spirituall death of the soule, let us make sure a spirituall resurrection too. *Audacter dicam*, saies S. *Hierome*, I say confidently, *Cum omnia posset Deus, suscitare Virginem post ruinam, non potest;* Howsoever God can do all things, he cannot restore a Virgin, that is fallen from it, to virginity againe. He cannot do this in the body, but God is a Spirit, and hath reserved more power, upon the spirit and soule, then upon the body, and therefore *Audacter dicam*, I may say, with the same assurance, that S. Hierome does, No soule hath so prostituted herselfe, so multiplied her fornications; but that God can make her a virgin againe, and give her, even the chastity of Christ himselfe. Fulfill therefore that which Christ saies, *The houre is comming, and now is, when the dead shall heare the voyce of the Son of God, and they that heare shall live:* Be this that houre, be this thy first Resurrection. Blesse Gods present goodnesse, for this now; and attend Gods leasure, for the other Resurrection hereafter. He that is *the first fruits of them that slept*, Christ Jesus is awake: he dyes no more, he sleepes no more. *Sacrificium pro te fuit, sed a te accepit, quo pro te obtulit:* He offered a Sacrifice for thee, but he had that from thee, that he offered for thee: *Primitiae fuit, sed tuae primitiae;* He was the first fruits, but the first fruits of thy Corne: *Spera in te futurum, quod praecessit in primitiis tuis:* Doubt not of having that in the whole Croppe, which thou has already in thy first fruits; that is, to have that in thy self, which thou hast in thy Saviour. And what glory soever thou hast had in this world, Glory inherited from noble Ancestors, Glory acquired by merit and service, Glory purchased by money, and observation, what glory of beauty and proportion, what glory of health and strength soever thou hast had in this house of clay, *The glory of the later house, shall be greater then of the former.* To this glory, the God of this glory, by glorious or inglorious waies, such as may most advance his own glory, bring us in his time, for his Son Christ Jesus sake. Amen.

THE FIRST SUNDAY AFTER EASTER

Text: John 20:19-31

1. John Chrysostom

As to believe carelessly and in a random way comes of an over-easy temper, so to be beyond measure curious and meddlesome marks a most gross understanding. On this account Thomas is held to blame. For he believed not the Apostles when they said, "We have seen the Lord"; not so much mistrusting them, as deeming the thing to be impossible, that is to say, the Resurrection from the dead, since he saith not, "I do not believe you," but, "Except I put my hand—I do not believe." But how was it, that when all were collected together, he alone was absent? Probably after the dispersion which had lately taken place, he had not returned even then. But do thou, when thou seest the unbelief of the disciple, consider the lovingkindness of the Lord; how for the sake of a single soul He showed Himself with His wounds, and cometh in order to save even the one, though he was grosser than the rest; on which account indeed he sought proof from the grossest of the senses, and would not even trust his eyes. For he said not, "Except I see," but, "Except I handle," he saith, lest what he saw might somehow be an apparition. Yet the disciples who told him these things were at the time worthy of credit, and so was He that promised; yet, since he desired more, Christ did not deprive him even of this.

And why doth He not appear to him straightway, instead of "after eight days"? In order that being in the meantime continually instructed by the disciples, and hearing the same thing, he might be inflamed to more eager desire, and be more ready to believe for the future. But whence knew he that His side had been opened? From having heard it from the disciples. How then did he believe partly, and partly not believe? Because this thing was very strange and wonderful. But observe, I pray you, the truthfulness of the disciples, how they hide no faults, either their own or others', but record them with great veracity.

Jesus again presenteth Himself to them, and waiteth not to be requested by Thomas, nor to hear any such thing, but before he had spoken, showing that even when he spake those words to the disciples, He was present. For He used the same words, and in a manner conveying a sharp rebuke and instruction for the future. For having said, "Reach hither thy finger, and behold my hands; and reach hither thy hand, and thrust it into my side," He added, "And be not faithless, but believing."

Seest thou that his doubt proceeded from disbelief? But it was before he had received the Spirit; after that, it was no longer so, but, for the future, they were perfected.

259

And not in this way only did Jesus rebuke him, but also by what follows; for when he, being fully satisfied, breathed again, and cried aloud, "My Lord, and my God," He saith, "Because thou hast seen me, thou hast believed; blessed are they who have not seen, and yet have believed."

For this is of faith, to receive things not seen, since, "Faith is the substance of things hoped for, the evidence of things not seen" (Hebrews 11:1). And here He pronounceth blessed not the disciples only, but those who after them should believe. "Yet," saith someone, "the disciples saw and believed." Yes, but they sought nothing of the kind, but from the proof of the napkins, they straightway received the word concerning the Resurrection, and before they saw the body, exhibited all faith. When therefore anyone in the present day say, "I would that I had lived in those times, and had seen Christ working miracles," let them reflect that, "Blessed are they who have not seen, and yet have believed."

It is worth inquiring how an incorruptible body showed the prints of the nails and was tangible by a mortal hand. But be not thou disturbed; what took place was a matter of condescension. For that which was so subtle and light as to enter in when the doors were shut was free from all density; but this marvel was shown that the Resurrection might be believed, and that men might know that it was the crucified One Himself, and that another rose not in His stead. On this account He arose bearing the signs of the Cross, and on this account He eateth. At least the Apostles everywhere made this a sign of the Resurrection, saying, "We, who did eat and drink with him" (Acts 10:41). As therefore when we see Him walking on the waves before the Crucifixion, we do not say that that body is of a different nature, but of our own; so after the Resurrection, when we see Him with the prints of the nails we will no more say that He is therefore corruptible. For He exhibited these appearances on account of the disciple.

AND MANY OTHER SIGNS TRULY DID JESUS. Since this Evangelist hath mentioned fewer signs than the others, he tells us that neither have all the others mentioned them all, but as many as were sufficient to draw the hearers to belief. For, "If," it saith, "they should be written every one, I suppose that even the world itself could not contain the books" (John 21:25). Whence it is clear that what they have mentioned they wrote not for display, but only for the sake of what was useful. For how could they who omitted the greater part, write these others for display? But why went they not through them all? Chiefly on account of their number; besides, they also considered, that he who believed not those they had mentioned, would not give heed to a greater number; while he who received these, would have no need of another in order to believe. And here too he seems to me to be for the time speaking of the miracles after the Resurrection. Wherefore He saith, "in the presence of his disciples."

For as before the Resurrection it was necessary that many should be done in order that they might believe that He was the Son of God, so was it also after the Resurrection, in order that they might admit that He had arisen. For another reason also he has added, "in the presence of his disciples," because He conversed with them alone after the Resurrection; wherefore also He said, "The world seeth me no more" (John 14:19).

Then, in order that thou mayest understand that what was done was done only for the sake of the disciples, he added, "that believing ye might have life in his name."

Speaking generally to mankind, and showing that not on Him Who is believed on, but on ourselves, He bestows a very great favor. "In his name," that is, "through Him"; for He is the Life.

2. Martin Luther

The Gospel praises the fruit of faith, and illustrates its nature and character. Among the fruits of faith are these two: peace and joy, as St. Paul writes to the Galatians, where he mentions in order all kinds of fruit saying: "But the fruit of the Spirit is love, joy, peace, longsuffering, kindness, goodness, faithfulness, meekness, self-control" (Galatians 5:22). Thus these two fruits are also mentioned in our text. In the first place, Christ stands there among the disciples, who sit in fear and terror, and whose hearts are greatly troubled every hour expecting death; to them He comes and comforts them, saying: "Peace be unto you." This is one fruit. In the second place there follows from this sweet word the other fruit, that they were glad when they saw the Lord. Then He further bestows upon faith, power and authority over all things in heaven and on earth, and truly extols it in that He says: "As the Father hath sent me, even so send I you." And again: "Receive ye the Holy Spirit: whose soever sins ye forgive, they are forgiven unto them; whose soever sins ye retain, they are retained." Let us now consider each thought in order.

Faith, as we have often said, is of the nature, that every one appropriates to himself the resurrection of the Lord Jesus Christ, of which we have already said enough; namely, that it is not sufficient simply to believe Christ rose from the dead, for this produces neither peace nor joy, neither power nor authority, but you must believe that He rose for your sake, for your benefit, and was not glorified for His own sake; but that He might help you and all who believe in Him, and that through His resurrection sin, death, and hell are vanquished and the victory given to you.

This is signified by Christ entering through closed doors, and standing in the midst of His disciples. For this standing denotes nothing else than that He is standing in our hearts; there He is in the midst of us, so that He is ours, as He stands there and they have Him among them. And when He thus stands within our hearts, we at once hear His loving voice saying to the troubled consciences: Peace, there is no danger; your sins are forgiven and blotted out, and they shall harm you no more.

And this entrance the Lord made here through barred doors, going through wood and stone, and still leaving everything whole, breaking nothing, yet getting in among his disciples. This illustrates how the Lord comes into our hearts and stands in us, namely, through the office of the ministry. Therefore, since God has commanded men to preach His Word, one should in no wise despise a mortal man into whose mouth He has put His Word, lest we get the idea that everyone must expect a special message from heaven, and that God should speak to him by the word of His mouth. For if He imparts faith to anyone, He does it by means of the preaching of man and the external word of man.

This is going through closed doors, when He comes into the heart through the Word, not breaking nor displacing anything. For when the Word of God comes, it neither injures the conscience, nor deranges the understanding of the heart and the external senses; as the false teachers do who break all the doors and windows, breaking through like thieves, leaving nothing whole and undamaged, and perverting, falsifying and injuring all life, conscience, reason, and the senses. Christ does not do thus. Such now is the power of the Word of God. Thus we have two parts, preaching and believing. His coming to us is preaching; His standing in our hearts is faith. For it is not sufficient that He stands before our eyes and ears; He must stand in the midst of us in our hearts, and offer and impart to us peace.

For the fruit of faith is peace; not only that which one has outwardly, but that of which Paul speaks to the Philippians (4:7), saying it is a peace that passeth all reason, sense, and understanding. And where this peace is, one shall not and cannot judge according to reason. This we shall see further in our Gospel lesson.

First, the disciples sit there behind barred doors in great fear of the Jews, afraid to venture outside, with death staring them in the face. Outwardly they indeed have peace, no one is doing them any harm; but inwardly their hearts are troubled, and they have neither peace nor rest. Amid their fear and anguish the Lord comes, quiets their hearts, and makes them glad, so that their fear is removed, not by removing the danger, but in that their hearts were no more afraid. For thereby the malice of the Jews is not taken away nor changed; they rave and rage as before, and outwardly everything remains the same. But they are changed inwardly, receiving such boldness and joy as to declare: "We have seen the Lord." Thus He quiets their hearts, so that they become cheerful and fearless, not caring how the Jews rage.

This is the true peace that satisfies and quiets the heart; not in times when no adversity is at hand, but in the midst of adversity, when outwardly there is nothing but strife before the eyes. And this is the difference between worldly and spiritual peace. Worldly peace consists in removing the outward evil that disturbs the peace, as when the enemies besiege a city there is no peace, but when they depart peace returns. Such is the case with poverty and sickness. While they afflict you, you are not contented; but when they are removed and you are rid of the distress, there is peace and rest again from without. But he who experiences this is not changed, being just as faint-hearted whether the evil be present or not; only he feels it and is frightened when it is present.

Christian or spiritual peace, however, just turns the thing about, so that outwardly the evil remains, as enemies, sickness, poverty, sin, death, and the devil. These are there and never desist, encompassing us on every side; nevertheless, within there is peace, strength, and comfort in the heart, so that the heart cares for no evil, yea, is really bolder and more joyful in its presence than in its absence. Therefore it is peace which passeth and transcendeth all understanding and all the senses. For reason cannot grasp any peace except worldly or external peace, for it cannot reconcile itself to it nor understand how that is peace if evil is present, and it knows not how to satisfy and comfort a person; hence it thinks if the evil depart, peace departs also. When, however, the Spirit comes, He lets outward adversity remain, but strengthens the person, making the timid fearless, the trembling bold, changing the troubled into a quiet, peaceful conscience, and such an one is bold, fearless and joyful in things by which all the world otherwise is terrified.

Whence does he receive this? From his faith in Christ. For if I truly believe in the Lord from the real depth of my heart, that my heart can truly say: My Lord Christ has by His resurrection conquered my need, my sin, death, and all evil, and will be thus with and in me, so that body and soul shall want nothing, that I shall have all I need, and no evil shall harm me: if I believe this, it is impossible for me to be faint-hearted and timid no matter how much sin and death oppress me. For faith is ever present and says: Does sin burden you, does death terrify you, look to Christ who died for your sake and rose again, and conquered every evil; what can harm you? Why will you then fear? So also in case other misfortunes burden you, as sickness or poverty, turn your eyes from it, lock the door to reason, and cast yourself upon Christ and cleave to Him; so shall you be strengthened and comforted. If you look to Christ and believe on Him, no evil that may befall you is so great that it can harm you and cause you to despair. Therefore it is impossible for this fruit to remain outside, where faith is, so that peace does not follow.

From peace the other fruit now follows, as is taught in this Gospel. When Christ came to the disciples and said: "Peace be unto you!" and showed them His hands and feet; then they were glad that they saw the Lord. Yes, to be sure they had to be glad, for that they saw Christ was the greatest joy the heart of man can experience. Hitherto we have been permitted to see our hands, that is, we have been taught to trust in our works; this brought no gladness. But to see Christ makes us glad. And this takes place by faith; for thus St. Paul in Romans 5:1-2 says: "Being therefore justified by faith, we have peace with God through our Lord Jesus Christ; through whom also we have had our access by faith into this grace wherein we stand; and we rejoice in hope of the glory of God."

Thus we have the fruit whereby we know who are true Christians. For he who has no peace in that in which the world finds nothing but unrest, and is joyful in that which in the world is nothing but gloom and sorrow, is not yet a Christian, and does not yet believe. This truth is being also sung at this season everywhere in the hymn on the Lord's resurrection; but hardly anybody understands it. He who composed it surely understood it aright. He does not stop at "the Lord is risen" when he says: "Christ is risen from His Passion," as though this were sufficient, but brings it home to us and adds: "Let us all rejoice in this." But how can we rejoice in it, if we have nothing of it and it is not ours? Therefore, if I am to rejoice in it, it must be mine, that I may claim it as my own property, that it may profit me. And finally he closes: "Christ will be our consolation, that we can and shall have no other consolation but Christ." He wants to be it Himself and He alone, that we should cling to Him in every time of need; for He has conquered all for our benefit, and by His resurrection He comforts all troubled consciences and sad hearts. This the Gospel teaches concerning faith and its fruits.

3. John Calvin

WHEN, THEREFORE, IT WAS EVENING. The Evangelist now relates that the resurrection of Christ was proved to the disciples by His presence. It did not happen without the providence of God, that all were assembled in one place, that the event might be more certain and more manifest. It is worthy of notice how gently Christ acted toward them, in not keeping them in suspense any longer than till the evening. Besides, He enlightened them, bringing the pledge of a new life, while darkness was overspreading the world.

WHERE THE DISCIPLES WERE ASSEMBLED. As to their having "assembled," it was an indication of faith, or, at least, of religious feelings. As to the circumstance of their keeping themselves concealed by "shut doors," we perceive in it some proof of their weakness; for though the strongest and boldest minds are sometimes seized with fear, yet it may easily be inferred that the apostles, at that time, trembled in such a manner as to manifest the deficiency of their faith. This example is worthy of notice; for, though they are less courageous than they ought to have been, still they do not give way to their weakness. True, they seek concealment for the sake of avoiding danger, but they gather courage so far as to remain together; otherwise they would have been scattered hither and thither and no man would have ventured to look at his neighbor. In this manner we ought to struggle against the weakness of our flesh, and not to indulge fear, which tempts us to apostasy. Christ also blesses their zeal, when He appears to them while they are assembled; and Thomas is justly deprived of the favor bestowed on all his brethren because, like a wandering soldier, he had withdrawn from the standard of union. Here, then, is a lesson for those who are excessively timid to sharpen and encourage themselves to correct their carnal fear; and particularly they ought to beware lest fear should cause them to scatter.

PEACE BE TO YOU! This is the ordinary form of salutation among the Hebrews; and by the word "peace" they denote all that cheerfulness and prosperity which is usually desired for a happy life. The phrase, therefore, means, "May you be well and prosperous!" I mention this, because there are some who, in explaining these words, enter into unnecessary discussions about peace and harmony, though Christ intended nothing else than to desire that His disciples might be happy and prosperous.

HE SHOWED THEM HIS HANDS AND SIDE. It was necessary to add this confirmation that by all these methods they might be fully assured that Christ was risen. If any person think it strange and inconsistent with the glory of Christ that He should bear the marks of His wounds even after

His resurrection, let him consider, first, that Christ rose not so much for Himself as for us, and, secondly, that whatever contributes to our salvation is glorious to Christ; for, when He humbled Himself for a time, this took nothing away from His majesty, and now, since those "wounds," of which we are speaking, serve to confirm the belief of His resurrection, they do not diminish His glory. But if any person should infer from this that Christ has still the wounded "side," and the pierced "hands," that would be absurd; for it is certain that the use of the wounds was temporary, until the Apostles were fully convinced that He was risen from the dead.

THEN WERE THE DISCIPLES GLAD WHEN THEY SAW THE LORD. This means that all the grief which had been occasioned to them by the death of Christ was dispelled by His new life.

JESUS SAITH TO THEM AGAIN, PEACE BE TO YOU. This second salutation appears to me to have no other object than that the Lord should receive such a degree of attention as was due to the greatness and importance of the subjects on which He was about to speak.

AS THE FATHER HATH SENT ME. By these words, Christ, as it were, instals them in the office to which He had previously appointed them. True, they had been already sent throughout Judea, but only as heralds, to issue a command that the supreme Teacher should be heard, and not as apostles, to execute a perpetual office of teaching. But now the Lord ordains them to be His ambassadors, to establish His kingdom in the world. Let it therefore be held by us as an ascertained truth, that the apostles were now, for the first time, appointed to be ordinary ministers of the Gospel.

His words amount to a declaration that hitherto He has discharged the office of a Teacher, and that, having finished His course, He now confers on them the same office; for He means that the Father appointed Him to be a Teacher on this condition, that He should be employed, for a time, in pointing out the way to others and should, afterward, put those persons in His room to supply His absence. For this reason Paul says that "he gave some, apostles; some, evangelists; some, pastors," to govern the Church till the end of the world (Ephesians 4:11). Christ therefore testifies, first, that, though He held a temporary office of teaching, still the preaching of the Gospel is not for a short time, but will be perpetual. Again, that His doctrine may not have less authority in the mouth of the apostles, He bids them succeed to that office which He has received "from his Father," places them in His room, and bestows on them the same authority. And it was proper that their ministry should be ratified in this manner, for they were unknown persons and of mean condition. Moreover, though they had the highest splendor and dignity, yet we know that all that belongs to men does not approach to the excellence of faith.

It is not without reason, therefore, that Christ communicates to His apostles the authority which He received "from the Father," that thus He may declare that the preaching of the Gospel was committed to Him, not by human authority, but by the command of God. But He does not substitute them in His room in such a manner as to resign to them the highest authority as a teacher, which the Father intended to be vested in Him alone. He therefore continues, and will eternally continue to be, the only

Teacher of the Church; but there is only this difference, that He spoke with His mouth so long as He dwelt on earth, but now speaks by the apostles. The succession or substitution, therefore, is of such a nature that it takes nothing from Christ, but His authority remains full and entire and His honor unimpaired; for that decree by which we are enjoined to hear Him, and not others, cannot be set aside: "This is my beloved Son, in whom I am well pleased; hear ye him" (Matthew 17:5). In short, Christ intended here to adorn the doctrine of the Gospel and not men.

It ought likewise to be observed that the only subject which is handled in this passage is the preaching of the Gospel; for Christ does not send His apostles to atone for sins, and to procure justification, "as he was sent by the Father." Accordingly, He makes no allusion in this passage to anything which is peculiar to Himself, but only appoints ministers and pastors to govern the Church; and on this condition, that He alone keeps possession of the whole power, while they claim nothing for themselves but the ministry.

4. Friedrich Schleiermacher

If we try to apply the commandment of the Lord to His disciples—sending them as the Father had sent Him—to ourselves, a number of difficulties arise. They are of such a nature that if examined closely it becomes apparent they must have occurred to the disciples also.

First of all, when the Saviour says, "As the Father has sent me, even so I send you," he states that His disciples as His ambassadors stand in the same relationship to Him as He stands to His Father. He had come, as He frequently has stated, to bear witness to His Father, to reveal Him, to make His will known, in order that people might see the Father in Him.

If we are to stand in the same relationship to Him it is a great and glorious task. We are called to make His will known, this one great commandment which He left to His people, to love each other with His love. We are called to stand in the world as those in whom the Redeemer of the world may be seen, as those through whom His form—however long ago it may have disappeared from view—takes shape before all men.

These are great and glorious opportunities—but what will become of the communion of men with God, which He came to bring about, if we continue to look back to Christ? This question has caused differences of opinion in the past as well as the present. There are those who conclude from these words of the Lord that we are sent by Him and must go back to Him and Him alone. We must proclaim Him as Lord over all things, as the basis of man's peace, as the ruler of all things in His kingdom.

Everything that affects man in any way, the entire governance of the world as it takes place before our eyes, and as it occupies our mind, as it touches our life in a thousand ways is attributed to the Son of God—and thus His and our heavenly Father disappears into the background.

Others again, in order to avoid this very development, the disappearance of the Father, see the calling of the disciple as it was the calling of the Master to develop in man the living recognition of God and the point of view resulting from it. They speak constantly of the eternal, all-powerful being, of the all-governing benevolence of the Heavenly Father but they speak exactly as if they were speaking on their own authority, as if they had been sent as immediately by the Father as the Redeemer Himself. What is the result? The revelation of the Father in the Son, this divine action in one particular human life, the love disclosed in the sending of the Son to give Himself for a sinful and hostile mankind, recedes before an almighty goodness which they seek to proclaim everywhere. The Redeemer Himself fades into the background as an earlier, greater, and wiser teacher—yet as One Who was sent for His time as we are sent for our time.

Yet neither the response of the one group nor that of the other was the intention of the Redeemer, and neither is His commission to us. If we go back to Him as those who were sent by Him, if we try to show ourselves through the aid of His spirit as those in whom He is alive, must not, according to His own words, His and our heavenly Father reveal Himself in us through word and deed? How can we proclaim Him without proclaiming that it was the Father whose word He preached, the Father whose works He had to do and thus restore mankind? One thing can and must not exclude the other. We are only sent by Him when we, as He did, through Him try to reveal His will which was the will of His heavenly Father. But we are only sent by Him when we faithfully confess that we feel that all living knowledge of God, the divine flame of love, the divine life is poured into the hearts of men only through Him. Thus we bear witness to the Son with the Father, and the Father with the Son, as those who have been sent by the Son of God.

THE SECOND SUNDAY AFTER EASTER

Text: John 10:11-16

1. St. Augustine

The Lord mentioned three characters—and our duty is to search them out in the Gospel—that of the shepherd, the hireling, and the thief. I suppose you took notice, when the lesson was being read, that He marked out the shepherd, the hireling, and the thief. "The shepherd," said He, "layeth down his life for the sheep," and entereth in by the door. The thief and the robber, said He, go up by another way. "The hireling," He said, "if he seeth a wolf or even a thief, fleeth; because he careth not for the sheep"; for he is an hireling, not a shepherd. The one entereth in by the door, because he is the shepherd; the second goeth up another way, because he is a thief; the third seeing them who wish to spoil the sheep feareth and fleeth, because he is an hireling. If ye shall find these three characters, ye have found, holy brethren, those whom ye should love, and those whom ye should tolerate, and those of whom ye must beware. The Shepherd is to be loved, the hireling is to be tolerated, of the robber must we beware. There are men in the Church of whom the Apostle speaks, who preach the Gospel by occasion, seeking of men their own advantage, whether of money, or of honor, or human praise. They preach the Gospel, wishing to receive rewards in whatsoever way they can, and seek not so much his salvation to whom they preach, as their own advantage. But he who heareth the word of salvation from him who hath not salvation, if he believe Him whom he preacheth, and put not his hope in him by whom salvation is preached to him, he that preacheth shall have loss; he to whom he preacheth shall have gain.

You have the Lord saying of the Pharisees, "They sit in Moses' seat." The Lord did not mean them only; as if He would send those who should believe on Christ to the school of the Jews, that they might learn there wherein is the way to the kingdom of heaven. Did not the Lord come for this end, that He might establish a Church, and separate those Jews who had a good faith, and a good hope, and a good love, as wheat from the chaff, and might make them one wall of the circumcision, to which should be joined another wall from the uncircumcision of the Gentile, of which two walls coming from different directions, Himself should be the Corner-stone? Did not the same Lord therefore say of these two people who were to be one, "And other sheep I have, which are not of this fold"? Now He was speaking to the Jews; "Them also," said He, "must I bring that there may be one fold, and one shepherd." Therefore there were two ships out of which He had called His disciples. They figured these two peoples, when

269

they let down their nets, and took up so great a draught and so large a number of fishes, that the nets were almost broken. "And they laded," it is said, "both the ships." The two ships figured the one Church, but made out of two peoples, joined together in Christ, though coming from different parts. Of this, too, the two wives who had one husband Jacob, Leah and Rachel, are a figure. Of these two, the two blind men also are a figure, who sat by the wayside, to whom the Lord gave sight. And if ye pay attention to the Scriptures, ye will find the two Churches, which are not two but one, figured out in many places. For to this end the Cornerstone serveth, for to make of two one. To this end serveth that Shepherd, for to make of two flocks one. So then the Lord who was to teach the Church, and to have a school of His own beyond the Jews, as we see at present, would He be likely to send those who believe on Him unto the Jews to learn? But under the name of the Scribes and Pharisees He intimated that there would be some in His Church who would say and not do; but, in the person of Moses He designated Himself. For Moses represented Him, and for this reason did he put a veil before him, when he was speaking to the people; because as long as they were in the Law given up to carnal joys and pleasures, and looking for an earthly kingdom, a veil was put upon their face that they should not see Christ in the Scriptures. For when the veil was taken away, after that the Lord had suffered, the secrets of the Temple were discovered. Accordingly when He was hanging on the Cross, the veil of the temple was rent from the top even to the bottom; and the apostle Paul says expressly, "But when thou shalt turn to Christ, the veil shall be taken away." Whereas with him who turneth not to Christ, though he read the Law of Moses, the veil is laid upon his heart, as the Apostle says. When the Lord then would signify beforehand that there would be some such in His Church, what did He say? "The Scribes and Pharisees sit in Moses' seat. What they say, do; but do not what they do."

When wicked clerics hear this which is said against them, they would pervert it. For I have heard that some do wish to pervert this sentence. Would they not, if they might, efface it from the Gospel? But because they cannot efface it, they go about to pervert it. But the grace and mercy of the Lord is present, and allows them not to do so; for He hath hedged round all His declarations with His truth, and in such wise balanced them; that if anyone would wish to cut off anything from them, or to introduce anything by a bad reading or interpretation, any right-hearted man may join to the Scripture what has been cut off from the Scripture, and read what went above or below, and he will find the sense which the other wished to interpret wrongly. What then, think ye, do they say of whom it is said, "Do what they say"? That is (and in truth it is so) addressed to laymen. For what does the layman who wishes to live well say to himself, when he takes notice of a wicked cleric? "The Lord said, 'What they say, do; what they do, do not.' Let me walk in the way of the Lord, not follow this man's conversation. Let me hear from him not his words, but God's. I will follow God, let him follow his own lust. For if I should wish to defend myself in such wise before God as to say, 'Lord, I saw thy cleric living evilly, and therefore I lived evilly'; would He not say to me, 'Thou wicked servant, hadst thou not heard from me, "What they say, do, but what they do, do not"?'" But a wicked layman, an unbeliever, who belongs not to Christ's flock, who belongs not to Christ's wheat, who as chaff is only borne with in the flock, what does he say to himself when the word of God begins to reprove him? "Away; why talkest thou to me? The very bishops and clergy do not do it, and dost thou force me to do it?" Thus he seeks for himself not a patron for his bad cause, but a companion for punishment. For will that wicked one, whosoever he be that he has chosen to imitate, will he ever defend him in the day of judgment? For as with all whom the devil seduces, he seduces them not to be partakers of a kingdom, but of his damnation; so all who follow the wicked seek companions for themselves to hell, not protection unto the kingdom of heaven.

How then do they pervert this declaration, when it is said to them in their wicked lives, "With good reason was it said by the Lord, 'What they say, do; what they do, do not'"? "It was well said," say they. "For it was said to you, that ye should do what we say; but that ye should not do what we do. For we offer sacrifice, you may not." See the cunning craftiness of these men; what shall I call them—hirelings? For if they were shepherds, they would not say such things. Therefore the Lord, that He might shut their mouths, went on, and said, "They sit in Moses' seat; what they say, do; but what they do, do not; for they say, and do not." What is it then, brethren? If He had spoken of offering sacrifice, would He have said, "For they say, and do not"? For they do offer sacrifice, they do offer unto God. What is it that they say, and do not? Hear what follows: "For they bind heavy burdens, and grievous to be borne, and lay them on men's shoulders, and they themselves will not touch them with one of their fingers." So openly did He rebuke, describe, and point them out. But those men when they thus wish to pervert the passage, show plainly that they seek nothing in the Church but their own advantage; and that they have not read the Gospel; for had they known but this very page, and read the whole, they would never have dared to say this.

But attend to a more clear proof that the Church hath such as these. Lest anyone should say to us, "He spake entirely of the Pharisees, He spake of the Scribes, He spake of the Jews; for the Church hath none such." Who then are they of whom the Lord saith, "Not everyone that saith unto me, Lord, Lord, shall enter into the kingdom of heaven"? And He added, "Many shall say to me in that day, Lord, Lord, have we not prophesied in thy name, and in thy name done many mighty works, and in thy name have eaten and drunken?" What! Do the Jews do these things in Christ's name? Assuredly it is manifest that He speaks of them who have the name of Christ. But what follows? "Then will I say to them, I never knew you; depart from me, all ye that work iniquity." Hear the Apostle sighing concerning such as these. He says that some preach the Gospel "through charity," others "by occasion," of whom he says, "They do not preach the Gospel rightly." A right thing, but themselves not right. What they preach is right; but they who preach it are not right. Why is he not right? Because he seeketh something else in the Church, seeketh not God. If he sought God, he would be chaste; for the soul hath in God her lawful husband.

Whosoever seeketh from God ought besides God, doth not seek God chastely. Consider, brethren; if a wife love her husband because he is rich, she is not chaste. For she loves not her husband, but her husband's gold. Whereas if she love her husband, she loves him both in nakedness and poverty. For if she love him because he is rich; what if (as human chances are) he be outlawed, and all on a sudden be reduced to need? She gives him up, mayhap; because what she loved was not her husband, but his property. But if she love her husband indeed, she loves him even more when poor; for that she loves with pity too.

And yet, brethren, our God never can be poor. He is rich, He made all things, heaven and earth, the sea and angels. In the heaven, whatsoever we see, whatsoever we see not, He made it. But notwithstanding, we ought not to love these riches, but Him who made them. For He hath promised thee nothing but Himself. Find anything more precious, and He will give thee this. Beauteous is the earth, the heaven, and the angels; but more beauteous is He who made them. They then who preach God, as loving God, who preach God, for God's sake, feed the sheep, and are no hirelings. This chastity did our Lord Jesus Christ require of the soul, when He said to Peter, "Peter, lovest thou me?" What is "lovest thou me?" Art thou chaste? Is not thine heart adulterous? Dost thou seek not thine own things in the Church, but Mine? If then thou be such an one, and lovest Me, "feed my sheep." For thou shalt be no hireling, but thou shalt be a shepherd.

But they did not preach chastely, concerning whom the Apostle sighs. But what doth he say? "What then? Notwithstanding every way, whether by occasion or in truth, Christ is preached." He suffers then that hirelings there should be. The shepherd preacheth Christ in truth, the hireling by occasion preacheth Christ, seeking something else. Notwithstanding, both the one and the other preacheth Christ. Hear the voice of the shepherd Paul: "Whether by occasion or in truth, Christ is preached." Himself a shepherd, he was pleased to have the hireling. For they act where they are able, they are useful as far as they are able. But when the Apostle for other uses sought for those whose ways the weak ones might imitate, he saith, "I have sent unto you Timotheus, who shall bring you into remembrance of my ways." And what doth he say? "I have sent unto you a shepherd, to bring you into remembrance of my ways"; that is, who himself also walketh as I walk. And in sending this shepherd, what doth he say? "For I have no one so likeminded, who with sincere affection is anxious for you." Were there not many with him? But what follows? "For all seek their own, not the things which are Jesus Christ's"; that is, "I have wished to send unto you a shepherd; for there are many hirelings; but it were not meet for an hireling to be sent." An hireling is sent for the transaction of other affairs and business; but for those which Paul then desired, a shepherd was necessary. And he scarcely found one shepherd among the many hirelings; for the shepherds are few, the hirelings many. But what is said of the hirelings? "Verily I say unto you, they have received their reward." Of the shepherd, what saith the Apostle? "But whosoever shall cleanse himself from such as these shall be a vessel unto honour, sanctified, and useful to the Lord, prepared always unto every good work." Not unto certain things prepared, and unto certain not prepared, but "unto every good work prepared." So much have I said concerning the shepherds.

2. Martin Luther

This is a comforting Gospel, which so beautifully portrays the Lord Jesus and teaches us what manner of person He is, what kind of works He does, and how He is disposed toward men. And there is no better way to understand it than to contrast light and darkness and day and night; that is, the good shepherd with the wicked one, as the Lord Himself does.

Now you have often heard that God has given the world two different proclamations. One is that which is declared in the Word of God when it says: "Thou shalt not kill, not commit adultery, not steal" (Exodus 20:13-15) and when it adds the threat that all who do not keep these commandments shall die. But this declaration will make no one godly at heart. For though it may compel a man outwardly to appear godly before men, inwardly it leaves the heart at enmity with the Law, and wishing that there were no such Law.

The other proclamation is that of the Gospel. It tells where one may obtain that which will meet the demands of the Law. It does not drive or threaten, but tenderly invites us. It does not say, Do this and that, but rather: "Come, I will show you where you may find and obtain what you need to make you godly. See, here is the Lord Jesus; He will give it to you." Therefore, the two are as contrary to each other as taking and giving, demanding and presenting, and this distinction must be well observed. Thus God has ever ruled and still rules the world today. To coarse and rude persons, who are not influenced by the Gospel, the Law must be declared, and they must be driven until they are humbled and acknowledge their imperfections. When this has been accomplished, the Gospel is to be applied.

These are the two divine proclamations that come from heaven. Besides these there are others that are not from heaven, but are human prattle which the pope and our bishops have invented that they might terrify our consciences. Such men are not worthy of being called shepherds or hirelings, but they are here designated by the Lord Jesus as thieves, murderers, and wolves. For if men are to be savingly governed, it must be done with the Word of God; and if it is not done by the Word of God, they are not properly governed.

Now, here Jesus has in mind the second proclamation. He explains it and sets Himself forth as the chief shepherd, yea, as the only Shepherd; for that which He does not tend is not kept. This comforting and sweet proclamation we will now consider.

You have heard that after His sufferings and death Christ our Lord arose from the dead and entered upon, and was enthroned in, an immortal existence. Not that He might sit up there in heaven idly and find pleasure in Himself, but that He might take charge of the kingdom of which the prophets and all the Scriptures have so fully spoken, and might rule as a king. Therefore, we should think of Him as being present and reigning among us continually, and never think of Him as sitting up there doing nothing, but rather that He from above fills and rules all things, as Paul says to the Ephesians (4:10), and especially that He is taking care of His kingdom, which is the Christian faith, and that therefore His kingdom among us here on earth must prosper. This kingdom, as we have said, is so constituted that we all must daily increase and grow in holiness, and it is not governed by any other power save the oral proclamation of the Gospel.

This proclamation is not of men; but Christ Himself sent it forth, and then put it into the hearts of the apostles and their successors so that they understood it, and into their mouths so that they spake and declared it. This is His kingdom, and so does He rule that all of His power is comprehended in and connected with the Word of God. They who hear and believe it belong to this kingdom, and the Word then becomes so mighty that it provides all that man may need and bestows all the blessings that we may desire. For it is the power of God, and it can and will save all who believe it, as St. Paul declared to the Romans (1:16). If you believe that Christ died to save you from all evil, and will hold fast to that Word, you will find it so certain and sure that no creature can overthrow it; and as no one can overthrow the Word, neither can anyone harm you who believe it. Accordingly, with the Word you will overcome sin, death, devil, and hell, and you will find a refuge in the Word and attain that which is found where the Word is, namely, everlasting peace, joy, and life. In short, you will be participants in all the power that is in the Word. Therefore, it is a peculiar kingdom. The Word is present and is orally proclaimed to all the world, but its power is deeply hidden so that none but they who believe realize that it is so effective and that it accomplishes such great things. It must be experienced and realized by the heart.

Hence, all that we preachers can do is to become the mouthpieces and instruments of Christ our Lord, through whom He proclaims the Word bodily. He sends forth the Word publicly so that all may hear it; but that the heart inwardly experiences it, that is effected through faith and is wrought by Christ in secret where He perceives that it can be done according to His divine knowledge and pleasure. That is why He says: "I am the good shepherd." And what is a good shepherd? "The good shepherd," says Christ, "layeth down his life for the sheep; and I lay down my life for the sheep." In this one virtue the Lord comprehends and exemplifies all others in the beautiful parable of the sheep. Sheep, you know, are most foolish and stupid animals. When we want to speak of anybody's stupidity we say, "He is a sheep." Nevertheless, it has this trait above all other animals, that it soon learns to heed its shepherd's voice and will follow no one but its shepherd, and though it cannot help and keep and heal itself, nor guard itself against the wolf, but is dependent upon others, yet it always knows enough to keep close to its shepherd and look to him for help.

Now Christ uses this trait or nature of the animal as an illustration in explaining that He is the good Shepherd. In this manner He plainly shows what His kingdom is, and wherein it consists, and would say: "My kingdom is only to rule the sheep"; that is, poor, needy, wretched men, who well see and realize that there is no other help or counsel for them.

Therefore, we should so preach Christ as one who will reject nobody, however weak he may be, but will gladly receive and comfort and strengthen everybody; that we may always picture Him to ourselves as a good shepherd. Then hearts will turn to Him of their own accord, and need not be forced and driven. The Gospel graciously invites and makes men willing, so that they desire to go, and do go, to Him with all confidence. And it begets a love for Christ in their hearts, so that they willingly do what they should, whereas formerly they had to be driven and forced. When we are driven, we do a thing with displeasure and against our will. That is not what God desires; therefore it is done in vain. But when I see that God deals with me graciously, He wins my heart, so that I am constrained to fly to Him; consequently, my heart is filled with happiness and joy.

3. Charles Kingsley

I AM THE GOOD SHEPHERD. Here are blessed words. They are not new words. You find words like these often in the Bible, and even in ancient heathen books. Kings, priests, prophets, judges, are called shepherds of the people. David is called the shepherd of Israel. A prophet complains of the shepherds of Israel who feed themselves and will not feed the flock.

But the old Hebrew prophets had a vision of a greater and better shepherd than David, or any earthly king or priest—of a heavenly and almighty Shepherd. "The Lord is my shepherd," says one; "therefore I shall not want." And another says, "He shall feed his flock like a shepherd. He shall gather his lambs in his arms, and carry them in his bosom, and shall gently lead those who are with young."

This was blessed news; good news for all mankind, if there had been no more than this. But there is more blessed news still in the text. In the text, the Lord of whom those old prophets spoke, spoke for Himself, with human voice, upon this earth of ours; and declared that all they had said was true; and that more still was true.

"I am the good shepherd," He says. And then He adds, "The good shepherd giveth his life for the sheep." Oh, my friends, consider these words. Think what endless depths of wonder there are in them. Is it not wonderful enough that God should care for men, should lead them, guide them, feed them, condescend to call Himself their Shepherd? Wonderful, indeed; so wonderful that the old prophets would never have found it out but by the inspiration of Almighty God. But what a wider, deeper, nobler, more wonderful blessing, and more blessed wonder, that the Shepherd should give His life for the servant, the Good for the bad, the wise One for the fools, the pure One for the foul, the loving One for the spiteful, the King for those who had rebelled against Him, the Creator for His creatures. That God should give His life for man! "Truly," says St. John, "herein is love. Not that we loved him: but that he loved us." Herein, indeed, is love. Herein is the beauty of God, and the glory of God; that He spared nothing, shrank from nothing, that He might save man. Because the sheep were lost, the good Shepherd would go forth into the rough and dark places of the earth to seek and to save that which was lost. That was enough. That was a thousand times more than we had a right to expect. Had He done only that He would have been forever glorious, forever adorable, forever worthy of the praises and thanks of heaven and earth, and all that herein is. But that seemed little in the eyes of Jesus, little to the greatness of His divine love. He would understand the weakness of His sheep by being weak Himself; understand the sorrows of His sheep, by sorrowing Himself; understand the sins of His sheep, by bearing all their sins; the temptations of His sheep, by conquering them Himself; and lastly, He would understand and conquer the death of His sheep, by dying Himself. Because the sheep must die, He would die too, that in all things, and to the uttermost, He might show Himself the good Shepherd, Who shared all sorrow, danger, and misery with His sheep, as if they had been His children, bone of His bone and flesh of His flesh. In all things He would show Himself the good Shepherd, and no hireling, who cared for himself and his own wages. If the wolf came, He would face the wolf; and though the wolf killed Him, yet would He kill the wolf, that by His death He might destroy death, and him who had the power of death, that is, the devil. He would go where the sheep went. He would enter into the sheepfold by the same gate as they did, and not climb over into the fold some other way, like a thief and a robber. He would lead them into the fold by the same gate. They had to go into God's fold through the gate of death; and therefore He would go in through it also, and die with His sheep, that He might claim the gate of death for His own, and declare that it did not belong to the devil, but to Him and His heavenly Father; and then having led His sheep in through the gate of death, He would lead them out again by the gate of resurrection, that they might find pasture in the redeemed land of everlasting life, where can enter neither devil, nor wolf, nor robber, evil spirit, evil man, or evil thing. This, and more than this, He would do in the greatness of His love. He would become in all things like His sheep, that He might show Himself the good Shepherd. Because they died, He would die; that so, because He rose, they might rise also.

But there is, if possible, better news still behind—"I am the good shepherd; and know my sheep, and am known of mine."

I KNOW MY SHEEP. Surely some of the words which I have just spoken may help to explain that to you. "I know my sheep." Not merely, I know who are My sheep, and who are not. Of course, the Lord does that. We might have guessed that for ourselves. What comfort is there in that? No, He does not say merely, "I know *who* my sheep are; but I know *what* My sheep are. I know them; their inmost hearts. I know their sins and their follies: but I know, too, their longing after good. I know their temptations, their excuses, their natural weaknesses, their infirmities, which they brought into the world with them. I know their inmost hearts for good and for evil. True, I think some of them often miserable, the poor, and blind, when they fancy themselves strong, and wise, and rich in grace, and having need of nothing. But I know some of them, too, to be longing after what is good, to be hungering and thirsting after righteousness, when they can see nothing but their own sin and weakness, and are utterly ashamed and tired of themselves, and are ready to lie down in despair, and give up all struggling after God. I know their weakness—and of Me it is written, 'I will carry the lambs in mine arms.' Those who are innocent and inexperienced in the ways of this world, I will see that they are not led into temptation; and I will gently lead those that are with young, those who are weary with the burden of their own thoughts, those who are yearning and laboring after some higher, better, more free, more orderly, more useful life, those who long to find out the truth, and to speak it, and give birth to the noble thoughts and the good plans which they have conceived: I have inspired their good desires, and I will bring them to good effect; I will gently lead them," says the Lord, "for I know them better than they know themselves."

Yes. Christ knows us better than we know ourselves: and better, too, than we know Him. Thanks be to God that it is so. Or the last words of the text would crush us into despair—"I know my sheep, and am known of mine."

Is it so? We trust that we are Christ's sheep. We trust that He knows us: but do we know Him? What answer shall we make to that question, Do you know Christ? I do not mean, Do you know *about* Christ? You may know *about* a person without knowing the person himself when you see him. I do not mean, Do you know doctrines about Christ? though that is good and necessary. Nor, Do you know what Christ has done for your soul? though that is good and necessary also. But, Do you know Christ Himself? You have never seen Him. True: but have you never seen anyone like Him—even in part? Do you know His likeness when you see it in any of your neighbors? That is a question worth thinking over. Again—Do you know what Christ is like? What His character is—what His way of dealing with your soul, and all souls, is? Are you accustomed to speak to Him in your prayers as to one who can and will hear you; and do you know His voice when He speaks to you and puts into your heart good desires, and longings after what is right and true, and fair and noble, and loving and patient, as He Himself is? Do you know Christ?

Alas! my friends, what a poor answer we can make to that question! How little do we know Christ?

What would become of us, if He were like us?—If He were one who bargained with us, and said—"Unless you know Me, I will not take the trouble to know you. Unless you care for Me, you cannot expect Me to care for you." What would become of us, if God said, "As you do to Me, so will I do to you"?

But our only hope lies in this, that in Christ the Lord is no spirit of bargaining, no pride, no spite, no rendering evil for evil. In this is our hope; that He is the likeness of His Father's glory, and the express image of His person; perfect as His Father is perfect; that like His Father, He causeth His rain to fall on the evil and the good, and His sun to shine on the just and on the unjust, and is good to the unthankful and the evil—to you and me—and knows us though we know Him not, and cares for us though we care not for Him; and leads us His way, like a good shepherd, when we fancy in our conceit that we are going in our own way. This is our hope, that His love is greater than our stupidity; that He will not tire of us, and our fancies, and our self-will, and our laziness, in spite of all our peevish tempers, and our mean and fruitless suspicions of His goodness. No! He will not tire of us, but will seek us, and save us when we go astray. And some day, somewhere, somehow, He will open our eyes, and let us see Him as He is, and thank Him as He deserves. Some day, when the veil is taken off our eyes, we shall see, like those disciples at Emmaus, that Jesus has been walking with us, and breaking our bread for us, and blessing us all our lives long; and that when our hearts burned within us at noble thoughts, and stories of noble and righteous men and women, and at the hope that some day good would conquer evil, and heaven come down on earth, then—so we shall find—God had been dwelling among men all along—even Jesus, who was dead, and is alive for evermore, and has the keys of death and hell, and knows His sheep in this world, and in all worlds, past, present, and to come, and leads them, and will lead them for ever, and none can pluck them out of His hand. Amen.

THE THIRD SUNDAY AFTER EASTER

Text: John 16:16-22

1. John Chrysostom

It is permitted to us also to conquer, looking to the Author of our faith, and walking on that road which He cut for us. So neither shall death get the mastery of us. "What then, shall we not die?" saith someone. Why, from this very thing it is clear that he shall not gain the mastery over us. The champion truly will then be glorious, not when he hath not closed with his opponent, but when having closed he is not holden by him. We therefore are not mortal, because of our struggle with death, but immortal, because of our victory; then should we have been mortal, had we remained with him always. As then I should not call the longest-lived animals immortal, although they long remain free from death, so neither him who shall rise after death mortal, because he is dissolved by death. For, tell me, if a man blush a little, should we say that he was continually ruddy? Not so, for the action is not a habit. If one become pale, should we call him jaundiced? No, for the affection is but temporary. And so you would not call him mortal, who hath been for but a short time in the hands of death. Since in this way we may speak of those who sleep, for they are dead, so to say, and without action. But doth death corrupt our bodies? What of that? It is not that they may remain in corruption, but that they be made better. Let us then conquer the world, let us run to immortality, let us follow our King, let us too set up a trophy, let us despise the world's pleasures. We need no toil to do so; let us transfer our souls to heaven, and all the world is conquered. If thou desirest it not, it is conquered; if thou deride it, it is worsted. Strangers are we and sojourners, let us then not grieve at any of its painful things. For if, being sprung from a renowned country, and from illustrious ancestors, thou hadst gone into some distant land, being known to no one, having with thee neither servants nor wealth, and then someone had insulted thee, thou wouldest not grieve as though thou hadst suffered these things at home. For the knowing clearly that thou wast in a strange and foreign land would persuade thee to bear all easily, and to despise hunger, and thirst, and any suffering whatever. Consider this also now, that thou art a stranger and a sojourner, and let nothing disturb thee in this foreign land; for thou hast a City whose Artificer and Creator is God, and the sojourning itself is but for a short and little time. Let whoever will strike, insult, revile; we are in a strange land, and live but meanly; the dreadful thing would be to suffer so in our own country, before our fellow citizens, then is the greatest unseemliness and loss. For if a man be where he had none that knows him, he endures all easily,

279

because insult becomes more grievous from the intention of those who offer it. For instance, if a man insult the governor, knowing that he is governor, then the insult is bitter; but if he insult, supposing him to be a private man, he cannot even touch him who undergoeth the insult. So let us reason also. For neither do our revilers know what we are, as, that we are citizens of heaven, registered for the country which is above, fellow choristers of the Cherubim. Let us not then grieve nor deem their insult to be insult; had they known, they would not have insulted us. Do they deem us poor and mean? Neither let us count this an insult. For tell me, if a traveler, having got before his servants, were sitting a little space in the inn waiting for them, and then the innkeeper, or some travelers, should behave rudely to him, and revile him, would he not laugh at the other's ignorance? Would not their mistake rather give him pleasure? Would he not feel a satisfaction as though not he but someone else were insulted? Let us too behave thus. We too sit in an inn, waiting for our friends who travel the same road; when we are all collected, then they shall know whom they insult. These men then shall hang their heads; then they shall say, "This is he whom we" fools "had in derision" (Wisdom 5:3).

With these two things then let us comfort ourselves, that we are not insulted, for they know not who we are, and that, if we wish to obtain satisfaction, they shall hereafter give us a most bitter one. But God forbid that any should have a soul so cruel and inhuman. "What then, if we be insulted by our kinsmen? For this is the burdensome thing." Nay, this is the light thing. "Why, pray?" Because we do not bear those whom we love when they insult us, in the same way as we bear those whom we do not know. For instance, in consoling those who have been injured, we often say, "It is a brother who hath injured you, bear it nobly; it is a father; it is an uncle." But if the name of "father" and "brother" puts you to shame, much more if I name to you a relationship more intimate than these; for we are not only brethren one to another, but also members, and one body. Now if the name of brother shame you, much more than of member. Hast thou not heard that Gentile proverb which saith that "it behooveth to keep friends with their defects"? Hast thou not heard Paul say, "Bear ye one another's burdens"? Seest thou not lovers? For I am compelled, since I cannot draw an instance from you, to bring my discourse to that ground of argument. This also Paul doth, thus saying, "Furthermore we have had fathers in our flesh, which corrected us, and we gave them reverence" (Hebrews 12:9). Or rather, that is more apt which he saith to the Romans, "As ye have yielded your members servants to uncleanness and to iniquity unto iniquity, even so now yield your members servants to righteousness." For this reason let us confidently keep hold of the illustration. Now dost thou not observe lovers, what miseries these suffer when inflamed with desire for harlots, cuffed, beaten, and laughed at, enduring a harlot, who turns away from and insults them in ten thousand ways; yet if they see but once anything sweet or gentle, all is well to do with them, all former things are gone, all goes on with a fair wind, be it poverty, be it sickness, be it anything else besides these. For they count their own life as miserable or blessed, according as they may have her whom they love disposed toward them. They know nothing of mortal honor or disgrace, but even if one insult, they bear all easily through the great pleasure and delight which they receive from her; and though she revile, though she spit in their face, they think, when they are enduring this, that they are being pelted with roses. And what wonder, if such are their feelings as to her person? For her very house they think to be more splendid than any, though it be but of mud, though it be falling down. But why speak I of walls? When they even see the places which they frequent in the evening, they are excited. Allow me now for what follows to speak the word of the Apostle. As he saith, "As ye have yielded your members servants to uncleanness, so yield your members servants unto righteousness"; so in like manner now I say, "as we have loved these women, let us love one another, and we shall not think that we suffer anything terrible." And why say I, "one another"? Let us so love God. Do ye shudder when ye hear that I require as much love in the case of God as we have shown toward a harlot? But I shudder that we do not show even thus much. And, if you will, let us go on with the argument, though what is said be very painful. The woman beloved promises her lovers nothing good, but dishonor, shame, and insolence. For this is what the waiting upon a harlot makes a man, ridiculous, shameful, dishonored. But God promiseth us heaven, and the good things which are in heaven; He hath made us sons and brethren of the Only-begotten, and hath given thee ten thousand things while living, and when thou diest, resurrection, and promiseth that He will give us such good things as it is not possible even to imagine, and maketh us honored and revered. Again, that woman compels her lovers to spend all their substance for the pit and for destruction; but God biddeth us sow the heaven, and giveth us an hundredfold, and eternal life. Again, she uses her lover like a slave, giving commands more hardly than any tyrant; but God saith, "I no longer call you servants, but friends" (John 15:15).

Have ye seen the excess both of the evils here and the blessings there? What then comes next? For this woman's sake, many lie awake, and whatever she commands, readily obey: give up house, and father, and mother, and friends, and money, and patronage, and leave all that belongs to them in want and desolation; but for the sake of God, or rather for the sake of ourselves, we often do not choose to expend even the third portion of our substance, but we look on the hungry, we overlook him, and run past the naked, and do not even bestow a word upon him. But the lovers, if they see but a little servant girl of their mistress and her a barbarian, they stand in the middle of the market-place, and talk with her, as if they were proud and glad to do so, unrolling an interminable round of words; and for her sake they count all their living as nothing, deem rulers and rule nothing (they know it, all who have had experience of the malady), and thank her more when she commands, than others when they serve. Is there not with good reason a hell? Are there not with good reason ten thousand punishments? Let us then become sober, let us apply to the service of God as much, or half, or even the third part of what others supply to the harlot. Perhaps again ye shudder; for so do I myself. But I would not that ye should shudder at words only, but at the actions; as it is, here indeed our hearts are made orderly, but we go forth and cast all away. What then is the gain? For there, if it be required to spend money, no one laments his poverty, but even borrows it to give, perchance, when smitten. But here, if we do but mention almsgiving, they pretend to us children, and wife, and house, and patronage, and ten thousand excuses. "But," saith someone, "the pleasure is great there." This it is that I lament and mourn. What if I show that the pleasure here is greater? For there shame, and insult, and expense, cut away no little of the pleasure, and after these the quarreling and enmity; but here there is nothing of the kind. What is there, tell me, equal to this pleasure, to sit expecting heaven and the kingdom there, and the glory of the saints, and the life that is endless? "But these things," saith someone, "are in expectation, the others in experience." What kind of experience? Wilt thou that I tell thee the pleasures which are here also by experience? Consider what freedom thou enjoyest, and how thou fearest and tremblest at no man when thou livest in company with virtue, neither enemy, nor plotter, nor informer, nor rival in credit or in love, nor envious person, nor poverty, nor sickness, nor any other human thing. But there, although ten thousand things be according to thy mind, though riches flow in as from a fountain, yet the war with rivals, and the plots, and ambuscades, will make more miserable than any the life of him who wallows with those women. For when that abominable one is haughty and insolent, you needs must kindle quarrel to flatter her. This therefore is more grievous than ten thousand deaths, more intolerable than any punishment. But here there is nothing of the kind. For "the fruit," it saith, "of the Spirit is love, joy, peace" (Galatians 5:22). Here is no quarreling, nor unseasonable pecuniary expense, nor disgrace and expense too; and if thou give but a farthing, or a loaf, or a cup of cold water, He will be much beholden to thee, and He doth nothing to pain or grieve thee, but all so as to make thee glorious, and free from all shame. What defense therefore shall we have, what pardon shall we gain, if, leaving these things, we give ourselves up to the contrary and voluntarily cast ourselves into the furnace that burns with fire? Wherefore I exhort those who are sick of this malady to recover themselves, and return to health, and not allow themselves to fall into despair. Since that son also was in a far more grievous state than this, yet when he returned to his father's house, he came to his former honor and appeared more glorious than him who had ever been well-pleasing. Let us also imitate him and, returning to our Father, even though it be late, let us depart from that captivity and transfer ourselves to freedom, that we may enjoy the Kingdom of heaven, through the grace and lovingkindness of our Lord Jesus Christ, to whom with the Father and the Holy Ghost be glory, for ever and ever. Amen.

2. John Calvin

A LITTLE WHILE, AND YOU DO NOT SEE ME. Christ had often forewarned the apostles of His departure, partly that they might bear it with greater courage, partly that they might desire more ardently the grace of the Spirit, of which they had no great desire, so long as they had Christ present with them in body. We must, therefore, guard against becoming weary of reading what Christ, not without cause, repeats so frequently. First, He says that He will very soon be taken from them, that, when they are deprived of His presence, on which alone they relied, they may continue to be firm. Next, He promises what will compensate them for His absence, and He even testifies that He will quickly be restored to them, after He has been removed, but in another manner, that is, by the presence of the Holy Spirit.

AND AGAIN A LITTLE WHILE, AND YOU WILL SEE ME. Yet some explain this second clause differently: "You will see me when I shall have risen from the dead, but only for a short time; for I shall very soon be received into heaven." But I do not think that the words will bear that meaning. On the contrary, He mitigates and soothes their sorrow for His absence by this consolation, that it will not last long; and thus He magnifies the grace of the Spirit, by which He will be continually present with them; as if He had promised that, after a short interval, He would return, and that they would not be long deprived of His presence.

Nor ought we to think it strange when He says that He is *seen*, when He dwells in the disciples by the Spirit; for, though He is not seen with the bodily eyes, yet His presence is known by the undoubted experience of faith. What we are taught by Paul is indeed true, that believers, "so long as they remain on earth, are absent from the Lord, because they walk by faith, and not by sight" (2 Corinthians 5:6,7). But it is equally true that they may justly, in the meantime, glory in having Christ dwelling in them by faith, in being united to Him as members to the Head, in possessing heaven along with Him by hope. Thus the grace of the Spirit is a mirror, in which Christ wishes to be seen by us, according to the words of Paul, "Though we have known Christ according to the flesh, yet we know him no more; if any man be in Christ, let him be a new creature" (2 Corinthians 5:16,17).

BECAUSE I GO TO THE FATHER. Some explain these words as meaning that Christ will no longer be seen by the disciples because He will be in heaven, and they on earth. For my part, I would rather refer it to the second clause, "You will soon see me"; "for My death is not a destruction to separate Me from you, but a passage into the heavenly glory, from which My divine power will diffuse itself even to you." He intended, therefore, in my opinion, to teach what would be His condition after His death, that they might rest satisfied with His spiritual presence, and might not think that it would be any loss to them that He no longer dwelt with them as a mortal man.

JESUS, THEREFORE, KNEW THAT THEY WISHED TO ASK HIM. Though sometimes the Lord appears to speak to the deaf, He, at length, cures the ignorance of His disciples, that His instruction may not be useless. Our duty is to endeavor that our slowness of apprehension may not be accompanied by either pride or indolence, but that, on the contrary, we show ourselves to be humble and desirous to learn.

YOU WILL WEEP AND LAMENT. He shows for what reason He foretold that His departure was at hand and, at the same time, added a promise about His speedy return. It was that they might understand better that the aid of the Spirit was highly necessary. "A hard and severe temptation," says He, "awaits you; for, when I shall be removed from you by death, the world will proclaim its triumphs over you. You will feel the deepest anguish. The world will pronounce itself to be happy, and you to be miserable. I have resolved, therefore, to furnish you with the necessary arms for this warfare." He describes the interval that elapsed between His death and the day when the Holy Spirit was sent; for at that time their faith, so to speak, lay prostrate and exhausted.

YOUR SORROW WILL BE TURNED INTO JOY. He means the "joy" which they felt after having received the Spirit; not that they were afterward free from all "sorrow," but that all the sorrow which they would endure was swallowed up by spiritual joy. We know that the apostles, so long as they lived, sustained a severe warfare, that they endured base reproaches, that they had many reasons for "weeping and lamenting"; but, renewed by the Spirit, they had laid aside their former consciousness of weakness so that, with lofty heroism, they nobly trampled under foot all the evils that they endured. Here then is a comparison between their present weakness and the power of the Spirit, which would soon be given to them; for, though they were nearly overwhelmed for a time, yet afterward they not only fought bravely, but obtained a glorious triumph in the midst of their struggles. Yet it ought also to be observed that He points out not only the interval that elapsed between the resurrection of Christ and the death of the apostles, but also the period which followed afterward; as if Christ had said, "You will lie prostrate, as it were, for a short time; but when the Holy Spirit shall have raised you up again, then will begin a new *joy*, which will continue to increase, until, having been received into the heavenly glory, you shall have perfect *joy*."

3. John Wesley

After God had wrought a great deliverance for Israel, by bringing them out of the house of bondage, they did not immediately enter into the land which He had promised to their fathers; but "wandered out of the way in the wilderness," and were variously tempted and distressed. In like manner, after God has delivered them that fear Him from the bondage of sin and Satan, after they are "justified freely by his grace, through the redemption that is in Jesus," yet not many of them immediately enter into "the rest which remaineth for the people of God." The greater part of them wander, more or less, out of the good way into which He hath brought them. They come, as it were, into a "waste and howling desert," where they are variously tempted and tormented: and this, some, in allusion to the case of the Israelites, have termed, "A wilderness state."

Certain it is that the condition wherein these are has a right to the tenderest compassion. They labor under an evil and sore disease, though one that is not commonly understood; and for this very reason it is the more difficult for them to find a remedy. Being in darkness themselves, they cannot be supposed to understand the nature of their own disorder; and few of their brethren, nay, perhaps, of their teachers, know either what their sickness is or how to heal it. So much the more need there is to inquire, first, What is the nature of this disease? secondly, What is the cause? and, thirdly, What is the cure of it?

And, first, What is the nature of this disease into which so many fall after they have believed? Wherein does it properly consist; and what are the genuine symptoms of it? It properly consists in the loss of that faith which God once wrought in their heart. They that are "in the wilderness" have not now that divine "evidence," that satisfactory conviction, "of things not seen," which they once enjoyed. They have not now that inward demonstration of the Spirit which before enabled each of them to say, "The life I live, I live by faith in the Son of God, who loved me, and gave himself for me." The light of heaven does not now "shine in their hearts," neither do they "see him that is invisible"; but darkness is again on the face of their souls, and blindness on the eyes of their understanding. The Spirit no longer "witnesses with their spirits, that they are the children of God"; neither does He continue as the spirit of adoption, "crying" in their hearts, "Abba, Father." They have not now a sure trust in His love, and a liberty of approaching Him with holy boldness. "Though he slay me, yet will I trust in him," is no more the language of their heart; but they are shorn of their strength, and become weak and feeble-minded, even as other men.

Hence, secondly, proceeds the loss of love, which cannot but rise or fall, at the same time, and in the same proportion, with true, living faith. Accordingly, they that are deprived of their faith are deprived of the love of God also. They cannot now say, "Lord, thou knowest all things, thou knowest that I love thee." They are not now happy in God, as everyone is that truly loves Him. They do not delight in Him as in time past, and "smell the odour of his ointments." Once all their "desire was unto him, and to the remembrance of his name"; but now even their desires are cold and dead, if not utterly extinguished. And as their love of God is waxed cold, so is also their love of their neighbor. They have not now that zeal for the souls of man, that longing after their welfare, that fervent, restless, active desire of their being reconciled to God. They do not feel those "bowels of mercies" for the sheep that are lost, that tender "compassion for the ignorant, and them that are out of the way." Once they were "gentle towards all men," meekly instructing such as opposed the truth, and, "if any was overtaken in a fault, restoring such a one in the spirit of meekness"; but, after a suspense, perhaps, of many days, anger begins to regain its power; yea, peevishness and impatience thrust sore at them, that they may fall; and it is well if they are not sometimes driven even to "render evil for evil, and railing for railing."

In consequence of the loss of faith and love, follows, thirdly, loss of joy in the Holy Ghost. For if the loving consciousness of pardon be no more, the joy resulting therefrom cannot remain. If the Spirit does not witness with our spirit that we are the children of God, the joy that flowed from the inward witness must also be at an end. And, in like manner, they who once "rejoiced with joy unspeakable," "in hope of the glory of God," now they are deprived of that "hope full of immortality," are deprived of the joy it occasioned; as also of that which resulted from a consciousness of "the love of God," then "shed abroad in their hearts." For the cause being removed, so is the effect: the fountain being dammed up, those living waters spring no more to refresh the thirsty soul.

With loss of faith, and love, and joy, there is also joined, fourthly, the loss of that peace which once passed all understanding. That sweet tranquillity of mind, that composure of spirit is gone. Painful doubt returns; doubt, whether we ever did and, perhaps, whether we ever shall, believe. We begin to doubt whether we ever did find in our hearts the real testimony of the Spirit; whether we did not rather deceive our own souls, and mistake the voice of nature for the voice of God; nay, and perhaps, whether we shall ever hear His voice, and find favor in His sight. And these doubts are again joined with servile fear, with that fear which hath torment. We fear the wrath of God, even as before we believed: we fear, lest we should be cast out of His presence; and thence sink again into that fear of death from which we were before wholly delivered.

But even this is not all; for loss of peace is accompanied with loss of power. We know everyone who has peace with God, through Jesus Christ, has power over all sin. But whenever he loses the peace of God, he loses also the power over sin. While that peace remained, power also remained, even over the besetting sin, whether it were the sin of his nature, of his constitution, the sin of his education, or that of his profession; yea, and over those evil tempers and desires which, till then, he could not conquer. Sin had then no more dominion over him; but he hath now no more dominion over sin. He may struggle, indeed, but he cannot overcome; the crown is fallen from his head. His enemies again prevail over him, and more or less bring him into bondage. The glory is departed from him, even the kingdom of God which was in his heart. He is dispossessed of righteousness, as well as of peace and joy in the Holy Ghost.

Such is the nature of what many have termed, and not improperly, "The wilderness state." But the nature of it may be more fully understood by inquiring, secondly, What are the causes of it? These, indeed, are various. But I dare not rank among these, the bare, arbitrary, sovereign will of God. He "rejoiceth in the prosperity of his servants: he delighteth not to afflict or grieve the children." His invariable will is our sanctification, attended with "peace and joy in the Holy Ghost." These are His own free gifts; and we are assured "the gifts of God are," on His part, "without repentance." He never repenteth of what He hath given, or desires to withdraw them from us. Therefore He never *deserts us*, as some speak; it is we only that *desert Him*.

What is the cure of it? To suppose that this is one and the same in all cases, is a great and fatal mistake, and yet extremely common, even among many who pass for experienced Christians, yea, perhaps take upon them to be teachers in Israel, to be the guides of other souls. Accordingly they know and use but one medicine, whatever be the cause of the distemper. They begin immediately to apply the promises; to "preach the gospel," as they call it. To give comfort is the single point at which they aim; in order to which they say many soft and tender things concerning the love of God to poor, helpless sinners, and the efficacy of the blood of Christ. Now this is *quackery* indeed, and that of the worst sort, as it tends, if not to kill men's bodies, yet without the peculiar mercy of God, "to destroy both their bodies and souls in hell." It is hard to speak of these "daubers with untempered mortar," these promise-mongers, as they deserve. They well deserve the title, which has been ignorantly given to others: they are *spiritual mountebanks*. They do, in effect, make "the blood of the covenant an unholy thing." They vilely prostitute the promises of God by thus applying them to all, without distinction. Whereas, indeed, the cure of spiritual, as of bodily diseases, must be as various as are the causes of them. The first thing, therefore, is to find out the cause; and this will naturally point out the cure.

For instance: Is it sin which occasions darkness? What sin? Is it outward sin of any kind? Does your conscience accuse you of committing any sin, whereby you grieve the Holy Spirit of God? Is it on this account that He is departed from you, and that joy and peace are departed with Him? And how can you expect they should return, till you put away the accursed thing? "Let the wicked forsake his way"; "cleanse your hands, ye sinners"; "put away the evil of your doings"; so shall your "light break out of obscurity"; the Lord will return and "abundantly pardon."

If upon the closest search, you can find no sin of commission, which causes the cloud upon your soul, inquire next, If there be not some sin of omission which separates between God and you. Do you "not suffer sin upon your brother"? Do you reprove them that sin in your sight? Do you walk in all the ordinances of God? In public, family, private prayer? If not, if you habitually neglect any one of these known duties, how can you expect that the light of His countenance should continue to shine upon you? Make haste to "strengthen the things that remain"; then your soul shall live. "Today, if ye will hear his voice," by His grace, supply what is lacking. When you hear a voice behind you saying, "This is the way, walk thou in it," harden not your heart; be no more "disobedient to the heavenly calling." Till the sin, whether of omission or commission, be removed, all comfort is false and deceitful. It is only skinning the wound over, which still festers and rankles beneath. Look for no peace within till you are at peace with God, which cannot be without "fruits meet for repentance."

But perhaps you are not conscious of even any sin of omission, which impairs your peace and joy in the Holy Ghost. Is there not, then, some inward sin which, as a root of bitterness, springs up in your heart to trouble you? Is not your dryness, and barrenness of soul, occasioned by your heart's "departing from the living God"? Has not "the foot of pride come against" you? Have you not thought of yourself "more highly than you ought to think"? Have you not, in any respect, "sacrificed to your own net, and burned incense to your own drag?" Have you not ascribed your success in any undertaking to your own courage, or strength, or wisdom? Have you not boasted of something "you have received, as though you had not received it"? Have you not gloried in anything, "save in the cross of our Lord Jesus Christ"? Have you not sought after or desired the praise of man? Have you not taken pleasure in it? If so, you see the way you are to take. If you have fallen by pride, "humble yourself under the mighty hand of God, and he will exalt you in due time." Have not you forced Him to depart from you, by giving place to anger? Have you not "fretted yourself because of the ungodly," or "been envious against the evil doers"? Have you not been offended at any of your brethren, looking at their (real or imagined) sin, so as to sin yourself against the great law of love, by estranging your heart from them? Then look unto the Lord, that you may renew your strength; that all this sharpness and coldness may be done away; that love, and peace, and joy, may return together, and you may be invariably kind to each other, and tender-hearted, forgiving one another, even as God for Christ's sake hath forgiven you. Have not you given way to any foolish desire? To any kind or degree of inordinate affection? How then can the love of God have place in your heart till you put away your idols? "Be not deceived: God is not mocked:" He will not dwell in a divided heart. As long, therefore, as you cherish a Delilah in your bosom, He has no place there. It is vain to hope for a recovery of His light till you pluck out the right eye, and cast it from you. Oh let there be no longer delay! Cry to Him, that He may enable you so to do! Bewail your own impotence and helplessness; and, the Lord being your helper, enter in at the strait gate; take the kingdom of heaven by violence! Cast out every idol from His sanctuary, and the glory of the Lord shall soon appear.

Perhaps it is this very thing, the want of striving, spiritual sloth, which keeps your soul in darkness. You dwell at ease in the land; there is no war in your coasts; and so you are quiet and unconcerned. You go on in the same even track of outward duties, and are content there to abide. And do you wonder, meantime, that your soul is dead? Oh stir yourself up before the Lord! Arise, and shake yourself from the dust; wrestle with God for the mighty blessing; pour out your soul unto God in prayer, and continue therein with all perseverance! Watch! Awake out of sleep; and keep awake!—otherwise there is nothing to be expected, but that you will be alienated more and more from the light and life of God.

If upon the fullest and most impartial examination of yourself, you cannot discern that you at present give way either to spiritual sloth or to any other inward or outward sin, then call to mind the time that is past. Consider your former tempers, words, and actions. Have these been right before the Lord? "Commune with him in your chamber, and be still"; and desire of Him to try the ground of your heart; and bring to your remembrance whatever has at any time offended the eyes of His glory. If the guilt of any unrepented sin remain on your soul, it cannot be but you will remain in darkness till, having been renewed by repentance, you are again washed by faith in "the fountain opened for sin and uncleanness."

THE FOURTH SUNDAY AFTER EASTER

Text: John 16:4b-15

1. St. Augustine

The medicine for all the wounds of the soul, and the one propitiation for the offenses of men, is to believe on Christ; nor can anyone be cleansed at all, whether from original sin which he derived from Adam, in whom all men have sinned and become by nature children of wrath, or from the sins which they have themselves added, by not resisting the concupiscence of the flesh, but by following and serving it in unclean and injurious deeds: unless by faith they are united and compacted into His Body, who was conceived without any enticement of the flesh and deadly pleasure, and whom His mother nourished in her womb without sin, and "Who did no sin, neither was deceit found in his mouth." They verily, who believe on Him, become the children of God, because they are born of God by the grace of adoption, which is by the faith of Jesus Christ our Lord. Wherefore, dearly beloved, it is with good reason that the same Lord and our Saviour mentions this one sin only, of which the Holy Ghost convinces the world, that it believeth not on Him. "I tell you the truth," He saith, "It is expedient for you that I go away. For if I go not away, the Comforter will not come unto you; but if I depart, I will send him unto you. And when he shall come, he will convince the world of sin, and of righteousness, and of judgment. Of sin, because they believe not on me. Of righteousness, because I go to the Father, and ye shall see me no more. Of judgment, because the prince of this world is already judged."

Of this one only sin then He would have the world to be convinced, that they believe not on Him; to wit, because by believing on Him all sins are loosed, He would have this one imputed by which the rest are bound. And because, by believing, they are born of God, and become children of God; "For," saith He, "to them gave he power to become the sons of God, to them that believe on him." Whoso then believeth on the Son of God, insofar as he adhereth to Him, and becometh himself also by adoption a son and heir of God, and a joint-heir with Christ, insofar he sinneth not. Whence John saith, "Whosoever is born of God sinneth not." And therefore the sin of which the world is convinced is this, that they believe not on Him. This is the sin of which He also saith, "If I had not come, they had not had sin." For what! Had they not innumerable other sins? But by His coming this one sin was added to them that believed not, by which the rest should be retained. Whereas in them that believe, because this one was wanting, it was brought to pass that all should be remitted to them that believe. Nor is it with any other view that the Apostle

289

Paul saith, "All have sinned, and have need of the glory of God"; that, "whosoever believeth on him, should not be confounded"; as the Psalm also saith, "Come ye unto him, and be enlightened, and your faces shall not be confounded." Whoso then glorieth in himself shall be confounded; for he shall not be found without sins. Accordingly he only shall not be confounded who glorieth in the Lord. "For all have sinned, and have need of the glory of God." And so when He was speaking of the infidelity of the Jews, He did not say, "For if some of them have sinned, shall their sin make the faith of God of none effect?" For how should He say, "If some of them have sinned"; when He said Himself, "For all have sinned"? But He said, "If some of them believed not, shall their unbelief make the faith of God of none effect?" That He might point out more expressly this sin, by which alone the door is closed against the rest that they by the grace of God should not be remitted. Of which one sin by the coming of the Holy Ghost, that is by the gift of His grace, which is granted to the faithful, the world is convinced, in the Lord's words, "Of sin, because they believed not on me."

Now there would be no great merit and glorious blessedness in believing, if the Lord had always appeared in His risen Body to the eyes of men. The Holy Ghost then hath brought this great gift to them that they should believe, that Him whom they should not see with the eyes of flesh, they might have a mind sobered from carnal desires, and inebriated with spiritual longings, sigh after. Whence it was that when that disciple who had said that he would not believe unless he touched with the hands His scars, after he had handled the Lord's body, cried out as though awaking from sleep, "My Lord and my God"; the Lord said to him, "Because thou hast seen me, thou hast believed; blessed are they that have not seen, and yet have believed." This blessedness hath the Holy Ghost, the Comforter, brought to us, that the form of a servant which He took from the Virgin's womb, being removed from the eyes of flesh, the purified eye of the mind might be directed to this Form of God, in which He continued equal with the Father, even when He vouchsafed to appear in the Flesh; so as that with the same Spirit filled the Apostle might say, "Though we have known Christ after the flesh; yet now we know him so no longer." Because even the Flesh of Christ he knew not after the flesh, but after the Spirit, who, not by touching in curiosity, but in believing assured, acknowledgeth the power of His resurrection; not saying in his heart, "Who hath ascended into heaven? that is, to bring Christ down; or, Who hath descended into the deep? that is, to bring back Christ from the dead." "But," saith he, "the word is nigh thee, in thy mouth, that Jesus is the Lord; and if thou shalt believe in thine heart that God hath raised him from the dead, thou shalt be saved. For with the heart man believeth unto righteousness, and with the mouth confession is made unto salvation." These, brethren, are the words of the Apostle, pouring them forth with the holy inebriation of the Holy Ghost Himself.

Forasmuch then as we could in no way have had this blessedness by which we see not and yet believe, unless we received it of the Holy Ghost, it is with good reason said, "It is expedient for you that I go away. For if

I go not away, the Comforter will not come unto you; but if I depart, I will send him unto you." By His divinity indeed He is with us always; but unless He had in Body gone away from us, we had always seen His Body after the flesh, and never believed after a spiritual sort; by the which belief justified and blessed we might attain with cleansed hearts to contemplate the Very Word, God with God, "by whom all things were made," and "who was made Flesh, that he might dwell among us." And if not with the contact of the hand, but "with the heart man believeth unto righteousness"; with good reason is the world, which will not believe save what it sees, convinced of our righteousness. Now that we might have that righteousness of faith of which the unbelieving world should be convinced, therefore said the Lord, "Of righteousness, because I go to the Father, and ye shall see me no more." As if He had said, "This shall be your righteousness, that ye believe on Me, the Mediator, of whom ye shall be most fully assured that He is risen again and gone to the Father, though ye see Him not after the Flesh; that by Him reconciled, ye may be able to see God after the Spirit." Whence He saith to the woman who represents the Church, when she fell at His feet after His resurrection, "Touch me not, for I am not yet ascended to the Father." Which expression is understood mystically, thus: "Believe not in Me after a carnal manner by means of bodily contact; but thou shalt believe after a spiritual manner; that is, with a spiritual faith shalt touch Me, when I shall have ascended to the Father." For, "blessed are they who do not see, and believe." And this is the righteousness of faith, of which the world, which hath it not, is convinced of us who are not without it; for "the just liveth by faith." Whether it be then that as rising again in Him, and in Him coming to the Father, we are invisibly and in justification perfected; or that as not seeing and yet believing we live by faith, for that "the just liveth by faith"; with these meanings said He, "Of righteousness, because I go to the Father, and ye shall see me no more."

Nor let the world excuse itself by this, that it is hindered by the devil from believing on Christ. For to believers the prince of the world is cast out, that he work no more in the hearts of men whom Christ hath begun to possess by faith, as he worketh in the children of unbelief, whom he is constantly stirring up to tempt and disturb the righteous. For because he is cast out, who once had dominion interiorly, he wageth war exteriorly. Although then by means of his persecutions, "the Lord doth direct the meek in judgment"; nevertheless in this very fact of his being cast out, is he "judged already." And of this "judgment" is the world convinced; for in vain doth he who will not believe on Christ complain of the devil whom, judged, that is, cast out, and for the exercising of us allowed to attack us from without, not only men, but even women, and boys, and girls, Martyrs have overcome. Now in whom have they overcome, but in Him on whom they have believed, and Whom seeing not, they loved, and by whose dominion in their hearts they have got rid of a most oppressive lord. And all this by grace, by the gift, that is, of the Holy Ghost. Rightly then doth the same Spirit convince the world, both of "sin," because it believeth not on Christ, "and of righteousness," because they who have had the will have believed, though Him on Whom they believed they saw not; and by His resurrection have hoped that themselves also should be in the resurrection perfected; "and of judgment," because if they had had the will to believe, they could be hindered by none, "for that the prince of this world hath been judged already."

2. Martin Luther

Christ pictures to us in this Gospel what His kingdom is and what takes place in it, how it is governed and what it accomplishes. Here you learn that there is a kingdom upon the earth, and that it is invisible, and that it cleaves to and rests upon the Word of God alone. Christ does not say that He wishes His disciples to follow Him up into heaven at once, but that He will send them the Holy Spirit and that He departs from them for the very purpose of sending them the Holy Spirit in order that thereby His kingdom may be further developed. Therefore, He says: "I have yet many things to say unto you, but ye cannot bear them now." They could not understand that kingdom, how it should exist and be administered. Their reason and senses were still too carnal, they had never seen a spiritual kingdom, nor heard of one; therefore they continually thought of a temporal, outward kingdom. And here as in other Gospels, faith and trust in Christ are preached. We wish now to consider the leading thoughts in this Gospel and to explain them as far as God gives us His grace to do so. The Lord addresses His disciples thus: "When the Comforter is come, he will convict the world in respect of sin, and of righteousness, and of judgment; of sin, because they believe not on me."

Here we must let that be "sin" which is ascribed to, and included in, sin by the high majesty of heaven. In the text, only unbelief is mentioned as sin "because," says the Lord, "they believe not on me."

But what is it to believe on Christ? It is not simply to believe that He is God, or that He reigns in heaven in equal power with God the Father; many others believe that. But I believe on Christ when I believe that He is a gracious God to me and has taken my sins upon Himself and reconciled me with God the Father, that my sins are His and His righteousness mine, that there is an intermingling and an exchange, that Christ is a mediator between me and the Father. For the sins of the whole world were laid upon Christ, and the righteousness of the Father, that is in Christ, will swallow up all our sins.

No sins dare and can remain upon Christ. Such faith makes me pure and acceptable to the Father. Of this faith the pope and our highly educated leaders know nothing to speak, much less to believe. They teach that man should do many good works if he is to be acceptable to God and be free from sin, and that then God imparts to him His grace.

However, here the Lord speaks quite differently, and says: "The Holy Spirit will convict the world in respect of sin, because they believe not on me." Unbelief only is mentioned here as sin, and faith is praised as suppressing and extinguishing the other sins, even the sins in the saints. Faith is so strong and overpowering that no sin dare put it under any obligation. Although sins are present in pious and believing persons, they are not imputed to them, nor shall their sins condemn them. This is Paul's meaning when he says in Romans 8:1: "There is therefore now no condemnation to them that are in Christ Jesus, who walk not after the flesh, but after the Spirit." Their hearts are cleansed by faith, as Peter writes in Acts 15:9. Therefore, whatever they do in this faith, in this assurance is all good, pure, and pleasing to God. On the contrary, without this faith all their doings are sin and destruction, though their good works may shine and glitter as beautifully as they will, and even though they raise the dead. For Paul says: "Whatsoever is not of faith is sin" (Romans 14:23).

Christ further says: "Of righteousness, because I go to the Father." Here all the learned come armed, yea, the whole world besides, and tell us what kind of righteousness this is. Yes, and they shall err. For the world has never known this righteousness; it does not yet know it, and it does not wish to know it. Hence, the Lord says here that the Holy Spirit will convict the world of this righteousness.

But what are we to understand here by "the world"? We dare not understand by it the coarse, outward sins, as adultery, murder, stealing, and theft. There are instituted for such characters the wheels and gallows, with which the worldly powers, the kings, emperors, and princes, have to do. But we will interpret "the world" as the subtle and secret sins, of which the Holy Spirit convicts, which the world does not know as sin. Yea, it pronounces them divine works; it applauds them and will not permit them to be called sins. How else can unbelief and other secret sins live in the heart while the heart itself is not conscious of them and knows not that they are sins? But those who convict the world must, on that account, be reviled as heretics and be banished from the country, as we see at present. Therefore, the Holy Spirit must convict the world.

The rod, however, by which the world is convicted and punished, is the divine Word and the holy Gospel, proclaimed by the apostles and preachers, as God the Father says to His Son in Psalm 2:9: "Thou shalt break them with a rod of iron; thou shalt dash them in pieces like a potter's vessel." That is, you shall humble them with the holy Gospel. But the world resents such conviction and punishment; yet it punishes severely, and even more severely than the Holy Spirit does. The Holy Spirit takes rods, but the world uses swords and fire. Isaiah also speaks in like terms of Christ our Lord in Isaiah 11:4: "He shall smite the earth with the rod of his mouth; and with the breath of his lips shall he slay the wicked."

What is now the righteousness the Lord means here? Some say righteousness is a virtue that gives to every person his own. Although this is a fine definition, yet it is misleading, in that we do not know how we are indebted to everyone, to God and to man. This God desires and demands of us. Therefore, His righteousness is nothing more than the faith and grace of God, by which God makes us pious and righteous, if we are to be found righteous and unblamable before God, and not only before man. For the smallest letter or title of the Law shall not fail, but all will be fulfilled.

Noah was found to be such a righteous man. It is written of him in Genesis 6:8-9: "Noah was a righteous man, and blameless in his generation; he walked with God. Therefore he found favor in the eyes of Jehovah." It is also written of Job, that he was a perfect and upright man, one that feared God and turned away from evil (Job 1:1). But that is done only by faith, when one believes that God has strangled and swallowed up one's sins in His righteousness. For this righteousness is nothing but to believe that Christ is seated at the right hand of the Father; that He is equal with God, possessing equal power; that He has become Lord by virtue of His Passion, by which He has ascended to the Father, reconciled us with God and is there as our Mediator. This is what the prophet means in Psalm 110:1. "Jehovah saith unto my Lord, sit thou at my right hand, until I make thine enemies thy footstool." Therefore, St. Paul calls Christ now a mediator (1 Timothy 2:5; Hebrews 8:6); then a throne of grace (Romans 3:25); a propitiation (1 John 2:2), and other like names. God requires this honor from us and faith demands it, that we possess Him as our Lord and Saviour; and this glory He will not concede to anyone else, as He says through the prophet: "My glory will I not give to another" (Isaiah 42:8).

His way to the Father is His glory. For "to go" means to die, and to pass through death to the Father and enter upon another existence. He glories in His future course when He says: "I go unto the Father." Therefore, here righteousness is nothing more than traveling by faith the road through death unto the Father. This faith makes us righteous before God, this faith by which we believe that He delivered us from sin, death, Satan, and hell, through His Passion, and that thereby God, the Father, is reconciled and our sins are blotted out by His blood. This is also the reason that He mentions His going, when He says, in respect of righteousness, not that He is with the Father, but that He goes to the Father. In this going, sin is swallowed up in righteousness and Christ passes cheerfully through death, so that no one is even aware of it. Therefore it follows: "And ye behold me no more."

The nature and art of faith are here set forth: Faith neither feels nor gropes, nor do the things connected with it require a science; but it bestirs itself cheerfully to believe the things it neither feels nor can measure with all its powers inwardly or outwardly. Paul says in Romans 8:24: "Who hopeth for that which he seeth?" Therefore, the Lord aptly says: "And ye behold me no more." As if He would say that this way of good works which He is traveling will not be seen nor grasped by the senses, but it must be believed.

Now follows the third and last part of our Gospel. "Of judgment, because the prince of this world is judged."

The prince of this world is Satan, and his members include all unbelieving and godless persons, all flesh with all its powers is condemned by God, including both the godly and the ungodly, believers and unbelievers, friends and enemies, as St. Peter cites in his First Epistle (4:17), when he says: "For the time is come for judgment to begin at the house of God," that is, with the elect, in whom God dwells. The righteous, while they live here, have flesh and blood, in which sin is rooted. To suppress this sin God will lead them into great misery and anxiety, poverty, persecution, and all kinds of danger—as Paul writes to the Romans (7:18ff; 8:4); and to the Corinthians—until the flesh becomes completely subject to the Spirit.

That, however, does not take place until death, when the flesh is completely turned to ashes. We must be in all points like Christ. Since He was here despised, mocked, and tried, so that, as the prophet Isaiah (53:3) says, He was esteemed and held as one stricken and smitten of God, the most despised and unworthy, full of grief and sorrow. His disciples must also go through the same experiences. Everyone should carefully consider this. It is so decreed, as Christ Himself before declared to His disciples, saying: "Remember the word that I said unto you, A servant is not greater than his lord. If they persecuted me they will also persecute you" (John 15:20). Hence Paul says in very plain words in 2 Timothy 3:12: "All that would live godly in Christ Jesus shall suffer persecution."

Therefore, St. Peter carefully discriminates and says: "If judgment begin first at us, what shall be the end of them that obey not the Gospel of God? And if the righteous is scarcely saved, where shall the ungodly and sinner appear?" (1 Peter 4:17-18.) This discrimination is between the sufferings of the godly and of the wicked. Godly and believing persons know their sins; they bear all their punishment patiently, and are resigned to God's judgment without the least murmur; therefore, they are punished only bodily, and here in time, and their pain and suffering have an end. Unbelievers, however, since they are not conscious of their sins and transgressions, cannot bear God's punishment patiently, but they resent it and wish their life and works to go unpunished, yea, uncensured. Hence, their punishment and suffering are in body and soul, here in time, and last forever beyond this life. The Lord says here, "The prince of this world is already judged." As if He were to say, "All that the world and humanity in the world discover, praise, and condemn, amounts to nothing; and whatever God judges the world cannot suffer nor bear, but rejects, repudiates, and condemns."

Thus, three thoughts have been presented to us in this Gospel: Sin, righteousness, and, finally, the cross and persecution. We shall be freed from sin through faith. If we believe that Christ made satisfaction for our sins and that His satisfaction is ours, that is then the righteousness. When we are free from sin, and are just and pious, then the world, Satan, and the flesh will arise and contend and battle against us. Then come persecution and the cross. This we wish to have set forth in brief at present from this Gospel. May God grant His grace that we learn it thus, and know how to govern ourselves by it when we need it.

3. John Donne

We use two not three Advents, three commings of Christ. An Advent of Humiliation, when he came in the flesh; an Advent of glory, when he shall come to judgement; and between these an Advent of grace, in his gracious working in us, in this life; and this middlemost Advent of Christ, is the Advent of the Holy Ghost, in this text; when Christ works in us, the Holy Ghost comes to us. And so powerfull is his comming, that whereas he that sent him, Christ Jesus himself, *Came unto his own, and his own received him not*; The Holy Ghost never comes to his owne but they receive him; for, onely by receiving him, they are his owne; for, besides his title of Creation, by which we are all his, with the Father, and the Son, as there is a particular title accrewed to the Son by Redemption, so is there to the Holy Ghost, of certaine persons, upon whom he sheds the comfort of his application. The Holy Ghost picks out and chooses whom he will; *Spirat ubi vult*; perchance me that speake; perchance him that heares; perchance him that shut his eyes yester-night, and opened them this morning in the guiltinesse of sin, and repents it now: perchance him that hath been in the meditation of an usurious contract, of an ambitious supplantation, of a licentious solicitation, since he came hither into Gods house, and deprehends himselfe in that sinfull purpose now. This is his Advent, this is his Pentecost. As he came this day with a Manifestation, so, if he come into thee this evening, he comes with a Declaration, a Declaration in operation. *Pater meus usque modo operatur, & ego operor, My Father works even now, and I work,* was Christs answer, when he was accused to have broken the Sabbath day; that the Father wrought that day as well as he. So also Christ assignes other reasons of working upon the Sabbath; *Cujus Bos,* Whose Oxe is in danger, and the owner will not relieve him? *Nonne legistis,* Have ye not read how *David* ate the Shew-bread? And *Annon legistis,* Did not the Priests breake the Sabbath, in their service in the Temple? But the Sabbath is the Holy Ghosts greatest working day: The Holy Ghost works more upon the Sunday, then all the week. In other dayes, he picks and chooses; but upon these days of holy Convocation, I am surer that God speaks to me, then at home, in any private inspiration. For, as the Congregation besieges God in publique prayers, *Agmine facto,* so the Holy Ghost casts a net over the whole Congregation, in this Ordinance of preaching, and catches all that break not out.

If he be come into thee, he is come to reprove thee; to make thee reprove thy selfe; But doe that, *Cum venerit, when the Holy Ghost is come.* If thou have beene slack in the outward acts of Religion, and findest that thou art the worse thought of amongst men, for that respect, and the more open to some penall Laws, for those omissions, and for these reasons onely beginnest to correct, and reprove thy selfe, this is a reproofe, *Antequam Spiritus venerit,* before the Holy Ghost is come into thee, or hath breathed upon thee, and inanimated thine actions. If the powerfulnesse, and the piercing of the mercies of thy Saviour, have sometimes, in the preaching thereof, entendered and melted thy heart, and yet upon the confidence of the readinesse, and easinesse of that mercy, thou returne to thy vomit, to the re-pursuite of those halfe-repented sins, and thinkest it time enough to goe forward upon thy death-bed, this is a reproofe *Postquam abierit Spiritus,* After the Holy Ghost is departed from thee. If the burden of thy sins oppresse thee, if thou beest ready to cast thy selfe from the Pinacle of the Temple, from the participation of the comforts afforded thee in the Absolution, and Sacraments of the Church, If this appeare to thee in a kinde of humility, and reverence to the Majesty of God, That thou darest not come into his sight, not to his table, not to speake to him in prayer, whom thou hast so infinitely offended, this is a reproofe, *Cum Spiritus Sanctus simulatur*, when the Holy Ghost is counterfaited, when Satan is transformed into an Angel of light, and makes thy dismayed conscience beleeve, that that affection, which is truly a higher Treason against God, then all thy other sins, (which is, a diffident suspecting of Gods mercy) is such a reverend feare, and trembling as he looks for.

Reprove thy selfe; but doe it by convincing, not by a downeright stupefaction of the conscience; but by a consideration of the nature of thy sin, and a contemplation of the infinite proportion between God and thee, and so between that sin and the mercy of God; for, thou canst not be so absolutely, so intirely, so essentially sinfull, as God is absolutely, and intirely, and essentially mercifull. Doe what thou canst, there is still some goodnesse in thee; that nature that God made, is good still; Doe God what hee will, hee cannot strip himselfe, not devest himselfe of mercy. If thou couldst doe as much as God can pardon, thou wert a Manichaean God, a God of evill, as infinite as the God of goodnesse is. Doe it, *Cum venerit Spiritus*, when the Holy Ghost pleads on thy side; not *cum venerit homo*, not when mans reason argues for thee, and sayes, It were injustice in God, to punish one for another, the soule for the body: Much lesse *Cum venerit inimicus homo*, when the Devill pleads, and pleads against thee, that thy sins are greater then God can forgive. Reprove any over-bold presumption, that God cannot forsake thee, with remembering who it was that said, *My God, my God, why hast thou forsaken me?* Even Christ himselfe could apprehend a dereliction. Reprove any distrust in God, with remembring to whom it was said, *Hodie mecum eris in Paradiso*; Even the thief himselfe, who never saw him, never met him, but at both their executions, was carryed up with him, the first day of his acquaintance. If either thy cheerefulnesse, or thy sadnesse bee conceived of the Holy Ghost, there is good ground of thy *Noli timere*, feare neither. So the Angel proceeded with Joseph, *Feare not to take Mary, for that which is conceived in her, is of the Holy Ghost*. Feare not thou, that a chearefulnesse and alacrity in using Gods blessings, feare not that a moderate delight in musique, in conversation, in recreations, shall be imputed to thee for a fault, for, it is conceived by the Holy Ghost, and is the off-spring of a peacefull conscience. Embrace therefore his working, *Qui omnia opera nostra operatus est nobis, Thou, O Lord, hast wrought all our works in us*; And whose working none shall be able to frustrate in us; *Operabitur, & quis avertit? I will worke, and who shall let it?* And as the Son concurred with the Father, and the Holy Ghost with the Son, in working in our behalfe, so *Operemur & nos*, let us also *worke out our Salvation with feare and trembling*, by reproving the errors in our understanding, and the perversenesses of our conversation, that way, in which the Holy Ghost is our guide, by reproving, that is, chiding and convincing the conscience, but still with comfort, that is, stedfast application of the merits of Christ Jesus.

THE FIFTH SUNDAY AFTER EASTER

Text: John 16:23b-30

1. St. Augustine

"Hitherto," He says, "ye have not asked anything in my name. Ask, and ye shall receive, that your joy may be full." This that He calls a full joy is certainly no carnal joy, but a spiritual one; and when it shall be so great as to be no longer capable of any additions to it, it will then doubtless be full. Whatever, then, is asked as belonging to the attainment of this joy, is to be asked in the name of Christ, if we understand the grace of God, and if we are truly in quest of a blessed life. But if aught different from this is asked, there is nothing asked: not that the thing itself is nothing at all, but that in comparison with what is so great, anything else that is coveted is virtually nothing. For, of course, the man is not actually nothing, of whom the Apostle says, "He who thinketh himself to be something, when he is nothing." But surely in comparison with the spiritual man, who knows that by the grace of God he is what he is, he who makes vain assumptions is nothing. In this way, then, may the words also be rightly understood, "Verily, verily, I say unto you, if ye shall ask anything of the Father in my name, he will give (it) you"; that by the words, "if anything," should not be understood anything whatever, but anything that is not really nothing in connection with the life of blessedness. And what follows, "Hitherto ye have not asked anything in my name," may be understood in two ways: either, that ye have not asked in My name, because a name that ye have not known as it is yet to be known; or, ye have not asked anything, since in comparison with that which ye ought to have asked, what ye have asked is to be accounted as nothing. In order, then, that they may ask in His name, not that which is nothing, but a full joy (since anything different from this that they ask is virtually nothing), He addresses to them the exhortation, "Ask, and ye shall receive, that your joy may be full"; that is, ask this in My name, that your joy may be full, and ye shall receive. For His saints, who persevere in asking such a good thing as this, will in no wise be defrauded by the mercy of God.

"These things," said He, "have I spoken to you in proverbs: but the hour cometh, when I shall no more speak unto you in proverbs, but I shall show you plainly of my Father." I might be disposed to say that this hour, whereof He speaketh, must be understood as that future period when we shall see openly, as the blessed Paul says, "face to face"; that what He says, "These things have I spoken to you in proverbs," is one with what has been said by the same Apostle, "Now we see through a glass, in a riddle"; and "I will show you," because the Father shall be seen through the instrumentality of the Son, is akin to what He says elsewhere, "Neither knoweth any man the Father, save the Son, and (he) to whom the Son shall be pleased to reveal him." But such a sense seems to be interfered with by that which follows: "At that day ye shall ask in my name." For in that future world, when we have reached the kingdom where we shall be like Him, for we shall see Him as He is, what shall we then have to ask, when our desire shall be satisfied with good things? As it is also said in another Psalm: "I shall be satisfied when thy glory shall be revealed." For petition has to do with some kind of want, which can have no place there where such abundance shall reign.

It remains, therefore, for us, so far as my capacity to apprehend it goes, to understand Jesus as having promised that He would cause His disciples, from being carnal and natural, to become spiritual, although not yet such as we shall be when a spiritual body shall also be ours, but such as was he who said, "We speak wisdom among them that are perfect"; and, "I could not speak unto you as unto spiritual, but as unto carnal"; and, "We have received, not the spirit of the world, but the Spirit who is of God; that we might know the things that are freely given to us of God. Which things also we speak, not in the words which man's wisdom teacheth, but which the Spirit teacheth; comparing spiritual things with spiritual. But the natural man perceiveth not the things of the Spirit of God." And thus the natural man, perceiving not the things of the Spirit of God, hears in such a way whatever is told him of the nature of God, that he can conceive of nothing else but some bodily form, however spacious or immense, however lustrous and magnificent, yet still a body: and therefore he holds as proverbs all that is said of wisdom; not that he accounts them as proverbs, but that his thoughts follow the same direction as those who habitually listen to proverbs without understanding them. But when the spiritual man begins to discern all things, and he himself is discerned by no man, he perceives, even though in this life it still be through a glass and in part, not by any bodily sense, and not by any imaginative likenesses of all sorts of bodies, but by the clearest understanding of the mind, that God is not material, but spiritual; in such a way does the Son show us openly of the Father, that He, who thus shows, is also Himself seen to be of the same substance. And then it is that those who ask, ask in His name; for in the sound of that name they understand nothing else than what the reality is that is called by that name, and harbor not, in vanity or infirmity of mind, the fiction of the Father being in one place, and the Son in another, standing before the Father and making request in our behalf, with the material substances of both occupying each its own place, and the Word pleading verbally for us with Him whose Word He is, while a definite space interposes between the mouth of the speaker and the ears of the hearer; and other such absurdities which those who are natural, and at the same time carnal, fabricate for themselves in their hearts. For any such thing, suggested by the experience of bodily habits, as occurs to spiritual men when thinking of God, they deny and reject, and drive away, like troublesome insects, from the eyes of their mind; and resign themselves to the purity of that light by whose testimony and judgment they prove these bodily images that thrust themselves on their inward vision to be altogether false. These are able to a certain extent to think of our Lord Jesus Christ, in respect of His manhood, as addressing the Father on our behalf; but in respect to His Godhead, as hearing (and answering) us along with the Father. And this I am of opinion that He indicated, when He said, "And I say not that I will pray the Father for you." But the intuitive perception of this, how it is that the Son asketh not the Father, but that Father and Son alike listen to those who ask, is a height that can be reached only by the spiritual eye of the mind.

"For the Father himself," He says, "loveth you, because ye have loved me." Is it the case, then, that He loveth, because we love; or rather, that we love, because He loveth? Let this same Evangelist give us the answer out of his own epistle: "We love him," he says, "because he first loved us." This, then, was the efficient cause of our loving, that we were loved. And certainly to love God is the gift of God. He it was that gave the grace to love Him, who loved while still unloved. Even when displeasing Him we were loved, that there might be that in us whereby we should become pleasing in His sight. For we could not love the Son unless we loved the Father also. The Father loveth us, because we love the Son; seeing it is of the Father and Son we have received (the power) to love both the Father and the Son: for love is shed abroad in our hearts by the Spirit of both, by which Spirit we love both the Father and the Son, and whom we love along with the Father and the Son. God, therefore, it was that wrought this religious love of ours whereby we worship God; and He saw that it is good, and on that account He Himself loved that which He had made. But He would not have wrought in us something He could love, were it not that He loved ourselves before He wrought it.

"And ye have believed," He adds, "that I came out from God. I came forth from the Father, and am come into the world: again I leave the world, and go to the Father." Clearly we have believed. For surely it ought not to be accounted a thing incredible because of this, that in coming to the world He came forth in such a sense from the Father that He did not leave the Father behind; and that, on leaving the world, He goes to the Father in such a sense that He does not actually forsake the world. For He came forth from the Father because He is of the Father; and He came into the world, in showing to the world His bodily form, which He had received of the Virgin. He left the world by a bodily withdrawal, He proceeded to the Father by His ascension as man, but He forsook not the world in the ruling activity of His presence.

2. Martin Luther

First we note that in order for a prayer to be really right, and to be heard, five things are required. The first is that we have from God His promise or His permission to speak to Him, and that we remember the same before we pray and remind God of it, thereby encouraging ourselves to pray in a calm and confident frame of mind. Had God not told us to pray, and pledged Himself to hear us, none of His creatures could ever with all their prayers obtain so much as a grain of corn. From this, then, there follows that no one receives anything from God by virtue of his own merit or that of his prayer. His answer comes by virtue of the divine goodness alone, which precedes every prayer and desire, which moves us, through His gracious promise and call, to pray and to desire, in order that we may learn how much He cares for us, and how He is more ready to give than we are to receive. He would have us seek to become bold, to pray in a calm and confident spirit, since He offers all, and even more, than we are able to ask.

In the second place, it is necessary that we never doubt the pledge and promise of the true and faithful God. For even to this end did God pledge Himself to hear, yea, commanded us to pray, in order that we may always have a sure and firm faith that we will be heard; as Jesus says in Matthew 21:22: "All things, whatsoever ye shall ask in prayer, believing, ye shall receive." Christ says in Luke 11:9-13: "And I say unto you, Ask, and it shall be given you; seek, and ye shall find; knock, and it shall be opened unto you. For every one that asketh receiveth; and he that seeketh findeth; and to him that knocketh it shall be opened. And of which of you that is a father shall his son ask a loaf, and he give him a stone? or a fish, and he for a fish give him a serpent? Or if he shall ask an egg, will he give him a scorpion? If ye then, being evil, know how to give good gifts unto your children, how much more shall your heavenly Father give the Holy Spirit to them that ask him?" With this and like promises and commands we must consolingly exercise ourselves and pray in true confidence.

In the third place, if one prays doubting that God will hear him, and only offers his prayers as a venture, whether it be granted or not granted, he is guilty of two wicked deeds. The first is, that he himself makes his prayer unavailing and he labors in vain. For Jesus says: "Whoever will ask of God, let him ask in faith, nothing doubting: for he that doubteth is like the surge of the sea driven by the wind and tossed. For let not that man think that he shall receive anything of the Lord" James 1:6-7. He means that the heart of such a man does not continue stable, therefore God can give it nothing; but faith keeps the heart calm and stable and makes it receptive for the divine gifts.

The other wicked deed is that he regards his most true and faithful God as a liar and an unstable and doubtful being; as one who can not or will not keep His promise; and thus through his doubt he robs God of His honor and of His name of truth and faithfulness. In this, such a grievous sin is committed that by this sin a Christian becomes a heathen, denying and losing his own God, and thus he remains in his sin, and must be condemned forever, without comfort. Moreover, if he receives that for which he prays, it will be given, not for his salvation, but for his punishment in time and eternity and it is not for the sake of the prayers, but because of His wrath that God rewards the good words which were spoken in sin, unbelief, and divine dishonor.

In the fourth place, some say: "Yes, I would gladly trust that my prayer would be heard, if I were only worthy and prayed aright." My answer is: "If you do not pray until you know and experience that you are fit, then you will never need to pray." As I have said before, our prayers must not be founded nor rest upon ourselves or their own merits, but upon the unshakable truth of the divine promise. Where they are founded upon anything else, they are false and deceive us, even though the heart break in the midst of its great devotions and we weep drops of blood. The very reason we do pray is because of our unworthiness; and just through the fact that we believe we are unworthy and confidently venture upon God's faithfulness to His Word do we become worthy to pray and to be heard. Be you as unworthy as you may, only look to it, and with all earnestness accept it as true, that a thousandfold more depends upon this, that you know God's truth and not change His faithful promise into a lie by your doubting. Your worthiness does not help you, but your unworthiness is no barrier. Disbelief condemns you, and trust makes you worthy and sustains you.

Therefore, be on your guard all through life that you may never think yourself worthy or fit to pray or to receive; unless it be that you discover yourself to be a freebold character risking all upon the faithful and sure promises of your gracious God, Who thus wishes to reveal to you His mercy and goodness. Just as He, out of pure grace, has promised you, being so unworthy, an unmerited and unasked hearing, so will He also hear you, an unworthy beggar, out of pure grace, to the praise of His truth and promise. This He does in order that you may thank, not your worthiness, but His truth, by which He fulfills His promise, and that you thank His mercy that gave the promise, that the saying in Psalm 25:8-10 may stand: "Good and upright is Jehovah: Therefore will he instruct sinners in the way. The meek will he guide in justice; and the meek will he teach his way. All the paths of Jehovah are lovingkindness and truth unto such as keep his covenant and his testimonies." Lovingkindness or mercy in the promise; faithfulness and truth in the fulfilling or hearing of the promises. And in another Psalm he says: "Mercy and truth are met together; righteousness and peace have kissed each other" (Psalm 85:10). That is, they come together in every work and gift we receive from God through prayer.

In the fifth place, one should so act in this confidence of prayer as not to limit God and specify the day or place, nor designate the way or measure of the prayer's fulfillment, but leave all to His own will, wisdom, and almighty power. Then confidently and cheerfully await the answer, not even wishing to know how and where, how soon, how long, and through whom. His divine wisdom will find far better ways and measures, time and place, than we can devise, even should we perform miracles. So, in the Old Testament, the children of Israel all trusted in God to deliver them while yet there was no possible way before their eyes, nor even in their thoughts; then the Red Sea parted and offered them a way through the waters, and suddenly drowned all their enemies (Exodus 14).

Thus Judith, the holy woman, did when she heard that the citizens of Bethulia wished to deliver the city to their enemies within five days if God, in the meantime, did not help. She reproved them and said, "Now who are ye, that have tempted God? They are not designs by which one acquires grace; but they awaken more disgrace. Do you wish to set a time for God to show you mercy, and specify a day according to your own pleasure?" (Judith 8:10-12). Then the Lord helped her in a wonderful manner, in that she cut off the head of the great Holofernes and dispersed the enemies.

In like manner, St. Paul says that God's ability is thus proved, in that He does exceeding abundantly above and better than we ask or think (Ephesians 3:20). Therefore, we should know that we are too finite to be able to name, picture, or designate the time, place, way, measure, and other circumstances for that which we ask of God. Let us leave that entirely to Him, and immovably and steadfastly believe that He will hear us.

3. Friedrich Schleiermacher

In the first place, everyone will no doubt say to himself in contradiction of this, that, if God is love, His love must reach as far as His omnipotence, and there must be a universal love of God. And certainly we shall feel bound to admit that this special love of which the Saviour speaks in our text is only an outcome of that universal love. As surely as the highest knowledge which we have reached through the Son of God is this, that God is love, so surely must we believe that every work of God's hands is also an object of His love. Only, of course, dead things could not be an object of His love; nor could that which, though certainly alive, yet was incapable of any perception of Him be such an object; but the spiritual eye of those who know Him soon becomes so clear as to all outward things, that they perceive that anything which we can only regard as inanimate and dead is really in itself nothing at all. That which we could imagine as having no kind of connection with that life which alone among created things is the image of God, is not in some way allied to it. Everything endowed with mind, everything that can, even in a very imperfect and distant way, become conscious of God, everything that according to its nature can be reached by the beams of His love—all these are certainly in themselves objects of that love.

And so the ancient accounts in the Old Testament of the creation of the world are closed with the words, "And God saw everything which he had made, and behold it was very good." That was the breathing of love, the look of divine delight over all His works; and it reached as far as His almighty power had done in calling into being that which was not; but still all was good only as connected with that part of this created, finite being which could be the reflection of His own being; which was capable of knowing Him and of feeling after Him in His works. And yet when we reflect that the principal subject of that old story is this earth alone, the scene of our life and work—that it notices only insofar as they affect this world, all the rest of God's works, which our present knowledge shows us as being so much greater and of so much wider range; when we reflect further, that in this world man is the only intelligent being, with reference to whom everything is arranged, for whom everything is made that belongs to this world, or that has any bearing on it in other worlds—with these things before our minds, oh, how can we understand the statement that God the Lord pronounced it all very good, when He saw not only man as the noblest work of His hands, appointed to have dominion over the earth, but just as clearly the fall of man, and all the loss to his spiritual life and work which sin would bring to this man and to the whole human race? We may surely say that if at that time God the Lord said of man and of the earth, which was to be his possession, that all was good, it must have been because He had in view not only sin and the fall, but further—and that not merely as included in His satisfaction, but as being the essential ground of it—Him who was appointed to restore all things. Indeed it was only in reference to Him—only because human nature was capable of receiving into union with it the Word who was to become flesh, therefore only because through Him man was to be brought back to God, into a closer and more intimate relation than had been possible before—it was only in view of all this that God the Lord pronounced all good.

And therefore already in this Word He made Himself known as the God Who would have compassion on sinners, and Who would overlook the times of ignorance, if only in those times He in Whom God was already well pleased, should find in men the adherence, the faith, the love without which He could neither impart His thoughts to them nor bring them into perfect union with God. And thus this universal love of God is everywhere shown to man as to the creature made in His own image, in all his various conditions; this is the way in which the Scriptures throughout explain and make intelligible that love and compassion of God; that He has included all under sin and unbelief, that the promise might come through faith in Him in Whom alone it would be made plain to all for what a glorious destiny God had created man. Therefore all that we are told of the special love of God and His delight in individuals concerns those who, according to His unsearchable plan, were appointed to stand in a closer earthly connection with Him Who was to come. And so the nation from which the Saviour was to arise was His chosen nation; for this reason it was preserved and kept separate and again and again delivered from the distress into which it had brought itself by sin, in order that the revelation of God should be kept safe, and that from this nation should come the only-begotten Son of the Highest. And thus we must say that all mankind was from the beginning the object of the divine good pleasure and love: nothing that was created in His likeness, nothing connected in any way with this created image of Himself, was excluded from His fatherly care; but no one was an object of God's love and solicitude in himself and for his own sake.

This brings us, then, to the second point to be considered: namely, what is the distinctive nature of that special love of God to us on account of our faith in Christ and love to Him? But this special and that universal love are so joined that even what the Saviour here spoke of specially to His disciples signifies nothing different from that universal love. It was not His disciples in themselves, as they had been and as they would have continued to be without Him, who were the objects of the divine love He speaks of; but only, He says, for this reason does the Father love you, because you have learned to love Me, because you have attained to the faith that I came forth from God. For as the Saviour of the world was, even from the beginning, as the only-begotten Son of God the one immediate object of divine satisfaction in this whole world of men; God chose and drew to Himself in a special manner (as we lately saw in the case of Abraham), only those who were connected with Christ's future; although they received, in the greatest moments of their lives, only a far-off prevision of that future which, faint as it was, became their greatest possession and the most precious treasure of their lives. And just in the same way He chose the disciples of His Son, only because of their closer connection with Him; as indeed it was natural that their love to the Beloved of God should attract the love of God to them. How like man the Most High seems to speak in these words! And yet how directly obvious must their divine truth be to us as well as their human character! This is just what we all feel; he who loves those whom we love, becomes thereby the object of our love. And if he was already such in some degree, he becomes now the object of a different, a new and more fervent affection. It cannot be otherwise. If the Saviour was the direct object of the divine delight, how should not God have taken delight in those who recognized in that Saviour the glory of the only-begotten Son of the Father? If He was the object of the Father's delight because through Him the whole human race was to be brought to God and to glory; how should not those also have become objects of God's delight, and have been, as it were, flooded with a reflection of His glory, who not only recognized that in Him all the divine promises were actually fulfilled, and knew Him as the source from which alone flowed the words of life, but who, moreover, could not but serve Him with their whole being in the accomplishment of all the divine purposes for the salvation of the world?

And how does the Saviour Himself represent to us this love of God, of which we become the objects for His sake? He said to His disciples, "I will not say that when you have need of anything, when you wish to ask anything from the Father, I will pray for you to the Father; for the Father himself loveth you, because ye love me and believe that I have come forth from God." Now is not this the highest relationship in which man can stand toward God—that he should make requests and God grant them, that he should ask and God should answer? For each question is really a petition, and every answer is a gift. Nowhere among the human family, indeed, has this relationship been regarded or expressed otherwise than just in this way. If in any place there was a sanctuary specially consecrated to higher beings or to the Highest, it was in order that prayer might thus be presented before God, and that thence might flow forth the blessings granted, that doubting spirits might there propound their questions, and receive an answer out of some mysterious depth of the divine nature. And this is the peculiarity of our relationship to Him, the Father—that He is only called on to give us such things as the heart purified by the word of His Son desires, only to answer such questions as are connected with our love and faith, because just by reason of our love to the Saviour and our faith that He came forth from God, no other questions arise in our hearts. Oh, what grander imagination can we have of our relationship to God than this? Is the highest Being the source of all happiness and of all good? Well, then, all must be good that comes from Him. And if His gifts are granted in answer to our requests, that is a sign that we ask what it was in His mind to grant us, that our souls are in harmony with the principles on which He rules and arranges the world of intelligent beings whom He has created in His likeness—a sign that we are only desiring that which He has Himself appointed as best for us. For if we asked anything else than this, He would not grant what we asked. And the Saviour therefore regards this as the fruit of our love to Him; for how can those who love Him and believe that He came forth from God ask for anything but what belongs to the work for which He came from God and came into the world, and after it was accomplished left the world and returned to the Father? What can they ask but what belongs to the work of saving the world through Him? And if our prayers have no other object than what is suggested by our love and faith toward the Saviour—well, He says, I need not even say that I will pray the Father for you, for the Father Himself loveth you; that is, the things you ask will come directly from Himself. But in fact these two ideas are essentially connected, and are the real ground of the relationship which the Saviour means to establish between God and us; the fact that we have really learned to love Him as He was, in view of what He came for, what He lived for, what He laid down His life for; and further, that we have arrived at the conviction that He came forth from God, given by God to men for their salvation, to fulfill His purposes of blessing toward them. And so the Saviour says also to His disciples a little earlier, "Hitherto have ye asked nothing in my name." For that alone is a prayer in His name, which is prompted by this faith in Him and love to Him; and it is only what is asked in His name that He promises His disciples will be granted. And therefore He says, "When I am no longer among you, you will ask in My name; for not till then will your souls be quite purified from the misconceptions which before were still mixed with your love and faith; and then you will only wish to obtain by your prayers that which from the beginning has been the real object of your doings and efforts; that is to say, only what belongs to the great work which the Father has appointed Me to accomplish." So far, then, as we no longer ask anything but what can be asked for in Christ's name, the Father loves us, so that He grants us what we ask; and such love to the Saviour is inseparably connected with the faith that He came forth from God. How otherwise could we so utterly bind ourselves to the work and will of a single man?

Yet, my friends, let us still linger a moment to look particularly at these words. How long they have given occasion to ever-renewed keen dispute and painful dissension among Christians! How have believers longed and striven to penetrate more and more deeply the mystery of this doctrine of the Saviour's proceeding from God! And how often has some particular way or another of thinking about it been the cause of utterly dividing Christians, and of rending apart their loving fellowship! If such mysterious doctrines, if any such exact definitions of the manner in which the Saviour proceeded from God were a part of the faith on which God's special love to us depends, oh, how was it possible that He who was the very brightness of that love should have been so careless of His own as not to have given them the plainest and most definite explanation of this in the most impressive way! How could He have left it, as it were, to chance, whether they should attain to this knowledge or not, if yet their share in this special love of the Father depended on it? How easily has now one, now another, been always falling on some new interpretation of the doctrine, how difficult Christians have always found it to agree on one and the same view, while yet each supported his own from Scripture! But how ruinous is this apparently so unavoidable difference of opinion, if it is not enough to believe that the Saviour came forth from God; if the love of God does not rest on him who holds that it is to be understood in this particular way and not in that other way. But, my friends, just because the Saviour brings our love to Him and our faith into so immediate connection, we may be sure that what only affects our belief that He came forth from God, in such a way that it has no influence on our love to Him, can just as little affect God's love to us; and we may tranquilly allow all such differences to take their course, so that this subject may always be coming up anew for Christian investigation. But that which cannot contribute to the growth of our love to the Saviour, for that very reason, does not determine God's love to us; and oh, still less let it mar our love to each other, still less let it break the bond of unity in which we show our love to the Saviour by helping forward His work. So we may let all that rest; if we are only sure of this, that to the question John sent to ask the Lord, "Art thou he that should come, or look we for another," there can be no answer but this: "Yes, truly, in Him all the promises of God are yea and amen; there is no other to be looked for after Him; in Him the whole fullness of divine love and grace is revealed to us, and the true life communicated to us through Him; yea, all saving truth is set before us in Him." And if we know this, that is believing that He came forth from God. For the fulfillment of the divine decrees can only proceed from God, and He must have come forth from God, who was to solve the mystery of man's so chequered and intricate and often so dark destiny—so to solve it that the issue of all shall be that very peace that comes from above, and that very eternal life to which all who believe in Him have made their way through death.

THE ASCENSION OF OUR LORD

Text: Mark 16:14-20

1. Leo the Great

THE ASCENSION COMPLETES OUR FAITH IN HIM, WHO WAS GOD AS WELL AS MAN. The mystery of our salvation, dearly beloved, which the Creator of the universe valued at the price of His blood, has now been carried out under conditions of humiliation from the day of His bodily birth to the end of His Passion. And although even in "the form of a slave" many signs of divinity have beamed out, yet the events of all that period served particularly to show the reality of His assumed Manhood. But after the Passion, when the chains of death were broken, which had exposed its own strength by attacking Him Who was ignorant of sin, weakness was turned into power, mortality into eternity, contumely into glory, which the Lord Jesus Christ showed by many clear proofs in the sight of many, until He carried even into heaven the triumphant victory which He had won over the dead. As therefore at the Easter commemoration, the Lord's resurrection was the cause of our rejoicing; so the subject of our present gladness is His ascension, as we commemorate and duly venerate that day on which the nature of our humility in Christ was raised above all the host of heaven, over all the ranks of angels, beyond the height of all power, to sit with God the Father. On which providential order of events we are founded and built up, that God's Grace might become more wondrous, when, notwithstanding the removal from men's sight of what was rightly felt to command their awe, faith did not fail, hope did not waver, love did not grow cold. For it is the strength of great minds and the light of firmly faithful souls unhesitatingly to believe what is not seen with the bodily sight, and there to fix one's affections whither you cannot direct your gaze. And whence should this godliness spring up in our hearts, or how should a man be justified by faith, if our salvation rested on those things only which lie beneath our eyes? Hence our Lord said to him who seemed to doubt of Christ's resurrection, until he had tested by sight and touch the traces of His Passion in His very Flesh, "because thou hast seen me, thou hast believed: blessed are they who have not seen and yet have believed."

THE ASCENSION RENDERS OUR FAITH MORE EXCELLENT AND STRONGER. In order, therefore, dearly beloved, that we may be capable of this blessedness, when all things were fulfilled which concerned the Gospel preaching and the mysteries of the New Testament, our Lord Jesus Christ, on the fortieth day after the Resurrection, in the presence of the disciples, was raised into heaven, and terminated His presence with us in the body, to abide on the Father's right hand until the times divinely fore-ordained for

309

multiplying the sons of the Church are accomplished, and He comes to judge the living and the dead in the same flesh in which He ascended. And so that which till then was visible of our Redeemer was changed into a sacramental presence, and that faith might be more excellent and stronger, sight gave way to doctrine, the authority of which was to be accepted by believing hearts enlightened with rays from above.

THE MARVELOUS EFFECTS OF THIS FAITH ON ALL. This faith, increased by the Lord's ascension and established by the gift of the Holy Ghost, was not terrified by bonds, imprisonments, banishments, hunger, fire, attacks by wild beasts, refined torments of cruel persecutors. For this faith throughout the world not only men, but even women, not only beardless boys, but even tender maids, fought to the shedding of their blood. This faith cast out spirits, drove off sicknesses, raised the dead: and through it the blessed Apostles themselves also, who after being confirmed by so many miracles and instructed by so many discourses, had yet been panic-stricken by the horrors of the Lord's Passion and had not accepted the truth of His resurrection without hesitation, made such progress after the Lord's ascension that everything which had previously filled them with fear was turned into joy. For they had lifted the whole contemplation of their mind to the Godhead of Him that sat at the Father's right hand, and were no longer hindered by the barrier of corporeal sight from directing their mind's gaze to That Which had never quitted the Father's side in descending to earth, and had not forsaken the disciples in ascending to heaven.

HIS ASCENSION REFINES OUR FAITH: THE MINISTERING OF ANGELS TO HIM SHOWS THE EXTENT OF HIS AUTHORITY. The Son of Man and Son of God, therefore, dearly beloved, then attained a more excellent and holier fame, when He betook Himself back to the glory of the Father's majesty, and in an ineffable manner began to be nearer to the Father in respect of His Godhead, after having become farther away in respect of His Manhood. A better instructed faith then began to draw closer to a conception of the Son's equality with the Father without the necessity of handling the corporeal substance in Christ, whereby He is less than the Father, since, while the nature of the glorified Body still remained the faith of believers was called upon to touch not with the hand of flesh, but with the spiritual understanding the Only-begotten, Who was equal with the Father. Hence comes that which the Lord said after His resurrection, when Mary Magdalene, representing the Church, hastened to approach and touch Him: "Touch me not, for I have not yet ascended to my Father": that is, I would not have you come to Me as to a human body, nor yet recognize Me by fleshly perceptions: I put thee off for higher things, I prepare greater things for thee: when I have ascended to My Father, then thou shalt handle Me more perfectly and truly, for thou shalt grasp what thou canst not touch and believe what thou canst not see. But when the disciples' eyes followed the ascending Lord to heaven with upward gaze of earnest wonder, two angels stood by them in raiment shining with wondrous brightness, who also said, "Ye men of Galilee, why stand ye gazing into heaven? This Jesus who was taken up from you into heaven shall so come as ye saw him going into heaven." By which words all the sons of the Church were taught to believe that Jesus Christ will come visibly in the same Flesh wherewith

He ascended, and not to doubt that all things are subjected to Him on Whom the ministry of angels had waited from the first beginning of His birth. For, as an angel announced to the blessed Virgin that Christ should be conceived by the Holy Ghost, so the voice of heavenly beings sang of His being born of the Virgin also to the shepherds. As messengers from above were the first to attest His having risen from the dead, so the service of angels was employed to foretell His coming in very Flesh to judge the world, that we might understand what great powers will come with Him as Judge, when such great ones ministered to Him even in being judged.

WE MUST DESPISE EARTHLY THINGS AND RISE TO THINGS ABOVE, ESPECIALLY BY ACTIVE WORKS OF MERCY AND LOVE. And so, dearly beloved, let us rejoice with spiritual joy, and let us with gladness pay God worthy thanks and raise our hearts' eyes unimpeded to those heights where Christ is. Minds that have heard the call to be uplifted must not be pressed down by earthly affections, they that are fore-ordained to things eternal must not be taken up with the things that perish; they that have entered on the way of Truth must not be entangled in treacherous snares, and the faithful must so take their course through these temporal things as to remember that they are sojourning in the vale of this world, in which, even though they meet with some attractions, they must not sinfully embrace them, but bravely pass through them. For to this devotion the blessed Apostle Peter arouses us, and entreating us with that loving eagerness which he conceived for feeding Christ's sheep by the threefold profession of love for the Lord, says, "dearly beloved, I beseech you, as strangers and pilgrims, abstain from fleshly lusts which war against the soul." But for whom do fleshly pleasures wage war, if not for the devil, whose delight it is to fetter souls that strive after things above, with the enticements of corruptible good things, and to draw them away from those abodes from which he himself has been banished? Against his plots every believer must keep careful watch that he may crush his foe on the side whence the attack is made. And there is no more powerful weapon, dearly beloved, against the devil's wiles than kindly mercy and bounteous charity, by which every sin is either escaped or vanquished. But this lofty power is not attained until that which is opposed to it be overthrown. And what so hostile to mercy and works of charity as avarice from the root of which spring all evils? And unless it be destroyed by lack of nourishment, there must needs grow in the ground of that heart in which this evil weed has taken root, the thorns and briars of vices rather than any seed of true goodness. Let us then, dearly beloved, resist this pestilential evil and "follow after charity," without which no virtue can flourish, that by this path of love whereby Christ came down to us, we too may mount up to Him, to Whom with God the Father and the Holy Spirit is honor and glory for ever and ever. Amen.

2. John Calvin

HE WHO SHALL BELIEVE AND BE BAPTIZED SHALL BE SAVED. This promise was added in order to allure all mankind to believe; as it is followed, on the other hand, by a threatening of awful destruction, in order to terrify unbelievers. Nor is it wonderful that salvation is promised to believers; for, by *believing* in the only begotten Son of God, not only are they reckoned among the children of God, but receiving the gift of free justification and of the Spirit of regeneration, they possess what constitutes eternal life. *Baptism* is joined to the *faith* of the Gospel, in order to inform us that the mark of our salvation is engraven on it; for had it not served to testify the grace of God, it would have been improper in Christ to have said, that "they who shall believe and be baptized shall be saved." Yet, at the same time, we must hold that it is not required as absolutely necessary to salvation, so that all who have not obtained it must perish; for it is not added to faith, as if it were the half of the cause of our salvation, but as a testimony. I readily acknowledge that men are laid under the necessity of not despising the sign of the grace of God; but though God uses such aids in accommodation to the weakness of men, I deny that His grace is limited to them. In this way we will say that it is not necessary in itself, but only with respect to our obedience.

BUT HE WHO SHALL NOT BELIEVE SHALL BE CONDEMNED. By this second clause, in which Christ condemns those who shall not believe, He means that rebels, when they reject the salvation offered to them, draw down upon themselves severer punishment, and not only are involved in the general destruction of mankind, but bear the guilt of their own ingratitude.

AND THESE SIGNS SHALL FOLLOW THEM THAT SHALL BELIEVE. As the Lord, while He still lived with men in the world, had ratified the faith of His gospel by miracles, so now He extends the same power to the future, lest the disciples should imagine that it could not be separated from His bodily presence. For it was of very great importance that this divine power of Christ should continue to be exerted amongst *believers*, that it might be certainly known that He was risen from the dead, and that thus His doctrine might remain unimpaired, and that His name might be immortal. When He says that *believers* will receive this gift, we must not understand this as applying to every one of them; for we know that gifts were distributed variously, so that the power of working miracles was possessed by only a few persons. But as that which was bestowed on a few was common to the whole Church, and as the miracles performed by one individual served for the confirmation of all, Christ properly uses the word "believers" in an indefinite sense. The meaning, therefore, is, that believers will be ministers of the same power which had formerly excited admiration in Christ, that during His absence the sealing of the Gospel may be more fully ascertained, as He promises that "they will do the same things, and greater" (John 14:12). To testify the glory and the divinity of Christ, it was enough that a few of the believers should be endued with this power.

Though Christ does not expressly state whether He intends this gift to be temporary, or to remain perpetually in His Church, yet it is more probable that miracles were promised only for a time, in order to give luster to the Gospel while it was new and in a state of obscurity. It is possible, no doubt, that the world may have been deprived of this honor through the guilt of its own ingratitude; but I think that the true design for which miracles were appointed was that nothing which was necessary for probing the doctrine of the Gospel should be wanting at its commencement. And certainly we see that the use of them ceased not long afterward, or, at least, that instances of them were so rare as to entitle us to conclude that they would not be equally common in all ages.

Yet those who came after them, that they might not allow it to be supposed that they were entirely destitute of miracles, were led by foolish avarice or ambition to forge for themselves miracles which had no reality. Thus was the door opened for the impostures of Satan, not only that delusions might be substituted for truth, but that, under the pretense of miracles, the simple might be led aside from the true faith. And certainly it was proper that men of eager curiosity who, not satisfied with lawful proof, were every day asking new miracles, should be carried away by such impostures. This is the reason why Christ, in another passage, foretold that the reign of Antichrist would be full of "lying signs" (Matthew 24:24); and Paul makes a similar declaration (2 Thessalonians 2:9).

That our faith may be duly confirmed by miracles, let our minds be kept within that moderation which I have mentioned. Hence, also, it follows that it is a silly calumny, which is advanced by those who object against our doctrine, that it wants the aid of miracles; as if it were not the same doctrine which Christ long ago has abundantly sealed.

AND AFTER THE LORD HAD THUS SPOKEN TO THEM. The Evangelist Matthew, having extolled in magnificent language the reign of Christ over the whole world, says nothing about His ascension to heaven. Mark, too, takes no notice of the place and the manner, both of which are described by Luke; for he says that "the disciples were led out to Bethany," that from "the Mount of Olives" (Matthew 24:3), whence He had descended to undergo the ignominy of the cross, He might ascend the heavenly throne. Now as He did not, after His resurrection, appear indiscriminately to all, so He did not permit all to be the witnesses of His ascension to heaven, for He intended that this mystery of faith should be known by the preaching of the Gospel rather than beheld by the eyes.

AND SAT DOWN AT THE RIGHT HAND OF GOD. In other passages I have explained what is meant by this expression, namely, that Christ was raised on high, that He might be exalted above angels and all creatures; that by His agency the Father might govern the world and, in short, that "before him every knee might bow" (Philippians 2:10). It is the same as if He were called God's Deputy, to represent the person of God; and, therefore, we must not imagine to ourselves any one place, since "the right hand" is a metaphor which denotes the power that is next to God. This was purposely added by Mark in order to inform us that Christ "was taken up into heaven," not to enjoy blessed rest at a distance from us, but to govern the world for the salvation of all believers.

3. John Donne

The Gospell is repentance, and remission of sinnes; For he came, *That repentance and remission of sinnes should be preached in his Name*; If then they will tell you, that you need no such repentance for a sinne, as amounts to a contrition, to a sorrow for having offended God, to a detestation of the sinne, to a resolution to commit it no more, but that it is enough to have an attrition, (as they will needs call it) a servill feare, and sorrow, that you have incurred the torments of hell; or if they will tell you, that when you have had this attrition, that the clouds of sadnesse, and of dejection of spirit have met, and beat in your conscience, and that the allision of these clouds have brought forth a thunder, a fearfull apprehension of Gods Judgements upon you; And when you have had your contrition, too, that you have purged your soule in an humble confession, and have let your soule blood with a true and sharpe remorse, and compunction, for all sinnes past, and put that bleeding soule into a bath of repentant teares, and into a bath of blood, the blood of Christ Jesus in the Sacrament, and feele it faint and languish there, and receive no assurance of remission of sinnes, so as that it can levy no fine that can conclude God, but still are afraid that God will still incumber you with yesterdayes sinnes againe tomorrow; If this be their way, they doe not preach the Gospell, because they doe not preach all the Gospell; for the Gospell is repentance and remission of sinnes; that is, the necessity of repentance, and then the assurednesse of remission, goe together.

Thus farre then the *Crediderit* is carried, wee must beleeve that there is a way upon earth to salvation, and that Preaching is that way, that is, the manner, and the matter is the Gospell, onely the Gospell, and all the Gospell, and then the seale is the administration of the Sacraments, as we said at first, of both Sacraments; of the Sacrament of Baptisme there can be no question, for that is literally and directly within the Commission, *Goe and Baptize,* and then *Qui non crediderit, Hee that beleeves not,* not onely he that beleeves not, when it is done, but he that beleeves not that this ought to be done, *shall bee damned;* wee doe not joyne Baptisme to faith, *tanquam dimidiam solatii causam,* as though Baptisme were equall to faith, in the matter of salvation, for salvation may bee had in divers cases by faith without Baptisme, but in no case by Baptisme without faith; neither doe wee say, that in this Commission to the Apostles, the administration of Baptisme is of equall obligation upon the Minister as preaching, that he may be as well excusable if hee never preach, as if hee never Baptize; Wee know S. *Peter* commanded *Cornelius* and his family to be Baptized, wee doe not know if hee Baptized any of them with his owne hand; So S. Paul sayes of himselfe, that Baptizing was not his principall function; *Christ sent not me to Baptize, but to preach the Gospell,* saith he; In such a sense as God said by *Jeremy, I spake not unto your fathers, nor commanded them concerning burnt offerings, but I said, obey my voyce,* so S. *Paul* saith, hee was not sent to Baptize; God commanded our fathers obedience rather then sacrifice, but yet sacrifice too; and hee commands us preaching rather then Baptizing, but yet Baptizing too; For as that is true, *In adultis,* in persons which are come to yeares of discretion, which S. *Hierome* says, *Fieri non potest,* It is impossible to receive the Sacrament of Baptisme, except the soule have received *Sacramentum fidei,* the Sacrament of faith, that is the Word preached, except he have been instructed and catechized before, so there is a necessity of Baptisme after, for any other ordinary meanes of salvation, that God hath manifested to his Church; and therefore *Quos Deus conjunxit*, those things which God hath joyned in this Commission, let no man separate; *Except a man bee borne againe of water and the Spirit, he cannot enter into the Kingdome of heaven;* Let no man reade that place disjunctively, *Of Water or the Spirit,* for there must bee both; S. *Peter* himselfe knew not how to separate them, *Repent and bee baptized every one of you,* saith he; for, for any one that might have beene, and was not Baptized, S. *Peter* had not that seale to plead for his salvation.

The Sacrament of Baptisme then, is within this *Crediderit*, it must necessarily be beleeved to be necessary for salvation: But is the other Sacrament of the Lords Supper so too? Is that within this Commission? Certainly it is, or at least within the equity, if not within the letter, pregnantly implyed, if not literally expressed: For thus it stands, they are commanded, *To teach all things that Christ had commanded them;* And then S. *Paul* sayes, *I have received of the Lord, that which also I delivered unto you, That the Lord Jesus tooke bread,* etc. (and so hee proceeds with the Institution of the Sacrament) and then he addes, that Christ said, *Doe this in remembrance of mee;* which is, not onely remember me when you doe it, but doe it that you may remember me; As well the receiving of the Sacrament, as the worthy receiving of it, is upon commandment.

In the Primitive Church, there was an erronious opinion of such an absolute necessity in taking this Sacrament, as that they gave it to persons when they were dead; a custome which was growne so common, as that it needed a Canon of a Councell, to restraine it. But the giving of this Sacrament to children newly baptized was so generall, even in pure times, as that we see so great men as *Cyprian* and *Augustine,* scarce lesse than vehement for the use of it; and some learned men in the Reformed Church have not so far declined it, but that they call it, *Catholicam consuetudinem,* a Catholique, an universall custome of the Church. But there is a farre greater strength both of naturall and spirituall faculties required for the receiving of this Sacrament of the Lords Supper, then the other of Baptisem. But for those who have those faculties, that they are now, or now should be able, to discerne the Lords body, and their owne soules, besides that inestimable and inexpressible comfort, which a worthy receiver receives, as often as he receives that seale of his reconciliation to God, since as Baptisme is *Tessera Christianorum,* (I know a Christian from a Turke by that Sacrament) so this Sacrament is *Tessera orthodoxorum* (I know a Protestant from a Papist by this Sacrament) it is a service to God, and to his Church to come frequently to this Communion, for truly (not to shake or afright any tender conscience) I scarce see, how any man can satisfie himselfe, that he hath said the Lords Prayer with a good conscience, if at the same time he were not in such a disposition as that he might have received the Sacrament too; for, if he be in charity, he might receive, and if he be not, he mocked almighty God, and deluded the Congregation, in saying the Lords Prayer.

There remains one branch of that part, *Docete servare,* Preach the Gospell, administer the Sacraments, and teach them to practise and doe all this: how comes matter of fact to be matter of faith? Thus; *Qui non crediderit,* he that does not beleeve, that he is bound to live well, as well as to beleeve aright, is within the penalty of this text. It is so with us, and it is so with you too; Amongst us, he that sayes well, presents a good text, but he that lives well, presents a good Comment upon that text. As the best texts that we can take, to make Sermons upon, are as this text is, some of the words of Christs owne Sermons: so the best arguments we can prove our Sermons by, is our owne life. The whole weekes conversation, is a good paraphrase upon the Sundayes Sermon; It is too soone to aske when the clocke stroke eleven, Is it a good Preacher? for I have but halfe his Sermon then, his owne life is the other halfe; and it is time enough to aske the Saterday after, whether the Sundayes Preacher preach well or no; for he preaches poorely that makes an end of his Sermon upon Sunday; He preaches on all the weeke, if he live well, to the edifying of others; If we say well, and doe ill, we are so far from the example of Gods children, which built with one hand, and fought with the other, as that, if we doe build with one hand, in our preaching, we pull down with the other in our example, and not only our own, but other men's buildings too; for the ill life of particular men reflects upon the function and ministry in generall.

And as it is with us, if we divorce our words and our works, so it is with you, if you doe divorce your faith and your workes. God hath given his Commission under seale, *Preach and Baptize;* God lookes for a returne of this Commission, under seale too; *Believe, and bring forth fruits worthy of beliefe.* The way that *Jacob* saw to Heaven, was a ladder; It was not a faire and an easie staire case, that a man might walke up without any holding. But *manibus innitendum,* sayes S. *Augustine,* in the way to salvation there is use of hands, of actions, of good works, of a holy life; *Servate omnia,* doe then all that is commanded, all that is within the Commission: If that seeme impossible, doe what you can, and you have done all; for then is all this done, *Cum quod non sit ignoscitur,* When God forgives that which is left undone, out of a wilfull and vincible ignorance. And therefore search thy conscience, and then Christs commandement enters, *Scrutamini Scripturas,* then search the Scriptures; for till then, as long as thy conscience is foule, it is but an illusion to apprehend any peace, or any comfort in any sentence of the Scripture, in any promise of the Gospell: search thy conscience, empty that, and then search the Scriptures, and thou shalt finde abundantly enough to fill it with peace and consolation; for this is the summe of all the Scriptures, *Qui non crediderit hoc, He that believes not his,* that he must be saved by hearing the word preached, by receiving the Sacraments, and by working according to both, is within the penalty of this text, *Damnabitur, He shall be damned.*

That God should let my soule fall out of his hand, into a bottomlesse pit, and roll an unremobeable stone upon it, and leave it to that which it finds there, (and it shall finde that there, which it never imagined, till it came thither) and never thinke more of that soule, never have more to doe with it. That of that providence of God, that studies the life and preservation of every weed, and worme, and ant, and spider, and toad, and viper, there should never, never any beame flow out upon me; that that God, who looked upon me, when I was nothing, and called me when I was not, as though I had been, out of the womb and depth of darknesse, will not looke upon me now, when, though a miserable, and a banished, and a damned creature, yet I am his creature still, and contribute something to his glory, even in my damnation; that that God, who hath often looked upon me in my foulest uncleannesse, and when I had shut out the eye of the day, the Sunne, and the eye of the night, the Taper, and the eyes of all the world, with curtaines and windowes and doores, did yet see me, and see me in mercy, by making me see that he saw me, and sometimes brought me to a present remorse, and (for that time) to a forbearing of that sinne, should so turne himselfe from me, to his glorious Saints and Angels, as that no Saint nor Angel, nor Christ Jesus himselfe, should ever pray him to looke towards me, never remember him, that such a soule there is; that that God, who hath so often said to my soule, *Quare morieris?* Why wilt thou die? and so often sworne to my soule, *Vivit Dominus,* As the Lord liveth, I would not have thee dye, but live, will never let me dye, nor let me live, but dye an everlasting life, and live an everlasting death; that that God, who, when he could not get into me, by standing, and knocking, by his ordinary meanes of entring, by his Word, his mercies, hath applied his judgements, and hath shaked the house, this body, with agues and palsies, and set this house on fire, with fevers and calentures, and frighted the Master of the house, my soule, with horrors, and heavy apprehensions, and so made an entrance into me; That that God should loose and frustrate all his owne purposes and practises upon me, and leave me, and cast me away, as though I had cost him nothing, that this God at last, should let this soule goe away, as a smoake, as a vapour, as a bubble, and that then this soule cannot be a smoake, nor a vapour, nor a bubble, but must lie in darknesse, as long as the Lord of light is light it selfe, and never a sparke of that light reach to my soule; What Tophet is not Paradise, what Brimstone is not Amber, what gnashing is not a comfort, what gnawing of the worme is not a tickling, what torment is not a marriage bed to this damnation, to be secluded eternally, eternally, eternally from the sight of God? Especially to us, for as the perpetuall losse of that is most heavy, with which we have been accustomed; so shall this damnation, which consists in the losse of the sight and presence of God, be heavier to us then others, because God hath so graciously, and so evidently, and so diversely appeared to us, in his pillar of fire, in the light of prosperity, and in the pillar of the Cloud, in hiding himselfe for a while from us; we that have seene him in the Execution of all the parts of this Commission, in his Word, in his Sacraments, and in good example, and not beleeved, shall be further removed from his sight, in the next world, then they to whom he never appeared in this. But *Vincenti & credenti,* to him that beleeves aright, and overcomes all tentations to a wrong beliefe, God shall give the accomplishment of fulnesse, and fulnesse of joy, and joy rooted in glory, and glory established in eternity, and this eternity is God; To him that beleeves and overcomes, **God** shall give himselfe in an everlasting presence and fruition, *Amen.*

THE SUNDAY AFTER ASCENSION DAY

Text: John 15:26–16:4a

1. St. Augustine

The Lord Jesus, in the discourse which He addressed to His disciples after the supper, when Himself in immediate proximity to His Passion and, as it were, on the eve of departure, and of depriving them of His bodily presence while continuing His spiritual presence to all His disciples till the very end of the world, exhorted them to endure the persecutions of the wicked, whom He distinguished by the name of the world: and from which He also told them that He had chosen the disciples themselves, that they might know it was by the grace of God they were what they were, and by their own vices they had been what they had been. And then His own persecutors and theirs He clearly signified to be the Jews, that it might be perfectly apparent that they also were included in the appellation of that damnable world that persecuteth the saints. And when He had said of them that they knew not Him that sent Him, and yet hated both the Son and the Father, that is, both Him who was sent and Him who sent Him—of all which we have already treated in previous discourses—He reached the place where it is said, "This cometh to pass, that the word might be fulfilled that is written in their law, They hated me without a cause." And then He added, as if by way of consequence, the words whereon we have undertaken at present to discourse: "But when the Comforter is come, whom I will send unto you from the Father, even the Spirit of truth, who proceedeth from the Father, he shall bear witness of me: and ye also shall bear witness, because ye have been with me from the beginning." But what connection has this with what He had just said, "But now have they both seen and hated both me and my Father: but that the word might be fulfilled that is written in their law, They hated me without a cause"? Was it that the Comforter, when He came, even the Spirit of truth, convicted those, who thus saw and hated, by a still clearer testimony? Yea, verily, some even of those who saw, and still hated, He did convert, by this manifestation of Himself, to the faith that worketh by love. To make this view of the passage intelligible, we recall to your mind that so it actually befell. For when on the day of Pentecost the Holy Spirit fell upon an assembly of one hundred and twenty men, among whom were all the apostles—and when they, filled therewith, were speaking in the language of every nation—a goodly number of those who had hated, amazed at the magnitude of the miracle (especially when they perceived in Peter's address so great and divine a testimony borne in behalf of Christ, as that He, who was slain by them and accounted amongst the dead, was proved to have risen again, and

319

to be now alive), were pricked in their hearts and converted; and so became aware of the beneficent character of that precious Blood which had been so impiously and cruelly shed because themselves redeemed by the very blood which they had shed. For the blood of Christ was shed so efficaciously for the remission of all sins that it could wipe out even the very sin of shedding it. With this therefore in His eye, the Lord said, "They hated me without a cause: but when the Comforter is come, he shall bear witness of me"; saying, as it were, They hated me, and slew me when I stood visibly before their eyes; but such shall be the testimony borne in my behalf by the Comforter, that He will bring them to believe in me when I am no longer visible to their sight.

"And ye also," He adds, "shall bear witness, because ye have been with me from the beginning." The Holy Spirit shall bear witness, and so shall ye. For, just because ye have been with me from the beginning, ye can preach what ye know; which ye cannot do at present, because the fullness of that Spirit is not yet present within you. "He therefore shall testify of me, and ye also shall bear witness": for the love of God shed abroad in your hearts by the Holy Spirit, who shall be given unto you, will give you the confidence needful for such witness-bearing. And that certainly was still wanting to Peter when, terrified by the question of a lady's maid, he could give no true testimony; but, contrary to his own promise, was driven by the greatness of his fear thrice to deny Him. But there is no such fear in love, for perfect love casteth out fear. In fine, before the Lord's Passion, his slavish fear was questioned by a bond-woman; but after the Lord's resurrection, his free love by the very Lord of freedom: and so on the one occasion he was troubled, on the other tranquillized; there he denied the One he had loved, here he loved the One he had denied. But still even then that very love was weak and straitened, till strengthened and expanded by the Holy Spirit. And then that Spirit, pervading him thus with the fullness of richer grace, kindled his hitherto frigid heart to such a witness-bearing for Christ, and unlocked those lips that in their previous tremor had suppressed the truth that, when all on whom the Holy Spirit had descended were speaking in the tongues of all nations to the crowds of Jews collected around, he alone broke forth before the others in the promptitude of his testimony in behalf of the Christ, and confounded His murderers with the account of His resurrection. And if anyone could enjoy the pleasure of gazing on a sight so charming in its holiness, let him read the Acts of the Apostles: and there let him be filled with amazement at the preaching of the blessed Peter, over whose denial of his Master he had just been mourning; there let him behold that tongue, itself translated from diffidence to confidence, from bondage to liberty, converting to the confession of Christ the tongues of so many of His enemies, not one of which he could bear when lapsing himself into denial. And what shall I say more? In him there shone forth such an effulgence of grace, and such a fullness of the Holy Spirit, and such a weight of most precious truth poured from the lips of the preacher, that he transformed that vast multitude of Jews who were the adversaries and murderers of Christ into men that were ready to die for His name, at whose hands he himself was formerly afraid to die with his Master. All this did that Holy Spirit, when sent, who had previously only been promised. And it was these great and marvelous gifts of His own that the Lord foresaw, when He said, "They have both seen and hated both me and my Father: that the word might be fulfilled that is written in their law, They hated me without a cause. But when the Comforter is come, whom I will send unto you from the Father, even the Spirit of truth, who proceedeth from the Father, he shall testify of me: and ye also shall bear witness." For He, in bearing witness Himself, and inspiring such witnesses with invincible courage, divested Christ's friends of their fear, and transformed into love the hatred of His enemies.

2. Martin Luther

Beloved, you have heretofore heard much about faith. Today you hear also of the witness of faith and of the cross that follows. Paul says to the Romans, "With the heart man believeth unto righteousness" (Romans 10:10). If one be pious, he must begin in his heart and believe. That serves only unto godliness; it is not enough for salvation. Therefore, one must also do what the Christian life requires, and continually abide in that life. Hence, Paul adds: "If thou shalt confess with thy mouth Jesus as Lord, thou shalt be saved." It is these two things that constitute our salvation, faith and confession of faith. Faith rescues from sin, hell, Satan, death, and all misfortunes. Now, when we have this, we have enough. We then let God live here that we may reach a hand to our neighbor and help him. Besides, God desires to have His name praised and His kingdom developed and extended. Therefore, we must praise His name, confess our faith and win others to do the same, so that God's kingdom may be extended and His name praised.

Thus, faith must be exercised, worked, and polished; be purified by fire, like gold. Faith, the great gift and treasure from God, must express itself and triumph in the certainty that it is right before God and man, and before angels, devils and the whole world. Just as a jewel is not to be concealed, but to be worn in sight, so also will and must faith be worn and exhibited, as it is written in 1 Peter 1:7: "That the proof of your faith, being more precious than gold that perisheth though it is proved by fire."

Now, by confession I must take upon myself the load of Satan, hell, death, and the whole world—kings and princes, pope and bishops, priests and monks. By faith, everything falls that reason can or ever has devised for the salvation of the soul. It must chastise the apish tricks of the whole world, and its jewel alone must be praised. The world cannot endure this, therefore it rushes in, destroys, kills, and says: "It is expedient for you that one man should die for the people, and that the whole nation perish not," as Caiaphas says in John 11:50. Thus, the confession must break forth, that God alone is the Saviour; and the same confession brings us into danger of losing our lives. As the Lord says later to the disciples: "They shall put you out of the synagogues."

One cannot paint the cross differently than it is here painted; that is its true color. But the cross of illness—to lie in bed at home ill—is nothing compared with the cross of persecution. The first is indeed suffering: but the suffering is golden when we are persecuted and put to death with ignominy; when our persecutors have the praise; when right and honor apparently are on their side, while shame, disgrace and injustice are on our side, compared with the world that wishes them thereby to have God's honor defended, so that all the world says we are served right and that God, the Scriptures, and all the angels witness against us. There can be no right in our cause, and without trial we must be banished and isolated in shame and disgrace. So it also was the lot of Christ—they put Him to death in the most scornful and disgraceful way, and crucified Him between two thieves or murderers; He was regarded as chief of sinners, and they said, with blasphemous words: "Aye, He called Himself God's Son; let God help Him now, if He wills it differently. Since He does not, God and all the angels must be against Him." So Christ says in our Gospel, "They will kill you," and not in an ordinary way, but in an infamous manner, and all the world will say that they thereby offer God a service. It is, indeed, hard to hold and confess that God is gracious to us and that we have a Saviour who opposes all the world, all its glitter and shine. But, let the struggle be as hard and sharp as it will, faith must express itself, even though we would like to have it otherwise.

Faith must expect all this, and nothing follows its confession more surely than the cross. For it is certain to come to us, either in life or at death, that all our doings will appear to be opposed to God and the Scriptures. It is better that it be learned during life, from the people, than from the devil at death; for the people cannot force it further than into the ears, but Satan has a pointed tongue that pierces the heart and makes the heart tremble. Satan torments you until you conclude that you are lost and ruined, that heaven and earth, God and all the angels, are your enemies. This is what the prophet means in Psalm 6:7-8, when he says: "I am weary with my groaning; every night make I my bed to swim; I water my couch with my tears. Mine eye wasteth away because of grief; it waxeth old because of all mine adversaries." It is hard to endure this. Now you see how weak you are who are permitted to bear witness of this faith. One fears his wife, another his children and riches, and a third fears himself.

Faith is in vain where it does not continue steadfast to the end. Christ says in Matthew 10:22 and 24:13: "But he that endureth to the end, the same shall be saved." Hence it is better to experience persecution here than punishment at the end. If one flees persecution, there is no faith in his heart—only a dead knowledge or erroneous belief, without sap and strength, marrow and bone; but where there is a true, living faith, it presses forward through sword and fire. Let us now notice how the Lord comforts His disciples.

He says: "But when the Comforter is come." That we may, under no circumstances, despair, Christ says, "I will send you a Comforter, even One Who is almighty." And he calls the Holy Spirit here a Comforter; for although both my sins and fear of death make me weak and timid, He comes and stirs up the courage in my heart, and says: "Ho, cheer up!"

Thus He trumpets courage into us; He encourages us in a friendly and comforting manner not to despair before death but to cheerfully go forward, even though we had ten necks for the executioner, and says: "Aye, although I have sinned, yet I am rid of my sins; and if I had still more, so that they overwhelmed me, I would hope, that they should do me no harm." Not that one should not feel his sins, for the flesh must experience them; but the Spirit overcomes and suppresses diffidence and timidity, and conducts us through them. He is powerful enough to do that.

Therefore, Christ says further: "Whom I will send unto you from the Father." For he, the Father, is the person that takes the initiative: I am the Son; and from us the Holy Spirit proceeds. And the three persons are one, and one essence, with equal power and authority, as He better expresses it when He says: "The Spirit of truth, who proceedeth from the Father." That is as much as to say: He Who comforts you is almighty and Lord over all things. How can the creatures now harm us, if the Creator stands by us? Notice how great the comfort of the Holy Spirit is. Now let all the Turks attack us. As long as He is our guard and rearguard, there is no danger. John also says in his First Epistle (3:19-20): "Hereby shall we know that we are of the truth, and shall assure our heart before him; because if our heart condemn us, God is greater than our heart, and knoweth all things." Likewise, in the following chapter, verse 4, he says: "Ye are of God, my little children, and have overcome them: because greater is he that is in you than he that is in the world." So the Lord now says, "Him will I send unto you, so that nothing can harm you." Is not that liberal comfort? Who would not be fearless and cheerful in view of this? And Christ calls him "the Spirit of truth"; that is, where He is and comes there is a rock foundation through and through, the real truth. Neither falsehood nor hypocrisy is there, for the Spirit is not hypocritical. But wherever He is not, there is nothing but hypocrisy and falsehood. Therefore, we fall when the test comes because the Spirit of truth is not present.

Christ now further says: "He shall bear witness of me." That is, if He is in the heart He speaks through you, and assures and confirms you in the belief that the Gospel is true. Then, as a result, the confession of the Gospel springs forth. What, then, is the Gospel? It is a witness concerning Christ, that He is God's Son, the Saviour, and beside Him there is none other. This is what Peter means when he says: "Ye are a royal priesthood, that we are elected thereto, that we preach and show forth the excellencies of Christ" (1 Peter 2:9). Hence, there must always be witnessing. Witnessing loads upon itself the wrath of the whole world. Then the cross follows, then rebellions rise, then the lords and princes and all who are great become angry; for the world cannot hear, nor will it tolerate, this kind of preaching. Therefore, the Gospel is hated and spoken against.

Reason thinks: Aye, one can, nevertheless, easily preach the Gospel in a beautifully simple and plain way, without a revolution in the world, and then it will be heartily welcomed. This is the utterance of Satan; for if I believe and say that faith in Christ alone does and accomplishes all, I overthrow the monkey play of the whole world; and that they cannot allow. Therefore, Christ's teachings and man's teachings cannot stand together;

one must fall. Priests and monks, as they are at present, are dependent in name, character, and works upon human institutions, which the Gospel thrusts to the ground. Hence, they dare not accept the Gospel, and they continue as they are.

Thus, I say that the Christian faith is founded upon Christ alone, without anything additional. The priests will not permit their affairs and institutions to fall; in consequence, seditions and rebellions follow. Therefore, there must be dissension where the Gospel and the confession of Christ are; for the Gospel opposes everything that is not of its own spirit. If the teachings of Christ and the priests were not antagonistic, they could easily stand together. They are now pitted against one another. As impossible as it is for Christ not to be Christ, so impossible is it for a monk or priest to be a Christian. Therefore, a fire must be kindled. The Lord himself, in Matthew 10:34 and Luke 12:51 says: "I came not to send peace, but a sword."

Then follows in our text: "And ye also bear witness, because ye have been with me from the beginning." Yes; then, first, when you become certain of your faith through the Holy Spirit, who is your witness, you must also bear witness of me, for to that end I chose you to be apostles. You have heard My words and teachings and have seen My works and life and all things that you are to preach. But the Holy Spirit must first be present; otherwise you can do nothing, for the conscience is too weak. Yes, there is no sin so small that the conscience could vanquish it, even if it were so trifling a one as laughing in church. Again, in the presence of death the conscience is far too weak to offer resistance. Therefore another must come and give to the timid, despairing conscience courage to go through everything, although all sins be upon it. And it must, at the same time, be an almighty courage, like He alone can give who ministers strength in such a way that the courage, which before a rustling leaf could cause to fear, is now not afraid of all the devils, and the conscience that before could not restrain laughing, now restrains all sins.

The benefit and fruit of the Holy Spirit is that sin will be changed to the highest and best use. Thus Paul boasts to Timothy, when he was converted, that whereas he had lived such a wicked life before, he now held his sin to be so contemptible that he composed a hymn and sang about it thus, in 1 Timothy 1:12-17: "I thank him that enabled me, even Christ Jesus our Lord, for that he counted me faithful, appointing me to his service; though I was before a blasphemer, and a persecutor, and injurious: howbeit I obtained mercy, because I did it ignorantly in unbelief; and the grace of our Lord abounded exceedingly with faith and love which is in Christ Jesus. Faithful is the saying, and worthy of all acceptation, that Christ Jesus came into the world to save sinners; of whom I am chief: howbeit for this cause I obtained mercy, that in me as chief might Jesus Christ show forth all his long-suffering, for an example of them that should thereafter believe on him unto eternal life. Now unto the King eternal, immortal, invisible, the only God, be honor and glory for ever and ever. Amen."

3. Charles Kingsley

[People] think of the Holy Spirit as only a gentle, and what they call a dove-like, being; and they forget what a powerful, awful, literally formidable being He is. They lose respect for the Holy Spirit. They trifle with Him; and while they sing hymns about His gentleness and sweetness, they do things which grieve and shock Him, forgetting the awful warning which He, at the very outset of the Christian Church, gave against such taking of liberties with God the Holy Ghost—how Ananias and Sapphira thought that the Holy Spirit was One Whom they might honor with their lips, and more, with their outward actions, but who did not require truth in the inward parts and did not care for their telling a slight falsehood that they might appear more generous than they really were in the eyes of men; and how the answer of the Holy Spirit of God was that He struck them both dead there and then for a warning to all such triflers, till the end of time.

Another mistake, which really pious and good people commit, is that they think the Holy Spirit of God to be merely, or little beside, certain pleasant frames, and feelings, and comfortable assurances, in their own minds. They do not know that these pleasant frames and feelings really depend principally on their own health: and, then, when they get out of health, or when their brain is overworked, and the pleasant feelings go, they are terrified and disheartened, and complain of spiritual dryness, and cry out that God's Spirit has deserted them, and are afraid that God is angry with them, or even that they have committed the unpardonable sin: not knowing that God is not a man that He should lie, nor a son of man that He should repent; that God is as near them in the darkness as in the light; that whatever their own health, or their own feelings, may be, yet still in God they live, and move, and have their being; that to God's Spirit they owe all which raises them above the dumb animals; that nothing can separate them from the love of Him who promised that He would not leave us comfortless, but send to us His Holy Ghost to comfort us and exalt us to the same place whither He has gone before.

Now, why do I say all this? To take away comfort from you? To make you fear and dread the Spirit of God? God forbid! Who am I, to take away comfort from any human being! I say it to give you true comfort, to make you trust and love the Holy Spirit utterly, to know Him—His strength and His wisdom as well as His tenderness and gentleness.

You know that afflictions do come—terrible bereavements, sorrows sad and strange. My sermon does not make them come. There they are, God help us all, and too many of them, in this world. But from whom do they come? Who is Lord of life and death? Who is Lord of joy and sorrow? Is not that the question of all questions? And is not the answer the most essential of all answers? It is the Holy Spirit of God; the Spirit who proceedeth from the Father and the Son; the Spirit of the Father Who so loved the world that He spared not His only begotten Son; the Spirit of the Son Who so loved the world, that He stooped to die for it upon the

Cross; the Spirit Who is promised to lead you into all truth, that you may know God, and in the knowledge of Him find everlasting life; the Spirit who is the Comforter, and says, "I have seen thy ways and will heal thee, I will lead thee also, and restore comforts to thee and to thy mourners." "I speak peace to him that is near, and to him that is far off," saith the Lord; "and I will heal him." Is it not the most blessed news, that He who takes away is the very same as He who gives? That He who afflicts is the very same as He who comforts? That He of whom it is written that "as a lion, so will he break all my bones; from day even to night wilt thou make an end of me"; is the same as He of whom it is written, "He shall gather the lambs in his arms, and carry them, and shall gently lead those that are with young"; and, again, "As a beast goeth down into the valley, so the Spirit of the Lord caused him to rest"? That He of whom it is written, "Our God is a consuming fire," is the same as He who has said, "When thou walkest through the fire, thou shalt not be burned"? That He who brings us into "the valley of the shadow of death," is the same as He of whom it is said, "Thy rod and thy staff they comfort me"? Is not that blessed news? Is it not the news of the Gospel; and the only good news which people will really care for, when they are tormented, not with superstitious fears and doctrines of devils which man's diseased conscience has originated, but tormented with the real sorrows, the rational fears of this stormy human life.

We all like comfort. But what kind of comfort do we not merely like but need? Merely to be comfortable?—To be free from pain, anxiety, sorrow?—To have only pleasant faces round us, and pleasant things said to us? If we want that comfort, we shall very seldom have it. It will be very seldom good for us to have it. The comfort which poor human beings want in such a world as this is not the comfort of ease, but the comfort of strength. The comforter whom we need is not one who will merely say kind things, but give help—help to the weary and heavy-laden heart which has no time to rest. We need not the sunny and smiling face, but the strong and helping arm. For we may be in that state that smiles are shocking to us, and mere kindness—though we may be grateful for it—of no more comfort to us than sweet music to a drowning man. We may be miserable, and unable to help being miserable, and unwilling to help it too. We do not wish to flee from our sorrow, we do not wish to forget our sorrow. We dare not; it is so awful, so heart-rending, so plain-spoken, that God, the master and tutor of our hearts, must wish us to face it and endure it. Our Father has given us the cup—shall we not drink it? But who will help us to drink the bitter cup? Who will be the comforter, and give us not mere kind words, but strength? Who will give us the faith to say with Job, "Though he slay me, yet will I trust in him?" Who will give us the firm reason to look steadily at our grief, and learn the lesson it was meant to teach? Who will give us the temperate will, to keep sober and calm amid the shocks and changes of mortal life? Above all, I may say—Who will lead us into all truth? How much is our sorrow increased—how much of it is caused by simple ignorance! Why has our anxiety come? How are we to look at it? What are we to do? Oh, that we had a comforter who would lead us into all truth—not make us infallible, or all knowing, but lead us into truth; at least put us in the way of truth, put things in their true light to us, and give us sound and rational views of life and duty. Oh, for a comforter who would give us the spirit of wisdom and understanding, the spirit of counsel and ghostly strength, the spirit of knowledge and true godliness, and fill us with that spirit of God's holy fear, which would make us not superstitious, not slavish, not anxious, but simply obedient, loyal, and resigned.

If we had such a Comforter as that, could we not take evil from His hands, as well as good? We have had fathers of our flesh who corrected us, and we gave them reverence. They chastised us, but we loved and trusted them, because we knew that they loved and trusted us—chastised us to make us better—chastised us because they trusted us to become better. But if we can find a Father of our spirits, of our souls, shall we not rather be in subjection to Him and live? If He sent us a Comforter, to comfort and guide, and inspire, and strengthen us, shall we not say of that Comforter—"Though he slay me, yet will I trust in him."

If we had such a Comforter as that, we should not care if He seemed at times stern, as well as kind; we could endure rebuke and chastisement from Him, if we could only get from Him wisdom to understand the rebuke, and courage to bear the chastisement. Where is that Comforter? God answers: "That Comforter am I, the God of heaven and earth." There are comforters on earth who can help thee with wise words and noble counsel, can be strong as man, and tender as woman. The God can be more strong than man, and more tender than woman likewise. And when the strong arm of man supports thee no longer, yet under thee are the everlasting arms of God.

Oh, blessed news, that God Himself is the Comforter. Blessed news, that He Who strikes will also heal: that He Who gives the cup of sorrow, will also give the strength to drink it. Blessed news, that chastisement is not punishment, but the education of a Father. Blessed news, that our whole duty is the duty of a child—of the Son who said in His own agony, "Father, not my will, but thine be done." Blessed news, that our Comforter is the Spirit who comforted Christ the Son Himself; Who proceeds both from the Father and from the Son; and Who will therefore testify to us both of the Father and the Son, and tell us that in Christ we are indeed, really and literally, the children of God who may cry to Him, "Father," with full understanding of all that that royal word contains. Blessed, too, to find that in the power of the divine Majesty, we can acknowledge the unity, and know and feel that the Father, Son, and Holy Ghost are all one in love to the creatures whom they have made—their glory equal, for the glory of each and all is perfect charity, and their majesty co-eternal, because it is a perfect majesty; whose justice is mercy, whose power is goodness, its very sternness love, love which gives hope and counsel, and help and strength, and the true life which this world's death cannot destroy.

PENTECOST

Text: John 14:23-31a

1. Leo the Great

Today's festival, dearly beloved, which is held in reverence by the whole world, has been hallowed by that advent of the Holy Ghost, which on the fiftieth day after the Lord's resurrection, descended on the apostles and the multitude of believers, even as it was hoped. And there was this hope, because the Lord Jesus had promised that He should come, not then first to be the Indweller of the saints, but to kindle to a greater heat, and to fill with larger abundance, the hearts that were dedicated to Him, increasing, not commencing His gifts, not fresh in operation because richer in bounty. For the majesty of the Holy Ghost is never separate from the omnipotence of the Father and the Son, and whatever the divine government accomplishes in the ordering of all things, proceeds from the Providence of the whole Trinity. Therein exists unity of mercy and lovingkindness, unity of judgment and justice: nor is there any division in action where there is no divergence of will. What, therefore, the Father enlightens, the Son enlightens, and the Holy Ghost enlightens: and while there is one Person of the Sent, another of the Sender, and another of the Promiser, both the Unity and the Trinity are at the same time revealed to us, so that the Essence which possesses equality and does not admit of solitariness is understood to belong to the same Substance but not the same Person.

EACH PERSON IN THE TRINITY TOOK PART IN OUR REDEMPTION. The fact, therefore, that, with the co-operation of the inseparable Godhead still perfect, certain things are performed by the Father, certain by the Son, and certain by the Holy Spirit, in particular belongs to the ordering of our redemption and the method of our salvation. For if man, made after the image and likeness of God, had retained the dignity of his own nature, and had not been deceived by the devil's wiles into transgressing through lust the law laid down for him, the Creator of the world would not have become a Creature, the Eternal would not have entered the sphere of time, nor God the Son, Who is equal with God the Father, have assumed the form of a slave and the likeness of sinful flesh. But because "by the devil's malice death entered into the world," and captive humanity could not otherwise be set free without His undertaking our cause, Who without loss of His majesty should both become true Man, and alone have no taint of sin, the mercy of the Trinity divided for Itself the work of our restoration in such a way that the Father should be propitiated, the Son should propitiate, and the Holy Ghost enkindle. For it was necessary that those who are to be saved should also do something on their part, and by the turning of their hearts to the Redeemer should quit the dominion of the enemy, even as the Apostle says, "God sent the Spirit of his Son into our hearts, crying Abba, Father"; "And where the Spirit of the Lord is, there is liberty"; and "no one can call Jesus Lord except in the Holy Spirit."

BUT THIS APPORTIONMENT OF FUNCTIONS DOES NOT MAR THE UNITY OF THE TRINITY. If, therefore, under guiding grace, dearly beloved, we faithfully and wisely understand what is the particular work of the Father, of the Son, and of the Holy Ghost, and what is common to the three in our restoration, we shall without doubt so accept what has been wrought for us by humiliation and in the body as to think nothing unworthy about the One and Selfsame Glory of the Trinity. For although no mind is competent to think, no tongue to speak about God, yet whatever that is which the human intellect apprehends about the essence of the Father's Godhead, unless one and the selfsame truth is held concerning His Only-begotten or the Holy Spirit, our meditations are disloyal, and beclouded by the intrusions of the flesh, and even that is lost which seemed a right conclusion concerning the Father, because the whole Trinity is forsaken, if the Unity therein is not maintained; and That Which is different by any in equality can in no true sense be One.

IN THINKING UPON GOD, WE MUST PUT ASIDE ALL MATERIAL NOTIONS. When, therefore, we fix our minds on confessing the Father and the Son and the Holy Ghost, let us keep far from our thoughts the forms of things visible, the ages of beings born in time, and all material bodies and places. Let that which is extended in space, that which is enclosed by limit, and whatever is not always everywhere and entire be banished from the heart. The conception of the Triune Godhead must put aside the idea of interval or of grade, and if a man has attained any worthy thought of God, let him not dare to withhold it from any Person therein, as if to ascribe with more honor to the Father that which he does not ascribe to the Son and Spirit. It is not true godliness to put the Father before the Only-begotten; what is detracted from the One is detracted from Both. For since Their Eternity and Godhead are alike common, the Father is not accounted either Almighty and Unchangeable, if He begat One less than Himself or gained by having One Whom before He had not.

CHRIST AS MAN IS LESS THAN THE FATHER; AS GOD CO-EQUAL. The Lord Jesus does, indeed, say to His disciples, as was read in the Gospel lection, "if ye loved me, ye would assuredly rejoice, because I go to the Father, because the Father is greater than I"; but those ears, which have often heard the words, "I and the Father are One," and "He that sees me, sees the Father also," accept the saying without supposing a difference of Godhead or understanding it of that Essence which they know to be co-eternal and of the same nature with the Father. Man's uplifting, therefore, in the Incarnation of the Word, is commended to the holy Apostles also, and they, who were distressed at the announcement of the Lord's departure from them, are incited to eternal joy over the increase in their dignity. "If ye loved me," He says, "ye would assuredly rejoice, because I go to the Father": that is, if, with complete knowledge ye saw what glory is bestowed on you by the fact that, being begotten of God the Father, I have been born of a human mother also, that being eternal "in the form of God" I accepted the "form of a slave," "ye would rejoice because I go to the Father." For to you is offered this ascension, and your humility is in Me raised to a place above all heavens at the Father's right hand. But I, Who am with the Father that which the Father is, abide undivided with My Father, and in coming from Him to you I do not leave Him, even as in returning to Him from you I do not forsake you. Rejoice, therefore, "because I go to the Father, because the Father is greater than I." For I have united you with Myself, and am become Son of Man that you might have power to be sons of God. And hence, though I am One in both forms, yet in that whereby I am conformed to you I am less than the Father, whereas in that whereby I am not divided from the Father I am greater even than Myself. And so let the Nature, which is less than the Father, go to the Father, that the Flesh may be where the Word always is, and that the one Faith of the catholic Church may believe that He Whom as Man it does not deny to be less, is equal as God with the Father.

AND THIS EQUALITY WHICH THE SON HAS WITH THE FATHER, THE HOLY GHOST ALSO HAS. Accordingly, dearly beloved, let us despise the vain and blind cunning of ungodly heretics, which flatters itself over its crooked interpretation of this sentence, and when the Lord says, "All things that the Father hath are mine," does not understand that it takes away from the Father whatever it dares to deny to the Son, and is so foolish in matters even which are human as to think, that what is His Father's has ceased to belong to His Only-begotten, because He has taken on Him what is ours. Mercy in the case of God does not lessen power, nor is the reconciliation of the creature whom He loves a falling off of eternal glory. What the Father has the Son also has, and what the Father and the Son have, the Holy Ghost also has, because the whole Trinity together is One God. But this faith is not the discovery of earthly wisdom nor the conviction of man's opinion: the Only-begotten Son has taught it Himself, and the Holy Ghost has established it Himself, concerning Whom no other conception must be formed than is formed concerning the Father and the Son. Because albeit He is not the Father nor the Son, yet He is not separable from the Father and the Son: and as He has His own personality in the Trinity, so has He One substance in Godhead with the Father and the Son, filling all things, containing all things, and with the Father and the Son controlling all things, to Whom is the honor and glory for ever and ever. Amen.

2. Martin Luther

In today's Gospel Christ says plainly and bluntly: "If a man love me, he will keep my Word; he that loveth me not, keepeth not my words." The text stands there clear: whoever loves God keeps His commandments, and, on the contrary, whoever does not love God does not keep His commandments. Christ here simply casts out of His kingdom all who do not keep His commandments with pleasure and love. Let us thoroughly understand this. It is briefly pictured to us here who are and who are not Christians. No one is a Christian unless he keeps Christ's Word, as He here says. And no one can keep it, unless he first loves God. God had tested the plan of making people godly by means of force. For, in olden times, God dealt severely with His people, so that they were forced to keep His Word, and not to blaspheme God, to observe the Sabbath, and to obey all the other commandments. To this end He threatened to afflict and punish them, severely, as is written in Leviticus 26:14ff. Thus, God from without coerced the people to be pious by means of the fear of punishment; but their hearts were not obedient. The result is the same in the present day. Therefore, to keep God's Word is a thing that can be accomplished only by divine love.

Accordingly, in the New Testament, God ceased to punish and only administered the Word; for the means must yet come to the point that the divine love be present. Neither the stake, nor bulls nor bans help in the least. Where this love is not, all amounts to nothing, do as we will. If one were to take all the swords in the world in his hands, he would not bring a single heretic to the faith. The people may, indeed, appear to accept the Word, but in their inward hearts there is no faith. Hence God has abolished the sword in this matter and His plan of salvation aims to possess the heart. The bishops are commanded first to take the heart captive, so that it may find love and pleasure in the Word, and the work is then accomplished. Hence, he who wishes to be a true bishop arranges all his administration to the end that he may win souls and develop a love for and a delight in God's Word and be able to oppose the false babblers with sound teaching, and to stop their mouths (Titus 1:11). This will never be accomplished by means of commandments, bans and bulls.

Thus the true spiritual leaders fight. They strike Satan dead and rescue souls from him; for to pierce Satan to death is nothing else than to rescue from him a human being whom he has taken captive by deceitful teaching. And that is the right kind of spiritual tactics. But in case people will not outwardly obey the Word, their parents should educate their children, and the civil government its subjects, to obedience. However, by this method, none are yet brought to believe. For it is affirmed in our text: "He that loveth me not keepeth not my words." Thus you hear what a Christian life is, namely to love God; it is not to storm about, eat flesh, destroy pictures in churches, become monks or nuns—neither a married nor a single life avails here. It means to love, and they do this who keep his Word.

Now, what is God's Word? It is that we love one another as Christ loved us, and that we believe on Him. If one truly possesses the Word, it must break forth out of the heart from pure love. One may possess the words and commands of man, even if he does not love; he may receive the command of a superior and execute it. But the only thing that will keep God's commandments and Word is love. Therefore, observe how foolishly our princes and bishops act, in that they coerce and constrain the people to believe by means of force.

How does one now acquire this love? The human heart is so false that it cannot love unless it first sees the benefit of loving. When, in the Old Testament, God struck blows among the people as if among dogs, and He dealt severely and fearfully with them, they naturally had not love for Him. Then God thought: I must show my love to you and be so affectionate that you cannot help but love Me. Then He took His Son and sent Him into our filth, sin, and misery, pouring out His mercy so freely and fully that we had to boast of all His treasures as if they were our own. He thus became a loving Father, and He declared His mercy and caused it to go forth into all the world that whosoever believes this and lays hold of it with his heart shall have a gracious and merciful God, Who never becomes angry nor deals blows, but Who, instead, is kind and affectionate. Now, where a heart believes and experiences this, and gets glimpses of so much, then it must place all its confidence and affection in God, and deal with its neighbor as God has dealt with itself. As a result the Word of God goes forth out of the heart, and His commandments will be kept with pleasure. Thus, first, there is no other God; secondly, man calls upon the name of the Lord; and thirdly, he lets God reign—God can do as He will, and he possesses his soul in quiet and observes the Sabbath. In this way, the commandments of the First Table are fulfilled. Henceforth, he is kindly and humbly disposed toward all persons, he honors his father and mother and serves his neighbor as his highest pleasure and with all the love of his heart. His thought is ever this: I will do to my neighbor as God has done to me. Thus love alone is the fulfillment of the Law, as Paul says to the Romans (13:10).

Now, no man can bring this love into the heart. Therefore, God struck in among the people with the law that man might experience and feel that no human being could love the divine, righteous, just, and holy Law. In view of this He gave us His Son, thus graciously poured out His greatest treasures, and sunk and drowned all our sins and filth in the great ocean of His love, so that this great love and blessing must draw man to love, and cheerfully be ready to fulfill the divine commandments with willing heart. In no other way can the heart love or have any love; it must be assured that it was first loved. Now, man cannot do this; therefore, Christ comes and takes the heart captive and says: Learn to know Me. Then the heart replies: Aye, Who art Thou? I am Christ, who placed Myself in your misery to drown your sins in My righteousness. This knowledge softens your heart, so that you must turn to Him. Thus love is awakened when one learns Who Christ is.

And a Christian should glory in this knowledge, as God says in Jeremiah 9:23-24: "Thus saith Jehovah, Let not the wise man glory in his wisdom, neither let the mighty man glory in his might, let not the rich man glory in his riches; but let him that glorieth glory in this, that he hath understanding, and knoweth me, that I am Jehovah who exerciseth loving-kindness, justice, and righteousness, in the earth: for in these things I delight, saith Jehovah." So also, Peter in his Second Epistle (3:18) says: "But grow in the knowledge of our Lord and Saviour Jesus Christ." In all the prophets and especially in the Psalms and in many places in the Bible there is much written about this knowledge. It is this knowledge of Christ that must convert or it will never be accomplished. No one is so hardened that he will not be converted and made tender if once his heart knows Christ. And the same knowledge causes one to steadfastly live a godly life. Isaiah says, "The time will come when this knowledge shall flow forth like a deluge." This came to pass in the time of the apostles. Therefore, whoever loves God will keep His commandments, and that love brings a knowledge of God.

Now Christ says, further, in our Gospel: "And my Father will love him." It comes to pass in this way: I know first, that Christ has served me by His whole life, and that Christ is God; thus I see that it is God's will that Christ should give Himself for me and that the Father commissioned Him to that end. Thus, I climb to the Father through Christ. Then my confidence in and love to God grow in me; this I must feel. Christ also says here: "And my Father will love him"; that is, the convert will feel that he is placed with Me in the same kingdom and co-inheritance, and will, through Me and with Me and with My voice, say to the Father in comforting confidence: "Dearly beloved Father."

Then the text continues: "And we will come unto him, and make our abode with him." Father, then I let Him rule in my heart according to His pleasure, and allow Him to be all in all. Therewith, my heart becomes a quiet, humble abode of God. Thus, God is a co-laborer with me and assists me as He says in Isaiah 66:1-2 and in Acts 7:49-50: "Thus saith Jehovah, Heaven is my throne, and the earth is my footstool: What manner of house will ye build unto me? and what place shall be my rest? For all these things hath my hand made, and so all these things came to be, saith Jehovah: but to this man will I look, even to him that is poor and of a contrite spirit, and that trembleth at my Word." The heart must come to the point where it knows God's glory, God's power, and God's wisdom, and lets God rule in everything. It knows that all is God's work; therefore, it cannot fear anything, cold, hunger, hell, death, Satan, poverty, or any like thing. Then the heart says: "My God, Who has made His abode in me, is greater than Satan, and all the powers of hell."

Thus there develops in man a confident defiance of everything upon earth, for he has God and all that is God's. He does all that he is now required to do, and fears not. On the contrary, where there is no love of God, that heart does not keep God's Word; and if the heart does not keep God's Word, the hand never will. There God will never enter and make His abode. There the devil dwells, until the weak and despairing soul will even fear the sound of a driven leaf, as Moses says in Leviticus 26:36. Man cannot endure the gnawing of conscience. The conscience can never know any peace when oppressed by sin, nor can it experience a joyful confidence in God; yea, it will sink lower than hell, while confidence is higher than the heavens. There is then nothing but despair and fear for that heart. All creatures are above it. Such is a picture of the kingdom of Satan.

Christ continues by saying: "And the word which ye hear is not mine, but the Father's who sent me." These words Christ speaks only in order to bring us to the Father, either in a gracious or ungracious way, either with pleasure and love or with fear, for all must lean and depend upon Him. Hence, whoever will not understand these words scorns God. Then no teaching, no words, nor anything else will help in his case. Now Christ comes and says: "These things have I spoken unto you, while yet abiding with you. But the Comforter, even the Holy Spirit, whom the Father will send in my name, he shall teach you all things, and bring to your remembrance all that I said unto you."

3. John Calvin

THE HOLY SPIRIT WILL BRING TO YOUR REMEMBRANCE ALL THINGS THAT I HAVE SAID TO YOU. It is indeed a punishment threatened by Isaiah against unbelievers, that the Word of God shall be to them "as a book that is sealed" (Isaiah 29:11); but in this manner, also, the Lord frequently humbles His people. We ought, therefore, to wait patiently and mildly for the time of revelation, and must not, on that account, reject the Word. When Christ testifies that it is the peculiar office of the Holy Spirit to teach the apostles what they had already learned from His mouth, it follows that the outward preaching will be in vain and useless if it be not accompanied by the teaching of the Spirit. God has therefore two ways of teaching; for, *first*, He sounds in our ears by the mouth of men; and, *second*, He addresses us inwardly by His Spirit; and He does this either at the same moment, or at different times, as He thinks fit.

But observe what are "all these things" which He promises that the Spirit will teach. "He will suggest," He says, "or bring to your remembrance, *all that I have said*." Hence it follows that He will not be a builder of new revelations. By this single word we may refute all the inventions which Satan has brought into the Church from the beginning, under the pretence of the Spirit. Mahomet and the Pope agree in holding this as a principle of their religion, that Scripture does not contain a perfection of doctrine, but that something loftier has been revealed by the Spirit. From the same point the Anabaptists and Libertines, in our own time, have drawn their absurd notions. But the spirit that introduces any doctrine or invention apart from the Gospel is a deceiving spirit, and not the Spirit of Christ. What is meant by "the Spirit being sent by the Father in the name of Christ," I have already explained.

PEACE I LEAVE WITH YOU. By the word "peace" He means prosperity, which men are wont to wish for each other when they meet or part; for such is the import of the word "peace" in the Hebrew language. He therefore alludes to the ordinary custom of His nation, as if He had said, "I leave you my farewell." But He immediately adds that this "peace" is of far greater value than that which is usually to be found among men, who generally have the word "peace" but coldly in their mouth, by way of ceremony or, if they sincerely wish peace for anyone, yet cannot actually bestow it. But Christ reminds them that His peace does not consist in an empty and unavailing wish, but is accompanied by the effect. In short, He says that He goes away from them in body, but that "His peace" remains with the disciples; that is, that they will be always happy through His blessing.

LET NOT YOUR HEART BE TROUBLED. He again corrects the alarm which the disciples had felt on account of His departure. It is no ground for alarm, He tells them; for they want only His bodily presence, but will enjoy His actual presence through the Spirit. Let us learn to be always satisfied with this kind of presence, and let us not give a loose rein to the flesh, which always binds God by its outward inventions.

IF YOU LOVED ME YOU WOULD REJOICE. The disciples unquestionably *loved* Christ, but not as they ought to have done; for some carnal affection was mixed with their love, so that they could not endure to be separated from Him; but if they had loved him spiritually, there was nothing which they would have had more deeply at heart than His return to the Father.

FOR THE FATHER IS GREATER THAN I. This passage has been tortured in various ways. The Arians, in order to prove that Christ is some sort of inferior God, argued that He is less than the Father. The orthodox Fathers, to remove all ground for such a calumny, said that this must have referred to His human nature; but as the Arians wickedly abused this testimony, so the reply given by the Fathers to their objection was neither correct nor appropriate; for Christ does not now speak either of His human nature, or of His eternal Divinity, but, accommodating Himself to our weakness, places Himself between God and us; and, indeed, as it has not been granted to us to reach the height of God, Christ descended to us, that He might raise us to it. "You ought to have rejoiced," He says, "because I return to the Father"; for this is the ultimate object at which you ought to aim. By these words He does not show in what respect He differs in Himself from the Father, but why He descended to us, and that was that He might unite us to God; for until we have reached that point, we are, as it were, in the middle of the course. We, too, imagine to ourselves but a half-Christ, and a mutilated Christ, if He does not lead us to God.

There is a similar passage in the writings of Paul, where he says that "Christ will deliver up the kingdom to God his Father, that God may be all in all," (1 Corinthians 25:24). Christ certainly reigns, not only in human nature, but as He is God manifested in the flesh. In what manner, therefore, will He lay aside the kingdom? It is, because the divinity which is now beheld in Christ's face alone, will then be openly visible in Him. The only point of difference is that Paul there describes the highest perfection of the divine brightness, the rays of which began to shine from the time when Christ ascended to heaven. To make the matter more clear, we must use still greater plainness of speech. Christ does not here make a comparison between the divinity of the Father and His own, nor between His own human nature and the divine Essence of the Father, but rather between His present state and the heavenly glory to which He would soon afterward be received; as if He had said, "You wish to detain Me in the world, but it is better that I should ascend to heaven." Let us therefore learn to behold Christ humbled in the flesh, so that He may conduct us to the fountain of a blessed immortality; for He was not appointed to be our guide, merely to raise us to the sphere of the moon or of the sun, but to make us one with God the Father.

4. Jonathan Edwards

PEACE I LEAVE WITH YOU, MY PEACE I GIVE UNTO YOU: NOT AS THE WORLD GIVETH, GIVE I UNTO YOU. These words are a part of a most affectionate and affecting discourse that Christ had with His disciples the same evening in which He was betrayed, knowing that He was to be crucified the next day. This discourse begins with the thirty-first verse of the thirteenth chapter, and is continued to the end of the sixteenth chapter. Christ began His discourse after He partook of the passover with them, after He had instituted and administered the sacrament of the Supper, and after Judas was gone out, and none were left but His true and faithful disciples whom He now addresses as His dear children. This was the last discourse that Christ had with them before His death. As it was His parting discourse, and, as it were, His dying discourse, so it is of many accounts the most remarkable we have recorded in our Bibles.

It is evident this discourse made a deep impression on the minds of the disciples; and we may suppose that it did so, in a special manner, on the mind of John the beloved disciple, whose heart was especially full of love to Him, and who had just then been leaning on His bosom. In this discourse Christ had told His dear disciples that He was going away, which filled them with sorrow and heaviness. The words of the text are given to comfort them, and to relieve their sorrow. He supports them with the promise of that peace which He would leave with them, and which they would have in Him and with Him when He was gone.

This promise He delivers in three emphatic expressions which illustrate one another. "Peace I leave with you"; as much as to say, though I am going away, yet I will not take all comfort away with Me. While I have been with you, I have been your support and comfort, and you have had peace in Me in the midst of the losses you have sustained, and troubles you have met with from this evil generation. This peace I will not take from you, but leave it with you in a more full possession.

"My peace I give unto you." Christ by calling it His peace signifies two things: That it was His *own*, that which He had to give. It was the peculiar benefit that He had to bestow on His children, now He was about to leave the world as to His human presence. Silver and gold He had none, for, while in His estate of humiliation, He was poor. The foxes had holes, and the birds of the air had nests; but the Son of man had not where to lay his head (Luke 9:58). He had no earthly estate to leave to His disciples, who were as it were his family: but He had *peace* to give them.

It was *His* peace that He gave them; as it was the *same kind* of peace which He Himself enjoyed. The same excellent and divine peace which He ever had in God, and which He was about to receive in His exalted state in a vastly greater perfection and fullness: for the happiness Christ gives to His people is a participation of His own happiness: agreeable to

John 15:11: "These things have I said unto you, that my joy may remain in you." And in His prayer with His disciples at the conclusion of this discourse, John 17:13: "And now come I to thee, and these things I speak in the world, that they might have my joy fulfilled in themselves." And John 17:22: "And the glory which thou gavest me, I have given them."

Christ here alludes to men making their wills before death. When parents are about to leave their children by death, they are wont in their last will and testament to give them their estate; that estate which they themselves were wont to possess and enjoy. So it was with Christ when He was about to leave the world, with respect to the peace which He gave His disciples; only with this difference, that earthly parents, when they die, though they leave the same estate to their children which they themselves heretofore enjoyed, yet when the children come to the full possession of it, they enjoy it no more; the parents do not enjoy it with their children. The time of the full possession of parents and children is not together. Whereas with respect to Christ's peace, He did not only possess it Himself before His death, when He bequeathed it to His disciples; but also afterward more fully: so that they were received to possess it with Him.

The third and last expression is, "not as the world giveth, give I unto you." Which is as much as to say, "My gifts and legacies, now I am going to leave the world, are not like those which the rich and great men of the world are wont to leave to their heirs, when they die. They bequeath to their children their worldly possessions; and it may be, vast treasures of silver and gold, and sometimes an earthly kingdom. But the thing that I give you, is My peace, a vastly different thing from what they are wont to give, and which cannot be obtained by all that they can bestow, or their children inherit from them."

The use that I would make of this doctrine is to improve it as an inducement unto all to forsake the world, no longer seeking peace and rest in its vanities, and to cleave to Christ and follow Him. Happiness and rest are what all men pursue. But the things of the world, wherein most men seek it, can never afford it; they are laboring and spending themselves in vain. But Christ invites you to come to Him, and offers you this peace, which He gives His true followers, and that so much excels all that the world can afford (Isaiah 55:2, 3).

You have hitherto spent your time in the pursuit of satisfaction in the profit or glory of the world, or in the pleasures and vanities of youth, have this day an offer of that excellent and everlasting peace and blessedness, which Christ has purchased with the price of His own blood. As long as you continue to reject those offers and invitations of Christ, and continue in a Christless condition, you never will enjoy any true peace or comfort; but will be like the prodigal, that in vain endeavored to be satisfied with the husks that the swine did eat. The wrath of God will abide upon you, and misery will attend you, wherever you go, which you never will be able to escape. Christ gives peace to the most sinful and miserable that come to Him. He heals the broken in heart and bindeth up their wounds. But it is impossible that they should have peace while they continue in their sins (Isaiah 57:19, 20, 21). There is no peace between God and them; for, as

they have the guilt of sin remaining in their souls, and are under its dominion, so God's indignation continually burns against them, and therefore
they travail in pain all their days. While you continue in such a state, you
live in dreadful uncertainty what will become of you, and in continual
danger. When you are in the enjoyment of things most pleasing to you,
where your heart is best suited, and most cheerful, yet you are in a state of
condemnation. You hang over the infernal pit, with the sword of divine
vengeance hanging over your head, having no security one moment from
utter and remediless destruction. What reasonable peace can anyone enjoy
in such a state as this? What though you clothe him in gorgeous apparel,
or set him on a throne, or at a prince's table, and feed him with the rarest
dainties the earth affords? How miserable is the ease and cheerfulness that
such have! What a poor kind of comfort and joy it is that such take in their
wealth and pleasures for a moment, while they are the prisoners of divine
justice, and wretched captives of the devil! They have none to befriend
them, being without Christ, aliens from the commonwealth of Israel,
strangers from the covenant of promise, having no hope, and without God
in the world!

I invite you now to a better portion. There are better things provided
for the sinful, miserable children of men. There is a surer comfort and
more durable peace: Comfort that you may enjoy in a state of safety, and
on a sure foundation: a peace and rest that you may enjoy with reason,
and with your eyes open. You may have all your sins forgiven, your greatest
and most aggravated transgressions blotted out as a cloud, and buried as in
the depths of the sea, that they may never be found more. And being not
only forgiven, but accepted to favor, you become the objects of God's complacency and delight; being taken into God's family and made His children
you may have good evidence that your names were written on the heart
of Christ before the world was made, and that you have an interest in that
covenant of grace that is well ordered in all things and sure; wherein is
promised no less than life and immortality, an inheritance incorruptible
and undefiled, a crown of glory that fades not away. Being in such circumstances, nothing shall be able to prevent your being happy to all
eternity; having for the foundation of your hope, that love of God which
is from eternity to eternity; and His promise and oath, and His omnipotent
power, things infinitely firmer than mountains of brass. The mountains
shall depart, and the hills be removed, yea, the heavens shall vanish away
like smoke, and the earth shall wax old like a garment, yet these things
will never be abolished.

In such a state as this you will have a foundation of peace and rest
through all changes, and in times of the greatest uproar and outward
calamity be defended from all storms, and dwell above the floods (Psalm
32:6, 7). And you shall be at peace with every thing, and God will make
all his creatures throughout all parts of his dominion, to befriend you (Job
5:19, 24). You need not be afraid of any thing that your enemies can do
unto you (Psalm 3:5, 6). Those things that now are most terrible to you,
namely, death, judgment, and eternity, will then be most comfortable, the
most sweet and pleasant objects of your contemplation, at least there will

be reason that they should be so. Hearken therefore to the friendly counsel that is given you this day, turn your feet into the way of peace, forsake the foolish and live; forsake those things which are no other than the devil's baits, and seek after this excellent peace and rest of Jesus Christ, that peace of God which passes all understanding. Taste and see; never was any disappointed that made a trial (Proverbs 24:13, 14). You will not only find those spiritual comforts that Christ offers you to be of a surpassing sweetness for the present, but they will be to your soul as the dawning light that shines more and more to the perfect day; and the issue of all will be your arrival in heaven, that land of rest, those regions of everlasting joy, where your peace and happiness will be perfect, without the least mixture of trouble or affliction, and never be interrupted nor have an end.

BIOGRAPHICAL SKETCHES

Saint Augustine (354-430)

No theological persuasion remains completely uninfluenced by this great theologian, who himself tested various philosophies of his time (for example, Manichaeism and Ciceronian skepticism) before giving his energies to Christianity. He was born at Tagaste in Numidia, North Africa, and received a first-rate education. In Carthage and Milan he was variously a teacher of grammar and rhetoric. Through the prayerful patience and persuasion of his mother, Monica, and through the influence of Bishop Ambrose of Milan, Augustine became Christian, submitting to baptism on Easter, 387. He became bishop of Hippo in North Africa in 395, where his fame as a great preacher and theologian was established. His own writing was prodigious, and the volume and earnestness of studies of his theology testify to his eminent importance to the history of Christianity. His *City of God* is a defense of the faith amidst the tragic and horrible collapse of the Roman Empire—Augustine died in 430 to the sounds of the Vandal siege of Hippo. His *Confessions* tells of his dramatic conversion from what he saw as a wasted and libertine life. Augustine's preaching, therefore, derives from a rich experience of judgment and suffering, and from the great hope of faith.

Saint Bernard of Clairvaux (1090-1153)

Bernard's parents, of Fontaines, Burgundy, in France, where Bernard was born, decided early upon an ecclesiastical career for him, and he was educated by the canons of St. Vorles at Chatillon. The unusually strict Benedictine monastery at Citeaux received Bernard in 1113, though he had to overcome the opposition of relatives and friends to this decision for monastic severity. In 1115 Bernard became the first abbot of a new Cistercian monastery at Clairvaux, from which sanctuary of writing and study he was often called, against his preference, to the Church outside as an arbiter of difficulties in theology and polity. His theology was Christ centered, and he is reported to have been a spell-binding preacher. His publications include letters, sermons, and treatises (many of them elaborations of his sermons), and his reputation as a defender of the faith (notably against Abelard) and a mystic is well established. After his death, Bernard was designated a doctor of the Church.

Phillips Brooks (1835-1893)

Born into a Boston family rich in Protestant traditions, Brooks attended Boston Latin School, and graduated from Harvard in 1855. After a short teaching career in Boston Latin School, he attended the Protestant Episcopal Seminary in Alexandria, Virginia, taking ordination as a deacon in 1859 and as a priest in 1860. Before he became rector of Trinity Church in Boston in 1869, he had been rector of two Philadelphia parishes. His service as Episcopal Bishop of Massachusetts, which office he assumed in 1891, was remarkable, especially for the skillful patience and charity which he brought to the tensions created in the Church by the Civil War. His cause was the North's, and his eloquent and pastoral preaching reflected his sensitivity to the national tragedy. Though he declined a professorship of Christian Ethics at Harvard, he influenced the university community through many years as University Preacher. As a writer of verse, Brooks is best remembered for his composition, "O Little Town of Bethlehem."

John Calvin (1509-1564)

Beyond the fact that Calvin, born at Noyon, Picardy, in northern France, was destined for a career in the Church, little is known of his early life. In 1521 he became Chaplain of Noyon Cathedral, and in 1523 he became a student at the Collège de la Marche in Paris. The study of law, theology, and the classics claimed his attention from 1528 to 1532, in which latter year he left the Roman Catholic Church. Basel, Switzerland, became Calvin's home when King Francis I settled France's religious controversy in favor of the Roman Catholics, and here, in 1536, his monumental *Institutes of the Christian Religion* was published. The theocratic experiment of Geneva, originally with the reformer William Farel, and interrupted by three years of writing, preaching and teaching Reformed theology in Strasbourg, commanded Calvin's energies until his death in 1564. His brilliant, stern, and disciplined mind fashioned a faith of God's triumphant grace, a theology always derived from a careful exposition of the Scripture; his continuous commentary of the Bible still proves worthy of careful study.

Saint John Chrysostom (about 345-407)

Saint John's early training in rhetoric with the Sophist and orator Libanus is reflected in his receiving the name Chrysostom, which means *golden-mouthed*. His was a pulpit eloquence unmatched in his time. He was born in Antioch, and was baptized there, around 370, by Bishop Meletius. For ten years, following his baptism, he lived in study and self-denial in the desert, returning in 381 to become a deacon in the Church, and in 386 a priest. In 398 he went to Constantinople as Patriarch, where he became extremely popular with the people through his devout homilies and his zeal for charity. But incisive preaching frequently cuts the comfort of the mighty, and Emperor Arcadius ordered him into exile for his reformist tactics and his homilies against worldliness. Chrysostom died at Comana in Pontus in 407, on his way to the desert Pithyus on the Black Sea, which was to have been his place of punishment.

John Donne (1572-1631)

The luxury of birth into a wealthy London merchant family, and a handsome inheritance, did not blunt Donne's brilliant legal and literary career. Acclaimed as the most eloquent pulpit orator of his day, he was ordained in 1615, when he was appointed preacher at Lincoln's Inn (where he had studied law), and chaplain to King James I. Donne was educated at Hart Hall, Oxford, and at Cambridge, and his early career involved defending cases in law and writing poetry, largely lyrical sonnets. In November, 1621, Donne became Dean of St. Paul's Church in London. The remaining ten years of his life were most rich in poetry and preaching, though, unfortunately, his health steadily deteriorated as his fame grew. His sermons were extraordinarily popular and, published as they were preached, they still justify his reputation. Donne was to have been promoted to Bishop of the Anglican Church, but his death in March, 1631, prevented his achieving this honor.

Jonathan Edwards (1703-1758)

It has been said of Jonathan Edwards that he is the greatest indigenous theologian the United States has produced. Born into the Congregational parsonage of Timothy Edwards in East Windsor, Connecticut, Jonathan's twelfth year found him publishing a tract on The Nature of the Soul. He graduated from Yale College, and in 1729 was ordained. He became at first the assistant and then the pastor of his grandfather's church at Northampton, Massachusetts. He remained in this charge until his dismissal in 1750 over sacramental and discipline issues. Until his election to the presidency of the College of New Jersey (later Princeton University) in 1758, in which year he died of smallpox, Edwards was a missionary to the American Indians in Stockbridge, Massachusetts. The Great Awakening of 1734 enhanced his already effective preaching ministry, and his zealous and reasoned homilies place his name among the great revivalists.

John Keble (1792-1866)

The son of a Church of England clergyman, Keble entered Corpus Christi College, Oxford, in 1807, graduating with extraordinary honors in 1811. A deacon in 1815 and a priest in 1816, Keble renounced an inclination toward a country parish to remain at Oxford where, from 1831 to 1841, he was Professor of Poetry. In 1827 he published his famous book The Christian Year, poems for each Sunday, Saint's day, and festival observed by the Anglican Church. Between 1823 and 1831 he assisted his father and brother in country parishes, and in 1836 he became vicar of Hursley, near Winchester, a position he maintained till his death. A zealous high-churchman, Keble was involved in the Tractarian Movement, a precedence, begun in 1823, to the anglo-catholic Oxford Movement. From 1833, Keble joined John Henry Newman in writing some of the Tracts for the Times, from which the Tractarians gained their name. Keble's sermons are known for their beauty of language, their clarity, and their faithfulness to the Church's liturgical drama.

Charles Kingsley (1819-1875)

Following his education in private schools and at King's College, London, Kingsley, who was born in Dartmouth, Devonshire, England, entered Magdalene College, Cambridge. Completing studies which had begun in 1838, he graduated in 1842 with high honors, and was ordained a priest the same year. His busy career included positions as rector of Eversley in Hampshire, Chaplain to Queen Victoria (from 1859), Professor of Modern History at Cambridge (1860-1869), and a canon of Westminster Cathedral (from 1873). Kingsley earned the reputation of a radical among his peers in the Church through his devotion to the Christian Socialist movement in England, and by his general unflagging efforts to improve the social conditions of the English working class. A broad churchman, and an opponent of the Tractarians, Kingsley was called the "Chartist clergyman" because of his support of the Chartist Movement, a militant English working-class force whose purpose was the attainment of certain political and social reforms. Typically, his sermons have a certain biting, direct, and simple quality to them.

Leo the Great (?-461)

It is 421, while Leo was an influential deacon in the Roman Church under Pope Celestine I, when first reference to him is found. When Pope Sixtus III died in 440, Leo was unanimously chosen to the throne of Peter, and the five sermons he preached on anniversaries of his elevation reflect his high conception of the papal office and his dedication to the primacy of the Roman Catholic Church. Leo was an extraordinarily able pope, co-ordinating the doctrine of papal supremacy, suppressing heresy, regulating discipline, and enforcing his authority in East and West. Reigning during the barbarian settlements in western Europe, Leo is remembered for stopping the ravaging journey of Attila the Hun short of the city of Rome. His sermons are brief, but excellent, and upon them are based many of the lessons of the Roman breviary; also, his teaching on papal supremacy became a classical source for later canon lawyers. Leo died on November 10, 461, and ranks as a doctor of the Western Church. He is one of two popes to whom the appellation "great" has been given.

Martin Luther (1483-1546)

The great reformer's father, a small mine operator of Eisleben, Saxony, intended Luther to become a lawyer, and his education, culminating in a

Master's degree in 1505 from Erfurt University, was directed to this end. Instead, the Augustinian monastery in Erfurt attracted him, and he took ordination in 1507. Wittenberg University, which made him a Doctor of Divinity in 1512, called Luther, the year after he became a priest, to be an instructor. While lecturing on the Bible, Luther came to his insight on justification by faith, and fashioned and structured the evangelical principles that were to characterize much of Evangelical Christianity. His excommunication after the Diet of Worms in 1521 resulted from his refusal to mitigate this theology. The temper of the time required Luther to become involved in polemic against Church immorality and abuses, peasant revolution, and German politics. Luther was of rather volatile temperament, and had a keen theological mind; the great volume and broad scope of his publications witness to his vigor and devotion to Christ and Church. Preaching always tested his teaching and action, and his characteristic "Law and Gospel" sermons, faithful to the Church's liturgical year, remain of high importance.

Friedrich Schleiermacher (1768-1834)

Moravian influence shaped the life of Schleiermacher, who was born at Breslau, Germany, the son of a Prussian army chaplain of the Reformed faith. He entered the University of Halle in 1787, and in 1796 he became chaplain at the Berlin Charite Hospital. His intricate theological persuasion included the influence of Kant, Spinoza, Plato, Jacobi, Fichte and Schelling, Pietism and German Romanticism; as a master apologist for the faith, his influence upon more recent and contemporary apologists is striking. Following a ministry in Stolp, Pommerania, and teaching at Halle University, Schleiermacher became, in 1807, pastor of Trinity Church in Berlin; in 1810 he received a theological chair at Berlin University. His eloquent preaching, which was characterized by great beauty of style, attracted a large and influential following, notably among the cultured agnostics of his time. Schleiermacher's important and provocative theology commands serious attention because of his unceasing willingness to submit it to the test of the pulpit.

Charles Haddon Spurgeon (1834-1892)

Spurgeon, an English non-conformist preacher, who was born on June 19, 1834 in Kelvedon, Essex, joined the Baptist Church in 1850, and in 1852 he became pastor of Waterbeach. After a remarkable career as a boy preacher, and after this early charge, he moved, in 1853, to Park Street Chapel, Southwark. In 1854 he began a London ministry, which soon outgrew available quarters, necessitating the building in 1861 of the mammoth Metropolitan Tabernacle, seating 6,000, for his vast congregations. A zealous preacher, not afraid to use humor and unconventional homiletic together with his appeal to the emotions, he continued to attract and move large crowds; his printed sermons, too, found a large audience. Theologically, Spurgeon was of Puritan-Calvinist persuasion, and he was an avid controversialist, distrusting the rationalizing tendencies of biblical criticism, and denying baptismal regeneration. In 1887 he withdrew from the Baptist Union, fearing what he thought to be biblical liberalism. Awareness of Spurgeon's fine work as a preacher is revived in our time through the recent work of Helmut Thielicke.

John Wesley (1703-1791)

John Wesley was the fifteenth child of Samuel Wesley, Anglican rector in Epworth, Lincolnshire, to which parish he was to return as priest in 1729. After graduating from Christ Church, Oxford, in 1724, Wesley was ordained to the priesthood in 1728. Meanwhile he had been a lecturer in Greek, a moderator, and a fellow at Lincoln College. His return to Oxford found him with a small group of students who met for prayer and Bible study—the "Holy Club" whose disciplines inspired the term *Methodists*. In 1738, after a chaplaincy to the Georgia colony, Wesley's well-known Aldersgate "experience" occurred, and his astonishing career of preaching and organizing Methodist Societies was launched. Anglican disapproval of his teaching sent him on an itinerant ministry, preaching four or five sermons on days when he would cover 40 to 60 miles on horseback. His simple direct preaching to people wherever he found them won an overwhelming response of heart and conscience. Wesley also trained lay preachers, and in 1744, with a few other ministers, met in the first organized conference of the new Societies—the origin of the Methodist Church.

SOURCES AND ACKNOWLEDGMENTS

1. St. Augustine (14 sermons)

The sermons for the First Sunday after Christmas and Easter are reprinted from *Sermons on the Liturgical Seasons*, trans. by Sister Mary Sarah Muldowney. New York: The Fathers of the Church, Inc., 1959; vol. 38. Used by permission of The Catholic University of America Press.

All other sermons are reprinted from *A Select Library of the Nicene and Post-Nicene Fathers of the Christian Church*, ed. by Philip Schaff. New York: Charles Scribner's Sons, 1888; vols. VI and VII.

2. Bernard of Clairvaux (5 sermons)

All sermons reprinted from *St. Bernard on the Christian Year*, trans. and ed. by a Religious of the C.S.M.V. London: A. R. Mowbray & Co., Ltd., 1954. Used by permission.

3. Phillips Brooks (6 sermons)

All sermons reprinted from *Sermons*. New York: E. P. Dutton & Co., 1895-1910; 10 vols.

4. John Calvin (16 sermons)

All sermons reprinted from *Commentary on a Harmony of the Evangelists Matthew, Mark and Luke* (3 vols.) and *Commentary on the Gospel according to John* (2 vols.), trans. by William Pringle. Grand Rapids, Michigan: William B. Eerdmans Publishing Co., 1949.

5. John Chrysostom (10 sermons)

All sermons reprinted from *A Select Library of the Nicene and Post-Nicene Fathers of the Christian Church*, ed. by Philip Schaff. New York: Charles Scribner's Sons, 1888; vols. X and XIV.

6. John Donne (3 sermons)

These sermons are reprinted from *Sermons*, ed. by George R. Potter and

Evelyn M. Simpson. Berkeley: University of California Press, 1953-1962; 10 vols. (Late Ed.). The old spelling has been retained.

7. Jonathan Edwards (1 sermon)

This sermon is reprinted from *The Works of President Edwards.* New York: G. & C. & H. Carvill, 1830; 10 vols.

8. John Keble (6 sermons)

All these sermons are reprinted from *Sermons for the Christian Year.* Oxford: James Parker and Co., 1875; 8 vols.

9. Charles Kingsley (7 sermons)

The sermon for the First Sunday after Christmas is reprinted from *All Saints Day and Other Sermons.* London and New York: Macmillan & Co., 1890.

The sermons for the Sunday Called Quinquagesima, the First Sunday in Lent, and the Fifth Sunday in Lent are reprinted from *The Good News of God.* London and New York: Macmillan & Co., 1890.

The sermons for Palm Sunday, the Second Sunday after Easter, and the Sunday after Ascension Day are reprinted from *Sermons on National Subjects.* London and New York: Macmillan & Co., 1890.

10. Leo the Great (5 sermons)

These sermons are reprinted from *A Select Library of the Nicene and Post-Nicene Fathers of the Christian Church,* second series, ed. by Philip Schaff. Grand Rapids: William B. Eerdmans, 1956; vol. XII.

11. Martin Luther (26 sermons)

The sermon for the Second Sunday after Christmas is reprinted from *Works,* ed. by Jaroslav Pelikan. St. Louis: Concordia Publishing House, 1957; vol. 22. Used by permission.

The sermon for the First Sunday in Advent is translated by George W. Forell.

The remainder of the sermons are reprinted from *Works,* ed. by John

Nicholas Lenker. Minneapolis: Lutherans in All Lands Co., 1905; vols. 10-14.

12. Friedrich Schleiermacher (5 sermons)

The sermons for the Second Sunday after Christmas and the Fifth Sunday after Easter are reprinted from *Selected Sermons*, trans. by Mary F. Wilson. London: Hodder & Stoughton, 1890.

The other sermons have been translated by George W. Forell, from Friedrich Schleiermacher, *Predigten*. Berlin: G. Reimer, 1843-1856; 6 vols.

13. Charles Spurgeon (1 sermon)

This sermon is reprinted from *Twelve Striking Sermons*. New York and Chicago: Fleming Revell, n.d.

14. John Wesley (2 sermons)

These sermons are reprinted from *Wesley's Standard Sermons*, ed. by Edward H. Sugden. London: The Epworth Press, 1921; 2 vols.